WHO GETS REPRESENTED?

D1572492

WHO GETS REPRESENTED?

PETER K. ENNS AND CHRISTOPHER WLEZIEN,
EDITORS

Russell Sage Foundation • New York

The Russell Sage Foundation

The Russell Sage Foundation, one of the oldest of America's general purpose foundations, was established in 1907 by Mrs. Margaret Olivia Sage for "the improvement of social and living conditions in the United States." The Foundation seeks to fulfill this mandate by fostering the development and dissemination of knowledge about the country's political, social, and economic problems. While the Foundation endeavors to assure the accuracy and objectivity of each book it publishes, the conclusions and interpretations in Russell Sage Foundation publications are those of the authors and not of the Foundation, its Trustees, or its staff. Publication by Russell Sage, therefore, does not imply Foundation endorsement.

Library of Congress Cataloging-in-Publication Data

Who gets represented? / Peter K. Enns and Christopher Wlezien, editors.
    p. cm.
  Includes bibliographical references and index.
  ISBN 978-0-87154-242-7 (alk. paper)
  1. Majorities.   2. Social classes—Political aspects.   3. Representative government and representation.   I. Enns, Peter K., 1976–   II. Wlezien, Christopher.
  JF1051.W46 2011
  321.8—dc22   2010028684

The paper used in this publication meets the minimum requirements of American National Standard for Information Sciences—Permanence of Paper for Printed Library Materials. ANSI Z39.48-1992.

Text design by Suzanne Nichols.

RUSSELL SAGE FOUNDATION
112 East 64th Street, New York, New York 10065
10 9 8 7 6 5 4 3 2 1

For Louis and Sonia

and

For Nicholas and Alexander

May their voices be heard.

Contents

Contributors

Peter K. Enns is assistant professor in the Department of Government at Cornell University and faculty director of Cornell's Prison Education Program.

Christopher Wlezien is professor of political science and faculty affiliate in the Institute for Public Affairs at Temple University. He also is associate member of Nuffield College, Oxford.

Marisa Abrajano is associate professor of political science at the University of California, San Diego.

Yosef Bhatti is Ph.D. fellow at the University of Copenhagen.

James N. Druckman is the Payson S. Wild Professor of Political Science and faculty fellow at the Institute for Policy Research at Northwestern University. He is also the Honorary Professor of Political Science at Aarhus University, in Denmark.

Christopher Ellis is assistant professor of political science at Bucknell University.

Robert S. Erikson is professor of political science at Columbia University.

Martin Gilens is associate professor of politics at Princeton University.

David A. Hopkins is assistant professor of political science at Boston College.

Wesley Hussey is assistant professor of government at California State University, Sacramento.

Lawrence R. Jacobs is the Walter F. and Joan Mondale Chair for Political Studies and director of the Center for the Study of Politics and Governance at the Hubert H. Humphrey Institute and Department of Political Science at the University of Minnesota.

Keith T. Poole is professor of political science at the University of Georgia.

Elizabeth Rigby is assistant professor of public policy and public administration at George Washington University.

Stuart N. Soroka is associate professor and the William Dawson Scholar at McGill University, director of the Canadian Opinion Research Archive, and codirector of the Media Observatory at the McGill Institute for the Study of Canada.

James A. Stimson is the Raymond Dawson Professor of Political Science at the University of North Carolina, Chapel Hill.

Laura Stoker is associate professor and director of graduate affairs at the University of California, Berkeley.

Joseph Daniel Ura is assistant professor of political science at Texas A&M University.

Katherine Cramer Walsh is associate professor of political science and the Morgridge Center for Public Service Faculty Research Scholar at the University of Wisconsin–Madison.

Gerald C. Wright is professor of political science at Indiana University, Bloomington.

John Zaller is professor of political science at the University of California, Los Angeles.

Acknowledgments

THERE ARE MANY people to thank. Most of all, we thank our sponsors, especially the Russell Sage Foundation. This staunch supporter of social science scholarship paid for the bulk of the costs of the conference from which this book sprang and, of course, provided this publication venue. Without Russell Sage, the conference and the book simply would not have been possible. We owe a debt of special thanks to Eric Wanner, the president of the Russell Sage Foundation. We also recognize the efforts of many others at Russell Sage, including Lianne Addington, Caroline Carr, Helen Glenn Court, who copyedited the manuscript, Suzanne Nichols, the director of publications, and April Rondeau, the production editor.

Cornell University also provided substantial support, both financial and administrative. Financial support came from the university's Department of Government, the Center for the Study of Inequality, and the Institute for the Social Sciences. We especially want to thank Laurie Coon, Matthew Evangelista, Michael Jones-Correa, Mary Katzenstein, Peter Katzenstein, and Judy Virgilio of the Department of Government, Kelly Andronicos and Stephen Morgan of the Center for the Study of Inequality, and Beta Mannix and Anneliese Truame of the Institute for the Social Sciences. We also thank David R. Harris, Cornell's vice provost for social sciences, Yasamin Miller, the director of Cornell's Survey Research Institute. The Canadian Opinion Research Archive provided generous financial support as well, and we are grateful to the archive's director, Stuart Soroka.

Of course, we thank the contributors to the book. Without them, the book quite obviously would not exist. We are flattered and delighted that so many outstanding scholars wanted to be included and contributed such original, important work.

The final product benefited tremendously from the others who attended the conference: Scott Althaus, Christopher Anderson, Adam Berinsky, Alan Gerber, Sunshine Hillygus, Gregory Huber, Jan Leighley, Jeff Manza, Suzanne Mettler, Jonathan Nagler, and especially John Griffin,

Michael Hagen, Richard Johnston, and Emily Thorson. We were fortunate that they agreed to spend the weekend with the rest of us and that they were such active participants. Suzanne Mettler deserves special mention for her gracious support, advice, and assistance. We would also like to thank Michael Miller for helping organize conference logistics.

We also thank the two anonymous reviewers. They put all of us through our paces and, in doing so, pushed us to produce a more focused and nuanced book.

Finally, we thank our families for letting this book take up so much of their time as well as ours.

Chapter 1

Group Opinion and the Study of Representation

PETER K. ENNS AND CHRISTOPHER WLEZIEN

W E CELEBRATE THE principle of one person, one vote. Even though we have learned in recent years that counting ballots is not as straightforward as we might have thought, procedural equality remains an important standard in modern democracies. On election day, we expect all votes to count equally. Of course, we are not interested only in whether our votes count. We care about which parties and candidates win. We also care about what happens afterward, that is, what elected officials actually do once in office. Just because my vote is counted and my preference is heard—and even the fact that my party or candidate won—does not mean that representatives follow my ideal policy position. In fact, citizens in a democracy should rarely expect policy to match their specific policy preferences. This partly reflects institutional features that lead some votes to be weighted more than others—for example, in the United States, the electoral college, gerrymandered house districts, and the structurally malapportioned Senate. However, even where political equality exists and all votes—or voices—count the same, a more fundamental aspect of democracy ensures that policy will not align with many citizens' preferences. If people's preferences differ, after all, actual policy simply cannot satisfy everyone.

In theory, politicians represent populations, whether districts, cities, states, or countries. Were politicians to give everyone equal weight, they would represent the distribution of the preferences of their constituents. It is common in the social sciences to theorize that, if all voters count equally, politicians will place policy at the median voter. In so doing, politicians would not choose the preferred positions of those on the left or the right. Policy representation would be unequal, and the degree of inequality would depend on the variation in underlying preferences— the more preferences vary, the greater the potential for policy to match some groups' interests but not others'. The point is not that other voters do not count, which they do, but that only one position can win. When we consider *policy outputs*, inequality in representation is inescapable.[1] The pertinent question before us is not whether unequal representation exists; rather, we want to know who gets represented. This is the central question that the chapters in this book seek to answer.

Despite the emphasis often placed on the median voter (for example, Downs 1957), it may be that some people's policy preferences, particularly the rich, matter more than others'. After all, they not only vote, they also participate in other ways, such as volunteering time and donating money to campaigns (Verba and Nie 1972; Verba, Nie, and Kim 1978; Nagel 1987; Brady, Verba, and Schlozman 1995). Thus, there is reason—if the supply of policy matches the expressed demand—to suppose that the wealthy have more impact on the policymaking process.[2] Some research supports the suspicion. David Weakliem, Robert Andersen, and Anthony Heath (2005) hint at a connection between the preferences of the wealthy and policy outcomes in their analysis of income inequality across countries. Focusing on the United States, Martin Gilens (2005) and Larry Bartels (2008) provide evidence for unequal policy responsiveness favoring the rich. Bartels considers general roll-call voting behavior (and abortion roll calls) in the U.S. Senate and demonstrates that they best reflect the ideological self-identification of high-income citizens. Gilens examines a wide range of policy decisions and shows that, though there tends to be a bias toward the status quo, when the rich prefer policies different from ones that the poor or those in the middle prefer, policy change corresponds most with the preferences of the rich. Other research comports with what Bartels and Gilens show; specifically, Lawrence Jacobs and Benjamin Page (2005) demonstrate that business leaders exert more influence than the general public on foreign policy decision makers.

The possibility that politicians are more likely to take their cues from the rich has not escaped the attention of scholars of economic inequality. Jacobs and Theda Skocpol observe that "Public officials . . . are much more responsive to the privileged than to average citizens and the less affluent" (2005, 1). This conclusion holds important implications for distributional outcomes. In the United States, more than three decades of prolific economic expansion at the top of the income distribution has produced levels of income inequality not seen since the Gilded Age (Danziger and Gottschalk 1995; Ryscavage 1999; Piketty and Saez 2006,

2007; Bartels 2008; Hungerford 2008; Kelly 2009). Perhaps the government's failure to offer policies designed to stem rising inequality reflects the importance that policymakers place on the preferences of the wealthy.

Another line of scholarship emphasizes the importance of being organized, which includes more than just being rich (for example, Truman 1951; Schattschneider 1960; Dahl 1961; Olson 1965; Walker 1991; Baumgartner and Leech 1998; Lowery and Brasher 2004). Interest groups can mobilize issue publics (Kollman 1998), provide relevant information to policymakers (Burstein and Hirsh 2007), and help fund campaigns (Wright 2003). Thus, politicians face numerous incentives to represent the expressed interests of organized groups. These include business interests to be sure, but also labor and numerous others in society, including racial, religious, and partisan groups. For issues salient to these groups, we might expect policies to reflect the preferences of the strongest and most organized groups or parties.

Do politicians follow the middle? The wealthy? The organized? Although we expect policy to reflect some citizens' interests at the expense of others, we have conflicting expectations about who gets represented. Regardless of our expectations, of fundamental importance is whether and to what extent preferences differ across groups. As we have noted, to the extent that preferences vary, all groups cannot have their preferences represented in policy, and the more variation the greater the disparity. Importantly, the converse also is true—where preferences are identical, actual policy will align with everyone's interests. By representing one group's opinions, policymakers will, by definition, represent the preferences of all groups. Thus, to understand who gets represented, we need to understand when and how preferences differ across groups.[3]

In the next section, we offer a brief overview of the ways in which scholars expect the opinions of certain prominent groups to differ in the United States. We then present an array of evidence showing that classic assumptions about group preferences often do not hold. This contrast—between expectations in the literature and the available data—motivates the studies of group opinion and group representation in the rest of the volume.

On Differences in Preferences

There are good reasons to expect preferences to differ along group lines in the United States. Most theories of group opinion stress objective interests. Prominent economic models of redistribution (such as Meltzer and Richard 1981; Bénabou 2000) assume that preferences for redistribution vary across income groups. Indeed, it would not be surprising if, based on their respective economic situations, the highest, middle, and lowest income groups have different levels of support for government spending and taxes. Income differences may also correlate with other group divisions, such as education level. Thus the opinions of low- (or high-) income groups may correspond with the opinions of low- (or high-) education groups.[4] Additionally, we might expect other aspects of group-based objective interest that extend beyond financial consider-ations. For example, African Americans may show a greater interest than whites, on average, in expanding civil rights.

Information and knowledge can also matter. Varying abilities to con-nect self-interest to policy preferences may produce nuanced patterns of group differences in opinion. Evidence suggests those who pay more at-tention to politics are better able to connect vote choice or policy prefer-ence to their self-interest than those who are uninterested in or unclear about policy options (Althaus 1998; Bartels 1996; Gilens 2001). Thus, we might find group differences more pronounced between the politically informed members of different groups. Similarly, because the wealthy tend to be the most politically informed, we might expect their attitudes to most closely reflect their economic self-interest.[5]

For similar reasons, we might expect group opinion to change differ-ently over time. Group interest could lead different groups to update their opinions in distinct ways. For example, as economic inequality has increased, we might expect support for redistributive policies, such as welfare or taxing the rich to polarize as the poor increasingly support more redistribution and the wealthy support less. Similarly, as policy moves in a liberal (or a conservative) direction we might expect polar-ization along partisan lines, as Democratic support for the policy in-creases (or decreases) and Republican support for the policy decreases (or increases). Information and knowledge may also influence patterns of opinion change (see, for example, Converse 1990; Delli Carpini and Keeter 1996; Zaller 1992). Even if groups do not update their policy opinions according to their own self-interest, it would not be surprising if different amounts of information and information sources led to dif-ferences in how the politically aware and unaware update their opin-ions.[6]

To summarize, there are strong reasons to believe that group prefer-ences differ and shift differently over time. Yet, emerging empirical evi-dence shows that such heterogeneity is not pervasive. Building on previ-ous research (Citrin and Green 1990; Sears and Funk 1991), Stuart Soroka and Christopher Wlezien (2008) and Page and Jacobs (2009) show that policy preferences across income groups are often similar.[7] Furthermore, recent research shows that over-time similarity, that is, parallel publics, also appears to be the norm (Page and Shapiro 1992; Soroka and Wlezien 2008; Ura and Ellis 2008; Enns and Kellstedt 2008; Kelly and Enns 2010).[8] This evidence suggests that patterns of group opinion may be more complicated than previously thought. To this end, the following analysis considers responses to a variety of survey questions over an extended period of time. The analysis reinforces the conclusion that before we can understand who gets represented, we must first understand group differences in policy preferences.

Preferences for Government Spending and Taxes

We begin with preferences for government spending in specific policy domains. These items are especially useful for our purposes. Data are available on a regular basis for an extended time, and preferences in most of these domains have been shown to affect both budgetary policy and actual spending (Wlezien 1996, 2004; Soroka and Wlezien 2010). Our data are based on the following question, included regularly in the General Social Survey (GSS) and elsewhere: "Do you think the government is spending too much, too little or about the right amount on [health care]?" Respondents are asked consistently about spending in other categories besides health care in the GSS in almost every year from 1973 to 1994 and subsequently in even-numbered years. Using responses to these questions, where question wording is identical over time and across domains, allows us to assess whether and to what extent differences are truly systematic and not unique to particular times and domains. We focus here on defense, the major social domains (welfare, health, and education), the environment, and crime.[9]

From the responses, we generate a standard summary measure of "net support" for spending in each domain across years. The measure is the percentage of people who think we are spending "too little" less the percentage of those who think we are spending "too much" in each domain.[10] With this measure, we can assess whether one group wants more spending than another.[11] We calculate net support separately for the highest, middle, and lowest income terciles based on the income levels reported in the GSS.[12] Figure 1.1 plots the mean level of net support, from 1973 to 2008, for each income group across the six policy domains.[13]

In figure 1.1, we see relatively little heterogeneity in preferences across income levels in all domains but welfare. The difference in means between high- and low-income citizens is five points on average for the nonwelfare domains, and none of these differences are even close to being statistically significant. Focusing on the top and bottom deciles—instead of terciles—of the income distribution has little effect (Gilens 2009). These similarities challenge conventional wisdom. As Pablo Beramendi and Christopher Anderson note, "Insofar as politics is about 'who gets what,' the distribution of income becomes an important factor shaping the preferences of voters, parties, and politicians" (2008, 5). At least for government spending on defense, health care, education, the envi-

Figure 1.1   Net Spending Support for Different Programs, by Income Level

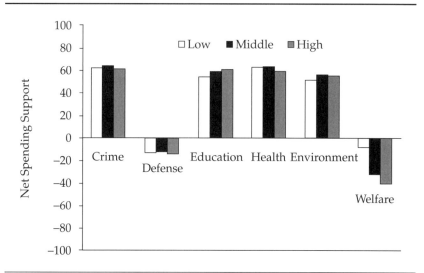

Source: Authors' calculations based on data from the General Social Surveys (Davis, Smith, and Marsden 1973–2008).

ronment, and crime, income does not appear to shape the preferences of citizens.[14]

Things are different for the welfare domain, where the high- and low-income means differ by more than thirty points. The differences across income levels are not symmetrical, however; the mean preference for people with middling incomes is much more like that for those with upper incomes. This pattern has important implications where representation is concerned (Soroka and Wlezien 2008). We already have noted the theoretical bases for representing the middle- or upper-income groups. Given the similarity in welfare preferences, if politicians follow the welfare preferences of those in the middle, they, to a large extent, would represent the preferences of upper-income earners; likewise, in representing the preferences of those with upper incomes, politicians would effectively represent the preferences of those in the middle. The welfare spending preferences of the middle and upper terciles are not identical, however, and it is important to determine what these differences mean for policy. It may be, after all, that what seems to be a small difference in preferences makes a big difference for policy. What is clear is that the welfare spending preferences of the lowest income group are least likely to be represented—not only is there a relatively large differ-

Figure 1.2   Net Support for Welfare Spending, by Income Level, 1973 to 2008

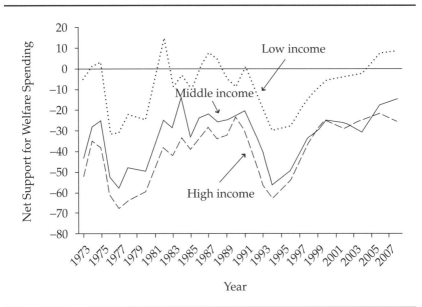

Source: Authors' calculations based on data from the General Social Surveys (Davis, Smith, and Marsden 1973–2008).

ence between their preferences and those of the middle and upper terciles, there is also little theoretical basis for representing the poor vis-à-vis the rest of the income distribution.

Spending preferences across income groups also largely track one another over time. That is, the similarities and differences that we see in figure 1.1 tend to hold over time. In effect, there is substantial parallelism in preference change—"parallel publics" in Benjamin Page and Robert Shapiro's words (1992). Welfare spending preferences in figure 1.2 exemplify the pattern. This parallelism tells us a lot about the dynamics of public preferences over time—namely, that people tend to respond to many of the same things in similar ways (Page and Shapiro 1992; Wlezien 1995; Enns 2006; Soroka and Wlezien 2008; Enns and Kellstedt 2008; Ura and Ellis 2008; Kelly and Enns 2010). The parallelism also carries implications for representation—in responding to the preferences of one group, politicians at least to some extent would follow the changes in preferences of the others. This may allow politicians to gain support from all groups even if preference levels differ across groups. Preference change is not perfectly parallel across groups, however. Of special note

Figure 1.3   Tax Preferences, by Income Level, 1976 to 2008

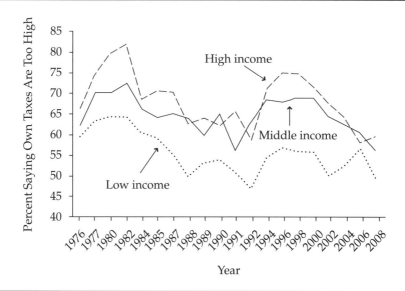

Source: Authors' calculations based on data from the General Social Surveys (Davis, Smith, and Marsden 1973–2008).

in figure 1.2 is that welfare preferences for middle- and high-income groups appear to have converged over time; by the end of the series, there is little difference whatsoever. As discussed, this convergence has important implications for policy; as the series converge, whether one represents the preferences of those with middling or upper incomes makes no real difference.

Next, we consider opinions about taxes. The GSS regularly asks respondents the question, "Do you consider the amount of federal income tax which you have to pay as too high, about right, or too low?" Figure 1.3 plots the percentages saying "too high" between 1976 and 2008. By comparison with spending preferences on welfare (and other domains), these data show less parallelism over time. This is fairly predictable, because tax rates have fluctuated unevenly over time, increasing for some groups—especially high-income citizens—in some periods, for example, the 1990s, and decreasing in other periods, for example, the 1980s and the 2000s. The pattern across income groups still is quite similar to what we observe for welfare: significant differences between the preferences for lower-income respondents and the rest of the distribution. On average, about 68 percent of people in the upper tercile think their taxes are too high, versus 56 percent of those in the lower tercile. Among middle-income people, 65 percent think so, revealing a similar asymmetry to what we saw on welfare spending. Notice that the differences for tax preferences are just one-half the size of those for welfare. Furthermore, much as we saw for welfare spending, the differences that we do observe between the middle- and high-income groups have largely disappeared.

Our analysis of spending and tax preferences reveals a high level of similarity across income groups. Differences are limited to taxes and one spending program—welfare—and, when they exist, are mostly between the poor on the one hand and middle- and high-income groups on the other. Differences simply are not as pervasive as one might expect.

Policy Mood

Although spending and taxing are much of what the federal government does, policy involves more than that. This is the main point of Gilens's (2009) recent analysis. Gilens analyzes 1,784 survey questions that were asked between 1981 and 2002. Looking at preferences among the tenth and ninetieth percentiles of the income distribution, he finds large differences in preferences for specific policies, such as whether to increase government regulation of the oil industry, approve the abortion pill RU-486, apply term limits for welfare recipients, or support development aid to the former Soviet Union (Gilens 2009, table 2).[15]

James Stimson provides another way to assess group differences across issues (1999, 2004; Erikson, MacKuen, and Stimson 2002). He averages across hundreds of political survey questions to create an over-time measure of the public's policy mood. This measure, which captures the public's support for more or less government, shows whether and how opinion differs generally across the various specific issues. The measure is of special interest because policy outputs in all branches of government have been shown to be influenced by changes in the public's mood (Stimson, MacKuen, and Erikson 1995; Erikson, MacKuen, and Stimson 2002). We begin by generating Stimson's policy mood by income level. We use every question in Stimson's mood index for which individual-level data are available to estimate the policy mood of the lowest quintile, the highest quintile, and the middle 60 percent of respondents. Relying on the General Social Surveys, the American National Election Study, and data from the Roper Center, we were able to obtain individual-level data for seventy-five question items that Stimson had used. More than 60 percent of these were asked at least fourteen times. In total, our series includes 1,019 survey questions.[16]

Figure 1.4 presents Stimson's policy mood by income from 1956 to 2006.[17] Here we can see that the highest income level shows the most conservative opinions in virtually every year. The lowest income level,

Figure 1.4   Stimson's Policy Mood, by Income Level, 1956 to 2006

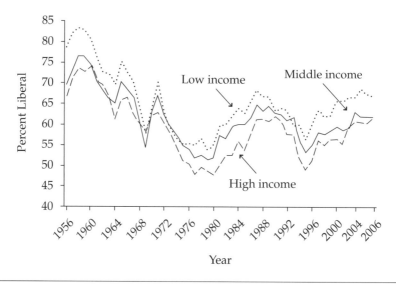

Source: Authors' calculations based on data from the General Social Surveys (Davis, Smith, and Marsden 1972–2008), American National Election Studies (Sapiro, Rosenstone, and the National Election Sudies 2004), and the iPoll Databank (Roper Center Public Opinion Archives, various years).

in contrast, is consistently most liberal. Still, the opinions of the different groups appear to be quite close, and they also track together over time. An analysis of variance (ANOVA) shows that income groups account for only 12.3 percent of the total variance of the three series. By contrast, 84.3 percent of the variance of mood across income groups and time is a function of parallel movement over time. The public's policy mood thus differs only modestly across income groups—of course the differences may matter for policy. Interestingly, for the middle and upper terciles, the differences that we do observe have declined in recent years. This is as we saw for welfare spending and taxes.

Ultimately, how income level influences policy preferences is not straightforward. Conclusions vary depending on which policies are analyzed, the period of analysis, and whether the measure of public opinion is policy-specific or global. How we understand representation of different income groups will necessarily also depend on these factors.

As discussed, we also are interested in other divisions and whether and how they matter for politics and policy. One important division is education. To consider its effects, figure 1.5 plots policy mood by education level.[18] Peter Enns and Paul Kellstedt (2008) show that from 1972 to

Figure 1.5   Stimson's Policy Mood, by Education Level, 1956 to 2006

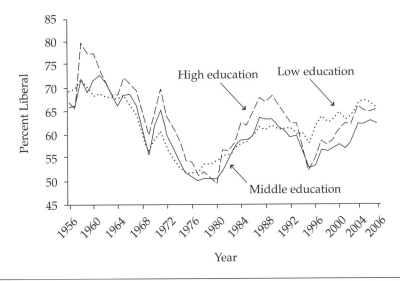

Source: Authors' calculations based on data from the General Social Surveys (Davis, Smith, and Marsden 1972–2008), American National Election Studies (Sapiro, Rosenstone, and the National Election Sudies 2004), and the iPoll Databank (Roper Center Public Opinion Archives, various years).

2004, different information groups typically updated their policy mood synchronously in response to changing economic conditions. Here, we extend the period of their analysis and observe a similar result. Notice first that for most of the period, the highest education group displays the most liberal opinions. This is in contrast with the finding in figure 1.4 that the highest income group consistently showed the most conservative preferences. Although income and education level are highly correlated in the United States, they do not produce the same policy preferences. There is less systematic difference in opinion for the middle and lower education groups, as the latter drifts much more liberally beginning in the late 1970s. Even though differences across the groups are not the same at all points in time, a high level of over-time parallelism between the three series remains—more than 87 percent of the variance across education groups and time is a function of parallel over-time movement. People with quite different education levels respond to new information in much the same way.[19]

Party identification is another important cleavage. To provide a general summary of how much it matters, we generate policy mood separately for Republicans, independents, and Democrats.[20] These are plot-

Figure 1.6   Stimson's Policy Mood, by Party Identification, 1956 to 2006

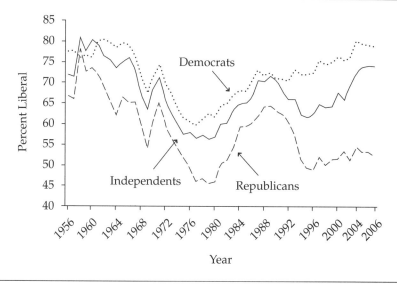

Source: Authors' calculations based on data from the General Social Surveys (Davis, Smith, and Marsden 1972–2008), American National Election Studies (Sapiro, Rosenstone, and the National Election Sudies 2004), and the iPoll Databank (Roper Center Public Opinion Archives, various years).

ted in figure 1.6, which shows much larger cross-sectional differences than those for education and income. Two additional patterns are particularly striking in this figure. First, during most of the last fifty years, independents' policy mood is closer to that of Democrats. Thus, if politicians follow the median voter model and represent those in the middle, Democrats would benefit more often than Republicans.[21] Second, the opinions of Democrats and Republicans polarize in the later part of the series, particularly through the 1990s (also see DiMaggio, Evans, and Bryson 1996; Evans 2003; Hetherington 2009).[22] Although some recent accounts of polarizing public opinion focus on George W. Bush's presidency (Jacobson 2006), our analysis suggests that polarization occurred during the Clinton years and simply persisted through the Bush years (also see Bafumi and Shapiro 2009). This polarization may have had important consequences for opinion representation; indeed, it may have encouraged more extreme policies.

Opinion About Race

Race offers another basis for group differences. Existing research finds important differences across racial groups and important policy implications (Griffin and Newman 2007, 2008). Here, we seek to provide a picture of what these differences look like over time. Our starting point is Kellstedt's work on racial policy preferences (2000, 2003). Kellstedt finds that responses to survey questions on a variety of racial policies, such as busing, integration, and affirmative action move together over time in meaningful ways—the public's racial policy liberalism ebbs and flows over time. For our analyses, we disaggregate by race, looking at the over-time racial policy liberalism of white and African American respondents. The strategy parallels our analysis of Stimson's policy mood. We use the General Social Surveys, the American National Election Studies, and the Roper Center to identify all questions in Kellstedt's racial policy index for which individual-level data are available. Twelve such survey questions have each been asked nine times or more. We combine these to formulate an index of racial policy preferences from 1962 to 2006 and display the scores for the general public as well as African American and white respondents in figure 1.7.

First, we focus on the racial liberalism of all respondents. As expected, the series corresponds closely with Kellstedt's. We observe a minor dip in the public's racial liberalism around 1963, followed by a larger dip in the late 1960s, and then an even more sustained drop in racial liberalism until around 1980. The public then becomes more racially liberal until the early 1990s.[23] Not surprisingly, white respondents, who make up the overwhelming majority of survey responses, track closely with the aggregate series. It is also not surprising that the racial policy preferences of African Americans are much more liberal than white respondents. What is surprising, however, is that African American and white respondents do not appear to respond to the same messages in the same way—while whites have become more liberal, African Americans have become less so. The lack of parallelism is distinct from the patterns we observed above with income and education groups. These differences also contrast with previous analyses of the over-time policy preferences of different racial groups (Page and Shapiro 1992; Kellstedt 2003). The differences in white and African American racial policy preferences, both cross-sectionally and over time, indicate that unequal representation could exist—aligning policy with either white or African American preferences would mean not aligning policy with the other group's preferences. [24]

Understanding Group Opinions

The foregoing analyses illustrate the complexity of group opinions. Differences can be meaningful across groups, but we cannot simply assume that they exist. Across income levels, for instance, preferences often do not differ. These results indicate that either (1) there is little difference in self-interest across income groups in many domains or (2) people do not

Figure 1.7   Kellstedt's Racial Policy Liberalism, by Race, 1962 to 2006

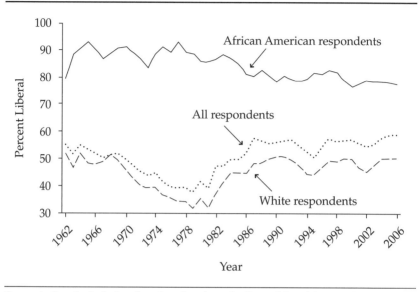

Source: Authors' calculations based on data from the General Social Surveys (Davis, Smith, and Marsden 1972–2008), American National Election Studies (Sapiro, Rosenstone, and the National Election Sudies 2004), and the iPoll Databank (Roper Center Public Opinion Archives, various years).

realize their interests. Either way, there is little difference for policymakers to represent. Additionally, when differences do emerge, as on welfare spending and taxes, the differences are largely between the middle and the rich on one hand and the poor on the other. Even these differences are dwarfed by the powerful changes we observe over time that affect income groups similarly. Differences across other groups are significant, including race and partisanship.[25] African Americans and whites hold very different positions on racial policy issues and have done so for a long time, though the difference has declined slightly. Partisans also have different positions, and these seem to have widened dramatically in recent years. Winning and losing politically matters a great deal for race and party. If we want to understand whose preferences best match policy, we need to understand how and why groups differ in their opinions. This is the focus of the first half of this book.

On the Representation of Difference

In addition to assessing differences in preferences, we want to know whether differences ultimately matter for policy. Is there inequality in representation? Do policymakers follow partisans or those middling independent voters? Do they follow the rich? The highly educated? The white majority?

Research on the representation of public opinion almost exclusively presumes that policymakers represent the "average" person (for reviews of the literature, see Burstein 2003; Brooks 2006; Manza and Cook 2002; Weakliem 2003; Soroka and Wlezien 2007). This is as one would expect were there perfect equality, where each person had equal power in the political process. As we have discussed, even where there is perfect political equality—and politicians represent the median person—not everyone would be equally represented in policy, unless of course our preferences were identical. To the extent that preferences differ, therefore, inequality in policy outputs is an unavoidable fact of democratic political life (Soroka and Wlezien 2008). We also have discussed that there is reason to think that citizens are not politically equal. Those who vote may matter more than those who do not, and this can have powerful implications for representation (Griffin and Newman 2005; McCarty, Poole, and Rosenthal 2006). Even all voters may not be equal, however, and politicians may privilege some voices over others, such as the wealthy or the organized.

Yet, for some groups, such as the poor, there is little theoretical basis for politicians to privilege their interests. They are not like the median voter or, obviously, those with upper incomes. They also are not organized (Schlozman and Tierney 1986).[26] We do not expect politicians to pay special attention to them. To find that the rich, those in the middle, or the organized are better represented than the poor would not startle or challenge us to revise our theories. In fact, this is what democratic theories predict. The question of theoretical interest is whether the rich command more attention than those in the middle. To find that the rich are better represented than the median person or voter would constitute important information about the functioning of representative democracy. It also would suggest that some of our theories are too Pollyannaish. The median person or voter just would not be as powerful as some models would predict. The representation of different groups is the focus of the second half of the book.

The Book

This book emerged from a conference we organized at Cornell University in 2008. In many ways, the final product differs from what we first had in mind. Our original focus was on the extent of differences and similarities (both cross-sectionally and over time) in public preferences between groups and what explains such patterns of similarity and difference. To address these questions, we invited many of the top scholars of public preferences and its representation in policy to the conference "Homogeneity and Heterogeneity in Public Opinion." What emerged was a conference not only on what explains similarities and differences in opinion but also on whether and how these differences (or the lack of) matter for representation. We discovered that no real consensus exists on how different groups influence policy. Not only were there debates about differences between groups, there were also serious disagreements about whether these differences matter. In essence, despite vast advances in research on public opinion and representation, the conference made clear that we do not yet have a good answer to the question of who gets represented, hence the title of this book.

The book is in two parts: the first about group preferences for policy and the second about representation of group interests. The first part of this volume—chapters 2 through 5—extend the analysis presented thus far, looking closely at policy preferences among income, education, racial, and partisan groups. The second part—chapters 6 through 11—shows that when the differences and similarities of group opinion are taken seriously, our understanding of representation and who gets represented advances greatly.

Chapter 2 examines policy preferences across racial and ethnic groups. We have already seen evidence that policy preferences can differ across racial groups in important ways. Marisa Abrajano and Keith T. Poole's "Assessing the Ethnic and Racial Diversity of American Public Opinion" develops a survey "matching" technique to provide a comprehensive assessment of ethnic and racial group political opinion. They show how this methodology can become an important tool for those who study group opinion. Its utility is borne out in their analysis, which shows that racial group opinions, particularly support for government and redistribution, do not necessarily align with the expectations of scholars or pundits.

The next two chapters in the section offer two new perspectives on partisan polarization in the electorate. The preceding analysis showed that in recent years, differences in the policy preferences of Democrats and Republicans dwarf the differences across income and education groups. In chapter 3, "United We Divide? Education, Income, and Heterogeneity in Mass Partisan Polarization," Christopher Ellis and Joseph Daniel Ura examine the evolving role of issues and show that, although education and income groups seem to update their opinions in parallel, an important interaction effect between the two can occur. They demonstrate that polarization has reflected different things for different people—"economic" issues for those with more education and low incomes and "cultural" issues for those with less education and relatively high incomes. Chapter 4, David A. Hopkins and Laura Stoker's "The Political Geography of Party Resurgence," moves things forward further still, focusing on the evolving strength and structure of partisanship across states. This focus on geographic heterogeneity offers an important contrast to the aggregate data. Studies of partisanship at the national level will miss important state-level factors. For example, we learn that since the 1970s the effect of party affiliation on vote choice has become more uniform across states, and considerations other than party now are less likely to influence electoral outcomes. These changes not only influence elections but also the incentives (or the lack thereof) for candidates to represent broad electoral coalitions.

The section ends with chapter 5, Katherine Cramer Walsh's "Get Government Out of It: Heterogeneity of Government Skepticism and Its Connection to Economic Interests and Policy Preferences." Walsh uses "listening investigations"—a form of citizen interviewing—to assess how policy preferences and attitudes toward government vary across society. These show that even when different social groups appear to have similar policy preferences, the underlying structure of these preferences can be radically different. Thus, the analysis offers an important reminder that even when surveys show similarities across groups, important group variation can still exist. Equally important, the chapter's focus on opinions about health-care policy offers a timely look at the reasons that different groups resist the expansion of government services.

The second half of the book focuses on policy representation. James N. Druckman and Lawrence R. Jacobs begin, in chapter 6, with an assessment of the Reagan administration's responsiveness to the preferences of different groups in different policy areas. Their chapter, "Segmented Representation: The Reagan White House and Disproportionate Responsiveness," builds on the lessons of the first half of the book by taking the complexity of group opinion seriously. They show that from the perspective of the president, different groups' opinions matter differently for different policy areas. In other words, in their analysis, whose views President Reagan represented depended on the issue, the group, and the administration's coalition-building strategy.

The next four chapters telescope in on differences in representation across income groups. We have seen that in contrast to conventional wisdom, we cannot assume that different income groups hold different policy preferences. These chapters take this finding to heart. In chapter 7, "Whose Statehouse Democracy? Policy Responsiveness to Poor Versus Rich Constituents in Poor Versus Rich States," Elizabeth Rigby and Gerald C. Wright turn to state-level representation. They explore differences in the opinions across income groups in the American states and the representation of these opinions in policy. The next three chapters examine representation at the federal level. In chapter 8, Yosef Bhatti and Robert S. Erikson's "How Poorly Are the Poor Represented in the U.S. Senate?"

reconsiders Bartels's analysis of Senate roll-call voting and demonstrates that how one measures opinion matters for the results one gets. The next two pieces switch from Senate votes to actual policy outcomes. Chapter 9, Martin Gilens's "Policy Consequences of Representational Inequality," provides compelling evidence of an upper-income bias in representation across various issues. In chapter 10, "Inequality in Policy Responsiveness?" Christopher Wlezien and Stuart N. Soroka, by contrast, show that politicians' responsiveness to opinion change over time is surprisingly equal. Together, these chapters significantly refine our understanding of the relationship between income level and representation in the United States.

Wesley Hussey and John Zaller conclude the section with chapter 11, "Who Do Parties Represent?" In it, they examine how party affiliation structures congressional responsiveness to constituency opinion and how this relationship has evolved over time. We learn that the study of representation must take into account more than just public opinion; the authors show that the party in charge consistently matters more than constituent preferences.

James A. Stimson has the last word. In his concluding essay, chapter 12, "The Issues in Representation," he summarizes and expands on thoughts that he offered during the closing session of the conference. His comments (and banter with John Zaller) during that session served as important inspiration for the title and the structure of this book. We really cannot thank Stimson and Zaller enough, though we have tried, and Jim's chapter couldn't be a more perfect ending to this volume. His chapter also opens new doors, suggesting how virtually equal representation can propagate inequality over time.

This chapter is based on a presentation at the Conference on Homogeneity and Heterogeneity in Public Opinion, at Cornell University, in Ithaca, New York, on October 3–5, 2008. For helpful comments, we thank Aileen Cardona Arroyo, Michael Dichio, Michael Hagen, Jason Hecht, Caitlin Hill, Desmond Jagmohan, Julianna Koch, Aleksandar Matovski, Stuart Soroka, Danielle Thomsen, Alexis Walker, John Zaller, and the two anonymous reviewers. We also thank Brian Richman for help with data collection.

Notes

1. Our interest in the congruence (or lack thereof) between policy outputs and constituent preferences has theoretical roots in Hannah Pitkin's notion of substantive representation (Pitkin 1967). The focus on opinion-policy con-

gruence is also of particular relevance for understanding the extent to which different social outcomes reflect different groups' ablility to see their ideal policies enacted. Of course, a lack of congruence between policy outputs and opinion does not preclude other types of representation, such as descriptive representation (Pitkin 1967).

2. Additionally, politicians tend to be richer than the median voter, so a politician representing the interests of the rich would likely be representing his or her own self-interest.

3. Of course, even when the preferences across groups are the same, we want to know whose preferences policymakers represent. Knowing who politicians pay attention to tells us why there is representation and where policy is likely to go should differences in preferences emerge.

4. To the extent that this is true, unequal representation favoring the rich may not always be a bad thing. This is not to say that it would not make any difference, of course.

5. Certainly, self-interest—economic or otherwise—does not tell the whole story of group preferences. We know, for example, that many high-income individuals support redistribution. For these individuals, socialization or values might better predict policy preferences than economic self-interest. Thus, group opinion differences might result from common socialization experiences that members of groups are likely to experience. For example, group cleavages might coincide with regional differences, such as North and South or urban and rural, or cleavages might correspond to political values, which often begin, and are reinforced, through family and group socialization (Lazersfeld, Berelson, and McPhee 1944; Campbell et al. 1960). There simply are many good reasons to think that group opinions sometimes reflect group interest and that unequal representation would have important distributional consequences.

6. For a different perspective on political awareness and opinion updating, see Enns and Kellstedt (2008).

7. Some early literature also notes patterns of homogeneity in preferences across groups. Angus Campbell and Homer C. Cooper's study of group attitudes in the 1954 congressional election concludes, "Most groups do not have an integrated pattern of political attitudes that distinguishes them from other groups. Many groups react in an individual way to specific issues but broad patterns of response are found only in the most homogenous and sophisticated groups" (1956, 106).

8. A similar pattern also holds cross-nationally (Soroka and Wlezien 2010).

9. Results for other areas, including cities, foreign aid, space, and transportation, present a similar story. Much of the same is true for Canada. These results are available on request.

10. In theory this measure captures both the direction and the magnitude of the preference for policy change. In practice, the measure has little utility as an indicator of the "direction" of preferences—whether the public wants more or less spending—at particular times. One problem is that question wording can fundamentally alter expressed support for policy (see, for example, Weaver, Shapiro, and Jacobs 1995 on differential support for "assistance to

the poor" and "welfare"). We cannot assume from responses to any particular survey question that the public "supports" or "opposes" a particular policy. For additional concerns with treating survey marginals as an indicator of the direction of preferences, see Soroka and Wlezien (2010, 70–71, and this volume).

11. We can also evaluate whether support increases or decreases over time. We take advantage of this possibility in subsequent analyses.

12. Using terciles from the GSS has the advantage of keeping our three categories equal in size—that is, the number of respondents in each category is the same, and no one category is more (or less) susceptible to measurement error. For income categories, and others, the total sample size is just over 1,100 on average. Approximately 5 percent of respondents do not answer the income question, leaving an average N of about 1,050, or 350 in each income category. Given that the income distribution reported to the GSS always is lower than what we see in census data, we also calculated using terciles from the U.S. Census Bureau. This makes virtually no difference to any of the results—specifically, using the census distribution slightly expands the range of differences. To determine preferences by income tercile, we begin with preferences aggregated by whatever income response categories exist in the individual-level survey file. We then collapse these into income terciles. When survey response categories overlap two income terciles, the respondents in this category are assigned the mean score (in the category) and allocated to the two income terciles proportionally, based on where the tercile division lies.

13. The levels of net support move roughly in parallel across income groups, so the observed differences and similarities in figure 1.1 are approximately the same at each time point (see also Soroka and Wlezien, this volume).

14. This does not mean that there is little heterogeneity in spending preferences. Soroka and Wlezien (2008) show that dividing respondents by education generates larger differences on average. The gaps in spending preferences typically are greater still across categories of party identification.

15. Although Gilens (2009, table 2) finds more differences than similarities, some interesting similarities emerge between the highest and lowest income deciles, such as support for job training for welfare recipients, child care for welfare recipients, and work requirements for welfare recipients (see also Gilens, chapter 9, this volume).

16. Because Stimson's policy mood aggregates across hundreds of survey questions, the margin of error associated with each estimate is much smaller than had we relied on a single survey. Thus, we are comfortable analyzing smaller income subgroups than our earlier analysis (that is, income quintiles instead of terciles). Of course, income group categories offered in surveys do not always correspond exactly with income quintiles. Coding was done to ensure that for each survey, the number of respondents in the high- or low-income category never exceeded 30 percent. For the overwhelming majority of surveys, however, the percentage of respondents in the high or low category is roughly equivalent to or less than 20 percent.

17. Following Stimson (1999, 2004), we calculate the percent liberal divided by the percent liberal plus the percent conservative. We used Stimson's (Wcalc)

dyad ratios algorithm to generate the mood indices. For all respondents, our measure of mood is highly correlated with Stimson's (Pearson's r = 0.85). See Kelly and Enns (2010) for an additional discussion of this measure.

18. Education levels correspond with upper and lower quintiles and then the middle 60 percent. Percentiles were calculated for each year. As with our categorization of income groups, the high and low categories never exceeded 30 percent and often fell below 20 percent.

19. The pattern also holds for specific policy domains (see Soroka and Wlezien 2008).

20. When surveys asked about degrees of partisanship, we coded strong Democrats and weak Democrats as Democrats, strong Republicans and weak Republicans as Republicans, and independents and independents who lean toward one party or the other as independents.

21. Of course, not all theories of voting predict that politicians will move to the middle (see, for example, Rabinowitz and Macdonald 1989).

22. As we would expect, an analysis of variance shows much more heterogeneity across partisan groups than for income or education groups. Partisan affiliation explains 45.7 percent of the total variance in preferences across the three partisan groups and 43.5 percent of the variance reflects common movement over time.

23. Kellstedt's series begins in 1950. However, not enough individual-level data are available for the early years, so we cannot begin our series until 1962. Consistent with the visual similarities reported for all respondents, our racial policy series correlates with Kellstedt's updated series at r = 0.68. This correlation actually understates the similarity between the series because we have more variability in the first few years of our survey as there are fewer questions with individual-level data available. The correlation between our measure and Kellstedt's measure jumps to r = 0.80 if we begin the comparison in 1966 rather than in 1962.

24. The figure also shows that the potential for policy to match one group's preferences more than others' varies over time and that this potential has declined in recent years.

25. Of course, this is true for other groups too, including gender (Box-Steffensmeier, De Boef, and Lin 2004; Clarke et al. 2004; Eichenberg 2003; Shapiro and Mahajan 1986).

26. This does not preclude significant mobilization (Piven and Cloward 1978).

References

Althaus, Scott L. 1998. "Information Effects in Collective Preferences." *American Political Science Review* 92(3): 545–58.

Bafumi, Joseph, and Robert Y. Shapiro. 2009. "A New Partisan Voter." *Journal of Politics* 71(1): 1–24.

Bartels, Larry M. 1996. "Uninformed Votes: Information Effects in Presidential Elections." *American Journal of Political Science* 40(1): 194–230.

———. 2008. *Unequal Democracy: The Political Economy of the New Gilded Age.* Princeton, N.J.: Princeton University Press.

Baumgartner, Frank R., and Beth L. Leech. 1998. *Basic Interests: The Importance of Groups in Politics and Political Science*. Princeton, N.J.: Princeton University Press.

Bénabou, Roland. 2000. "Unequal Societies: Income Distribution and the Social Contract." *American Economic Review* 90(1): 96–129.

Beramendi, Pablo, and Christopher J. Anderson. 2008. "Income Inequality and Democratic Representation." In *Democracy, Inequality, and Representation*, edited by Pablo Beramendi and Christopher J. Anderson. New York: Russell Sage Foundation.

Box-Steffensmeier, Janet M., Suzanna De Boef, and Tse-Min Lin. 2004. "The Dynamics of the Partisan Gender Gap." *American Political Science Review* 98(3): 515–28.

Brady, Henry E., Sidney Verba, and Kay Lehman Schlozman. 1995. "Beyond SES: A Resource Model of Political Participation." *American Political Science Review* 89(2): 271–94.

Brooks, Clem. 2006. "Voters, Satisficing and Public Policymaking: Recent Directions in the Study of Electoral Politics." *Annual Review of Sociology* 32:191–211.

Burstein, Paul. 2003. "The Impact of Public Opinion on Public Policy: A Review and an Agenda." *Political Research Quarterly* 56(1): 29–40.

Burstein, Paul, and C. Elizabeth Hirsh. 2007. "Interest Organizations, Information, and Policy Innovation in the U.S. Congress." *Sociological Forum* 22(2): 174–99.

Campbell, Angus, Philip E. Converse, Warren E. Miller, and Donald E. Stokes. 1960. *The American Voter*. New York: John Wiley & Sons.

Campbell, Angus, and Homer C. Cooper. 1956. *Group Differences in Attitudes and Votes*. Ann Arbor: Survey Research Center of the University of Michigan.

Citrin, Jack, and Donald Phillip Green. 1990. "The Self-Interest Motive in American Public Opinion." *Research in Macropolitics* 3(1): 1–28.

Clarke, Harold D., Marianne C. Stewart, Mike Alt, and Euel Elliott. 2004. "Men, Women, and the Dynamics of Presidential Approval." *British Journal of Political Science* 35(1): 31–51.

Converse, Philip E. 1990. "Popular Representation and the Distribution of Information." In *Information and Democratic Processes*, edited by John A. Ferejohn and James H. Kuklinski. Chicago: University of Illinois Press.

Dahl, Robert A. 1961. *Who Governs? Democracy and Power in an American City*. New Haven, Conn.: Yale University Press.

Danziger, Sheldon, and Peter Gottschalk. 1995. *America Unequal*. New York: Russell Sage Foundation.

Davis, James A., Tom W. Smith, and Peter V. Marsden. 1972–2008. "General Social Surveys, 1972–2008" [cumulative file] [computer file]. ICPSR25962-v2. Storrs, Conn.: Roper Center for Public Opinion Resarch, University of Connecticut/Ann Arbor, Mich.: Inter-University Consortium for Political and Social Research [distributors], 2010-02-08. doi:10.3886/ICPSR25962.

Delli Carpini, Michael X., and Scott Keeter. 1996. *What Americans Know About Politics and Why It Matters*. New Haven, Conn.: Yale University Press.

DiMaggio, Paul, John Evans, and Bethany Bryson. 1996. "Have Americans' Social Attitudes Become More Polarized?" *American Journal of Sociology* 102(3): 690–755.

Downs, Anthony. 1957. *An Economic Theory of Democracy*. New York: Harper and Row.

Eichenberg, Richard C. 2003. "Gender Differences in Public Attitudes Toward the Use of Force by the United States, 1990–2003." *International Security* 28(1): 110–41.

Enns, Peter K. 2006. "The Uniform Nature of Opinion Change." Paper presented at the Annual Meeting of the American Political Science Association. Philadelphia (September 2006).

Enns, Peter K., and Paul M. Kellstedt. 2008. "Policy Mood and Political Sophistication: Why Everybody Moves Mood." *British Journal of Political Science* 38(3): 433–54.

Erikson, Robert S., Michael B. MacKuen, and James A. Stimson. 2002. *The Macro Polity*. Cambridge: Cambridge University Press.

Evans, John H. 2003. "Have Americans' Attitudes Become More Polarized? An Update." *Social Science Quarterly* 84(1): 71–90.

Gilens, Martin. 2001. "Political Ignorance and Collective Policy Preferences." *American Political Science Review* 95(2): 379–96.

———. 2005. "Inequality and Democratic Responsiveness." *Public Opinion Quarterly* 69(5): 778–96.

———. 2009. "Preference Gaps and Inequality in Representation." *PS: Political Science & Politics* 42(2): 335–41.

Griffin, John D., and Brian Newman. 2005. "Are Voters Better Represented?" *Journal of Politics* 67(4): 1206–27.

———. 2007. "The Unequal Representation of Latinos and Whites." *Journal of Politics* 69(4): 1032–46.

———. 2008. *Minority Report: Evaluating Political Equality in America*. Chicago: University of Chicago Press.

Hetherington, Marc J. 2009. "Putting Polarization in Perspective." *British Journal of Political Science* 39(3): 413–48.

Hungerford, Thomas L. 2008. *Income Inequality, Income Mobility, and Economic Policy: U.S. Trends in the 1980s and 1990s*. CRS Report RL34434. Washington: Congressional Research Service.

Jacobs, Lawrence R., and Benjamin I. Page. 2005. "Who Influences U.S. Foreign Policy?" *American Political Science Review* 99(1): 107–23.

Jacobs, Lawrence R., and Theda Skocpol. 2005. "American Democracy in an Era of Rising Inequality." In *Inequality and American Democracy: What We Know and What We Need to Learn*, edited by Lawrence R. Jacobs and Theda Skocpol. New York: Russell Sage Foundation.

Jacobson, Gary C. 2006. *A Divider, Not a Uniter: George W. Bush and the American People*. New York: Pearson Longman.

Kellstedt, Paul M. 2000. "Media Framing and the Dynamics of Racial Policy Preferences." *American Journal of Political Science* 44(2): 245–60.

———. 2003. *The Mass Media and the Dynamics of American Racial Attitudes*. New York: Cambridge University Press.

Kelly, Nathan J. 2009. *The Politics of Income Inequality in the United States*. New York: Cambridge University Press.

Kelly, Nathan J., and Peter K. Enns. 2010. "Inequality and the Dynamics of Public Opinion: The Self-Reinforcing Link Between Economic Inequality and Mass Preferences." *American Journal of Political Science*. Forthcoming.

Kollman, Ken. 1998. *Outside Lobbying: Public Opinion and Interest Group Strategies*. Princeton, N.J.: Princeton University Press.

Lazersfeld, Bernard R., Paul F. Berelson, and William N. McPhee. 1944. *The People's Choice*. New York: Duell, Sloan, and Pearce.

Lowery, David, and Holly Brasher. 2004. *Organized Interests and American Government*. New York: McGraw-Hill.

Manza, Jeff, and Fay Lomax Cook. 2002. "Policy Responsiveness to Public Opinion: The State of the Debate." In *Navigating Public Opinion: Polls, Policy, and the Future of American Democracy*, edited by Jeff Manza, Fay Lomax Cook, and Benjamin I. Page. Oxford: Oxford University Press.

McCarty, Nolan, Keith T. Poole, and Howard Rosenthal. 2006. *Polarized America: The Dance of Ideology and Unequal Riches*. Cambridge, Mass.: MIT Press.

Meltzer, Alan H., and Scott F. Richard. 1981. "A Rational Theory of the Size of Government." *Journal of Political Economy* 89(4): 914–27.

Nagel, Jack H. 1987. *Participation*. Englewood Cliffs, N.J.: Prentice-Hall.

Olson, Macur, Jr. 1965. *The Logic of Collective Action*. Cambridge, Mass.: Harvard University Press.

Page, Benjamin I., and Lawrence R. Jacobs. 2009. *Class War? What Americans Really Think About Economic Inequality*. Chicago: University of Chicago Press.

Page, Benjamin I., and Robert Y. Shapiro. 1992. *The Rational Public: Fifty Years of Trends in Americans' Policy Preferences*. Chicago: University of Chicago Press.

Piketty, Thomas, and Emmanuel Saez. 2006. "The Evolution of Top Incomes: A Historical Perspective." *American Economic Review* 96(2): 200–205.

———. 2007. "Income and Wage Inequality in the United States, 1913–2002." In *Top Incomes over the Twentieth Century: A Contrast Between European and English-Speaking Countries*, edited by A. B. Atkinson and Thomas Piketty. Oxford: Oxford University Press.

Pitkin, Hanna F. 1967. *The Concept of Representation*. Los Angeles: University of California Press.

Piven, Frances Fox, and Richard A. Cloward. 1978. *Poor People's Movements: Why They Succeed, How They Fail*. New York: Vintage Books.

Rabinowitz, George, and Stuart Elaine Macdonald. 1989. "A Directional Theory of Issue Voting." *American Political Science Review* 83(1): 93–121.

Roper Center Public Opinion Archives. Various years. iPOLL Databank. Roper Center for Public Opinion Research, University of Connecticut. Available at http://www.ropercenter.uconn.edu/data_access/ipoll/ipoll.html (accessed August 23, 2010).

Ryscavage, Paul. 1999. *Income Inequality in America: An Analysis of Trends*. Armonk, N.Y.: M.E. Sharpe.

Sapiro, Virginia, Steven J. Rosenstone, and the National Election Studies. 2004. "American National Election Studies Cumulative Data File, 1948–2004" [computer file]. ICPSR08475-v13. Ann Arbor, Mich.: University of Michigan, Center for Political Studies [producer], 2004. Ann Arbor, Mich.: Inter-University Consortium for Political and Social Research [distributor], 2007-09-25. doi:10.3886/ICPSR08475.

Schattschneider, Elmer E. 1960. *The Semisovereign People: A Realist's View of Democracy in America*. New York: Holt, Rinehart and Winston.

Schlozman, Kay Lehman, and John T. Tierney. 1986. *Organized Interests and American Democracy.* Princeton, N.J.: Princeton University Press.

Sears, David O., and Carolyn L. Funk. 1991. "The Role of Self-Interest in Social and Political Attitudes." *Advances in Experimental Social Psychology* 24(1): 1–91.

Shapiro, Robert Y., and Harpreet Mahajan. 1986. "Gender Differences in Policy Preferences: A Summary of Trends from the 1960's to the 1980's." *Public Opinion Quarterly* 50(1): 42–61.

Soroka, Stuart N., and Christopher Wlezien. 2007. "The Relationship Between Public Opinion and Policy." In *Oxford Handbook of Political Behavior*, edited by Russell J. Dalton and Hans-Dieter Klingemann. Oxford: Oxford University Press.

———. 2008. "On the Limits to Inequality in Representation." *PS: Political Science & Politics* 41(2): 319–27.

———. 2010. *Degrees of Democracy.* Cambridge: Cambridge University Press.

Stimson, James A. 1999. *Public Opinion in America: Moods, Cycles, and Swings,* 2nd ed. Boulder, Colo.: Westview Press.

———. 2004. *Tides of Consent: How Public Opinion Shapes American Politics.* New York: Cambridge University Press.

Stimson, James A., Michael B. MacKuen, and Robert S. Erikson. 1995. "Dynamic Representation." *American Political Science Review* 89(3): 543–65.

Truman, David B. 1951. *The Governmental Process: Political Interests and Public Opinion.* New York: Alfred A. Knopf.

Ura, Joseph Daniel, and Christopher R. Ellis. 2008. "Income, Preferences, and the Dynamics of Policy Responsiveness." *PS: Political Science & Politics* 41(4): 785–94.

Verba, Sidney, and Norman H. Nie. 1972. *Participation in America.* New York: Harper and Row.

Verba, Sidney, Norman H. Nie, and Jae-On Kim. 1978. *Participation and Political Equality.* Cambridge, Mass.: Cambridge University Press.

Walker, Jack L., Jr. 1991. *Mobilizing Interest Groups in America.* Ann Arbor, Mich.: University of Michigan Press.

Weakliem, David. 2003. "Public Opinion Research and Political Sociology." *Research in Political Sociology* 12(1): 49–80.

Weakliem, David, Robert Andersen, and Anthony F. Heath. 2005. "By Popular Demand: The Effect of Public Opinion on Income Inequality." *Comparative Sociology* 4(3–4): 260–84.

Weaver, R. Kent, Robert Y. Shapiro, and Lawrence R. Jacobs. 1995. "Trends: Welfare." *Public Opinion Quarterly* 59(4): 606–27.

Wlezien, Christopher. 1995. "The Public as Thermostat: Dynamics of Preferences for Spending." *American Journal of Political Science* 39(4): 981–1000.

———. 1996. "Dynamics of Representation: The Case of U.S. Spending on Defense." *British Journal of Political Science* 26(1): 81–103.

———. 2004. "Patterns of Representation: Dynamics of Public Preferences and Policy." *Journal of Politics* 66(1): 1–24.

Wright, John R. 2003. *Interest Groups and Congress.* New York: Longman.

Zaller, John R. 1992. *The Nature and Origins of Mass Opinion.* New York: Cambridge University Press.

PART I

Group Opinions

Part I

Introduction

PETER K. ENNS AND CHRISTOPHER WLEZIEN

T HIS BOOK BEGAN with the observation that where preferences differ, all groups cannot have their preferences represented in policy. That is, not everyone's policy preferences will win. Understanding group opinion—how it differs or agrees across various segments of society—thus provides an important first step toward understanding the nature of representation. To this end, chapter 1 looked at policy preferences by income, education, partisanship, and race. Although meaningful differences do exist, we also saw surprising similarities in group preferences. Where scholars have assumed unequal representation, group preferences often are indistinguishable. In such cases, policy cannot align with one group's preferences more than another's; representation in policy outcomes—that is, substantive representation—will be equal.

The next four chapters build on this analysis by exploring the similarities and differences in group opinions. We see additional evidence that common perceptions about differences in opinions across socioeconomic and racial groups do not receive support. We also see evidence that assumptions about similarities in partisan polarization must be updated. Together, these chapters offer a nuanced picture of public opinion that challenges conventional wisdom. They also show that before we can draw meaningful inferences about representation, we must first understand what policies different groups prefer.

Marisa Abrajano and Keith T. Poole start the section. In addition to offering a new methodology for studying group survey opinion, their chapter provides new insight into the policy preferences of different racial and ethnic groups. Their findings offer an important contrast with what scholars and pundits often assume about racial and ethnic group opinion. For example, in terms of support for government services, Asian policy preferences match more closely with African American preferences than do Latino preferences. Although existing scholarship has often presumed that racial-ethnic groups hold similar policy prefer-ences (such as Garcia 2003; Hero 1992) and that Latinos and blacks are most likely to share common preferences (Kaufman 2003), we see that the story is more complex. Knowing whether policymakers follow the preferences of one minority group does not tell us whether this represen-tation conflicts or coincides with the preferences of other racial minori-ties. Their analysis also shows that racial-ethnic group support for vari-ous policy programs does not always reflect the income status of the group. In other words, socioeconomic indicators are not necessarily the driving force in racial-ethnic group opinion.

The next two chapters examine heterogeneity in partisan polariza-tion. We saw in the introductory chapter (see figure 1.6) that partisan opinion differences have emerged as one of the most important areas of policy disagreement in contemporary politics. Thus, partisanship is one of the most likely areas for differential representation. Exploring this heterogeneity, Christopher Ellis and Joseph Daniel Ura add an impor-tant new dimension to the debate (see, for example, Frank 2004; Bartels 2006) on whether low-income voters have moved to the Republican party on account of moral issues and against their economic self-interest. Furthermore, their chapter shows that even when different income and education groups appear to update their opinions in parallel—as we saw in the introductory chapter for the general public mood—the inter-action between income and education can produce distinct patterns of results. This finding suggests that even when group opinions seem to move in tandem, room for differential representation may exist. David A. Hopkins and Laura Stoker also examine the increasing influence of partisanship in the electorate. Their focus is geographic heterogeneity and its influence on presidential voting. Specifically, they show that the increasing partisan structure of the presidential vote has not evolved uniformly across the states. The finding offers insight into historical pat-terns of voting, future presidential-campaign strategies, and incentives for presidents to increasingly cater to their partisan base. Their state-level analysis also suggests that which party holds power will increas-ingly determine who gets represented.

In the final chapter of part 1, Katherine Cramer Walsh provides fur-ther evidence that the seemingly innocuous assumption that policy pref-erences will coincide with group "self-interest" does not always receive support. Her listening investigations reveal that upper- and lower-class individuals both tend to withhold support for universal health care. Walsh's qualitative approach enables her to go beyond the subgroup analysis reported in the introductory chapter and offer an explanation of *why* different social classes have similar health care preferences. Specifically, she finds that the structure underpinning these expressed opinions varies in important ways across social class. Furthermore, her listening investigations demonstrate that even if a policy corresponded with both groups' preferences, lower-class respondents would be unlikely to *perceive* that politicians had represented their interests. These findings indicate that simply knowing whether a policy matches the expressed opinions of a particular group does not tell us *who* the policy is most likely to benefit or which group individuals *believe* the policy benefits.

Individually, each of these chapters makes an important contribution to the public opinion literature. Together, the first half of this volume combines to offer an important lesson for the study of representation. When asking whose preferences policymakers represent, scholars must avoid common assumptions about groups' self-interests and policy preferences. To understand who gets represented, we must first understand what policy outcomes are preferred by various constituent groups.

References

Bartels, Larry. 2006. "What's the Matter with *What's the Matter with Kansas?*" *Quarterly Journal of Political Science* 1(2): 201–26.

Frank, Thomas. 2004. *What's the Matter with Kansas? How Conservatives Won the Hearts of America*. New York: Henry Holt.

Garcia, John A. 2003. *Latino Politics in America: Community, Culture, and Interests*. Lanham, Md.: Rowman and Littlefield.

Hero, Rodney. 1992. *Hispanics and the U.S. Political System*. Philadelphia: Temple University Press.

Kaufman, Karen. 2003. *The Urban Voter: Group Conflict and Mayoral Voting Behavior in American Cities*. Ann Arbor: University of Michigan Press.

Chapter 2

Assessing the Ethnic and Racial Diversity of American Public Opinion

MARISA ABRAJANO AND KEITH T. POOLE

RESEARCHERS WHO ARE interested in understanding subgroup behavior typically face a series of trade-offs in their research design, most notably those pertaining to sample size and the types of questions available in public opinion surveys. Consider the 2004 National Annenberg Election Survey, which is a companion to the 2000 survey conducted by the Annenberg team of scholars at the University of Pennsylvania (Romer et al. 2006). This survey is highly desirable for most social scientists because it contains more than 150 questions about individual political attitudes, behaviors, and perceptions. Moreover, because it interviews more than eighty thousand people, the number of subgroup populations captured is also sizable—approximately five thousand Latinos and seven thousand blacks. A major drawback, however, is that key questions on issue attitudes are yes or no responses. More fine-grained measures such as 7-point issue-scale questions were not used.

On the other hand, the preeminent survey on American political attitudes and behavior, the American National Election Study (NES), contains numerous 7-point issue scales, as well as several detailed issue questions and feeling-thermometer questions. The main problem with this dataset is its small sample size (N = 1,212) and thus the limited sample of subgroup populations. In 2004 the NES interviewed 81 Latinos, 180 blacks, and 876 whites.

We resolve these two concerns by developing a method that combines the desirable qualities of separate surveys by linking survey respondents based on their reported internal (subjective) utility for political stimuli.

In our application, we combine the large sample size of the Annenberg survey and the detailed issue questions provided by the NES survey. By doing so, we are able to overcome the "small sample size" and "detailed question" trade-off encountered by researchers studying subgroup populations.

More specifically, our method of linking respondents is rather straightforward. For each respondent in the larger yet less comprehensive sample (Annenberg), we search for the respondent in the smaller and more comprehensive sample (NES) with the closest set of thermometer scores for a given set of political stimuli.[1] We use feeling-thermometer questions since, as we will discuss in more detail, they are likely to be the most accurate indicator of an individual's *subjective utility* because they are measures of *affect*. Because feeling thermometers ask individuals to provide their subjective feelings of "warmth" toward a politician, a political party, and the like, we believe that such responses are a good measure of one's preference for the stimuli in question. By matching respondents on their subjective utility for these types of political stimuli, we create a "linked" sample in which we now have Annenberg respondents answering all the NES questions. To illustrate this point, say, for instance, that Annenberg did not ask respondents whether they prefer blue to orange, but the NES did. By using our linking procedure, we now can accurately estimate whether the respondent from the linked sample prefers blue to orange.[2] Our analyses in this chapter focus on subgroup populations based on race and ethnicity, though this technique can certainly be applied to other subgroup populations. In particular, we examine their opinions on policies pertaining to social welfare and redistribution.

We make several contributions to the existing literature. First, racial-ethnic group opinion provides another lens to determine "who gets represented" in American politics. Second, our analysis of racial-ethnic group preference offers a deeper understanding of the relationship between social class and representation, as one's social class and racial-ethnic identity tend to overlap with each other.[3] Finally, we also hope to reintroduce the usefulness of feeling thermometers not only to researchers interested in understanding voter attitudes and perceptions but also to those who wish to study new methodological techniques for expanding the amount of data available to scholars studying subgroup populations.

In the next section, we discuss the literature on the various strands of research focusing on feeling-thermometer questions.

Using Feeling Thermometers to Capture Affect

Feeling-thermometer questions were originally developed for group evaluations by Aage Clausen and were first used in the American National Election Study in 1964. The group feeling-thermometer questions were for Protestants, Catholics, Jews, blacks, whites, southerners, big business, labor unions, liberals, and conservatives. Herbert Weisberg and Jerrold Rusk added feeling-thermometer questions for individuals (either prominent politicians or candidates) in the 1968 NES. A feeling thermometer asks respondents to respond to a set of stimuli (made up of individuals or groups) based on their subjective views of warmth toward each. The thermometer ranges from 0 to 100 degrees with 100 indicating a warm and very favorable feeling, 50 indicating neutrality toward the group or the politician, and 0 indicating that the respondent feels cold and very unfavorable toward the group or the politician.

Since their inception in the 1964 NES, feeling thermometers have remained a constant not only in this preeminent survey on American political behavior and attitudes but also in other fields (such as psychology). Feeling thermometers emerged as a standard tool in survey-based political research for several reasons. As Weisberg and Rusk (1970) note, feeling thermometers allow respondents to evaluate candidates on "those dimensions which come naturally to them, [those] which are [their] normal guidelines for thinking about candidates." Because feeling thermometers do not impose any types of frames on respondents, they can tap into those evaluative dimensions that they consider most important to them. Feeling thermometers have also been shown to accurately capture an individual's affective sentiments. As such, we expect the responses from a set of feeling thermometers to be an excellent proxy for an individual's internal subjective utility.

We assume that an individual's reported feeling for a politician or a group is generated by the individual's subjective utility function over the relevant issue-policy space in question, along with all nonpolicy attributes, related to the individual's psychological makeup. That is,

$$\text{Thermometer Score} = f\,[U_i(X, Z)]$$

where f is a simple mapping function that takes the subjective utility and translates it into the 0 to 100 scale, U_i is the utility function for individual i, X are the relevant issue-policy dimensions, and Z are dimensions such as likability, leadership, and, for ethnic-racial groups, possibly one pertaining to group identity. The combination of X and Z is in part determined by the standard demographic characteristics that we are concerned with as social scientists. With respect to the X dimensions, we assume that, consistent with a standard spatial model of choice (Downs 1957; Enelow and Hinich 1984), the individual has an ideal point (or most preferred point) on each dimension. The Z dimensions are best thought of as *valence* dimensions (Enelow and Hinich 1984); that is, either the politician or group has the attribute or doesn't—likable, not likable; honest, corrupt; and so on. Here we assume that individuals prefer the positive side of the valence dimension and politicians or groups that have the attributes that produce a higher subjective utility. When we pair respondents based on sets of thermometers we are actually linking people with similar internal-utility functions.[4] If this logic holds, pairing respondents based on their feeling-thermometer scores should be more accurate than pairing respondents based on demographics if what we are interested in is distributions of subpopulations over political issues.

Feeling-thermometer questions sparked a great deal of research in the 1970s and early 1980s with a primary focus on modeling the latent dimensions underlying the thermometers as well as testing theories of spatial voting (see Weisberg and Rusk 1970; Wang, Schonemann, and Rusk 1975; Rabinowitz 1976; Cahoon, Hinich, and Ordeshook 1978; Poole and Rosenthal 1984; Poole 1984, 1990). Other scholars explored the reasons behind the variations in feeling-thermometer responses and cautioned in the interpretation of these responses (see Knight 1984; Giles and Evans 1986; Wilcox, Sigelman, and Cook 1989). This is because individuals can vary in their interpretation of the 0 to 100 scale: some may choose to use the entire scale, others may restrict themselves to only a certain part of the scale (Wilcox, Sigelman, and Cook 1989). As such, Kathleen Knight (1984) recommends adjusting thermometer ratings for groups by subtracting the average score for an individual's set of responses from the score for the group of interest. Micheal Giles and Arthur Evans (1986) also suggest accounting for both the mean and the standard deviation of the thermometer scores. Thus, when working with any type of survey data, potential concerns such as these exist.[5]

Since this burst of activity, for approximately twenty years, thermometers have been relatively understudied. Our method is somewhat similar in spirit to the increasingly popular method known as matching, but our procedure differs in several major ways. Essentially, what matching seeks to do is to isolate any other effects aside from the variable of interest identified by the researcher. For example, political scientists studying political behavior have long been interested in understanding whether voter mobilization efforts, such as being contacted by a campaign or receiving mailers, increase turnout (Arceneaux, Gerber, and Green 2006; Imai 2005; Gerber and Green 2000, 2005). The treatment group in these studies is those who were asked to vote, and the control group is those who were not asked. One way to assess the impact of voter contact on turnout is to match the treated group with the control group based on background variables, such as age, education, income, and the like. Matching on these demographic characteristics should control for other factors that may influence turnout, and thus any differences in turnout could be attributed to mobilization efforts. In this regard, the procedure mirrors a controlled trial design experiment used by medical researchers. The logic is that, after matching individuals from both groups based on specific background characteristics, any difference that arises can be attributed to the treatment being applied.

Our method also pairs individuals based on shared characteristics, which in our case pertain to measures of affect, but our goal is not to identify a specific causal mechanism between a treated and an untreated group. Instead, we match individuals based on their subjective utility to predict their political attitudes and preferences. The primary factor that distinguishes our technique from matching is that most, if not all, of the research using matching methods have done so by pairing individuals based on their demographic characteristics (for example, Nickerson 2005). This, though, is not the only observed data available to researchers. In fact, we find affect to do a better job at predicting individuals' political attitudes than do their demographics (which will be discussed in the following section).

Data and Methods

We use two datasets—the 2004 National Annenberg Election Survey and the 2004 NES. The 2004 NES interviewed 1,212 individuals, who were asked to give thermometer ratings to fourteen political stimuli: George W. Bush, John Kerry, Ralph Nader, Richard Cheney, John Edwards, Laura Bush, Hillary Clinton, Bill Clinton, Colin Powell, John McCain, John Ashcroft, the Democratic Party, the Republican Party, and Ronald Reagan.

The 2004 National Annenberg Election Survey was designed as a rolling cross-sectional panel in the field from October 27, 2003, to November 16, 2004,[6] and randomly selected and then interviewed 81,422 individuals during the period. Given the nature of the survey design, an average of 150 to 300 interviews were conducted on a daily basis. Altogether, twenty thermometer questions were asked in the Annenberg. Respondents were asked to evaluate the following political figures: George W. Bush, John Kerry, Richard Cheney, John Edwards, Ralph Nader, Wesley Clark, Howard Dean, Richard Gephardt, Joe Lieberman, John Ashcroft, Laura Bush, Bill Clinton, Hillary Clinton, Rudy Giuliani, Albert Gore, Teresa Heinz Kerry, Rush Limbaugh, John McCain, Condoleezza Rice, and Arnold Schwarzenegger. Unfortunately, respondents were not asked to evaluate all these individuals for each wave of the survey. And though the thermometer questions used in the NES do overlap, they are not identical. Thus we link respondents based only on the ten feeling-thermometer questions that were common to both datasets (Bush, Kerry, Cheney, Edwards, Nader, Laura Bush, Bill Clinton, Hillary Clinton, Ashcroft, and McCain).[7] In the Annenberg, respondents were given four to seven stimuli; in the NES, they were given all ten.

Our formula for pairing respondents is quite straightforward. For each respondent in the larger yet less comprehensive sample (Annenberg), we search for the respondent in the smaller and more comprehensive sample (NES) with the closest set of thermometer scores for a given set of political stimuli. We identify the respondent whose *link score* minimizes the following expression:

$$\text{Link Score} = \frac{\sum_{k=1}^{K} |r_i - r_j|}{K}$$

where K denotes the number of political stimuli in common, r_i is the ith respondent in one of the surveys and r_j is the jth respondent in the other survey. If a respondent pairs perfectly to all the stimuli, then his or her link score would be 0.

For example, suppose the Annenberg respondent answers five thermometer questions—giving Bush a score of 100, Kerry a score of 0, Cheney a score of 60, Edwards a score of 40, and Bill Clinton a score of 0. Our method then finds an NES respondent with the closest scores for all the stimuli. Thus, suppose an NES respondent gives Bush a score of 100, Kerry a score of 0, Cheney a score of 50, Edwards a score of 50, and Bill Clinton a score 0. Of these five answers, the Annenberg respondent and the NES respondent differ only on the scores for Cheney and Edwards. This respondent's link score would be as follows:

$$4 = \frac{(|100-100|)+(|0-0|)+(|60-50|)+(|40-50|)+(|0-0|)}{5}$$

If this is the lowest possible link score, then this is the NES respondent who is closest to this particular Annenberg respondent. Among the 61,980 Annenberg respondents with four or more thermometer scores, the algorithm matched 10,246 respondents (16.5 percent) with NES respondents who had identical scores. The link score ranges from a minimum of 0, indicating a perfect score, to a maximum of 25. The average link score is 3.38, with a standard deviation of 2.74. Considering that an individual responded to an average number of approximately 4.6 stimuli (with a standard deviation of 0.70), this means that the average link score is off on average by less than 1 unit on a scale of 0 to 100.[8]

Assessing the Validity of the Linking Procedure

We first present several checks to evaluate the accuracy and effectiveness of our linking procedure. The most basic test is to see how closely the distributions of the linked Annenberg respondents (who, because of our procedure, now have responses to all the questions from the NES survey) compare with the attitudinal distributions from respondents in the NES and the Annenberg data. It is helpful to compare these distributions in our linked data with those from these other two datasets because we know what the distributions look like in the NES and the Annenberg. Again, what we refer to as the "linked sample" consists of Annenberg respondents who have "hypothetically answered" all the questions from the 2004 NES survey.

But before turning to the distributions on attitudes and opinions, it is worthwhile to know the pairings of the respondents from the Latino, black, and white samples in the linked data with those in the NES data. That is, we are interested in determining whether blacks from the NES were primarily linked with blacks in the Annenberg and whether the majority of Latinos from the linked data map onto Latino respondents in the NES data. The breakdown of Latinos, blacks, and whites in the linked data (using the demographics from the linked-to NES respondents) is as follows: 45,892 whites, 8,630 blacks, and 3,457 Latinos. Latinos in the linked dataset paired with 244 NES Latinos and 300 NES black respondents. Therefore, the majority of Latino respondents from the linked dataset were actually whites from the NES (2,810 respondents). The same is true for the black sample in our linked dataset: 6,373 respondents were paired with white respondents from the NES, 1,413 respondents with black NES respondents, and 781 respondents with Latino NES respondents. Finally, for the white sample, the majority (39,805 respondents) mapped onto the affective signatures of white NES respondents, 2,667 onto black NES respondents, and 2,536 onto NES Latino respondents. Given that the distribution in the NES is heavily skewed toward whites, it is understandable why the majority of blacks and Latinos from the linked data mapped onto the subjective utilities of whites. These distributions suggest that demographic characteristics do not necessarily predict an individual's subjective internal utility function.

Given the small samples of blacks, Latinos, and Asians in the 2004 NES, we are fairly confident that the distribution of our much larger linked samples over the 7-point scales more accurately represent the distribution of these racial-ethnic groups in the general population. We recognize that that this depends on our claim that our linking procedure can ignore race-ethnicity by matching on subjective utility. As such, we are assigning whites' attitudes on policy issues in the NES to blacks or Latinos in the Annenberg survey. To some, our claim may seem radical or a big leap of faith. What it boils down to saying is that many whites share the opinions of blacks, Latinos, and Asians (note that the distributions of the NES respondents from the three groups greatly overlap in table 2.4), and our subjective utility method simply matches some whites with some blacks and some Latinos who share the same opinions.

Importantly, our analysis of public opinion across racial-ethnic groups is in line with previous research. It also offers a broader picture of American public opinion by situating the viewpoints of the other two major racial-ethnic groups, Latinos and Asians, onto the traditional black-white spectrum. Until now, how the attitudes of these two groups compare with those of whites and blacks has been underexplored in the public opinion literature.

We now turn to table 2.1, which presents several comparisons of demographic distributions, based on race, gender, age, and education, for our linked sample (here, we use the demographics from the linked-to NES respondents), the original Annenberg survey, and the original NES survey. We see that the gender distribution in the linked data is 44.8 percent male and 55.2 percent female, which is similar to the NES breakdown—46.7 percent male and 53.3 percent female. The breakdown for a respondent's education level is also quite close across the three sets of data, though it is not as precise as the gender breakdowns. In terms of race-ethnicity, the percentage of blacks appears to be overrepresented in our linked sample (13.9 percent) relative to both the Annenberg sample (8 percent) and the NES sample (9.9 percent). This suggests that several blacks in the NES sample had affective "signatures" that linked many nonblacks (mostly whites) in the Annenberg sample. However, it is impressive that the percentage of blacks in the linked data is nearly identical to the actual percentage of blacks in the U.S. population, 13.4 percent.[9] The percentage of whites in the linked sample is somewhat lower than it is for the other two datasets, 74 percent versus 83.3 percent and 78 percent. The Latino sample is much closer, with 5.6 percent in the linked data, 7.5 percent in the Annenberg, and 6.7 percent in the NES. In this case, these percentages underestimate the actual Latino population in the United States, as they now make up 15 percent of the total population.[10] Finally, for Asians the percentage in each dataset is very similar though it underestimates their actual share of the total U.S. population, which is 5 percent. The final demographic variable we consider is age. Here, the linked, Annenberg, and NES data are just about identical, with an average age of 48 in both the Annenberg and the linked data and 47.3 in the NES. Overall, this initial check makes us reasonably confident that our linking technique, along with its intended goal of being able to predict group political attitudes and preferences, is also doing an adequate job of inferring the demographic distributions of the linked sample.

These distributions are suggestive, but a key robustness check would compare the performance of the linking procedure in predicting key political attitudes to the predictions generated by standard demographic-matching methods. Table 2.2 compares the linking procedure with the standard procedure on matching that uses basic demographic characteristics, such as gender, age, education, and income.[11] In predicting one's vote intention, partisanship, and ideology, the linking procedure is ca-

Table 2.1   **Distribution of Demographic Indicators in the Linked, Annenberg, and NES Data**

	Linked	Annenberg	NES
Gender (percent)			
Male	44.8	44.7	46.7
Female	55.2	55.3	53.3
Education (percent)			
Eight grade or less	2.5	2.0	3.1
Grades 9 to 11	4.8	5.3	6.0
High school diploma	30.5	25.6	29.3
Some college	23.5	17.7	21.8
Two-year college	9.3	7.9	9.9
Bachelor's degree	17.8	20.0	18.4
Advanced	11.5	14.4	11.5
Race-ethnicity (percent)			
Black	13.9	8.0	9.9
Asian	2.0	1.5	1.6
White	74.0	83.3	78.0
Latino	5.6	7.5	6.7
Age (mean)	48.0	48.0	47.3
N	61,980	81,422	1,212

Source: Authors' compilation, based on the 2004 National Annenberg Election Survey (Romer et al. 2006) and the 2004 National Election Study (NES) (Center for Political Studies 2004).

pable of correctly classifying a larger percentage of respondents than does the matching procedure based on demographics. In particular, note the accuracy of the linking procedure's ability to correctly classify vote choice—90 percent for Kerry and 97 percent for Bush. Demographic matching did not perform nearly as well and classified only 52 percent of Kerry supporters and 53 percent of Bush voters. In terms of partisan and ideological preferences, the percentage of respondents correctly classified under the linking are not nearly as high as for vote choice but still outperforms the percentage correctly classified using the demographic matching procedure. This comparison provides us with ample reassurance that our linking technique is tapping into the subjective utility of individuals and can accurately predict their political preferences.

Figure 2.1 presents another way to assess how well demographics versus feeling thermometers can predict key political attitudes. This figure graphs the R-squared values of two sets of regression models—one in which the dependent variable is partisanship and the other in which it is ideology; in the first set of models, the independent variables are the

Table 2.2   Comparing the Linking Procedure with Demographic
                 Matching

Political Variable	Linking Procedure		Matching Procedure (Age, Education, Gender)	
	Percent Correctly Classified	Number of Exact Matches	Percent Correctly Classified	Number of Exact Matches
Vote choice				
Kerry	90	117	52	33
Bush	97	128	53	63
Party ID				
Democrats	42	80	26	26
Independents	27	8	16	8
Republicans	41	65	30	16
Ideology				
Liberal	31	16	22	4
Moderate	35	30	31	32
Conservative	44	39	31	22

Source: Authors' compilation, based on the 2004 National Annenberg Election Survey
(Romer et al. 2006) and the 2004 National Election Study (Center for Political Studies 2004).

Figure 2.1   Predicting Ideology and Partisanship as a Function of
               Demographics Versus Thermometer Scores

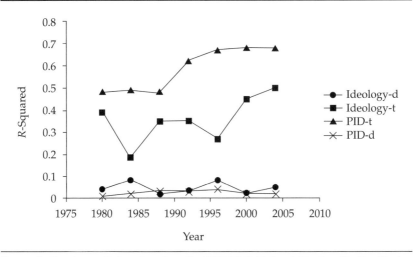

Source: Authors' compilation, based on the 1975–2004 National Election Studies (Sapiro,
Rosenstone, and the National Election Studies 2004).
Note: Ideology-d and PID-d reflect values based on demographic variables. Ideology-t and
PID-t reflect values based on thermometer scores.

demographic characteristics of the respondents, and in second set, the explanatory variables are the feeling-thermometer scores. We use the NES data from 1980 to 2004 and estimate these models for every presidential election year. The graph indicates that the fit for the partisanship and ideology models is significantly higher when the independent variables are the feeling-thermometer scores rather than demographics. Across this time period, the average R-squared value in the ideology model predicted by thermometers is .36, compared to an average R-squared value of .05 in the model predicted by demographics. Similarly, in the party identification model predicted by the thermometers, the average R-squared value is .59, relative to an average R-squared value of .02 in the model that uses demographics for its explanatory variables.[12]

An additional robustness check is to compare the racial-ethnic group distributions on a fundamental attitudinal variable—that of vote choice.[13] Because we know whom respondents reported voting for in both the NES and the Annenberg, we can compare the vote choice distributions from our linked data with these datasets. Overall, the vote choice distributions for all three datasets are quite comparable. In the linked data, 54.1 percent of Latinos supported Kerry, relative to 60.5 percent in the NES sample and 62 percent in the Annenberg survey who voted for Kerry. The linked estimate matches the closest to predictions from the Nation Election Pool (NEP), which estimates Latino support for Kerry at 53.3 percent.[14] A somewhat greater discrepancy emerges with respect to the Latino distributions on their support for Bush, with the linked data estimating 43.5 percent, the NES estimating 34.9 percent, and the Annenberg reporting 38 percent who voted for Bush. The NEP estimated 44 percent of the Latino vote going to Bush, which is the largest share that any Republican presidential candidate has ever received from the Latino electorate. The distribution for whites in the linked data slightly underestimates their support for Kerry, relative to the other two datasets. Note that the percentage of whites supporting Bush is nearly identical for all three datasets. In terms of actual support for Bush, which the NEP estimated at 58.1 percent, however, the linked estimates are once again the closest. Turning to the vote choice distributions for blacks, the percentage of support for Kerry (85.5 percent) is located between the estimates from the Annenberg and the NES, 89.7 percent and 84.5 percent, respectively. Black support for Bush was also comparable in the linked and the NEP data, 10.4 percent and 12.1 percent, respectively. An almost identical percentage of blacks in the Annenberg survey reported voting for Bush, 10.3 percent. Based on the distributions on both group attitudes and demographics presented thus far, it appears that our linking procedure recovers group characteristics fairly well from both of these dimensions.

Another way to determine how well the thermometer scores capture an individual's internal utility function is to look at the distributions of

Table 2.3   Group Thermometer Evaluations, by Ethnic-Racial Group

| R's Race | Group Thermometer Scores Toward . . . | | | | | | | |
	Latinos Linked	NES	Blacks Linked	NES	Whites Linked	NES	N Linked	NES
Latino	82.9	82.7	74.2	75.8	70.7	74.2	2814	66
	(14.0)	(15.5)	(20.1)	(18.7)	(19.6)	(18.3)		
Black	67.1	68.8	88.5	87.0	71.7	72.3	6971	154
	(17.5)	(18.2)	(14.7)	(15.5)	(23.0)	(20.0)		
White	66.6	66.6	68.9	69.2	74.3	73.8	39736	763
	(19.1)	(19.3)	(18.8)	(18.4)	(19.2)	(19.2)		

Source: Authors' compilation, based on the 2004 National Annenberg Election Survey (Romer et al. 2006) and the 2004 National Election Study (Center for Political Studies 2004). *Note:* Standard deviation in parentheses.

the ethnic-racial group thermometers in the NES for whites, blacks, and Latinos. These thermometer questions simply ask respondents how they feel toward whites, blacks, and Latinos. If these feeling thermometers are really tapping into an individual's attitudes and preferences, we would expect that for each ethnic group, on average, they would feel warmest toward their own group. We present these distributions in table 2.3 for both the linked data (using the group thermometers from the linked-to NES respondents) and for the original NES data. First, we see that, consistent with our expectations, each ethnic-racial group evaluates their respective ethnic-racial group most positively. For instance, in evaluating their own group, blacks' average thermometer score is 88.5 in the linked data and 87 in the NES data. Blacks then feel warmest toward whites, who are followed by Latinos. Likewise, Latinos rate themselves the highest with a mean score of 82.9. But unlike blacks, Latinos, after their own group, feel warmest toward blacks and then whites. For whites, they, too, rate themselves the highest, followed by blacks and then Latinos. Notice, though, that across these three racial-ethnic groups, it is blacks who evaluate their own group with the highest score (88.5), followed by Latinos (82.9) and then whites (73.8). Blacks may feel "warmest" toward their own group due to their shared historical experiences of discrimination in the United States, which as Michael Dawson (1995) argues, has created a very powerful and cohesive black group identity. On the other hand, given that the term Latino is a panethnic label that encompasses individuals from various Spanish-speaking countries of origin, their level of group cohesiveness and identity may not be as strong as it is for blacks. Along with validating the claim that thermometer scores tap into affect, table 2.3 further highlights how

Table 2.4   Mean Responses to 7-Point Issue Scales, Linked Versus NES Data

	Government Spending		Defense Spending		Government Jobs		Government Aid to Blacks	
	Linked	NES	Linked	NES	Linked	NES	Linked	NES
Race								
Latino	4.52	4.57	4.58	4.49	4.13	4.28	4.29	4.28
Black	5.41	5.25	4.42	4.30	3.15	3.31	3.13	3.31
White	4.38	4.36	4.76	4.65	4.45	4.82	4.88	4.82
Gender								
Men	4.26	4.32	4.84	4.74	4.49	4.61	4.70	4.61
Women	4.75	4.69	4.53	4.41	4.00	4.48	4.47	4.48
Vote choice								
Bush	3.89	3.71	5.30	5.19	5.06	5.17	5.34	5.30
Kerry	5.15	5.07	4.03	3.89	3.38	3.49	3.77	3.88
N	53,232	1,060	53,877	1,061	56,384	1,103	54,459	1,073

Source: Authors' compilation, based on the 2004 National Annenberg Election Survey (Romer et al. 2006) and the 2004 National Election Study (Center for Political Studies 2004).

closely the distributions from the linked data follow the distributions from the NES data. Again, affective signatures trump ethnicity in that our Latinos and blacks in the Annenberg sample are linked *mostly to whites* with nearly identical affective signatures in the NES sample. These results increase our confidence in the effectiveness of the linking procedure.

We now move on to table 2.4, which looks at the responses from the nine 7-point issue scale questions. In particular, we compare the mean responses of our respondents from the linked data with the mean responses of our respondents from the NES, by their race-ethnicity, gender, and vote choice (Bush or Kerry). Recall that the Annenberg data did not contain any of these 7-point issue scale questions; as such, the row entries in table 2.4 represent Annenberg survey respondents who have now "answered" the NES 7-point issue scale questions as a result of our linking procedure.

These issue scale questions ask individuals to place themselves on a 7-point scale on a number of issues, ranging from the U.S. intervention in Iraq to government aid in assisting blacks and Latinos.[15] Only the end points of the 7-point scales are labeled, and respondents are told these (usually) polar opposite positions. For example, the "government services" question is phrased as follows: "Some people think the govern-

Environment vs. Jobs		Women's Role		Government vs. Private Health Insurance		Government Aid to Latinos		U.S. Intervention	
Linked	NES	Linked	NES	Linked	NES	Linked	NES	Linked	NES
3.73	3.82	1.54	1.53	3.58	3.42	3.61	3.68	3.86	3.65
3.66	3.71	1.65	2.01	2.82	3.31	3.76	3.84	2.99	3.19
3.54	3.58	2.00	1.93	3.79	3.78	4.91	4.92	3.98	3.93
3.50	3.52	1.94	1.96	3.79	3.79	4.75	4.71	4.15	3.98
3.59	3.66	1.90	1.88	3.46	3.54	4.60	4.62	3.47	3.55
4.03	4.04	2.22	2.17	4.35	4.41	5.20	5.15	4.72	4.67
2.98	3.02	1.60	1.72	2.88	3.06	3.97	4.17	2.79	2.81
51,536	1,019	59,117	1,157	56,160	1,112	48,290	937	53,013	1041

ment should provide fewer services, even in areas such as health and education, in order to reduce spending. Suppose these people are at one end of a scale, at point 1. Other people feel it is important for the government to provide many more services even if it means an increase in spending. Suppose these people are at the other end, at point 7. And, of course, some other people have opinions somewhere in between, at points 2, 3, 4, 5, or 6."[16]

As these distributions indicate, the mean responses appear to be quite similar across these different subgroup populations. Responses by Latinos, blacks, and whites in the linked data are nearly identical to those in the NES for the scaling questions pertaining to government services, defense spending, jobs, aid to blacks, the environment, and aid to Latinos. Likewise, the distributions of the mean responses to the other demographic subgroup that we examine, gender, are comparable in both sets of data. For example, in the scaling question that asks about women's role in society, the mean response in the linked dataset for women is 1.90, and the average response of women from the NES is 1.88. The mean response by men in the linked data is 1.94, and in the NES, mean response of men is 1.96. In fact, the largest discrepancy in the NES and the linked distributions, based on gender, is only .48. Finally, we examine Kerry supporters versus those who supported Bush in 2004. Once again

Table 2.5   Distribution of Linked, Annenberg, and NES Data on a Common Issue Question

	Approve of the way the president is handling the economy (percent approving)		
	Linked	NES	Annenberg
Race			
Latino	36.5	35.8	43.9
Black	10.7	12.8	13.7
White	50.4	47.3	48.6
Gender			
Men	44.3	43.1	48.5
Women	41.5	38.1	42.0
Aggregate	42.8	40.4	44.9
N	61,948	1,121	84,122

Source: Authors' compilation, based on the 2004 National Annenberg Election Survey (Romer et al. 2006) and the 2004 National Election Study (Center for Political Studies 2004).

we find that the average responses to these 7-point issue scale questions from the two datasets are almost identical to one another, with the largest difference between them being .18. More important, this technique also increases, by a rather significant amount, the sample size of the racial-ethnic groups in the linked dataset.

Next, we compare the distributions to an issue question common to both the NES and the Annenberg survey. This is a particularly rigorous way to test the validity of our procedure, because if the distribution on the linked respondents, who are in fact the Annenberg respondents answering an NES question, reproduces a similar distribution to that of the Annenberg respondents, then we have every reason to believe that linking individuals based on subjective utility can recover groups' distributions on policy preferences and attitudes. Thus, in table 2.5, we present the distributions to this common issue question, which is one pertaining to opinions on George W. Bush's handling of the economy (approve or disapprove). We also include the distributions from the NES survey to check whether the linked distributions reflect the Annenberg distribution more so than that of the NES. As in our presentation of previous distributions, we look at groups' opinions by race-ethnicity and gender.

What is striking about these distributions is how well the linked data recovers the gender and racial-ethnic group distributions of the Annenberg survey. For instance, the distributions by race-ethnicity in the linked dataset are 36.5 percent for Latinos, 50.4 percent for whites and 10.7 percent for blacks, and in the Annenberg data, this breakdown is 43.9 percent, 48.6 percent, and 13.7 percent, respectively. Moreover, the distributions by gender are comparable in the linked and in the Annenberg data—44.8 percent of men in the linked data approved the president's performance on the economy while 48.5 percent of men in the Annenberg data held this opinion. The comparison on the distributions for women is even more precise—41.5 percent in the linked data and 42 percent in the Annenberg.

The similarity of these distributions makes us rather confident of the validity of the linking procedure. Currently, the small sample size of Latinos, blacks, and Asians in the NES has been a challenge to scholars studying racial and ethnic politics.[17] However, our linking procedure makes it possible for these researchers, as well as for researchers interested in other subgroups in the American electorate, to use the existing NES surveys to understand subgroup preferences with greater confidence and precision.

Assessing the Public Opinion of Racial and Ethnic Groups

Given all these robustness checks, we now use the information in the linked data to examine the public opinion on social welfare issues for the major racial and ethnic groups in the United States. The public opinion literature confirms the fact that significant variations exist in the attitudes and opinions of racial-ethnic groups. In particular, distinctions in the opinions on the role of government, social welfare policies, and race-related policies exist between blacks and whites (Kinder and Sanders 1990; Sigelman and Welch 1991; Tate 1994; Gilens 1999; Kinder and Sanders 1996; Kinder and Winter 2001; Winter 2008; for an explanation of why differences exist between black and white opinions, see Kinder and Winter 2001; Kinder and Sanders 1996). Blacks tend to be more supportive of such policies than whites are, particularly on the issue of welfare (Gilens 1999). However, much less is known about the opinions of the other major racial-ethnic groups in the United States—Latinos and Asians—on these policies and how they fit into this predominantly black-white framework. Understanding ethnic and racial group attitudes toward these issues is crucial, as the principles of equality and limited government are fundamental features of the American political tradition (Hofstadter 1948). In light of the fact that Latinos have now surpassed blacks as the largest minority group and that Asians are the second largest immigrant group, it is important to know how their opinions fit into this existing framework. Finally, given the economic differences that exist between ethnic-racial minorities and whites (DeNavas-Walt, Proctor, and Smith 2009), the variations in public opinion based on social class (as discussed by both Martin Gilens as well as Elizabeth

Rigby and Gerald C. Wright in this volume) may also be borne out when examining the public's attitudes by ethnicity-race. Due to their shared status as a minority group in the United States, race scholars have presumed that ethnic-racial groups will hold similar policy concerns and attitudes (Garcia 2003; Hero 1992). However, data limitations have made it a challenge to determine whether support for this assertion exists. Although some research shows that Latinos favor government-sponsored social welfare policies to a greater extent than whites (Abrajano and Alvarez 2010), no available data, to date, can compare attitudes toward the role of government across all the major ethnic-racial groups. Is support for social welfare policies just a function of their income status? Or is there also an ethnic-racial dimension to it? Moreover, a large percentage of the Latino and Asian populations are born outside of the United States, which means that their political-socialization processes and orientation to politics markedly differ from those of native-born Americans.[18] Thus, the means by which they learn about American politics and conceptualize basic political terms, such as conservative and liberal, may also vary from non-immigrants and, therefore, affect their issue opinions.

Figures 2.2, 2.3, and 2.4 compare the opinions of these four ethnic-racial groups across two fundamental elements of American politics—political ideology and the role of government.[19] Using these 7-point issue scale questions to draw any types of reliable inferences from minority policy preferences has been nearly impossible to do until now, given the extremely small number of Latinos, blacks, and Asians interviewed in the NES. Here, the number of observations has increased so that the linked-dataset respondents include approximately 6,700 blacks, 41,000 whites, 3,100 Latinos, and 1,100 Asians. Again, we use the issue scale responses of their linked-to NES respondents in our analyses. Figure 2.2 examines the responses to questions regarding the ideological position of Bush, Kerry, and their respective political parties. The responses to these questions ranged from 1 to 7, 1 being liberal and 7 being conservative. Across the ethnic-racial groups, distinctions clearly exist in their perceptions of the ideological positions of the major-party presidential candidates and the two political parties. Overall, blacks appear to evaluate the candidates and the parties as less ideologically extreme than whites, Latinos, and Asians do. In fact, blacks perceive the difference between the parties and their candidates to be much smaller than do the other ethnic-racial groups. Whites, Latinos, and Asians perceive a greater ideological divide between the parties and the two presidential candidates, with whites perceiving Kerry and the Democrats to be slightly more liberal than Latinos and Asians do. It is also worthwhile to note that Asians perceive Bush as being conservative far more than do blacks, whites, and Latinos.

Figure 2.2   Perceptions of Candidate and Party Ideology, by Ethnic-Racial Group

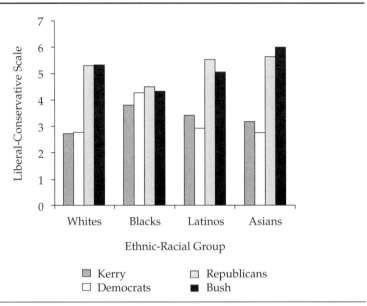

Source: Authors' compilation, based on the 2004 linked data, as discussed in the text.

Figure 2.3   Opinions on the Role of Government, by Ethnic-Racial Group

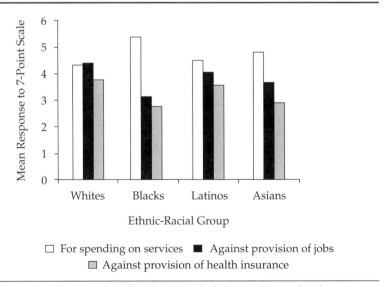

Source: Authors' compilation, based on the 2004 linked data, as discussed in the text.

Figure 2.4   Opinions on Government Aid to Minorities, by Ethnic-Racial Group

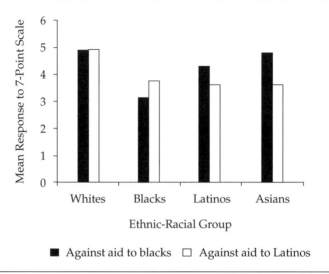

Source: Authors' compilation, based on the 2004 linked data, as discussed in the text.

In figures 2.3 and 2.4, we present the mean responses provided by each group on opinions toward the role of government. These questions include the amount of federal spending on government services, government provision of jobs, government versus private health insurance, and government aid to Latinos and blacks. Finding consistency with the previous research on public opinion and race, we see that blacks, more than any other ethnic-racial group, believe that the government should play an active role in the provision of jobs and services. Blacks believe that the government needs to play a larger role in providing health insurance to the American population than do the other ethnic-racial groups. Likewise, blacks are more likely to favor an increase in government spending on social services as well as government aid in the provision of jobs than Latinos or whites are. Note that of the ethnic-racial groups that we examine, blacks have both the lowest median household income and the highest poverty rate (DeNavas-Walt, Proctor, and Smith 2009); as such, their support for greater government involvement in health care is consistent with Gilens's findings (chapter 9, this volume) that the least affluent are more supportive of this measure than the more well-off.[20] These findings also reflect Rigby and Wright's observation (chapter 7, this volume) that the poor are more liberal on such policies than the wealthy. However, it is not always the case that an ethnic-racial group's median household income predicts their attitudes toward redistribution. After blacks, Asians are the most supportive of federal spending on social services. They are also more supportive of providing government aid to Latinos than whites are.[21]

Despite the commonly held belief that Latinos and blacks are the most likely to share preferences and concerns (Kaufman 2003), given their status as minority groups and similar life circumstances, their views toward the role of government differ. In fact, Latinos are more closely aligned with whites on the role of government, while Asians aligned more closely with blacks. Thus, it cannot be assumed that ethnic-racial groups have the same positions on these policies, or that all minority groups support an active government role in providing social services. Despite the median household income level and poverty rate of Latinos being nearly on par with blacks, these indicators do not seem to be the driving force in Latino attitudes toward social welfare policies.

Do these opinions change when a specific ethnic-racial group is the direct beneficiary from government provisions? Scholars such as Gilens (1999) have documented white opposition to social welfare policies that have largely benefited blacks, but it is unclear how other ethnic-racial groups feel about this issue and whether opinions change when government aid is directed toward a ethnic-racial group other than blacks. Regardless of the group receiving aid, however, we see that whites are the least supportive of such policies. Asian opposition to government aid for blacks is at about the same level as white opposition. Latinos are also more opposed than blacks are to government aid to blacks, but less so than Asians and whites are. With respect to Latinos receiving government aid, blacks, Latinos, and Asians have similar views, with blacks being just slightly more opposed than Latinos and Asians.[22] The opinions of each of these groups also vary according to the group receiving assistance. Asians are more opposed to government aid to blacks than they are to aid to Latinos, whereas blacks are more favorable toward federal aid for blacks than toward aid for Latinos. Similarly, Latinos are more supportive of federal assistance for Latinos than of aid for blacks. Of course, it is understandable why blacks and Latinos would favor government efforts directly benefiting their own group over efforts benefiting other groups; this pattern is similar to their ratings on the group thermometer questions. Asian opposition to federal aid to blacks may be attributed to the tensions between these two communities, as documented in the research by both Claire Kim (2000) and Min Song (2005). Survey data has also found that Asians report feeling the least close and least likely to get along with blacks relative to other ethnic-racial groups (Abrajano and Alvarez 2010).

For comparative purposes, table 2.6 presents opinions on social welfare issues that were included in the analyses of Gilens as well as those

Table 2.6   Opinions on Social Welfare Issues, by Ethnic-Racial Group

	Whites	Blacks	Latinos	Asians
Federal spending on welfare programs				
Increase	19.7	26.0	27.1	14.6
Keep the same	46.7	42.0	36.4	62.5
Decrease	33.7	31.9	36.1	22.9
Cut out entirely	0.0	0.1	0.4	0.0
Investing social security in the stock market				
Favor	46.7	30.5	45.9	32.9
Neither favor nor oppose	26.2	41.5	42.8	28.4
Oppose	26.8	26.3	11.3	35.5
Government should give parents in low-income families money to help pay for their children to attend a private or religious school instead of their local public school				
Favor	28.0	33.7	42.0	11.3
Neither favor nor oppose	2.2	2.5	4.7	5.7
Oppose	68.8	62.9	52.2	83.0
N	40,808	7,036	2,814	853

Source: Authors' compilation, based on the 2004 linked data, as discussed in the text.

of Rigby and Wright (chapters 9 and 7, respectively, this volume). On the question pertaining to federal spending on welfare programs, the modal category for each group was to keep federal spending on welfare programs at its current level. However, nearly twice as many blacks and Latinos (26 percent and 27.1 percent, respectively) than Asians (14.6 percent) favored an increase in welfare spending. In fact, Asians, who have the highest median household income of all ethnic-racial groups, are the least supportive of government efforts to expand welfare programs. This pattern is similar to the one reported by Gilens (chapter 9, this volume), which shows that individuals in the 90th income percentiles favor cuts in welfare spending to a greater degree than those in the 50th or 10th income percentiles. With regards to the idea of investing social security in the stock markets, the modal category across the groups varied. Most blacks were indifferent to the proposal (they neither favored or opposed it), but a plurality of Latinos and whites favored such a plan. The bulk of Asians, on the other hand, opposed the proposal. Here, the more affluent ethnic-racial group, Asians, do not appear to be supportive of a market-oriented reform to social security, which runs at odds with Gilens's findings.

The final question we examine relates to the school voucher program, that is, government efforts to enable low-income children to attend a private or religious school rather than a public one. Conventional wisdom expects affluent Americans to favor such a plan, given that they have the financial resources to take advantage of it (see Gilens, chapter 9, this volume). Based on this logic, we would expect Asians and whites to be the most supportive. Across all groups, however, the majority of respondents are against school vouchers. In fact, the most affluent group—Asians—expressed the greatest opposition (83 percent), followed by whites (68 percent), blacks (62.9 percent), and Latinos (52.2 percent). This consensus suggests that race-ethnicity may not be capturing the variations in opinions toward vouchers that arise when examining these opinions based on income level.

Conclusion

In this chapter, we have outlined a method for linking respondents from different surveys based on their *subjective utility* for salient political figures. In particular, we use feeling-thermometer questions, because they are an accurate measure of an individual's subjective utility. This is because they, in turn, are measures of *affect*. In applying our technique to the 2004 Annenberg survey and the 2004 NES survey, we find that pairing survey respondents based on their thermometer scores not only recovers the distributions on group demographics, such as race-ethnicity, gender, and education, extremely well but also predicts group distributions across an array of political attitudes and opinions. We also performed a number of robustness checks to ensure that the linking procedure produced reliable estimates—most notably, we compared the linking procedure with the standard method of matching that relies on demographics. The technique withstood all these external validity checks, providing us with ample reassurance that both the theoretical and the methodological aspects of the linking procedure are valid. Although our focus was subgroup populations based on race-ethnicity, state- and local-politics scholars can also benefit from this technique because they, too, face sampling issues when using public opinion surveys (see, for example, Brace et al. 2004). Finally, this technique enriches and expands the work on matching methods and survey research more broadly, inasmuch as we demonstrate that linking individuals based on their affective signatures can accurately predict their political attitudes better than those methods that use demographic characteristics can.

From a substantive standpoint, we were able to examine the ethnic-racial variations in American public opinion on fundamental issues regarding the role of government and social welfare policies, as well as perceptual data on political ideology. Recall that these questions were not part of the original Annenberg survey, and thus, by applying the linking procedure, we are able to understand ethnic-racial groups' views on national policies. This analysis also enabled us to discern whether income disparities among ethnic-racial groups translated into the same types of variations in public opinion that are examined in the other chapters of this volume. For some issues, such as government involvement in health care, we do find some overlap between race-ethnicity and social class. On the other hand, the issue of school vouchers did not appear to be consistent between ethnic-racial groups and income groups. Thus, in light of the country's vastly changing ethnic and racial composition, understanding the diversity in public opinion from both a social-class and ethnic-racial standpoint is critical for elected officials who wish to be responsive to the needs and concerns of all Americans.

Appendix

In this appendix, we provide more detailed evidence for the quality of our linking procedure. Specifically, we show the comparisons of our procedure to standard demographic methods of matching using a split sample and a standard ordinary least squares (OLS). A partial summary of these experiments is presented earlier in table 2.2 and figure 2.1.

Split Sample Experiment

To obtain the results shown in table 2.2, we split the 2004 NES in half and then used our linking procedure to match each respondent in part one of the split survey to a respondent in part two. This was done in the same way that we linked the NES and Annenberg surveys.

We also used standard demographics—gender, age, education, and income—to match each respondent from part one to a respondent in part two. The comparison is shown in table 2.2. We also randomly matched each respondent from part one to a respondent in part two. The random matching gives us a baseline for comparing our linking method to standard demographic matching.

Figure 2.A1 shows a smooth histogram of the three forms of matching for party identification (party ID). The horizontal axis shows the difference between the party ID of the part-one respondent and the party ID of the part-two respondent. This difference can run from −6 to +6. For example, a −6 would correspond to a strong democrat (0 on the party ID scale) being matched with a strong republican (6 on the party ID scale). The number of respondents in the 2004 survey was 1,212, so the split

Figure 2.A1   NES 2004 Survey Party ID Differences, by Thermometer Matching Versus Demographics Matching

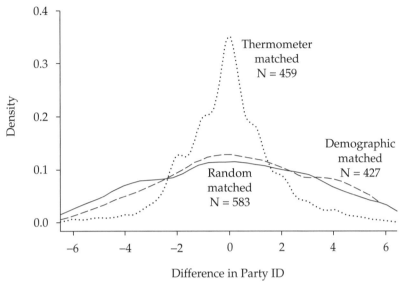

Source: Authors' compilation, based on the 2004 National Annenberg Election Survey (Romer et al. 2006) and the 2004 National Election Study (Center for Political Studies 2004).

was 606 versus 606. But, due to the missing data, the numbers varied with the three different matching methods (see figure 2.A1).

The linking method that we show in this chapter is clearly superior to demographic matching, which barely outperforms random matching. The mean difference when using our thermometer method is −0.041, with a standard deviation of 1.777. In contrast, the mean difference for demographic matching is 0.548, with a standard deviation of 2.855, and for random matching, the mean is 0.132, with a standard deviation of 3.073.

Figure 2.A2 is in the same format as Figure 2.A1, only now the horizontal axis shows the difference between the self-placement on the liberal-conservative 7-point scale of the part-one respondent and the self-placement of the part-two respondent. This difference can run from −6 to +6. For example, a −6 would correspond to a self-identified "Extremely Liberal" respondent (1 on the liberal-conservative scale) being matched with a respondent who identifies him- or herself as "Extremely Conservative" (7 on the liberal-conservative scale). Again, the number of observations varied with the three different matching methods because of missing data.

**Figure 2.A2   NES 2004 Survey Liberal-Conservative 7-Point Scale
Differences, by Thermometer Matching Versus
Demographics Matching**

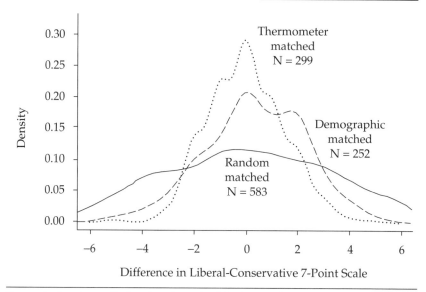

Source: Authors' compilation, based on the 2004 National Annenberg Election Survey
(Romer et al. 2006) and the 2004 National Election Study (Center for Political Studies 2004).

The linking method that we show in this chapter is once again clearly
superior to demographics. The mean difference when using our thermometer method is 0.017, with a standard deviation of 1.473. In contrast,
the mean difference for demographic matching is 0.373, with a standard
deviation of 1.913. The random-matching mean and standard deviation
are the same as in Figure 2.A1—0.132 and 3.073, respectively.

Regression Models Experiment

For our second test of our linking procedure, we ran a set of simple regression models using the 1980 through 2004 NES presidential election
surveys, where the dependent variables were the respondent's position
on the 0 to 6 party identification scale and the respondent's position on
the 1 to 7 liberal-conservative scale. We used two sets of independent
variables: standard demographics—gender, age, education, and income—and the feeling thermometers for the major political figures in
the survey.

We show four sets of regressions from the data: demographics on the party identification scale; demographics on the liberal-conservative scale; thermometers on the party identification scale, and thermometers on the liberal-conservative scale. We used all the thermometers in each survey except for those where the response level was so low that it greatly reduced the number of observations (for example, including Patrick Lucey in 1980 reduces the number of observations for the party identification regression from 699 to 428, and the number for the liberal-conservative scale drops from 642 to 391). The R-squares for these regressions are shown in figure 2.1. For more data tables, see the online appendix at http://www.russellsage.org/chap2_appendix.pdf.

Notes

1. This means that individuals are being linked to one another based on a vector of stimuli affect. When these individuals are paired based on these vectors of affect, we find that different groups (for example, race-ethnicity, gender) show distinctive affective signatures or patterns.
2. Essentially, we are taking the respondents (rows) in the Annenberg data and adding columns (responses to survey questions) to them.
3. For example, the U.S. Census Bureau estimates the 2008 poverty rate for non-Latino whites at 8.6 percent, 11.8 percent for Asians, 23.2 percent for Latinos, and 24.7 for blacks (DeNavas-Walt, Proctor, and Smith 2009). Thus more than a majority of individuals (68.3 percent) who are considered to be poor are ethnic-racial minorities.
4. We are thus not attempting to recover the utility function of a respondent. We are assuming that their responses to a set of feeling-thermometer questions serve as a proxy for their internal utility function.
5. However, given the large sample size of the 2004 Annenberg survey, we expect that any individual-level errors will be minimized at the aggregate level.
6. The survey was conducted by Daniel Romer, Kate Kenski, Kenneth Winneg, Christopher Adasiewicz, and Kathleen Hall Jamieson of the Annenberg Public Policy Center at the University of Pennsylvania (Romer et al. 2006).
7. The thermometers listed are from the NES.
8. Given that the Annenberg is much larger than the NES, certain NES respondents pair up with the Annenberg respondents more so than others. The frequency of these pairings ranges from 2 to 645.
9. Estimates from the 2008 U.S. Census, http://www.census.gov/PressRelease/www/releases/archives/facts_for_features_special_editions/010969.html.
10. Estimate from http://www.census.gov/population/www/socdemo/Hispanic/Hispanic.html.
11. This analysis was performed by dividing the 2004 NES sample in half; this produced two datasets. For the demographic matching procedure, respondents from the first half of the sample were matched to respondents in the second half of the sample based on age, education, and gender. A similar analysis was performed for the linking procedure, but we used the ther-

mometer scores instead of demographics. For additional details, see the appendix.

12. Based on this comparison of goodness of fit, we decided not to include demographics as part of the linking procedure.

13. The number of observations in the Annenberg data is significantly smaller than in the linked data since the question of vote choice was not asked of all the survey respondents. This question was asked only in the interview period right before the 2004 general election.

14. Created in 2003, the NEP is a consortium of media organizations (ABC, CBS, CNN, FOX, NBC, and the Associated Press) that conducts the exit polls for national elections.

15. Respondents are also asked to place candidates on these 7-point issue scale questions, making it possible to calculate the distance between an individual's position on an issue from his or her placement of the candidate's position on that issue.

16. The NES codebook contains the complete wording for all the 7-point issue scale questions that we examine.

17. Thus, any inferences about racial-ethnic group preferences have used datasets that focus specifically on one ethnic-racial group (such as the Latino National Political Survey, the Latino National Survey, and the National Black Election Studies).

18. Latinos currently comprise 15 percent of the U.S. population, and it is projected that 40 percent of this population is foreign-born. Asians make up 5 percent of the U.S. population.

19. Across these racial-ethnic groups, the overall distributions from the linked sample (recall that these are Annenberg respondents "answering" NES questions) reproduce the NES distributions exceptionally well. Refer to figure 2.A2 for comparative statistics.

20. As of 2008, the median household income of blacks is $34,218, compared to $37,913 for Latinos, $52,312 for whites, and $65,637 for Asians.

21. It is beyond the scope of this chapter to determine why this is so, but it may be because of the large number of foreign-born (40 percent) among the Asian population.

22. The difference in the mean response between blacks and Latinos is .15.

References

Abrajano, Marisa, and R. Michael Alvarez. 2010. *New Faces, New Voices: The Latino Electorate in America*. Princeton, N.J.: Princeton University Press.

Arceneaux, Kevin, Alan S. Gerber, and Donald P. Green. 2006. "Comparing Experimental and Matching Methods Using a Large-Scale Voter Mobilization Experiment." *Political Analysis* 14(1): 37–62.

Brace, Paul, Kevin Arceneaux, Martin Johnson, and Stacy G. Ulbig. 2004. "Does State Political Ideology Change over Time?" *Political Research Quarterly* 57(4): 529–40.

Cahoon, Lawrence S., Melvin J. Hinich, and Peter C. Ordeshook. 1978. "A Statistical Multidimensional Scaling Method Based on the Spatial Theory of Voting." In *Graphical Representation of Multivariate Data*, edited by P. C. Wang. New York: Academic Press.

Center for Political Studies. 2004. "The 2004 National Election Study" [dataset]. Ann Arbor: University of Michigan, Center for Political Studies [producer and distributor]. Available at http://www.electionstudies.org (accessed August 23, 2010).

Dawson, Michael C. 1995. *Behind the Mule: Race and Class in African-American Politics*. Princeton, N.J.: Princeton University Press.

DeNavas-Walt, Carmen, Bernadette D. Proctor, and Jessica C. Smith. 2009. "Income Poverty and Health Insurance Coverage in the United States: 2008." *Current Population Reports*, P260–236. Washington: U.S. Census Bureau. Available at http://www.census.gov/prod/2009pubs/p60-236.pdf.

Downs, Anthony. 1957. *An Economic Theory of Democracy*. New York: Harper and Row.

Enelow, James M., and Melvin J. Hinich. 1984. *The Spatial Theory of Voting*. New York: Cambridge University Press.

Garcia, John A. 2003. *Latino Politics in America: Community, Culture, and Interests*. Lanham, Md.: Rowman and Littlefield.

Gerber, Alan S., and Donald P. Green. 2000. "The Effects of Personal Canvassing, Telephone Calls, and Direct Mail on Voter Turnout: A Field Experiment." *American Political Science Review* 94(3): 653–64.

———. 2005. "Do Phone Calls Increase Voter Turnout? An Update." *Annals of the American Academy of Political and Social Science* 601(1): 142–54.

Gilens, Martin. 1999. *Why Americans Hate Welfare: Race, Media, and the Politics of Antipoverty Policy*. Chicago: University of Chicago Press.

Giles, Micheal, and Arthur Evans. 1986. "The Power Approach to Intergroup Hostility." *Journal of Conflict Resolution* 30(3): 469–86.

Hero, Rodney. 1992. *Latinos and the U.S. Political System*. Philadelphia: Temple University Press.

Hofstadter, Richard. 1948. *The American Political Tradition and the Men Who Made It*. New York: Alfred A. Knopf.

Imai, Kosuke. 2005. "Do Get-Out-the-Vote Calls Reduce Turnout? The Importance of Statistical Methods for Field Experiments." *American Political Science Review* 99(2): 283–300.

Kaufman, Karen. 2003. *The Urban Voter: Group Conflict and Mayoral Voting Behavior in American Cities*. Ann Arbor: University of Michigan Press.

Kim, Claire. 2000. *Bitter Fruit: The Politics of Black-Korean Conflict in New York City*. New Haven, Conn.: Yale University Press.

Kinder, Donald R., and Lynn M. Sanders. 1990. "Mimicking Political Debate with Survey Questions: The Case of White Opinion on Affirmative Action for Blacks." *Social Cognition* 8(1): 83–103.

———. 1996. *Divided by Color: Racial Politics and Democratic Ideals*. Chicago: University of Chicago Press.

Kinder, Donald, and Nicholas Winter. 2001. "Exploring the Racial Divide: Blacks, Whites, and Opinion on National Policy." *American Journal of Political Science* 45(2): 439–56.

Knight, Kathleen. 1984. "The Dimensionality of Partisan and Ideological Affect." *American Politics Quarterly* 12(3): 305–34.

Nickerson, David W. 2005. "Scalable Protocols Offer Efficient Design for Field Experiments." *Political Analysis* 13(3): 233–52.

Poole, Keith T. 1984. "Least Squares Metric, Unidimensional Unfolding." *Psychometrika* 49(3): 311–23.

———. 1990. "Least Squares Metric, Unidimensional Scaling of Multivariate Linear Models." *Psychometrika* 55:123–49.

Poole, Keith T., and Howard L. Rosenthal. 1984. "U.S. Presidential Elections 1968–1980: A Spatial Analysis." *American Journal of Political Science* 28(May): 282–312.

Rabinowitz, George. 1976. "A Procedure for Ordering Object Pairs Consistent with the Multidimensional Unfolding Model." *Psychometrika* 41(3): 349–73.

Romer, Daniel, Kate Kenski, Kenneth Winneg, Christopher Adasiewicz, and Kathleen Hall Jamieson. 2006. *Capturing Campaign Dynamics 2000 & 2004: The National Annenberg Election Survey*. Philadelphia: University of Pennsylvania Press.

Sapiro, Virginia, Steven J. Rosenstone, and the National Election Studies. 2004. "American National Election Studies Cumulative Data File, 1948–2004" [computer file]. ICPSR08475-v13. Ann Arbor: University of Michigan, Center for Political Studies [producer], 2004. Ann Arbor, Mich.: Inter-University Consortium for Political and Social Research [distributor], 2007-09-25. doi:10.3886/ICPSR08475.

Sigelman, Lee, and Susan Welch. 1991. *Black Americans' Views of Racial Inequality: The Dream Deferred*. New York: Cambridge University Press.

Song, Min H. 2005. *Strange Future: Pessimism and the 1992 Los Angeles Riot.* Durham, N.C.: Duke University Press.

Tate, Katherine. 1994. *From Protest to Politics: The New Black Voters in American Elections*. Cambridge, Mass.: Harvard University Press and Russell Sage Foundation.

Wang, Ming-Mei, Peter H. Schonemann, and Jerrold G. Rusk. 1975. "A Conjugate Gradient Algorithm for the Multidimensional Analysis of Preference Data." *Multivariate Behavioral Research*, 10:45–80.

Weisberg, Herbert F., and Jerrold G. Rusk. 1970. "Dimensions of Candidate Evaluation." *American Political Science Review* 64(4): 1167–85.

Wilcox, Clyde, Lee Sigelman, and Elizabeth Cook. 1989. "Some Like It Hot: Individual Differences in Responses to Group Feeling Thermometers." *Public Opinion Quarterly* 53(2): 246–57.

Winter, Nicholas. 2008. *Dangerous Frames: How Ideas About Race and Gender Shape Public Opinion*. Chicago: University of Chicago Press.

Chapter 3

United We Divide? Education, Income, and Heterogeneity in Mass Partisan Polarization

CHRISTOPHER ELLIS AND JOSEPH DANIEL URA

THE RESURGENCE OF mass partisanship over the last half century is among the most important developments in modern American politics. Party elites have polarized on a variety of issues, and citizens have responded by becoming better able to understand party issue conflict, more likely to hold an affective commitment to one party over another, and more apt to structure their attitudes to reflect the issue structure of elite party conflict (for example, Hetherington 2001; Pomper and Weiner 2002). In the aggregate, the result is a mass party system that is more polarized on a variety of domains (Abramowitz and Saunders 1998; Layman and Carsey 2002; Baldassarri and Gelman 2008).

Beyond this core result, though, considerable debate remains about who is polarizing on which issues, and what the implications are for the structure of the mass party system and the nature of political representation. For example, the prominent discussion over Thomas Frank's (2004) *What's the Matter with Kansas?* thesis—which asserts that poor, uneducated whites have become Republicans on the basis of their preferences on issues of traditional morality—has produced a variety of competing claims about the ways citizens balance their preferences regarding traditional New Deal–type economic issues and scope-of-government issues against their preferences concerning cultural or moral issues when making political decisions (see, for example, Ansolabahere, Rodden, and Snyder 2006; Bartels 2008; Gelman et al. 2008).

This chapter integrates and extends this literature, exploring changes in how preferences on the two issue dimensions relate to party identification for different citizens over the past four decades. We focus on heterogeneity across income and education, two individual-level characteristics that have received considerable attention in popular and scholarly debates regarding the nature of mass attitude change. More important, we address the oft-neglected intersection between income and education in shaping how citizens respond to changes in the political context and how these changes influence the issue bases of the American mass party system. Income and education are obviously highly correlated in the American context, but they are not one and the same. Expectations regarding the effects of the two concepts, considered separately, allow for a richer theoretical and substantive understanding of their joint effects in shaping mass attitude change: how the independent effects of income and education may either reinforce or counteract one another.

Drawing on research that addresses mass response to changing elite-party cues, and other studies that examine how income and education affect how citizens relate to the political world, we develop expectations regarding the roles of income and education—and the intersection of the two—in shaping mass response to elite polarization: who is polarizing, on which issues, and to what degree. We then assess these expectations, exploring how elite polarization has affected the relationship between partisanship and policy preferences, and the ways in which these relationships vary across income cohorts, levels of formal education, and across educational lines among income cohorts.

We find broad similarities in the types of issues most relevant to party identification, and in the changes in the relative importance of those issues, across different types of citizens: disparities across educational and income lines are typically a matter of degree rather than magnitude. But we also find substantively important differences across educational and income lines—and across educational levels within income groups—in response to elite polarization. In particular, we find that mass party polarization on economic and scope-of-government issues is most acute among relatively highly educated citizens with relatively low incomes, whereas mass party polarization on cultural issues has occurred mainly among less educated citizens with relatively high incomes.

These observations point to a more comprehensive view of mass polarization in the United States over the last three-plus decades. Claims that polarization is occurring among only a small subset of citizens, or is restricted to economic or cultural issues, or that certain types of citizens are driving a class war or a culture war, are incomplete. Likewise, polarization on either economic or cultural issues cannot be defined as strictly limited to the rich or the poor, or the educated or the uneducated. Examining the electorate as a whole, or examining the conditional effects of income or education alone, obscures critical effects that enrich our understanding of mass party system change and whose preferences get represented when Democrats or Republicans take office.

Elite Polarization and the Changing Issue Bases of Mass Party Coalitions

Scholars have devoted considerable attention to understanding the impact of elite-party polarization (beginning in the late 1970s and continuing through the present) on mass political behavior in the United States. The growing ideological distance between Democratic and Republican elites has been instrumental in clarifying and crystallizing citizens' understandings of major party positions on important public policy issues, as well as attitudes toward the parties themselves (see, for example, Levine, Carmines, and Huckfeldt 1997; Abramowitz and Saunders 1998; McCarty, Poole, and Rosenthal 2006). The sharpening of elite-party discourse brought about by polarization has been linked to growing awareness of differences between the parties, a greater ability among citizens to locate parties correctly in an ideological space, and an increase in the proportion of people who hold an affective preference for one party over the other (Hetherington 2001; Pomper and Weiner 2002).

Citizens have generally reacted to elite polarization by changing the structure of their own political attitudes, increasing the weight they give to issue preferences and ideological leanings—and decreasing that given to socialization and other factors (Brewer 2005; Saunders and Abramowitz 2004). The result, at least in the aggregate, is a mass party system that is increasingly polarized along ideological and issue lines (Bafumi and Shapiro 2009; Levendusky 2009). Disagreement remains, however, as to the qualitative level and importance of mass partisan polarization and to the types of issues on which mass parties are polarizing.

Many discussions of changes in the issue bases of party coalitions over the past forty years focus on two prominent dimensions: one encompassing the traditional conflicts over economics, redistribution, and the size and the scope of the federal government that have divided the parties since at least the New Deal era, and a second dealing broadly with culture, religion, and traditional morality.[1] Party elites have polarized on both dimensions, and, at least at the national level, the two dimensions have essentially been collapsed into one: the elite Republican Party now almost uniformly argues for a stronger government role in enforcing traditional social and religious values and a weaker government role in redistributing wealth and providing distributive services; the elite Democratic Party almost uniformly argues for the reverse.

At the mass level, however, preferences on these dimensions remain largely distinct from one another for many citizens (Layman and Carsey 2002). With the two sets remaining largely separate domains, the questions of which dimension matters more to political decision making, and which is more strongly associated with critical aspects of political identity, have become increasingly relevant to commentators and scholars of political behavior. Do the principal dividing lines in American mass party conflict remain based on economic concerns, or are they now cultural? Some, citing that most of what the government actually does in terms of policy outputs still deals largely with economic and redistributive matters (for example, Erikson, MacKuen, and Stimson 2002), say that traditional New Deal–style conflict over the proper size and reach of the federal government remains dominant to mass political choices (Ansolabahere, Rodden, and Snyder 2006). Others assert that changes in elite and activist cues on traditional morality issues have caused cultural concerns to displace economic ones as the predominant dividing lines in party politics (for example, Hunter 1994; Miller and Schofield 2003).

Income in the Theory of Mass Polarization

A growing body of research has moved beyond these aggregate level discussions to explore the extent to which changes in elite behavior have influenced all citizens equally (if at all). Perhaps the highest-profile debates have centered on the role of income to mass partisan change, in particular the degree to which citizens in different income strata are making political choices based on different issues. Thomas Frank (2004), for example, advances the claim that poorer citizens have become more likely to make political choices based on cultural and moral preferences rather than economic ones.

The implications of this argument are considerable. Most obviously, Frank implies poorer citizens are moving en masse to the Republican Party in violation of their own economic interests. But perhaps more significant, the argument implies that poor citizens are making important political decisions based on a different dimension of policy than the one that structures most elite policy conflict. Poorer citizens, in this view, make political choices and associate their political identities with preferences on cultural issues, whereas wealthy citizens are more strongly concerned with economic and scope-of-government matters. Political leaders thus have the opportunity to represent the interests and priorities of the wealthy over those of the poor—an opportunity that they, perhaps, often take (see Gilens, chapter 9, this volume; see also Ura and Ellis 2008; Wlezien and Soroka, chapter 10, this volume).

Frank's claims, however, have been subject to considerable empirical scrutiny and have not always stood up well. Larry Bartels, for example, shows that preferences on economic issues still drive choices even among the poor and that class-based politics are as prevalent as at any time in recent history (2006, 2008; see also Stonecash 2001). Andrew

Gelman and colleagues (2008) take a different perspective, arguing that cultural concerns are becoming most important to the affluent.

Education in the Theory of Mass Polarization

Citizens with more formal education, sophistication, and political awareness are generally more likely to receive elite-party messages, understand complex political concepts, and be able to relate their own personal circumstances and values to concrete political choices. The role of education is especially important: education is a primary route to becoming informed about and interested in politics and especially important for structuring the quantity and quality of citizens' political cognition (Delli Carpini and Keeter 1996). Formal education is important in its own right and is also strongly associated with other concepts of interest (such as sophistication and awareness) that enhance one's ability to receive and process political information (Abrajano 2005; Sigelman and Yaranella 1986).

The impact of education and awareness on the ability to receive and process polarizing elite cues is central to many models of mass response to elite polarization. Although polarization has made elite-party messages clearer, politics and policy remain distant for most, and some of these messages may still not be clear enough for less educated citizens to understand or react to. As a result, response to changing elite-party cues and mass polarization on either dimension may be restricted largely or exclusively to the more educated, politically aware subsets of the public (Layman and Carsey 2002).[2]

Education, Income, and the Issue Bases of Mass Party Change

Despite the importance of the independent influences of education and income in motivating the dynamics of partisan polarization, there has been surprisingly little investigation of the intersection of the two. This is a substantial oversight. In part, this results from the common conflation of education with social class. Frank (2004), for example, alternates between discussions of income and discussions of education, at times suggesting that educational attainment can be used as a proxy for social class. Income and education are, of course, highly correlated, but they are not one and the same. More to the point, research has suggested that at least in some contexts, income and education should have differential effects on the structure of mass political choices. Drawing on previous work, we develop theoretical expectations of the roles that education and income, considered independently, will have on mass response to elite polarization on these two dimensions. We then consider how the two factors may intersect.

Education

The more highly educated are typically better able to understand and process abstract, complex political information, and certain types of political issues are more abstract and complex than others. Elite signals and other contextual information on so-called hard political issues require relatively high levels of cognitive capacity to understand and process, and typically only the most educated and sophisticated segment of the electorate incorporates this information into the political decision-making process (Carmines and Stimson 1980). The less educated, by contrast, are typically less able to understand difficult political messages and thus comparably more likely to make political decisions—and respond to changing cues—on symbolic "easy" issues. We thus might expect more educated citizens to pay comparably more attention to elite cues on harder issues, and the less educated to rely more on easier issue cues.

Using this hard-easy distinction to distinguish cultural and economic issues, the cultural dimension is clearly the easier of the two. Issues such as gay marriage, abortion, and traditional morality fit most of Edward Carmines and James Stimson's (1980) criteria for easy issues: they are highly symbolic, emotionally charged, and typically focused on policy ends, rather than means (see also Leege et al. 2002; Joslyn and Haider-Markel 2002). A good deal of research, for example, has suggested that abortion is a clear example of an easy issue—highly symbolic, focused largely on ends (such as should abortion be legal or illegal), and related strongly to core social and religious values and beliefs (Carmines and Stimson 1980; see also Jelen and Wilcox 2003).

Economics, social welfare, and redistribution, in contrast, are harder issues—typically more complex and more means-focused: How do we achieve economic growth? How do we balance the goals of providing equal opportunity and rewarding individual initiative? These are more difficult for citizens with low levels of education or political awareness to discern clear left and right positions. Although specific economic issues can certainly be treated as easy in certain circumstances, generally issues on this dimensions are more likely to deal with how to achieve desired goals (quality education, economic growth, and the like) than with goals per se. These issues are, all else equal, more likely to be technical and thus make it more difficult for citizens to discern clear left-right positions (see also Luskin, McIver, and Carmines 1989; Bailey, Sigelman, and Wilcox 2003).

If this distinction is accurate, then to the extent that education mediates mass response to elite polarization, more educated citizens should respond more strongly to elite polarization on the harder economic and scope-of-government dimensions, and their less educated counterparts to the easier cultural dimension.

Income

Recent research suggests that wealthier, more affluent individuals are more likely to give more weight to religious and cultural concerns when making political choices (Gelman et al. 2008, 2007). This implies that less affluent citizens tend to weight economic and scope-of-government issues more heavily. This relationship may emerge from the comparably lower vulnerability to market forces and sensitivity to marginal changes in social welfare policies among wealthier citizens, who, as a result, can turn their attention to other things. Poorer citizens, in contrast, may have disproportionate incentives to tie their political identities to their preferences on economic concerns. If this is true, poorer citizens may be more apt to respond to changing elite cues on economic and scope-of-government concerns, and wealthier citizens to cues on cultural concerns.[3]

Despite their high correlation, then, we expect high levels of income and high levels of education to have differential effects on the nature of mass response to elite cues and changes in the issue bases of mass party choice. All else equal, we expect that higher levels of education will lead citizens to pay more attention to changing elite cues on economic and scope-of-government issues, and that higher levels of income will lead citizens to pay disproportionately more attention to changing cues on cultural issues.

Income and Education

Considering income and education as separate theoretical concepts provides a useful baseline for understanding their joint effects in shaping the changing structure of mass attitudes. Figure 3.1 presents a stylized description of the joint effects we expect high and low levels of income and education to have in shaping response to polarization. This simple representation provides a sense of how the effects of income and education may intersect in ways that might not be apparent when considering each independently, given the high correlation between them.

First, consider the "off-diagonal" groups: citizens with low levels of education but relatively high incomes, or relatively high education but low incomes. Those with high incomes and less education have both relatively greater immunity from a need for a social safety net and a heightened likelihood of relying on symbolic, easy issues in making political decisions. These citizens should be particularly responsive to

Figure 3.1   Theoretical Expectations of Income and Education in Shaping Response to Elite Polarization

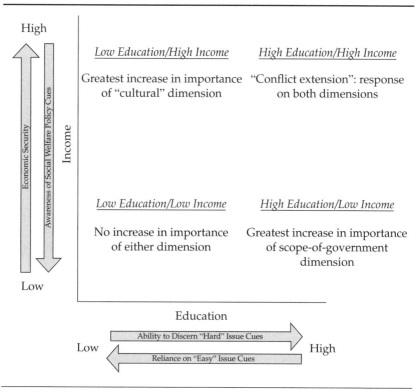

Source: Figure generated by authors.

changing elite cues on cultural issues: these are citizens with a high likelihood of being both interested in, and reliant on, cultural concerns.

High-education, low-income citizens, by contrast, should have both a greater interest in, and a greater ability to understand, elite partisan cues on hard issues. Citizens in this group should be especially responsive to polarizing elite cues on economic and scope-of-government issues.

Low-education, low-income citizens should exhibit both a relatively low propensity to care about cultural concerns and a lower likelihood to perceive and understand changes in party cues on the harder scope-of-government dimension. We expect that members of this group are the least likely to react to elite polarization: in our typology, they are among the least likely to understand polarizing elite cues on economic issues, and the least likely to care about polarizing elite cues on cultural issues.

Finally, our high-education, high-income group may best fit the framework of Geoffrey Layman and Thomas Carsey's (2002) "conflict extension" argument: in our typology, members of this group have both a disproportionate capacity to understand economic cues and a dispro- portionate likelihood of caring about cultural ones.

In sum, we expect important and systematic heterogeneity in how in- come, education, and the intersection of the two affect mass response to elite-party polarization. We expect that the growing association of eco- nomic and scope-of-government issues with partisan identification will be concentrated most heavily among the relatively highly educated, rel- atively low-income individuals. Conversely, to the extent that a culture war is growing within American mass party politics, the fighting should be concentrated primarily among affluent citizens with relatively low levels of formal education.

Measuring Economic and Cultural Issue Preferences

In the following sections, we assess these predictions, exploring pat- terns of similarity and difference in the changing issue bases of partisan choice over the past thirty-five years. We begin by operationalizing the concepts of proximate interest: mass preferences on the scope-of- government and cultural dimensions. Our goal is to produce reliable measures of preferences on these two dimensions that are available for a long enough period to be able to capture important shifts in how citizens relate preferences to partisanship. We turn to the General Social Survey (GSS), which offers a rich battery of issue questions consistently posed to respondents since the mid-1970s. The GSS asked eighteen policy ques- tions related to opinions on specific policy issues in each survey year from 1974 to 2006. Each of these questions can be coded for liberal or conservative content based on the positions of party elites (see the ap- pendix for questions and coding). Exploratory factor analysis suggests that responses to these questions load on two dimensions.

The first of these dimensions comprises a set of ten questions dealing with government spending in a variety of programmatic domains. It in- cludes preferences on traditional distributive and redistributive issues, representative of the issues that determine "who gets what" in American politics. But it goes beyond that, capturing preferences for a wide range of issues related to traditional liberal-conservative conflicts over the proper size and reach of the federal government. We thus use this mea- sure as a proxy for mass preferences on the conventional economic and scope-of-government dimensions that have divided the Democratic and Republican parties since at least the New Deal era.[4] Although this mea- sure consists of only spending questions, the aggregates of this ten-issue measure correlate at .83 with James Stimson's (1999) *policy mood*, the longitudinal measure of public opinion regarding the size and scope of government that is most commonly used in empirical work on democratic representation and mass-elite linkages.

The second dimension comprises seven questions regarding perceptions of homosexuality and the legality of abortion. We take this dimension as a measure of cultural preferences. Unlike the scope-of-government scale dimension, there is no commonly accepted benchmark from which to gauge the validity of this dimension. Although this measure contains preferences for only two central issues, abortion and gay rights, these issues are two of the most visible ones that represent the rise of cultural conflict (Hunter 1994).[5] Furthermore, measures on these issues are used in research that examines relationships between elite and mass preferences on issues of culture and traditional morality (see, for example, Lindaman and Haider-Markel 2002).

We thus have data to measure individuals' preferences on the two issue dimensions. For each dimension, we construct preference scores for all respondents by coding each response for ideological content and summing the responses to all policy questions in each set (coding available in the appendix), thus creating simple scales of preferences where higher scores indicate greater liberalism.

Modeling Strategy

With these series in hand, we turn to understanding the changing issue bases of mass party coalitions. We explore the ways in which citizens associate preferences on each of these dimensions to party identification, how the relative weight of these factors has changed as elite parties have polarized, and whether the nature of these changes varies across relevant income and educational cohorts.[6] Although disentangling the changing causal relationships between policy preferences and partisanship is outside the scope of this chapter (for a fuller treatment, see Carsey and Layman 2006), our theoretical discussion focuses on the degree to which citizens in different socioeconomic cohorts can recognize the connections between partisanship and preferences on these two dimensions and adjust their own attitudes accordingly. The empirical goal is thus to examine substantively important differences in how different types of citizens connect partisanship to preferences on these two dimensions.

Our modeling strategy is a straightforward one adapted from Marc Hetherington (2001). The data come from the pooled GSS dataset covering the years 1974 to 2006. The baseline for the analysis is a simple OLS regression model in which the dependent variable is the standard 7-point measure of party identification asked of all GSS respondents. The primary independent variables of interest are the scales of scope-of-government and cultural preferences, both recalibrated to a scale of 0 to 1 to make comparability across scales easier. We also include measures of other relevant sociodemographic and political correlates of party identification.

To capture the degree of polarization among party elites at the time that a respondent's survey was conducted, we assign to each respondent a measure of the level of *elite-party polarization* at the time of the survey, operationalized as the difference between the mean Republican and Democratic DW-NOMINATE scores in the House of Representatives during the year in which the survey was conducted (see Poole and Rosenthal 1997; McCarty, Poole, and Rosenthal 2006).[7] A survey respondent from 1974, for example, would be assigned the DW-NOMINATE score for the 93rd Congress (1973 to 1974). Our polarization measure is also reset to a scale of 0 to 1, with the period of lowest polarization in the thirty-two years of data that we have (1979 to 1980) set to 0 and the period of highest polarization (2005 to 2006) set to 1. To assess the moderating impact of polarization on each of the independent variables, we interact each predictor with the elite-polarization measure.[8] This procedure allows us to see how the expected association of each independent variable with partisanship changes as parties grow more (or less) polarized.

The analysis thus yields two coefficients of interest for each independent variable: a *baseline effect* and a *context-dependent effect*. The baseline effect estimates the expected association of the predictor when the elite-polarization measure is set to 0. The context-dependent effect measures the degree to which the impact of each predictor varies as a function of party polarization. A statistically significant context effect indicates that the relative impact of the predictor to party identification changes as a function of party polarization. Our main concern is with the context effects: the degree to which the impact of each of these predictors changes as parties polarize.

We run a number of iterations of this model in efforts to gauge both the changing impact of each of these issue dimensions to party choice in the aggregate, and the potential differences across income and educational groups that may underlie the aggregate findings. The first model examines the population as a whole, and the subsequent models divide the population into income and educational groups, modeling the association between partisanship and its individual-level correlates separately for each group.

To keep the groups large enough for meaningful analysis, we stratify the population into three income and two educational groups.[9] With respect to income, we divide citizens into three terciles based on real household income (upper, middle, and lower). With respect to education, we classify respondents into high- and low-education groups, based on whether the respondent's level of formal education is *above* or

Figure 3.2   Expected Impact of Issue Variables on Partisanship

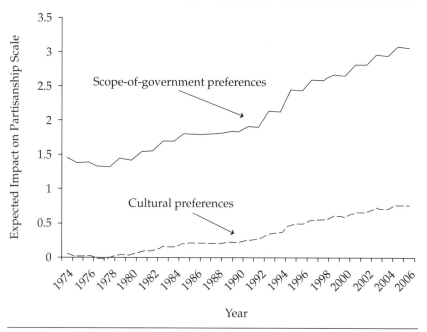

Source: Authors' compilation based on the General Social Surveys (Davis, Smith, and Marsden 1974–2006).
Note: All predictors have been scaled to a range of 0 to 1. Lines represent the expected impact on partisanship of moving from the most conservative possible position to the most liberal on each issue dimension.

at or below the median education level for a citizen born in the same birth cohort (as in, decade).[10] As expected, there is a strong, but not anything close to perfect, correlation between education and income (25 percent of low-income citizens, 37 percent of middle-income citizens, and 58 percent of high-income citizens fall into the high-education group).[11]

Aggregate Results

Results for the baseline model are presented in table 3.1, which builds on previous research and yields evidence that changes in the political context have changed the relationship between party identification and factors known to affect it. To provide a sense of the relative association of these factors to partisanship, in figure 3.2 we use the coefficients from the analysis, combined with levels of elite polarization, to graph the expected impact of the two issue sets on the 7-point partisanship scale at

Table 3.1   Context-Dependent Predictors of Partisanship, 1974–2006

	Baseline Impact	Variable * Polarization
Economic/scope-of-government liberalism	1.31 *	1.76 *
	(.16)	(.33)
Cultural-issue liberalism	−.09	.78 *
	(.09)	(.18)
Real income (tens of thousands)	−.61 *	−.17
	(.09)	(.16)
Ideological self-identification (7-point scale)	1.56 *	1.99 *
	(.13)	(.26)
Urban	.07	−.02
	(.05)	(.12)
Rural	−.11	−.24
	(.06)	(.14)
Catholic	.67 *	−.60 *
	(.05)	(.11)
Jewish	1.14 *	−.44
	(.13)	(.33)
Religious fundamentalist	.28 *	−.46 *
	(.06)	(.12)
Black	1.06 *	.28 *
	(.07)	(.14)
Female	−.10 *	.26 *
	.04	(.09)
Southern white	−.07	−.05
	(.06)	(.12)
Polarization (in DW-NOMINATE scores)	−.70 *	
	(.32)	
R^2	.20	
N	15,341	

Source: Authors' compilation based on the General Social Surveys (Davis, Smith, and Marsden 1974–2006).
Note: Table entries are OLS coefficients (cluster-corrected standard errors in parentheses). All predictors have been scaled to a range 0 to 1. Baseline impact taken when polarization is at the lowest level.
* $p < .05$, two-tailed tests

given points in time. The expected impact of a predictor in a given year is determined by adding its baseline-effect coefficient to its context-effect coefficient (multiplied by the level of polarization for the year of interest). The graph shows the expected impact on the partisanship scale of moving from the minimum issue scales value (most conservative) to the maximum value (most liberal) for each dimension in any given year.

We first see that, consistent with past work (for example, Layman and Carsey 2002), preferences on the scope-of-government and cultural dimensions are both becoming more important to partisanship. Scope-of-government preferences, important predictors of party identification in the 1970s, have become still more important, and cultural issues, previously not associated with partisanship, have become relevant as parties have polarized. The changing relative impact of the two dimensions is striking, however: scope-of-government preferences have become not only more strongly associated with partisanship in an absolute sense but also are increasing in importance at a rate significantly ($p < .01$) greater than that of cultural issues. In other words, scope-of-government issues are not only becoming more important to the mass party system, but their impact is also growing relative to that of cultural issues.[12] This further supports the idea that the party system is not, in the main, divided by cultural concerns.

These baseline results provide a straightforward description of how the issue bases of American party coalitions have changed. It is clear that though cultural issues have become increasingly important, they have not displaced scope-of-government issues as the dominant dimension of mass party conflict. Nor have they lessened the impact of social class itself (see also Stonecash, Brewer, and Moriani 2003). Rather, the scope-of-government dimension has remained dominant, becoming even more so over time.

Income, Education, and the Changing Issue Bases of Party Identification

We address our expectations regarding heterogeneity across income and educational lines in a straightforward way: by asking whether the impact of each of the predictors discussed varies significantly and substantively across our income and educational groups. We begin by replicating the aggregate model, running separate models for our two income groups and three educational groups. Results are presented in table 3.2, which to save space, reports results only for the issue preference scales.

The coefficients for both the baseline and interactive effects, with rare exceptions, have the same sign for each of the groups, and are of reasonably similar magnitude. Elite-party polarization is not causing different types of citizens to respond to the political world in fundamentally different ways. Nevertheless, there are systematic differences in the magnitude of changes across different groups that are important to understanding how the party system has evolved over the past three decades.

With respect to education, there are important differences, supportive of our expectations, in how high- and low-education citizens have updated their attitudes. Figure 3.3 graphs the expected associations between partisanship and preferences on these two issue dimensions for our high- and low-education groups. On scope-of-government issues,

Table 3.2   **Baseline and Context-Dependent Effect of Policy Preference Variables, by Income and Education**

	Low Education	High Education	Low Income	Middle Income	High Income
Scope-of-government issues (Baseline)	1.15 *	1.41 *	.69 *	1.53 *	1.58 *
	(.19)	(.27)	(.30)	(.27)	(.28)
Scope-of-government issues (Context effect)	.84 *	2.24 *	1.13 *	1.51 *	2.28 *
	(.43)	(.49)	(.61)	(.56)	(.56)
Cultural issues (Baseline)	.35 *	.09	−.15	−.57 *	−.00
	(.11)	(.14)	(.17)	(.15)	(.15)
Cultural issues (Context effect)	1.00 *	.33	.57 *	1.24 *	.66 *
	(.22)	(.26)	(.30)	(.30)	(.30)
R^2 (full model)	.12	.30	.12	.17	.26
N	10,627	6,242	5,147	5,264	4,958

Source: Authors' compilation based on the General Social Surveys (Davis, Smith, and Marsden 1974–2006).
Note: Table entries are OLS coefficients (cluster-corrected standard errors in parentheses). All predictors scaled to a range of 0 to 1. All other variables included in table 3.3 models are included in these models, but not shown in this table.
* $p < .05$, one-tailed tests

although both the high- and low-education groups structure their preferences similarly (with conservative preferences on economic issues leading to greater Republican identification in the baseline period, and the impact of these issues increasing as parties polarize), the growth in the importance of this dimension is significantly ($p < .05$) higher for the high-education group, nearly three times the rate of the low-education group. More educated citizens are becoming better able to relate scope-of-government issues to partisanship than their less educated counterparts. This is consistent with our expectation that education should make it easier for citizens to perceive and react to changing elite cues on hard issues.

With respect to the cultural dimension, however, we see precisely the opposite effect. The growing impact of cultural issues is nearly three times as large for the low-education cohort as for the high-education: in fact, for high-education citizens, we cannot say with confidence that cultural issues have increased in importance at all. For the low-education group, by contrast, cultural issues are becoming more relevant, significantly ($p < .05$) more so than for the more educated. In fact, the context-dependent effect on economic issues for the less educated is statistically

Figure 3.3   **Expected Impact of Issue Variables on Partisanship, by Education Level**

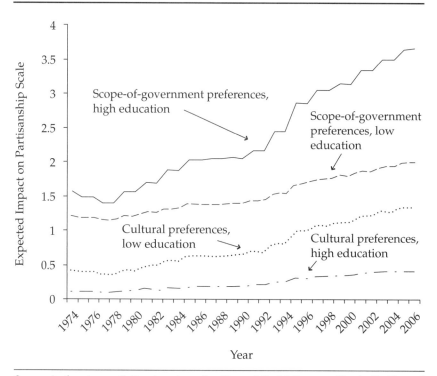

Source: Authors' compilation based on the General Social Surveys (Davis, Smith, and Marsden 1974–2006).
Note: All predictors are scaled to a range of 0 to 1.

indistinguishable from that on cultural issues. Although scope-of-government polarization is greatest among the most educated segment of the citizenry, growth in the weight attached to cultural issues is highest among the less educated.

There is also important heterogeneity across income levels (the final three columns of table 3.2) that, at least at the outset, runs somewhat counter to our expectations. Consistent with the work of Gelman and his colleagues (2008), the largest increase in the importance of culture to partisanship comes from the top two income cohorts. But the context-dependent effect for scope-of-government issues also becomes progressively larger for higher-income terciles. Figure 3.4 shows a growing class divide in how citizens of different income groups use economic issues. The difference in impact of economic preferences on party identification

Figure 3.4   Expected Impact of Issue Variables on Partisanship, by
              Income Level

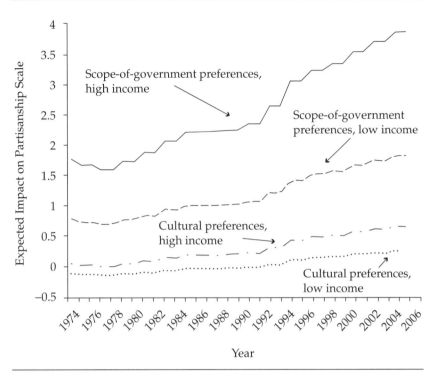

Source: Authors' compilation based on the General Social Surveys (Davis, Smith, and
Marsden 1974–2006).
Note: All predictors are scaled to a range of 0 to 1.

among high- and low-income citizens is expected to be about 1 point on
the 7-point scale at the lowest levels of polarization, but more than double that at the highest levels. Income, then, also appears to be related to
response to elite polarization: the partisan identifications of wealthier
people are becoming more issue-oriented than those of the poor, with
respect to both scope-of-government and cultural issues.

These findings are not perfectly consistent with Frank's (2004) culture-
wars argument. For all groups, the impact of economic issues is increasing, and these issues are still far more important than cultural issues in
predicting partisanship. Further, we see that poor citizens are the least
likely to have responded to elite cues on cultural issues, consistent with
the observation that their wealthy counterparts are those disproportionately fighting the culture wars. But these results are also not perfectly

Figure 3.5   Expected Impact of Issue Variables on Scope-of-Government Preferences Among High- and Low-Income Cohorts, by Education

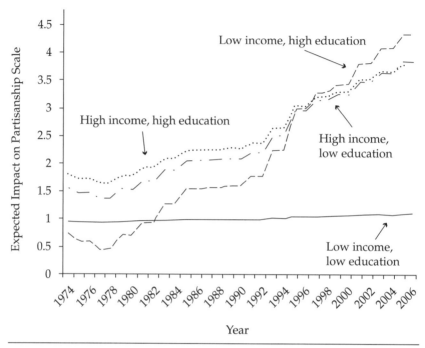

Source: Authors' compilation based on the General Social Surveys (Davis, Smith, and Marsden 1974–2006).
Note: All predictors are scaled to a range of 0 to 1.

consistent with many prominent critiques of Frank: the greatest increase in the importance of scope-of-government issues also appears among the rich. This speaks, perhaps, to the idea of a growing divide in the relevance of economic and scope-of-government preferences to political choices, a divide that falls largely along class lines.

The results so far consider differences across income and education levels independently, without controlling for the impact of the other. To test our expectations regarding the joint roles of income and education, we ask whether these results regarding baseline roles obscure findings that may be missed without considering their joint effects. Table 3.3 reports the estimated baseline and context-dependent effects on party identification of each of these issues for the high- and low-education cohorts within each of the three income terciles. We use these data to generate figures 3.5 and 3.6, which illustrate the expected associations be-

Table 3.3   Baseline and Context-Dependent Effect of Policy Preference Variables, by Education Level Within Income

	Low Income		Middle Income		High Income	
	Low Education	High Education	Low Education	High Education	Low Education	High Education
Scope-of-government issues (baseline)	.94*	.45	.95*	2.40*	1.37*	1.64*
	(.34)	(.63)	(.33)	(.48)	(.40)	(.41)
Scope-of-government issues (context effect)	.16	3.90*	1.72*	.68	2.46*	2.16*
	(.73)	(1.17)	(.76)	(.88)	(.91)	(.74)
Cultural issues (baseline)	-.12	.04	-.58*	-.20	.20	.36
	(.21)	(.35)	(.19)	(.26)	(.22)	(.21)
Cultural issues (context effect)	.56	.73	1.40*	.46	1.19*	.07
	(.38)	(.64)	(.41)	(.46)	(.47)	(.39)
R^2 (full model)	.10	.21	.12	.30	.16	.36
N	3,937	1,196	3,420	1,836	2,236	2,716

Source: Authors' compilation based on the General Social Surveys (Davis, Smith, and Marsden 1974–2006).
Note: Table entries are OLS coefficients (cluster-corrected standard errors in parentheses). All predictors scaled to a range of 0 to 1. Demographic control variables included in these models, but not shown in this table.
* $p < .05$, one-tailed tests

Figure 3.6   Expected Impact of Issue Variables on Cultural Preferences Among High- and Low-Income Cohorts, by Education

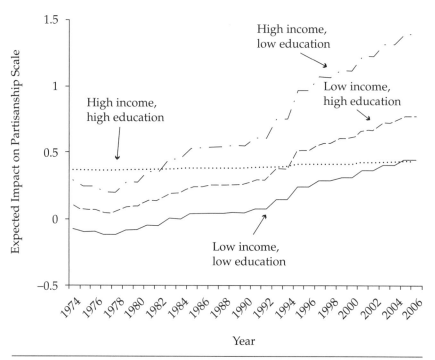

Source: Authors' compilation based on the General Social Surveys (Davis, Smith, and Marsden 1974–2006).
Note: All predictors are scaled to a range of 0 to 1.

tween partisanship and scope-of-government issues (figure 3.5), and between partisanship and cultural issues (figure 3.6) for our two education groups within the richest and poorest terciles. Although this analysis reflects the same broad similarity as the others (for all groups, preferences on scope-of-government issues remain dominant), differences across these groups that are not predicted from either the education or income results alone are significant and substantively important.

First, consider differences across educational lines for the poorest tercile. Consistent with our expectations, we find that for low-income citizens, the effects on the importance and the change in importance for each of these dimensions are strongly conditional on education. Low-income, high-education respondents are strongly responsive to changes in elite political context on scope-of-government issues, the highest among the six groups, in fact. For this group, there is no significant increase in the association between cultural issues and partisanship. For low-income, low-education citizens, by contrast, there has been no strengthening of the relationship between partisanship and scope-of-government preferences: this is the only group for which the interactive effect for the cultural dimension is actually larger than that for the scope-of-government dimension.

Poor citizens as a whole have reacted the least strongly on the scope-of-government dimension. Estimating the direct effects of income alone, however, obscures the fact that for the more highly educated among the poor, these issues have increased dramatically in importance. The largest increase comes from the low-income, high-education group, those with both the interest in and the ability to process changing cues on scope-of-government issues. By contrast, if the argument that culture is becoming disproportionately relevant holds for anyone, it does so for the low-income, low-education group. More accurately, however, we can say that this group has simply been the least likely to react in any way to changes in the elite context: for this group, neither issue dimension has become significantly more associated with partisan choice.

Taken together, these differences clearly indicate that education is an important intermediary in shaping how low-income citizens relate their issue preferences to partisanship. First and perhaps most important, figures 3.5 and 3.6 reflect the growing divergence in the importance of economic concerns between the preferences of the less educated poor, and the preferences of nearly everyone else. Poor, less educated citizens have remained unaware or uninterested in elite polarization on either issue dimension and appear to have almost entirely tuned out changes in the elite-party context of the past few decades. These differences are especially pronounced when considering economic issues. Whereas citizens in all other groups have become significantly more likely to structure their partisan attachments along economic lines, low-income, low-education citizens have not.

More highly educated, low-income citizens are a different story. These citizens—who are most likely, according to our expectations, both to place considerable importance on scope-of-government issues and to have the ability to process changing elite cues about them—have responded by organizing their partisanship considerably more strongly along scope-of-government lines.

We also find important heterogeneity when breaking down the high- and middle-income groups by education level. In the aggregate, wealthy and middle-income citizens have shown the greatest increase between cultural issues and partisanship. But for the more educated citizens in these cohorts, there has been no significant increase in the impact of these issues: it is actually for these groups that the impact of cultural issues has increased the least. To the extent that the culture wars are increasingly being fought among comparably wealthier citizens, it is clearly the less educated wealthy—those most likely, according to our expectations, to respond to the largely symbolic changes in elite rhetoric on this dimension—who are doing the fighting. Somewhat counter to our expectations, the differences between educated and less-educated citizens on this dimension are even larger than we had expected: wealthy, educated citizens appear not to be responding to elite polarization on the cultural dimension.

High- and low-education citizens within these two income cohorts exhibit similar rates of increase on the importance of the scope-of-government dimension. Because of higher baseline levels of importance of these issues for the well-educated citizens in both groups, scope-of-government issues remain more important for the high-education middle class than for the low-education middle class, and as important for the high-education rich as for the low-education rich. But, unlike with the poorest cohort, we cannot say with confidence that the more educated wealthy are more likely to react to elite polarization on the scope-of-government dimension.

In sum, issue preferences, particularly economic and scope-of-government ones, have become increasingly associated with Americans' partisan political choices over the last few decades. This basic result holds for most Americans across the important cleavages of education and income: citizens in all income and educational groups had divided, and continue to remain so, primarily based on preferences for economic and scope-of-government, not moral and cultural, issues. But the strength of the change in these associations—and the relative importance of the two issue dimensions—varies in systematic and important ways across education and income levels, and across education levels within income groups.

The wealthy have come to place a greater reliance on economic and scope-of-government concerns than the poor. But this finding is moderated strongly by education and driven largely, it appears, by the fact that wealthy citizens are on average more educated than the poor. For more highly educated poor citizens (those more likely to be able to perceive and react to changes in elite discourse on these harder scope-of-government concerns), the impact of scope-of-government concerns has increased dramatically, more so than for any other group. The impact for the less educated poor, by contrast, has changed little. In addition, to the extent that cultural issues are coming to define mass party conflict, it appears that they are doing so primarily among wealthy and middle-income citizens. This effect, however, is again mediated by education: the growing importance of culture to partisan choice is evident only among the less educated.

Discussion and Conclusions

Taken together, these findings show systematic heterogeneity across income and educational lines with respect to the issue structure of mass partisan attitudes. They also show that education and income, despite being correlated, have distinctive substantive effects: considering the intersectional effects of income and education provides for a richer, more nuanced view of the changing issue bases of party coalitions than considering each effect separately does. How citizens conceive of the relationship between issues and partisanship have changed over the past three-plus decades, in ways that have produced growing differences across class and educational lines. In the 1970s, these differences were relatively small. All types of citizens were about equally able (or unable) to connect partisanship and issue attitudes. For all groups, economic and scope-of-government attitudes were weakly connected to partisan identification, and cultural concerns simply did not matter. These differences have grown substantially over time in ways that have implications for the structure of American political conflict.

In substantive terms, the data show that relatively wealthy, less-educated citizens are the core of the culture-war dynamic in American politics: for them, the impact of culture on partisanship is becoming much stronger. Relatively poor, well-educated citizens, by contrast, have become especially attuned to the growing divide on economic and scope-of-government issues, and their partisan identities are becoming most strongly tied to scope-of-government preferences. The least educated poor are the least likely to have reacted in any meaningful way to changes in the political context. They are perhaps the only group for whom partisanship has not become more issue-oriented.

In some respects, our work dovetails with other recent research on mass opinion dynamics, showing broad similarity in how citizens in different groups respond to changes in the political context (Ellis, Ura, and Ashley-Robinson 2006; Enns and Kellstedt 2008; Soroka and Wlezien 2008). But the broad pattern of homogeneity in mass preference change over the past thirty-five years does not deny important heterogeneity in the degree and the relative magnitude of these changes. At a minimum, these differences have considerable implications for how campaigns should frame messages for various subgroups of the electorate, and for how citizens in different income or educational groups are equipped to understand elite-party messages on these dimensions and to hold leaders accountable for their actions on these issues.

The results also speak to the important role that concepts such as education and political awareness play in helping lower-income citizens relate their own preferences to the political world. It appears, for example, that lower-income citizens have responded the least strongly to changing elite messages on economic and scope-of-government issues. This limited response, however, is concentrated among the less-educated segment of the poorest income cohort; the relatively well-educated poor pay at least as much attention to economic and scope-of-government issues as the wealthy do. The limited response on the part of the poor, in other words, seems to be driven entirely by differing education levels: less educated people, on average, are less able to align scope-of-government preferences and partisanship. Poor citizens, on average, are comparably less educated than the rich.

This chapter has focused narrowly on changes in the issue bases of mass party choice, but the results have implications for theories of equality and inequality in representation and suggest different avenues for future research on both mass response and possible inequalities. Much recent work has explored the independent roles of education (for example, Stimson 2004; Enns and Kellstedt 2008) and income (for example, Soroka and Wlezien 2008) in mass preference change and representation, typically focusing on each concept independently. Our results show that though income and education are highly correlated, they should not be treated as additive concepts. Higher levels of education may matter to citizens in different economic cohorts in fundamentally different ways that may be obscured because of the high correlation between the two. Our results suggest that analysts of public opinion dynamics should more closely consider the joint roles of education, and related concepts of sophistication and engagement, and income in shaping how citizens update their preferences in response to changes in the political world, and how elected officials respond to dynamic shifts in public opinion.

More important, decades of research into representation of public opinion have shown that elected officials are strongly responsive to public opinion on issues that citizens find salient and easy to understand, and perhaps less attentive to mass opinion on issues that citizens know or care little about (see, for example, Arnold 1990; Jones 1994; Smith 2000; Erikson, MacKuen, and Stimson 2002). If we assume that citizens care more about the types of issues most closely aligned with their own partisanship and other political choices, we would expect public opinion to be represented more strongly on issues that citizens use to structure their partisanship (as well as expect political elites to spend more time addressing such issues).

This analysis suggests that the rich and the poor and the educated and the non-educated within these economic cohorts may have different preferences regarding the types of issues to which policymaking elites should be paying the most attention. Most studies which find broad patterns of equality in representation across socioeconomic lines (see Ura and Ellis 2008; Soroka and Wlezien, this volume) focus on the representation of the ideological type—whether preferences of a particular group more closely correspond with public policy than those of another group do or whether movements in a liberal or conservative direction of particular groups are associated with future changes in policy. But comparably less attention has been given to equality and inequality in the representation of the priorities of the rich and the poor or engaged and less engaged citizens (see Verba, Schlozman, and Brady 1995). Our basic analysis suggests that such research is in order.

Finally, we note that the evidence presented in this chapter is consistent with more fundamental changes in citizens' orientations toward the issue bases of partisan politics. We have principally addressed salience and association, how differences in income and education influence the changing association between citizens' preferences on New Deal and cultural issues and their partisan identities. In essence, this is an argument about conditional sorting (Fiorina 2005). As elite parties have polarized, it has become easier for citizens to match their partisanship with their issue preferences, though, as we have shown, the sorting process works differently across cleavages defined by income, education, and the intersection of the two. Layman and Carsey (2002) suggest that increased alignment of partisanship and any set of issue preferences may, in fact, catalyze attitude change, by pushing other issue attitudes to line up with partisan positions, catalyzing more extreme views, or both. Thus, for example, we might expect low-income, high-education citizens to become more liberal on economic issues over time as a consequence of the changing association between partisanship and the preferences that we observe here. Our data are consistent with this conflict extension perspective, but do not provide sufficient leverage to definitively assess whether the increased association between preferences and partisanship that we observe for some groups has contributed to over-time changes in those groups' absolute preferences. This deserves additional scholarly attention.

Appendix: Variables, Coding, and Dimensionality of Issue Measures

Economic and Scope-of-Government Issues   This measure is derived from ten questions dealing with the spending priorities of the federal government. All are of the following type:

> We are faced with many problems in this country, none of which can be solved easily or inexpensively. I'm going to name some of these problems, and for each one, I'd like you to tell me whether you think we're spending too much money on it, too little money, or about the right amount. Are we

spending too much money, too little money, or about the right amount on . . . [the military, armaments, and defense; foreign aid; solving the problems of big cities; halting the rising crime rate; dealing with drug addiction; improving the nation's education system; improving and protecting the environment; welfare; improving and protecting the nation's health; improving the conditions of blacks]?

All questions with the exception of the military, armaments, and defense item were scored as 1 for "too little spending" and -1 for "too much spending." The military, armaments, and defense question was reverse-coded. "Don't know," "about the right amount of spending," and "refused to answer" responses were scored as 0. The individual-level measure of preferences on this dimension is a simple summation of scores for each of the ten questions. (Individual-level factor scores correlate at 0.89 with the simple additive scales.)

Preferences for an eleventh spending issue, spending on space exploration, did not load on a single factor with the other ten items and is thus excluded from the measure.

Cultural Issues   This measure is derived from seven questions, six related to the legality of abortion in various circumstances and a seventh dealing with homosexual relations. The abortion questions are as follow:

Please tell me whether or not you think it should be possible for a pregnant woman to obtain a legal abortion if . . . [the woman's own health is seriously endangered by the pregnancy; if there is a strong chance of a serious defect in the baby; if the woman is single and does not want to marry the man; if the woman is pregnant as a result of rape or incest; if the woman is poor and cannot afford any more children; if the woman is married and does not want any more children]?

"Yes" responses (signifying support for legal abortion) were scored at 1. "No" responses were scored as −1.

The homosexuality question is as follows:

There's been a lot of discussion about the way morals and attitudes about sex are changing in this country. If two adults of the same sex have sexual relations, do you think it is always wrong, almost always wrong, wrong only sometimes, or not wrong at all?

"Always wrong" was scored as −1, "almost always wrong" and "wrong only sometimes" were scored as 0, and "not wrong at all" was scored as 1.

The individual-level measure of preferences on this dimension is a simple summation of individuals' responses to the seven questions (after reweighting the scores such that the abortion and homosexuality issues were weighted equally). Individual-level factor scores correlate at 0.94 with the simple additive scales.

Notes

1. Referring to the former as an economic dimension is a relatively standard practice (see Miller and Schofeld 2003; Gelman et al. 2008; Bartels 2008). But although the issues that load on this dimension do include purely economic concerns of taxation, redistribution, and regulation, this dimension is perhaps better understood as a broader scope-of- government dimension, dealing with the more general conflicts about the proper size and scope of the federal government in domestic affairs, particularly in redistributing wealth and providing social services. This New Deal basis of conflict includes, but goes beyond, purely economic matters.
2. There are many different ways to measure which types of citizens are best able to receive, understand, and react to complex information about the political world. Our focus, for both practical and substantive reasons, is with formal education. With respect to our substantive question of interest, scholars have used many different measures to stratify the public by level of political engagement—formal education, knowledge, political awareness, and the like—but the finding, regardless of measure, has been the same: citizens who are more likely to be able to understand and process changing political cues have been the most likely to respond to changes in elite-party polarization.
3. This does not mean that low-income citizens need hold universally left-of-center preferences on these issues. Attitudes on economic and scope-of-government issues are formed from a wide variety of considerations—including, but not limited to, one's own social standing—and the direct effects of income (or economic self-interest more broadly defined) on issue attitudes remain comparably small. Opposition to a greater government role in economic and domestic matters, for example, may stem from anti-government attitudes and skepticism of government's ability to solve social problems. These attitudes may be more common among low-income citizens (see Walsh, chapter 5, this volume). This does suggest, though, that low-income citizens, whatever their preferences, will be more likely to pay attention to elite behavior on this dimension and make connections between their own attitudes and partisanship accordingly.
4. Two of the issues, the military and foreign aid, also have a strong foreign policy component to them. Although we see valid theoretical and empirical reason to include these two issues alongside the others in a measure of scope-of-government liberalism, excluding them does not materially change the results to follow.
5. The greatest limitation of this measure is obviously that it contains preferences for essentially only two issues. Beginning in 1986, the GSS has consistently asked a number of other questions—school prayer, birth control, sex education, and assisted suicide—that attempt to get more broadly at

cultural-issue conflict. Preferences on this broader set of issues strongly load alongside the two issues that we have for a longer time frame on a single dimension of cultural preferences, and an individual-level scale of preferences on a broader measure of cultural preferences, including these other issues, correlates at .84 with our more limited issue set (in the years where both are available). These findings offer strong empirical support for our two-item measure.

6. The object of this chapter is to examine heterogeneity in the changing issue bases of American mass partisanship and the ways in which these dividing lines differ across relevant groups. We recognize, however, that debate on the nature of the causal relationship between partisanship and preferences at the individual level is considerable (see, for example, Abramowitz and Saunders 1998; Carsey and Layman 2006). Our analyses cannot adjudicate the underlying theoretical debate over the causal relationship between issue preferences and partisanship: our substantive interest is in the changing nature of the associations between issue preferences and partisanship (for a more extended discussion of this topic, see also Bafumi and Shapiro 2009).

7. This measure of polarization is unidimensional. It would, of course, be useful to have separate, valid measures of economic and cultural polarization, but at least with respect to key votes and policy platforms, elite polarization on both dimensions has happened more or less concurrently.

8. Elite-party polarization increased during all but two sessions of Congress during the observed period (the 94th and 95th Congresses, which opened in 1975 and 1974, respectively) and strongly corresponds with levels of aggregate income inequality and rates of immigration to the United States during the same period (McCarty, Poole, and Rosenthal 2006). Given the strong interrelationships among these variables, it is difficult to disentangle the effects of elite polarization, income inequality, and immigration for mass polarization. However, it is reasonably clear that changes in elite-level partisan orientations and national demographic conditions as a group influence mass partisanship (for example, Bartels 2000; Carmines and Stimson 1980; Hetherington 2001). Furthermore, recent analyses suggest that elite-party polarization may be a first cause of subsequent changes in income distribution and policies related to immigration (McCarty, Poole, and Rosenthal 2006). As such, it is reasonable to claim that elite-party polarization ultimately influences mass party polarization, though it is unclear whether its effect is direct or transmitted through the policy environment. Because our proximate interest lies with variance in how individuals respond to changes in macro political conditions rather than explaining those changes themselves, we rely on a direct account of the relationship between elite polarization and mass polarization in formulating our empirical analyses. The literature supports this approach, but we note that our results support other plausible interpretations with respect to what macro-level variable or variables (elite polarization, income inequality, immigration, and so on) act most directly on mass partisan polarization. Though our claims about the effects of income and education on individual-level behavior do not depend on a particular interpretation of the aggregate dynamics.

9. Keeping the size of the groups relatively large also helps to control for some of the self-selection effects that can be a problem in analyses such as this. Obviously, citizens are not placed into educational or income groups at random, or as a result of circumstances entirely beyond their control: placements into one of these groups reflects, at least to some extent, lifestyle priorities and choices (such as using a higher degree to secure a job that promotes social change rather than a job for simple economic mobility, which then reflect back on political priorities and choices. This may be especially problematic for citizens who fall into the nonconventional groups—those with high incomes and low levels of formal education, or the reverse. Keeping the classifications sufficiently broad (for most birth cohorts, for example, high education means anything more than a high school diploma) helps eliminate some of the more severe self-selection effects—not all low-income, high-education citizens are missionaries or social workers. We also explore some modeling strategies that attempt to control more explicitly for these effects—stratifying respondents based on occupational classification or age, for example. None of these considerations seem to affect our findings, though data limitations prevent us from exploring them too deeply. For now, we can simply say that self-selection does not dramatically affect the results to come, though surely it has some impact worthy of further exploration.

10. Operationalizing education relative to one's peers helps to circumvent some of the considerable comparability issues that arise when comparing educational attainment across years and generations (see Nie, Junn, and Stehlik-Barry 1996).

11. Education and income have modest effects on levels of preferences on these dimensions. Higher incomes are associated with more conservative, and higher levels of education more liberal, preferences on scope-of-government issues. Higher levels of both income and education are associated with greater liberalism on cultural issues. But the explanatory power of both is relatively modest—explaining less than 2 percent of the variance in scope-of-government preferences and less than 8 percent of cultural preferences.

12. Although not our proximate interest, the changing impact of some control variables is worth noting. The impact of ideological self-identification has increased considerably, at a rate statistically indistinguishable from that of scope-of-government issues. The independent impact of income has remained relatively constant over the past thirty-five years: after controlling for issue preferences and a variety of other factors, wealth is modestly associated with higher levels of Republican identification. The pure social-class basis of party politics has not increased over time, and income itself remains a very modest predictor of party identification. But its impact on partisanship has not diminished.

References

Abrajano, Marisa A. 2005. "Who Evaluates a Presidential Candidate by Using Non-Policy Campaign Messages?" *Political Research Quarterly* 58(1): 55–67.

Abramowitz, Alan I., and Kyle L. Saunders. 1998. "Ideological Realignment in the U.S. Electorate." *Journal of Politics* 60(3): 634–52.

Ansolabahere, Stephen, Jonathan Rodden, and James Snyder. 2006. "Purple America." *Journal of Economic Perspectives* 20(2): 97–118.

Arnold, R. Douglas. 1990. *The Logic of Congressional Action*. New Haven, Conn.: Yale University Press.

Bafumi, Joseph, and Robert Shapiro. 2009. "A New Partisan Voter." *Journal of Politics* 71(1): 1–24.

Bailey, Michael, Lee Sigelman, and Clyde Wilcox. 2003. "Presidential Persuasion on Social Issues: A Two-Way Street?" *Political Research Quarterly* 56(1): 49–58.

Baldassarri, Delia, and Andrew Gelman. 2008. "Partisans Without Constraint: Political Polarization and Trends in American Public Opinion." *American Journal of Sociology* 114(2008): 408–46.

Bartels, Larry M. 2000. "Partisanship and Voting Behavior, 1952–1996." *American Journal of Political Science* 44(1) 35–50.

———. 2006. "What's the Matter with *What's the Matter with Kansas?*" *Quarterly Journal of Political Science* 1(2): 201–26.

———. 2008. *Unequal Democracy: The Political Economy of the New Gilded Age*. Princeton, N.J.: Princeton University Press.

Brewer, Mark D. 2005. "The Rise of Partisanship and the Expansion of Partisan Conflict Within the American Electorate." *Political Research Quarterly* 58(2): 219–29.

Carmines, Edward G., and James A. Stimson. 1980. "The Two Faces of Issue Voting." *American Political Science Review* 74(1): 78–91.

Carsey, Thomas, and Geoffrey Layman. 2006. "Changing Sides or Changing Minds? Party Identification and Policy Preferences in the American Electorate." *American Journal of Political Science* 50(2): 464–77.

Davis, James A., Tom W. Smith, and Peter V. Marsden. 1974–2006. General Social Surveys, 1974–2008 [Cumulative file] [Computer file]. ICPSR25962-v2. Storrs, Conn.: Roper Center for Public Opinion Resarch, University of Connecticut/ Ann Arbor, Mich.: Inter-University Consortium for Political and Social Research [distributors], 2010-02-08. doi:10.3886/ICPSR25962.

Delli Carpini, Michael X., and Scott Keeter. 1996. *What Americans Know About Politics and Why It Matters*. New Haven, Conn.: Yale University Press.

Ellis, Christopher R., Joseph Daniel Ura, and Jenna Ashley-Robinson. 2006. "The Dynamic Consequences of Nonvoting in American National Elections." *Political Research Quarterly*. 59(2): 227–33.

Enns, Peter K., and Paul M. Kellstedt. 2008. "Policy Mood and Political Sophistication: Why Everybody Moves Mood." *British Journal of Political Science* 38(3): 433–54.

Erikson, Robert S., Michael B. MacKuen, and James A. Stimson. 2002. *The Macro Polity*. Cambridge: Cambridge University Press.

Fiorina, Morris P., with Samuel J. Abrams and Jeremy C. Pope. 2005. *Culture War? The Myth of a Polarized America*. New York: Pearson-Longman.

Frank, Thomas. 2004. *What's the Matter with Kansas? How Conservatives Won the Heart of America*. New York: Metropolitan Books.

Gelman, Andrew, David Park, Boris Shor, Joseph Bafumi, and Jeronimo Cortina.

2008. *Red State, Blue State, Rich State, Poor State: Why Americans Vote the Way They Do.* Princeton, N.J.: Princeton University Press.

Gelman, Andrew, Boris Shor, Joseph Bafumi, and David Park. 2007. "Rich State, Poor State, Red State, Blue State: What's the Matter with Connecticut?" *Quarterly Journal of Political Science* 2(4): 345–67.

Hetherington, Marc J. 2001. "Resurgent Mass Partisanship: The Role of Elite Polarization." *American Political Science Review* 95(3): 619–31.

Hunter, James. D. 1994. *Before the Shooting Begins: Searching for Democracy in America's Culture War.* New York: Macmillan.

Jelen, Ted G., and Clyde Wilcox. 2003. "Causes and Consequences of Public Attitudes Toward Abortion: A Review and Research Agenda." *Political Research Quarterly* 56(4): 489–500.

Jones, Bryan. 1994. *Reconceiving Decision Making in Democratic Politics.* Chicago: University of Chicago Press.

Joslyn, Mark R., and David Haider-Markel. 2002. "Framing Effects on Personal Opinion and Perception of Public Opinion: The Cases of Physician-Assisted Suicide and Social Security." *Social Science Quarterly* 83(3): 690–706.

Layman, Geoffrey C., and Thomas Carsey. 2002. "Party Polarization and 'Conflict Extension' in the American Electorate." *American Journal of Political Science* 46(4): 786–802.

Leege, David C., Kenneth D. Wald, Brian S. Kruger, and Paul D. Meuller. 2002. *The Politics of Cultural Differences.* Princeton, N.J.: Princeton University Press.

Levendusky, Matthew. 2009. *The Partisan Sort: How Liberals Became Democrats and Conservatives Became Republicans.* Chicago: University of Chicago Press.

Levine, Jeffrey, Edward G. Carmines, and Robert Huckfeldt. 1997. "The Rise of Ideology in the Post–New Deal Party System, 1972–1992." *American Politics Quarterly* 25(1): 19–34.

Lindaman, Kara, and Donald P. Haider-Markel. 2002. "Issue Evolution, Political Parties, and the Culture Wars." *Political Research Quarterly* 55(1): 91–110.

Luskin, Robert C., John P. McIver, and Edward G. Carmines. 1989. "Issues and the Transmission of Partisanship." *American Journal of Political Science* 33(2): 440–58.

McCarty, Nolan, Keith T. Poole, and Howard Rosenthal. 2006. *Polarized America: The Dance of Ideology and Unequal Riches.* Cambridge, Mass.: MIT Press.

Miller, Gary, and Norman Schofeld. 2003. "Activists and Partisan Realignment in the United States." *American Political Science Review* 97(2): 245–60.

Nie, Norman H., Jane Junn, and Kenneth Stehlik-Barry. 1996. *Education and Democratic Citizenship in America.* Chicago: University of Chicago Press.

Pomper, Gerald M., and Marc D. Weiner. 2002. "Toward a More Responsible Two-Party Voter." In *Responsible Partisanship? The Evolution of American Political Parties Since 1950,* edited by John C. Green and Paul S. Herrnson. Lawrence: Kansas University Press.

Poole, Keith T., and Howard L. Rosenthal. 1997. *Congress: A Political-Economic History of Roll Call Voting.* Oxford: Oxford University Press.

Saunders, Kyle L., and Alan I. Abramowitz. 2004. "Ideological Realignment and Active Partisans in the American Electorate." *American Politics Research* 32(3): 285–309.

Sigelman, Lee, and Ernest Yaranella. 1986. "Public Opinion on Public Issues: A Multivariate Analysis." *Social Science Quarterly* 67(3): 402–10.

Smith, Mark. 2000. *American Business and Political Power.* Chicago: University of Chicago Press.

Soroka, Stuart N., and Christopher Wlezien. 2008. "On the Limits to Inequality in Representation." *PS: Political Science & Politics* 41(2): 319–27.

Stimson, James A. 1999. *Public Opinion in America: Moods, Cycles, and Swings,* 2nd ed. Boulder, Colo.: Westview Press.

——. 2004. *Tides of Consent: How Public Opinion Shapes American Politics.* Cambridge: Cambridge University Press.

Stonecash, Jeffrey M. 2001. *Class and Party in American Politics.* Boulder, Colo.: Westview Press.

Stonecash, Jeffrey M., Mark D. Brewer, and Mack D. Moriani. 2003. *Diverging Parties.* Boulder, Colo.: Westview Press.

Ura, Joseph Daniel, and Christopher R. Ellis. 2008. "Income, Preferences, and the Dynamics of Policy Responsiveness." *PS: Political Science & Politics* 41(4): 785–94.

Verba, Sidney, Kay Lehman Schlozman, and Henry E. Brady. 1995. *Voice and Equality: Civic Voluntarism in American Politics.* Cambridge, Mass.: Harvard University Press.

Chapter 4

The Political Geography of Party Resurgence

DAVID A. HOPKINS AND LAURA STOKER

T HE GROWING ELECTORAL strength of American political parties is one of the most fruitful topics of recent empirical research. The phenomenon of increasing ideological polarization between Democratic and Republican elites, especially members of Congress, has long been acknowledged (for example, Rohde 1991; Poole and Rosenthal 2007). Mounting evidence also suggests that the growing divergence between party leaders on public policy matters over the past few decades has been increasingly echoed within the larger electorate, with a simultaneous rise in the rates at which party identifiers support their party's nominees for office. Since the 1970s, more Americans have come to perceive important differences between the parties (Hetherington 2001). Democratic and Republican identifiers within the mass public increasingly differ with respect to ideology (Abramowitz and Saunders 1998; Levine, Carmines, and Huckfeldt 1997; Levendusky 2009) and issue positions (Layman and Carsey 2002; Stoker and Jennings 2008). Over the same period, party labels have become more consequential to the electoral preferences of rank-and-file voters. The effect of individual party identification on vote choice has strengthened considerably since the 1970s in both presidential and congressional elections, reaching levels by 1996 that matched or exceeded those of the 1950s (Bartels 2000). As a result, the party-decline thesis commonly advanced a generation ago (see Wattenberg 1984) has been replaced with a growing scholarly consensus that for elites and masses alike, parties play as central a role as ever in American electoral politics.

Although political scientists increasingly acknowledge that parties in the electorate have become significantly stronger among individual voters over the past four decades, agreement is substantially less with respect to the potential consequences of these trends for aggregate electoral outcomes and political representation. Many contemporary journalists and pundits, who frequently describe—and often lament—the high levels of partisanship and ideological conflict that characterize the current political environment,[1] perceive the polarization of Washington elites over the past several decades as occurring simultaneously with a growing partisan divide among voters that falls along geographic lines. The striking regional pattern of party support that emerged in the 2000 presidential election, and has remained largely intact ever since, appears to reflect a widening rift in the electorate not only between Republicans and Democrats, or between conservatives and liberals, but between the so-called red states (which includes the South, the Great Plains, and the Rocky Mountains) and blue states (which includes the Northeast, the urban Midwest, and the Pacific Coast). According to this view, conflict in Washington among party elites reflects, or is reflected by, divisions out in the country among ordinary Americans—divisions that are increasingly apparent on the electoral map (Brooks 2001; Barone 2001; Farhi 2004). Even Democratic nominee Barack Obama's relatively decisive victory in the 2008 presidential election appeared to be a limited incursion into previously Republican territory; Obama carried only three of fourteen southern/border states and three of twelve Great Plains/Rocky Mountain states, in nearly all cases by narrow margins.

Several scholars have challenged this account of contemporary politics, arguing that variation in the partisan alignments of states has in fact been relatively modest in recent elections, despite exaggerated claims to the contrary by the news media (Fiorina 2005; Ansolabehere, Rodden, and Snyder 2006). Yet it seems likely that the massive increase over time in the strength of party identification as a predictor of vote choice among individual citizens has had an observable effect on aggregate outcomes at the level of electoral constituencies. If partisan loyalty is now the norm among the vast majority of voters in presidential elections, the relative number of voters identifying with the two parties within a state's electorate has presumably become a more reliable predictor of the state's likely partisan alignment in the electoral college. To the extent that the aggregate distribution of party identification differs from one state to the next, the growing strength of parties in the electorate could well produce an overall increase in the state-level variation of electoral outcomes.

We examine the growing strength of partisanship within and across states and consider the implications of these individual-level findings for the size and stability of state-level electoral outcomes. In the analysis that follows, we demonstrate that state-level electoral divisions have, in fact, increased substantially since the 1970s, concurrently with the rise in the individual-level effect of party identification on vote choice in national elections. However, we also show that the national trend of rising party strength among individual voters obscures substantial variation at the subnational level. The residents of some states have become much more party-loyal since the 1970s, whereas in others the relationship of party identification to the presidential vote has remained relatively constant. As a result, the effect of party on vote choice is now more uniform across states than it was forty years ago. At the same time, considerations other than party have become increasingly less likely to produce variation in state electoral outcomes. For both reasons, the aggregate partisan balance among the voters of a state has become an increasingly dependable predictor of that state's likely partisan alignment in the electoral college.

These trends have important implications for American politics. Political parties act as institutions of intermediation between voters and their representatives; in the United States, this mass-elite link is mediated further by the use of subnational geographic units as the basis of democratic elections. Congress may be an ostensibly national institution, but its members are elected independently within relatively small constituencies—a characteristic that exerts a powerful influence on their workways (Mayhew 1974; Fenno 1978). Even the president is chosen not by a true national popular electorate, but in effect by fifty-one simultaneous state-level elections in which virtually all electoral votes are allocated by states to candidates on a winner-take-all basis.[2] As a result, presidential candidates devote more attention and campaign resources to populous, competitive states than to the rest of the nation; the strategic implications of the electoral college appear to shape even the governing decisions of incumbent presidents (Doherty 2006).

Due to the nature of the nation's electoral institutions, party coalitions are, to a great degree, geographic; candidates and officeholders certainly have powerful reasons to think of them as such. As more states become increasingly safe territory for one party or other over time, we would expect the behavior of political actors to respond accordingly. Because rampant party-line voting now renders most states electorally noncompetitive, candidates may be less inclined than before to attempt the construction of a broad electoral coalition by courting voters in states that normally favor the opposition, and would have less incentive while in office to take into account the preferences of the electorate beyond their own partisan base of support. Changes over time in the strength of parties at the individual level, when aggregated into geographically defined electoral units, can therefore fundamentally affect the nature of political representation in America.

Our analysis begins by presenting evidence of growing electoral division at the state level and discussing how growing party loyalty among voters in some or all of the states could account for this trend. We then turn to an over-time analysis of the relationship between party identification and the presidential vote that considers variation within and across states. The final section of the chapter considers an array of possible explanations for the pattern of geographic heterogeneity in the resurgence of partisanship.

Party and Geography in American Elections

Is the United States becoming more politically divided along geographic lines? Some scholars have found significant variation among contemporary state-level partisan alignments (Gelman et al. 2008; Abramowitz and Saunders 2005), but others argue that the red-against-blue narrative is little more than a myth (Fiorina 2005; Ansolabehere, Rodden, and Snyder 2006). It is clear, however, that state-level differences in presidential election outcomes have grown markedly over the past four decades. Figure 4.1 displays the mean deviation of the state-level two-party vote from the national popular vote in each presidential election from 1972 to 2008. (The national vote is subtracted to account for nationwide swings in party support from election to election.) The average state differed from the national result by about 6 percentage points in most of the elections between 1972 and 1992. By 2008, this gap had increased to nearly 9 points. Weighting states by the number of their electoral votes slightly reduces the mean deviation across the time series, reflecting the tendency of populous states to be more representative of the national electorate. Even so, the average deviation has grown steadily from about 4 percentage points to more than 7 percentage points since the 1970s.

As a result, fewer states over time closely mirror the national division of the popular vote and are thus likely to act as pivotal battlegrounds in the electoral college. Figure 4.2 displays the percentage of electoral votes cast by states in which the state popular vote falls within 10, 5, and 3 points of the national vote from 1972 to 2008. Regardless of the specific threshold used to distinguish states that are representative of the national electorate from those that are not, the number of electoral votes cast by pivotal states has declined appreciably since the 1970s. As recently as 1988, more than half of all electoral votes were cast by states in which the presidential candidates finished within 3 percentage points of their national vote shares. By 2008 only 25 percent of the total electoral vote was cast by such states. The eleven states that fell within 3 percentage points of the national popular vote division in 2008 included the central electoral battlegrounds of the fall campaign, where both Barack Obama and John McCain focused their attention and resources.[3] The growth in state-level electoral variation over time has transformed a

Figure 4.1   State-Level Variation in Presidential Election Results, 1972 to 2008

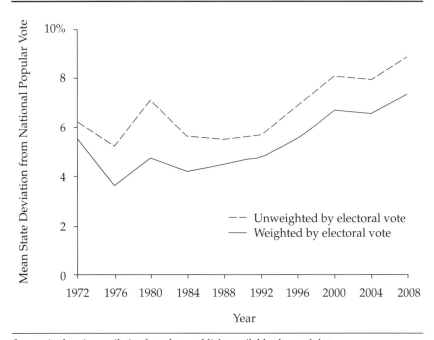

Source: Authors' compilation based on publicly available electoral data.

number of former swing states into dependable partisan strongholds, reducing the size of the competitive territory contested by both presidential candidates. Just as Texas, Georgia, and Tennessee have evolved from competitive to safely Republican states since the 1970s, California, New Jersey, and Illinois have moved in the opposite direction, becoming solidly Democratic over the same period.

It is clear that the widely recognized growth in the strength of parties in the electorate since the early 1970s has occurred at the same time as a less well-acknowledged increase in the geographic variation of presidential election results. How are these two trends connected? One hypothesis, derived not only from the common assumptions of political pundits but from academic scholarship as well (for example, Hetherington 2001), holds that the increasing importance of party identification (PID) in the electorate over the past four decades is a direct mass response to the ideological polarization of national party leaders. As voters see the two parties in Washington differ more sharply on a greater

Figure 4.2   Declining Scope of Competition in Presidential Elections, 1972 to 2008

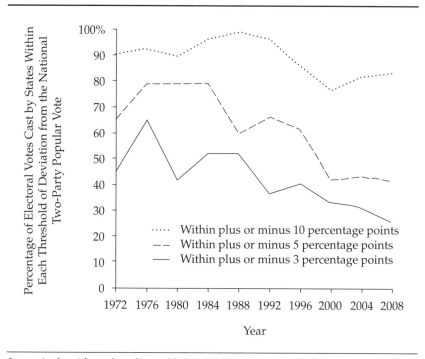

Source: Authors' figure based on publicly available electoral data.

number of issues, their own party loyalties are more commonly activated in the voting booth. If this reasoning is correct, we would expect to find that the increasing strength of PID in determining vote choice occurred uniformly across states, as the mass public responded consistently across the nation to the same stimulus: the polarization of national political elites.[4] The increased variation in state-level electoral outcomes would simply reflect differences among states in the aggregate distribution of PID within their electorates—differences that were becoming more consequential as the individual-level strength of PID rose over time. According to this view, voters everywhere were somewhat likely to defect from their favored party in presidential elections during the "weak party" era of the 1970s, but have collectively grown more loyal at similar rates as national party leaders have sharpened their differences.[5]

Alternatively, the individual-level relationship between PID and the vote may have differed not only over time but across states as well. The national rise in party strength could have been driven by change in a subset of states, while other states remained stable from one election to the next. Such a finding would suggest that other factors besides elite polarization also account for the size of the effect of partisanship on vote choice—that various state-level characteristics and dynamics, in addition to national trends, influence the strength of parties in the electorate.

Figure 4.3 illustrates these two scenarios. The first panel depicts the PID-vote relationship as moderately strong ($b = .25$) and identical across states. The second panel depicts the PID-vote relationship as equally strong on average, but also as varying substantially from state to state. In each panel, the differing intercepts represent the presence of other factors besides party identification operating within particular states or on their inhabitants to cause more Republican outcomes or more Democratic outcomes at the state level than would be predicted solely on the basis of the state's aggregate partisan balance and the effect of PID within the state.

The third panel depicts a later hypothetical time point when the connection between PID and voting has become stronger. Compared with panel 1, PID is now a better predictor of individuals' vote choices in each state, with the slope doubling in size ($b = .5$). Compared with panel 2, PID has become more important overall due to its increasing significance in the states where it was initially weak—that is, to the disappearance of heterogeneity across states in the strength of the relationship between PID and the vote. Here, the national resurgence of parties in the electorate is largely fueled by changes taking place within a subset of states.

The fourth panel depicts the erosion of state differences net of PID. Compared with the baselines depicted in panel 1 and panel 2, two things have changed: the PID effect on vote choice has increased, and factors influencing state-level electoral outcomes net of PID have declined.[6] Considerations other than party have become less likely to produce state-level differences in electoral outcomes. There is, of course, no logical reason to expect state differences net of PID to disappear just because PID effects have grown. If both developments occur simultaneously, however, the implications are important: party identification becomes a more powerful predictor of both how individuals will vote and how the state as a whole will vote. If state differences net of PID diminish, a state's aggregate partisan balance becomes an extremely powerful predictor of the electoral result within the state.

These illustrated outcomes set the stage for depicting two ideal, typical routes by which the relationship between party identification and vote choice may grow within a national sample over time, as it did, according to previous studies, in presidential elections since the 1970s. In the first scenario, the process generating the stronger linkage is operat-

Figure 4.3 Potential State-Level Patterns Behind Rising Party Identification–Vote Association

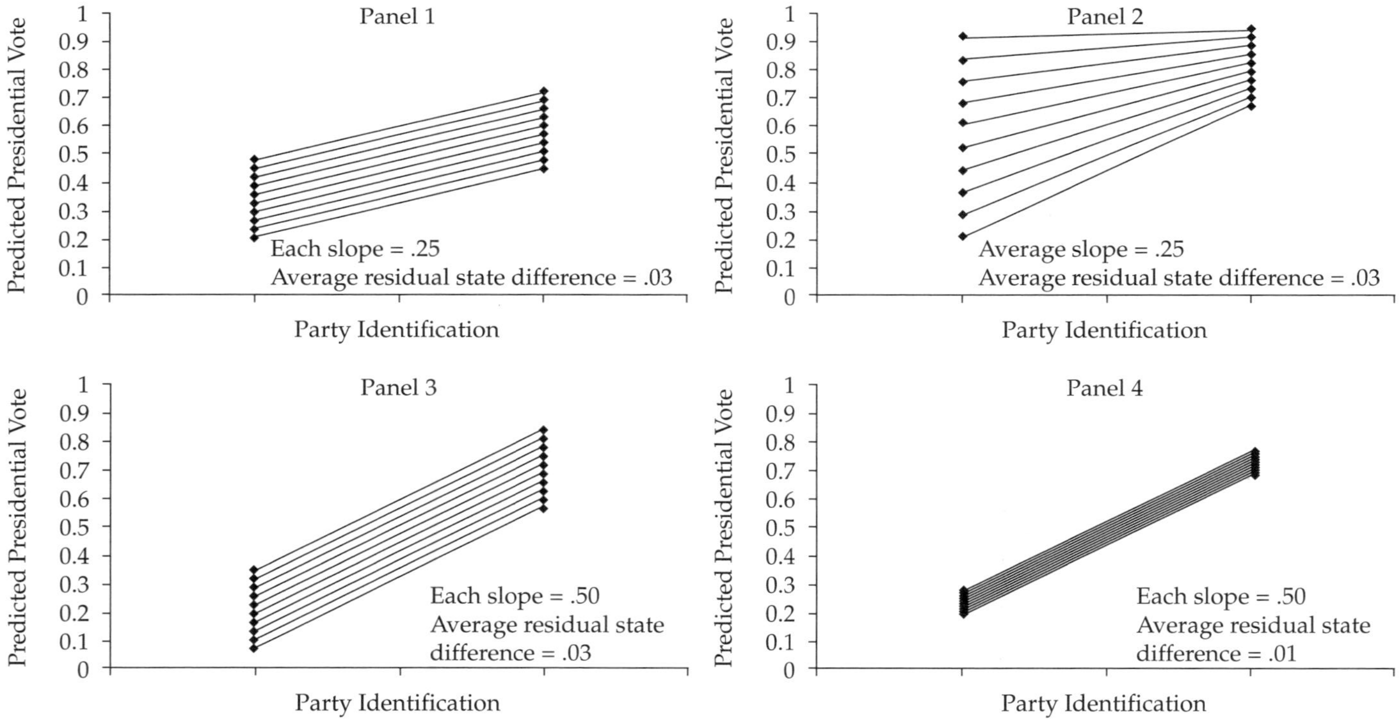
Panel 1
Predicted Presidential Vote
1
0.9
0.8
0.7
0.6
0.5
0.4
0.3
0.2
0.1
0
Each slope = .25
Average residual state difference = .03
Party Identification
Panel 2
Predicted Presidential Vote
Average slope = .25
Average residual state difference = .03
Party Identification
Panel 3
Predicted Presidential Vote
Each slope = .50
Average residual state difference = .03
Party Identification
Panel 4
Predicted Presidential Vote
Each slope = .50
Average residual state difference = .01
Party Identification

Source: Figure generated by authors.

ing uniformly on voters across states. As in Marc Hetherington's (2001) account, this phenomenon could be elite-driven in origin and operating at the level of individual psychology. According to this view, as the parties themselves have become more ideologically distinct—that is, as Democratic and Republican elites have polarized—individuals across the nation have responded by developing a keener sense of the differences between the parties, which has in turn made their party identification more meaningful and more consequential to how they vote. Even if the strength of PID in determining the vote continues to vary from one state to another, the changing national political environment increases the effect of PID by an equal amount in every state over the period. We call this the national tide hypothesis.

The second ideal, typical scenario explains the rise in PID effects evident in national samples by citing dynamics that have operated differently across the fifty states and resulted in the elimination of heterogeneity in PID effects among them. As illustrated, a rise in PID effects within the nation could reflect fundamentally different patterns of continuity and change within states. Some states remained stable in between the two points depicted in panels 2 and 3 of figure 4.3, but party strength was on the rise in others, leading to a convergence over time in the magnitude of the effect of PID on the vote across states. This we call the state variation hypothesis.

There are several reasons why PID effects may vary both across states and over time, and hence for the state variation account to be plausible. First, we would expect various short-term, election-specific forces to affect the influence of party identification on vote choice at the state level. Voters might desert their party to support a favorite-son candidate nominated by the opposition. An issue might arise of special concern to residents of particular states, prompting higher rates of partisan defection. In addition, the electoral strategies of candidates and parties, such as targeting campaign messages and resources to states considered competitive, might affect the relationship of vote choice to PID.

Second, the political environment within a state might also exert an influence on the effect of party identification. For example, the strength of party organizations varies substantially from state to state. States and local areas differ in the degree and nature of party competition for sub-presidential offices, which could well affect the importance of partisan identity among voters in different places. Social interactions and the political character of particular states or local communities could affect the propensity of party identifiers to defect or remain loyal.

Finally, heterogeneity in PID effects across states and time could also be a consequence of the diverse demographic profiles of states. States in which aggregate educational attainment tends to be low are also states whose inhabitants have depressed levels of political interest and knowledge, which would work to attenuate PID effects compared with those evident in states where the collective socioeconomic status is relatively high. Variation in state demographic profiles could thus lie behind variation in the PID-vote link. Notably, this explanation for varying effects cites nothing about the context itself as consequential. Varying effects are observed simply because the individual-level processes play out differently depending on voters' socioeconomic status (SES) or levels of political knowledge, attributes that on average vary substantially across states.

We present evidence from an analysis of survey data from the National Election Studies (NES) surveys from 1972 to 2008 that appears to confirm the state variation interpretation rather than the national tide interpretation of the dynamics of change in the PID-vote relationship in the American electorate. These findings suggest that the growing importance of PID as a determinant of individual voting decisions can be fully understood only by examining data at the subnational level. In some states, party identification today bears the same—usually very strong—relationship to the vote that it has shown for decades. In other states, one finds modest or sharp upward trends in the PID-vote link. This substantial variation challenges the simple account of mass response to elite polarization that is favored by many observers. The growing convergence in PID effects across states is part of the story behind the solidifying state-level electoral leanings.

We also find that state differences in vote outcomes other than those accounted for by variation in aggregate party identification are on the decline. Overall state-level differences in electoral results rose substantially from 1972 to 2008, as illustrated in figures 4.1 and 4.2. These differences, though, are increasingly explained by the balance of party identification within states; after accounting for state-level differences in partisan composition, little variation in the electoral outcome remains to be explained. Whereas in the past it was fairly common for state electoral results to diverge from what would be expected based on the state's partisan leanings, a state's overall PID balance is now an excellent predictor of its alignment in presidential elections.

After presenting evidence of these claims, we consider several potential causes of declining state-level differences in the centrality of party identification. Our analysis considers five possible explanations: southern realignment; variation across states in voters' perceptions of party differences, tied to state-level party polarization and differences in socioeconomic status; variation across states in the share of cross-pressured voters who hold issue positions at odds with their party's nominee; variation in the degree of competitiveness within states, which is associated with differences in the intensity of the presidential campaign; and variation in the strength of more general party competition within the state.

Data

We analyze survey data from the biennial National Election Studies (NES) for the last ten presidential elections, from 1972 to 2008. The NES data include information about the state and congressional districts of each respondent for each election, enabling analyses that link individuals to their place of residence. The NES studies also carry common instrumentation over the period, including measures of party identification and vote choice, feeling-thermometer evaluations of the presidential and congressional candidates, party placements, and issue attitudes. In addition, we make use of electoral data compiled for presidential and congressional elections at the state and district levels from 1972 through 2008, as well as, in one analysis, measures of the ideology of congressional delegations.

The primary drawback of the NES time series data as a tool for subnational analysis derives from the NES sampling design, which is itself a product of the face-to-face mode of interviewing used exclusively in almost all of the studies. The multistage cluster design, the first stage of which is redesigned every decade following the decennial census, dictates four attributes. First, the sample of individuals is representative of the nation (nonresponse bias set aside), but the sample of states is not representative of the population of states. Second, individuals are clustered within states, reducing the within-state "effective Ns" and, hence, the ability to generalize to the state level. Third, the actual (and effective) Ns vary across states, depending on whether the probability of the place being selected at the early stages of the sampling design is high or low. Fourth, the states that fall into the sample are changing over time (for further details of the NES samples and a discussion of their limitations for studying subnational units, see Stoker and Bowers 2002).

Arguably the most problematic of these limitations for the present purposes is the fact that the states falling into the NES samples have changed over time. Table 4.1 lists the sample sizes across the forty-eight states in the NES sample frame (which excludes Alaska and Hawaii) from 1972 to 2008. A number of states are almost completely absent from the NES. Vermont and Montana, for example, have each been represented by just one respondent during this period, whereas the total number of respondents from several other states remains in the low double digits. Because over-time comparisons across states are of interest to us, we limited our analysis to states that had a continual or nearly continual presence in the NES data over the entire period. We were left with an N of twenty-five states (in bold in table 4.1); because these tend to be the largest states, they include about 80 percent of the U.S. population.

We also decided to exclude any respondent interviewed by telephone in the preelection interview, out of concerns about noncomparability in-

Table 4.1 National Election Studies (NES) Sample Sizes Within States Over Time

State	NES ID no.	1972	1976	1980	1984	1988	1992	1996	2000	2004	2008
Alabama	41	27	31	29	53	55	48	44	63	64	22
Arizona	61	34	28	8			63	65	13		42
Arkansas	42	105	95	22	60	53	33	24	34	30	
California	71	225	189	144	262	214	243	140	191	138	287
Colorado	62	30	23	34	37	37	40	38	37	27	99
Connecticut	1	55	30	27	47	38	33	14	17	10	30
Delaware	11			7					2		20
Florida	43	77	78	76	78	57	97	90	92	48	173
Georgia	44	90	54	40	92	93	139	81	34	10	78
Idaho	63								5		
Illinois	21	130	124	75	64	59	83	46	56	35	29
Indiana	22	41	27	52	49	41	88	87	38	47	55
Iowa	31	70	70	11	52	44	33	24	28	22	
Kansas	32			8	66	54	59	11	14		28
Kentucky	51	67	53	23					16		
Louisiana	45	64	50	24			24	20	52	46	83
Maine	2	42	49	13					4		
Maryland	52	56	50	26	47	43	54	32	35	34	
Massachusetts	3	93	81	42	30	37	70	38	60	57	22
Michigan	23	110	90	73	147	114	134	97	72	59	114
Minnesota	33	61	50	32	54	57	78	53	63	47	25
Mississippi	46	44	26	19				1	4		63
Missouri	34	76	67	31	32	32	42	36	22	19	
Montana	64								1		

State											
Nebraska	35	44	30	21			18	22	2		
Nevada	65							2	5		31
New Hampshire	4				39	31	36	18	20	13	
New Jersey	12	104	83	59	58	51	83	56	42	36	23
New Mexico	66							17		3	64
New York	13	168	113	121	189	156	176	87	115	86	123
North Carolina	47	125	98	37	65	71	51	24	23		65
North Dakota	36							7	7		39
Ohio	24	172	127	97	97	98	79	38	73	33	85
Oklahoma	53	23	20	31				4	10		36
Oregon	72	41	59	23	59	50	44	37	36	26	27
Pennsylvania	14	157	135	77	54	55	76	47	52	16	36
Rhode Island	5								2		20
South Carolina	48	25	19	16				1	13		69
South Dakota	37	38	38					1	6		
Tennessee	54	28	34	33	102	124	88	49	42	22	77
Texas	49	75	55	127	153	143	186	136	137	84	365
Utah	67	30	32	25				11	39	32	
Vermont	6								1		
Virginia	40	45	36	48	48	49	115	123	91	78	34
Washington	73	52	45	28	34	42	44	32	49	40	23
West Virginia	56	45	30	13	52	30	38	12	4		
Wisconsin	25	26	23	29	59	65	56	43	69	52	21
Wyoming	68			13	78	47	34	11	5		

Source: Authors' compilation based on data from the National Election Studies (2010).
Note: Boldface indicates states included in this analysis.

troduced by mode effects. This restriction applied to about half of the 2000 sample and a smaller number of respondents in 1992 and 1996. Nonvoters were also excluded, as were respondents who were the lone representative of their congressional district. Because the decision to drop respondents interviewed by telephone significantly reduced the number of cases from 2000, we combined the 2000 and 2004 data in all analyses.

Party Strength in the Electorate Across States and over Time

Figure 4.4 presents initial findings indicating whether the rising strength of party identification (PID) as a predictor of presidential voting is consistent with the national tide hypothesis or instead reveals the existence of subnational dynamics as well. It also addresses the question of whether state differences net of PID have been increasing or decreasing over time. For each presidential election from 1972 to 2008, we estimated a two-level random coefficients model regressing presidential preference on party identification. Each model allowed the constants and slope coefficients to vary across states, but imposed the assumption that the variation in the constants or coefficients follows a normal distribution. Both PID and the presidential vote index were scaled to range from 0 (strongly Democratic) to 1 (strongly Republican).[7] The Y-axis of figure 4.4 shows the mean state-level slope coefficient for each year (for further exposition of the multilevel modeling approach and its application to political science, as well as a discussion of the virtues of recursive maximum-likelihood estimates [RMLE] when the number of macro-level units is small, see Steenbergen and Jones 2002).[8] The error bars indicate the degree of variation in slopes across states (the standard deviation of the distribution of slopes).

The analysis reveals a steady, almost linear increase in the average PID coefficient across the period. At the same time, the error bars are noticeably shrinking, with the variation in slopes across the sample of states reaching a minimum between 2000 and 2004, but with the greatest drop in variability evident when comparing the 1970s and 1980s to the 1990s and 2000s. The pattern of convergence across states in the strength of the PID-vote relationship is unmistakable, resulting in a steady increase in the average slope coefficient.

What is not clear from the figure, however, is exactly which states were changing and how, a question of utmost importance to any interpretation of the findings. We therefore turn from analyzing the NES data as yielding a series of consecutive cross sections to treating it as an 8- or 9-point time series for each state. An examination of the over-time find-

Figure 4.4   Relationship Between Party Identification and Presidential Vote Across States

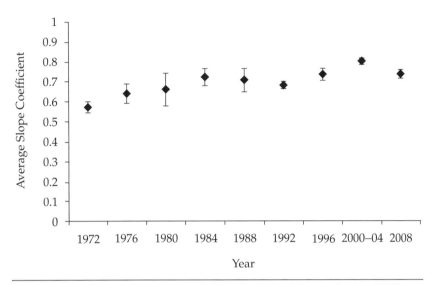

Source: Authors' compilation based on data from the National Election Studies (2010).

ings for each of the twenty-five states in our sample yields three main conclusions. First and most important, there is no discernable time trend in the coefficients for nine of the states, from all regions of the country. This group includes Massachusetts, Connecticut, and Maryland in the Northeast; Virginia, Florida, and Texas in the South; Michigan in the Midwest; and Colorado and Oregon in the West.[9] Second, in the remaining states there is frequently some fluctuation but typically a trend in the upward direction, especially after 1984. The coefficients within these states typically began at lower values than the first set of states, but grew closer over time to those of the stable states—yielding the convergence evident in figure 4.4.

Third, these trends cannot be explained by party realignment in the South. According to the standard account of southern realignment, conservative whites who once constituted the Democratic Party's most loyal base of support began to defect to Republican candidates in the 1960s, breaking up the "Solid South" that arose at the end of Reconstruction nearly a century before. These voters initially remained Democratic identifiers, even as they voted for Republican presidential nominees from Barry Goldwater and onward. Over time, due either to partisan conversion or cohort replacement, conservative southern whites increasingly identified as Republicans themselves, thus closing the partisan gap between identity and behavior that had first emerged during the civil rights era. Yet if the observed nationwide increase in the strength of parties in the electorate since the 1970s is principally due to southern realignment, with former conservative Dixiecrats (or their children) finally joining the Republican Party in the last few elections after decades of defecting to vote for Republican presidential candidates, the growth of the relationship between party identification and vote choice over time should be consistently stronger in the South than elsewhere. We find, however, echoing Larry Bartels (2000), that the increasing importance of party in determining presidential vote choice since the 1970s is occurring outside the South as well. In fact, substantial state-level differences exist in the relationship of party ID and the vote across states both within and outside the South.[10]

Thus, growth in the effect of party identification on vote choice since the 1970s has not occurred uniformly across the nation. States in which the PID-vote link was once weak have now joined others in which it has consistently been strong, producing a convergence across states in the strength of party effects on the vote. Surprisingly, the southern realignment is not responsible for this convergence; we consider other possible explanations below. The increasing magnitude and consistency of PID effects across the nation is part of the story behind the increasingly reliable state-level electoral divisions.[11]

Moreover, state electoral outcomes have become increasingly well explained by voters' partisan leanings. Put another way, differences across states net of PID have dwindled. To illustrate this, in figure 4.5 we plot the standard deviation of the state-level intercepts over time, drawn from the multilevel analyses described earlier.[12] Beginning in 1992, the variation across states in presidential voting unaccounted for by PID is consistently low; standard deviations on the order of .06 in the 1970s and 1980s (save for 1976) have given way to standard deviations on the order of .02 to .03. Thus, party identification increasingly accounts for not only how individuals vote but also which party's nominee carries the state. Further evidence of this trend from the NES data is given in figure 4.6, which plots the total amount of variation across states on the presidential index and the percentage of that variation statistically explained by PID.[13] Both show clear upward trends. As state-level electoral outcomes have diverged over time, differences in the statewide distributions of party identifiers increasingly account for state-level variation in election results.

However, states are not becoming more dissimilar in the aggregate party identification of their electorates. PID differences across states

Figure 4.5   Intercept Variation Across States

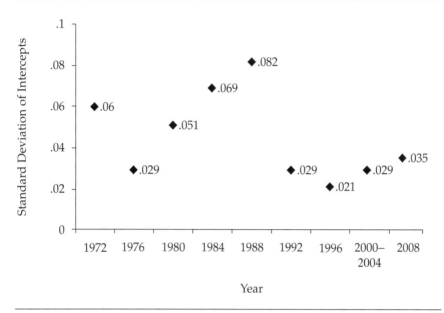

Source: Authors' compilation based on data from the National Election Studies (2010).
Note: From random effects model predicting presidential vote index from PID.

have not grown over time, at least in the subset of states included in our analysis. Instead, relatively stable partisan divisions can increasingly account for electoral outcomes at the state level, as PID effects have converged to a high level across states while differences net of PID have faded.

The findings illustrated in figures 4.4, 4.5, and 4.6 collectively reveal party identification to be an increasingly strong and stable predictor of both the voting habits of individuals and the aggregate electoral outcomes of states. Whereas the importance of parties in the electorate varied substantially across states in the 1970s, by the 2000s the growing effect of PID on the vote in a subset of states produced relative uniformity both across states in any given year and within particular states from one election to the next. This rising partisan stability among states over time is consistent with the findings of David Hopkins (2009), who demonstrates that state-level partisan alignments in the five presidential elections between 1992 and 2008 were more stable than in any other five-election sequence since the end of Reconstruction.

Figure 4.6   Variation Across States on Presidential Index, and Percent of that Variation Explained by Party Identification (PID)

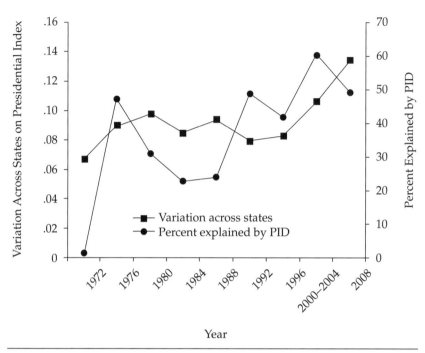

Source: Authors' compilation based on data from the National Election Studies (2010).

Explaining State Variation in Party Strength: The Role of Perceived Ideological Differences

If party resurgence in the electorate represents a direct mass response to sharpened ideological differences between national party officials, as many assume, we would expect little variation among states in the magnitude of the increase in the PID-vote relationship over time, given that voters everywhere presumably observed the same elite-level phenomena. Instead, the overall increase in party strength varies widely across states. Perhaps, however, voters' perceptions of party differences have grown unevenly across the states. This could happen if voters take their cues about the parties' relative ideological positions in part from the reputation and behavior of party officeholders representing their home states. If so, the greatest growth in PID effects would occur in states whose congressional delegations polarized the most. Alternatively, differential rates of growth in the socioeconomic status (SES) of state residents over time could produce a similar outcome. We would expect high-SES voters to be more aware of party differences, which would lead them to vote more loyally for their own party.

To measure the degree of elite polarization within each state over time, we calculated the difference in the mean first-dimension DW-NOMINATE score for each party's House of Representatives delegation for the Congress elected in each presidential year from 1972 and onward (see Poole and Rosenthal 2007).[14] In the 2007–2008 Congress, for example, the difference in party means in the Pennsylvania House delegation was .701, whereas in California it was 1.095. State-level variation was much higher in the early years of our time series; the difference in means between the parties in Virginia in the 1973–1974 Congress, for example, was just .064, reflecting the preponderance at that time of conservative Democrats within the state's congressional delegation. Perceptions of party differences were measured using respondent placement of each party on the 7-point liberal-conservative scale.[15]

Although it is plausible that citizens' perceptions of party differences would respond to state-level as well as national-level cues about the ideological positions of the parties, we found no evidence for this supposition. Controlling for the polarization of the national parties over time, the coefficient representing the effect of state-level party polarization on individual perceptions of ideological differences was essentially 0, with a t-statistic of .46 and a p-value of .664.[16] Similar null results appeared when state-level polarization was specified as interacting with PID in models predicting the presidential vote index. National-level changes in polarization over time, however, do help explain perceptions of party differences, as expected. As polarization grew from its minimum (.526) to its maximum (.946) across the period, the perceived ideological differences between the parties grew from .26 to .42 on the 0-to-1 scale.

Are differences in PID effects explained by variation in states' sociodemographic profiles, with the wealthy and well-educated more aware of partisan polarization? Three specific findings bear on this question. First, individuals of higher socioeconomic status (measured by both educational attainment and income level) are, unsurprisingly, much more likely to perceive party differences than are those of a lower SES. In a trivariate OLS regression with perceived party difference as the dependent variable, and with all variables scaled 0 to 1, the estimated coefficients for each effect of education and income are equal to .27 and .20, respectively, with the former a much more reliable predictor than the latter (with a t-statistic of about four times larger). Second, the populations of the nine states where the strength of PID tended to be stable over time had modestly higher levels of SES than those states where PID effects were relatively low at the beginning of the period. The residents of these states were, accordingly, more likely to perceive ideological differences between the parties (detailed findings to follow). Third, these state-level differences, though small at first, also tended to diminish over time. For example, in the 1972 to 1980 period, the gap in educational attainment between the two groups of states was .04, the income gap was .02, and the ideological perception gap was .03 (all significant at $p < .01$ according to a t-test, despite their size). In the later years, the gaps were .03, .01, and .01, respectively.

As a result, the convergence over time in the strength of PID among different states may be due in small part to decreasing differences in aggregate socioeconomic status between the two groups of states.[17] In the 1970s and early 1980s, PID effects were stronger in states with comparatively wealthy, highly educated residents, who were in turn more likely to perceive ideological differences between the parties. As state differences in SES declined over time, state-level variation in PID effects eroded as well.

For several reasons, however, differences between states in the perception of ideological differences between the parties cannot fully explain the variably growing strength of parties in the electorate. First, there is a substantial degree of homogeneity at the state level in the over-time differences in perceptions of party differences on the 7-point ideology scale. States where the strength of PID as a predictor of presidential vote choice remained constant over time showed patterns of change in party perceptions similar to those evident among states where the link between PID and the vote was on the rise. The full set of state means for each election is displayed in figure 4.7. A higher-order polynomial is fit to the means of the nine states with no trend in the link between PID and presidential vote (thick line), and a second is fit to the remaining states (thin line). Although the gap in perceptions between the two states is evident in the 1972 to 1980 period, it is quite modest in magnitude.[18] The stronger pattern in the figure, which is evident across nearly all the individual states when examined separately, is of large perceived party differences in the ideologically charged 1972 election between Richard Nixon and George McGovern that diminished dramatically by 1976 and then climbed once more in the Ronald Reagan era and afterward.

The second piece of evidence concerns the role played by perceptions of party differences in moderating the relationship between party and vote choice as revealed in an individual-level analysis. As would be expected from a perspective that treats party identification as a social identity (Campbell et al. 1960; Green, Palmquist, and Schickler 2002), the effects of PID on the vote are strong even among those who perceive no ideological differences between the parties. In a simple OLS regression analysis of the presidential vote index that included PID (scored 0 to 1),

Figure 4.7   Perceived Ideological Differences Between the Parties Across States and Time

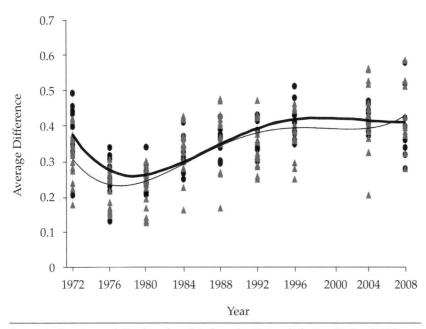

Year

Source: Authors' compilation based on data from the National Election Studies (2010).
Note: The thick line reflects the nine states with no trend in the link between PID and presidential vote. The thin line reflects the remaining states.

perceptions of party ideological differences (scored 0 to 1), and the interaction between the two, the PID main coefficient averages .58 across the nine time points, with an average *t*-statistic of 17.9. In other words, the expected difference on the dependent variable was a robust .58 among respondents who saw no differences between the parties. In addition, the main effect coefficient grew fairly steadily over time (but with a noticeable dip in 1996), from .46 in 1972 to .67 in 2008. Even voters who cannot distinguish the parties ideologically have become more loyal to their party's presidential candidates over time.

The interaction term, representing the extent to which the PID coefficient increases as the perceived ideological distance between the parties grows, is statistically significant in each year, with an average coefficient of .28 across the period and an average *t*-statistic of 4.4 (and no discernable trend over time). Thus, voters' perceptions of a widening ideological gap between the parties undoubtedly do play some role in explaining the resurgent strength of parties in the electorate since the 1970s.[19]

We conclude, then, that the increasing centrality of party identification as a determinant of individual vote choice can be only partially explained by voters' perceptions of the ideological polarization of party elites. Though voters increasingly do perceive ideological differences between the parties, and though such perceptions account in part for the growing aggregate party loyalty of the American electorate since the 1970s, substantial state-level differences in the growth of party strength over time remain even after accounting for variation across states in voters' perception of party differences—variation that cannot be explained by the degree of state-level elite polarization and can be attributed to state-level differences in socioeconomic status to only a limited extent.

Explaining State Variation in Party Strength: Other Potential Factors

We turn next to consideration of other possible causes of state-level variation in the effect of party identification on the presidential vote. Our analysis focuses in turn on the potential influence of crosscutting issues, variation in the degree of state-level partisan competition, and differences among states in the degree of competitiveness in congressional elections.

Crosscutting Issues

A further possible explanation for the observed variation in the potency of party identification across both states and time emphasizes the ability of crosscutting issues to provoke partisan defection. By the 1970s and early 1980s, divisions between the parties on issues involving race, gender, and morality had emerged among elites at the national level. In the mass electorate, differences on these issues initially tended to be within, rather than between, party identifiers, providing a basis for voters to desert their party's candidate; over time, however, partisans responded to elite differentiation by increasingly aligning with the positions taken by their own party's leadership (Layman and Carsey 2002; Levendusky 2009; Stoker and Jennings 2008). Figures 4.8 and 4.9 illustrate how the partisan divide on such cultural issues has grown since the early 1970s, matched by a decline in the percentage of cross-pressured voters—Republican identifiers holding culturally liberal views or Democratic identifiers holding conservative views.[20] If cross-pressured voters were more common in some states than others, we would expect to find variation across states in PID effects on the vote.

Further analysis shows that the behavior and geographic distribution of culturally conservative Democrats (rather than that of culturally liberal Republicans) can account in part for state-level variation in party

Figure 4.8   Partisan Divide on the Cultural-Issues Index over Time

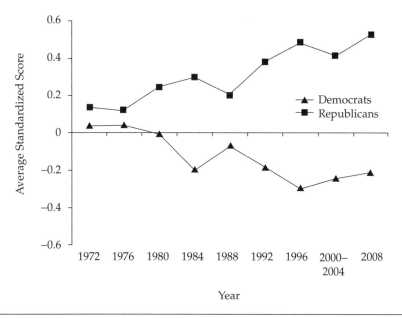

Source: Authors' compilation based on data from the National Election Studies (2010).

Figure 4.9   Percentage Cross-Pressured on Cultural Issues

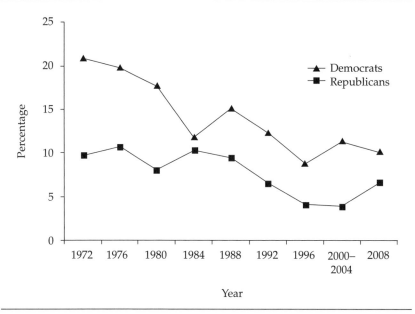

Source: Authors' compilation based on data from the National Election Studies (2010).

Figure 4.10   Effect of Party Identification Among Liberals and Conservatives on Cultural Issues

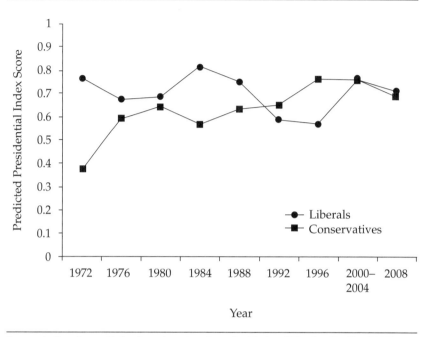

Source: Authors' compilation based on data from the National Election Studies (2010).

strength. In every election between 1972 and 1988 except 1980, defection rates among culturally conservative Democrats exceeded those of culturally liberal Republicans. Liberal Republicans tended to vote for Republican candidates despite being cross-pressured, whereas conservative Democrats often defected from their party's presidential nominees, especially George McGovern in 1972 and Walter Mondale in 1984. Figures 4.10 and 4.11 summarize these patterns. Figure 4.10 displays the coefficient on PID over time among voters who held liberal or conservative views on cultural issues.[21] Figure 4.11 depicts the predicted presidential index score by PID and issue attitude, first for the first four elections in the period (1972 to 1984) and then for more recent elections (1988 to 2008). As these results demonstrate, the relative weakness of party identification as a determinant of presidential voting in the 1970s and 1980s partly reflected the high defection rates of culturally conservative Democrats. By the 1990s, social issues continued to influence individual vote choice and to cause defections, but the fraction of cross-pressured voters had dropped and defection was no longer

Figure 4.11   Effect of Cultural Issues on Party Loyalty in Presidential Elections, 1972 to 2008

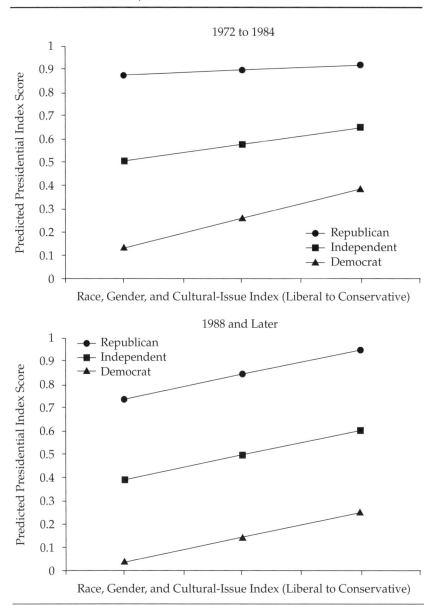

Source: Authors' compilation based on data from the National Election Studies (2010).

asymmetric; liberal Republicans were just as likely to defect as conservative Democrats.

Variation among states in the proportion of culturally conservative Democrats can therefore partially account for state differences in the effect of PID on the vote. In the 1970s and early 1980s, residents of states in which PID was a relatively weak predictor of the vote tended to hold more conservative views on already salient issues involving race and gender, as well as emerging issues concerning religion and morality (including abortion). For example, between 1972 and 1980, 25.8 percent of Democrats in the nine states where PID was already a strong predictor of the vote held conservative views (below the midpoint of the scale), compared with 35.7 percent of Democrats in states where PID was weak.

These findings are consistent with previous studies suggesting that cultural issues were effectively used by Republican candidates as wedge issues to splinter the Democratic electoral coalition, allowing for Republican dominance in presidential elections during the 1970s and 1980s despite the overall preponderance of Democratic identifiers in the electorate (Shafer and Claggett 1995; Hillygus and Shields 2008). Although this approach is usually associated with the so-called southern strategy pursued by Richard Nixon and other Republican candidates, our findings indicate that high defection rates among culturally conservative Democrats were hardly confined to the South. Over time, the increasing differentiation of the two parties in the electorate on cultural issues—whether due to conversion, persuasion, generational replacement, or a combination of causes—has reduced the population of cross-pressured voters and thus the opportunity for parties, and especially the Republican Party, to benefit from large-scale defection in states where those voters constitute a significant share of the population. This development has played an important part in the growing significance of PID to the vote nationwide, the variable rate of its ascendance across states, and the declining variation in state outcomes that remains to be explained after accounting for the overall state-level distribution of PID. Indeed, evidence is growing that the variation in voter opinion, especially that of affluent suburban voters, on social and moral issues is responsible for much of the contemporary geographic variation in party alignment; culturally conservative residents of red states now identify as, and vote for, Republicans, and blue-state cultural liberals consider themselves Democrats and vote accordingly (Gelman et al. 2008; Hopkins 2007).

Defection by partisans who are cross-pressured on economic rather than cultural issues does not similarly account for the growing size and homogeneity of PID effects in presidential elections. Several findings are relevant here. First, although Democrats and Republicans in the mass public became more polarized on economic issues between 1972 and 2008, the partisan divide on this dimension was already substantial in

1972. Using an index constructed from survey items on traditional New Deal conflicts over the scope of government and its involvement in the provision of social welfare programs,[22] we found a partisan gap of .8 standardized units in 1972, which expanded to 1.3 standardized units by 2008. Accordingly, the fraction of cross-pressured partisans was already low in 1972 (about 9 percent within each party), though it declined further to 3 to 5 percent in each party by 2008.[23]

Second, cross-pressured voters were equally numerous in states where the strength of party identification rose significantly over the past forty years and in states where the PID-vote relationship remained high throughout. For example, over the three elections between 1972 and 1980, 36.8 percent of Democrats in the nine states with the strongest PID effects held views that could be classified as economically conservative (below the scale midpoint), compared with 36.6 percent of Democrats in the remaining states. The proportion of Republicans holding liberal economic views (above the scale midpoint) across the two groups of states stood at 28.5 percent and 25.7 percent, respectively, during the same period.

Third, partisan defection rates tended to be symmetric across the period among economically liberal Republicans and economically conservative Democrats. Thus, defection on these issues tended to depress PID effects about equally in Democratic-leaning and Republican-leaning states. The one clear exception to this pattern occurred in the 1972 election, when economically cross-pressured Democrats defected from McGovern to Nixon at high rates and economically liberal Republicans remained loyal to their party.

In summary, though the decline in the proportion of partisans who are cross-pressured on economic issues has contributed to the national growth in the link between party identification and vote choice since the 1970s, it cannot explain the heterogeneity in this trend across states. The state-level variation in the share of Democrats who are relatively conservative on cultural issues, and who defected from their party's presidential nominees at unusually high rates during the elections from 1972 through 1984, is more important to understanding state-level variation in the PID-vote relationship over that period.

Party Competition in Presidential Races

The closeness of the presidential contest within the state might be expected to affect the relative importance of party identification in determining the presidential vote. Plausible hypotheses exist for either a positive or a negative association between these attributes. The anticipation of a close statewide race affects campaign strategy, with battleground or swing states receiving the vast majority of campaign resources and candidate visits. The presence of campaign activity within a state might convey more political information and stimulate higher interest among voters, thus activating party cues. Conversely, active campaign efforts might reduce the effect of party by increasing the salience of other factors known to influence vote choice, such as personal evaluations of the candidates, perceptions of the incumbent party's performance in office, or policy issues orthogonal to party identification (Keele and Wolak 2008).

To examine this possibility, we evaluated whether the degree of competitiveness within a state—as measured by the size of either the state two-party vote margin or its deviation from the national popular vote—moderated the strength of PID as a determinant of presidential voting. We found no evidence of an effect in either direction across any of a number of specifications (for example, bivariate and multivariate for some but not all elections) using either measure. It appears that either both hypotheses are incorrect, that both are at work but are canceling each other out, or that the dynamics involved require study through more nuanced cross-level specifications or more precise measures of campaign intensity. In any event, state-level variation in PID effects cannot be predicted by the basis of state-level variations in the competitiveness of the presidential election.

General Level of Party Competition Within the State

Studies of state party organizations and political cultures often distinguish between strong party states, where party labels are central to electoral outcomes, and weak party states, where candidates cultivate personal followings or mobilize issue publics outside of the institution of the party (see, for example, Mayhew 1986). This variation may also be relevant to understanding variation in PID effects on the presidential vote. Consider a state with little competition in down-ballot races. We might expect the voters in that state to exhibit weaker loyalty even in presidential elections than voters in states where widespread competition at the congressional level exposes voters to partisan messages, activates partisan cues, and solidifies party loyalties. To investigate this question, we used the outcomes of House elections to develop an indicator of the strength of state-level party competition. Specifically, we calculated the percentage of close House races in each state—the percentage in which the winner received no more than 55 percent of the two-party vote—for every presidential election year between 1972 and 2008. This measure of congressional competition varied from 0 to 80 percent across the twenty-five states included in our NES analysis, but with most cases clustered toward 0; the median over time and states was .11 (and was even smaller in the 2000s than in previous decades). We examined the extent to which PID effects on the presidential vote were elevated in states with more competitive congressional elections.[24]

Two findings are of note. First, House races from 1972 through 1980 tended to be more competitive in the nine states where PID effects were already high (and did not grow later) than in the remaining states. For example, 67 percent of the state-year observations were above the median in competitiveness within these nine states (compared to 44 percent for the remaining states), but 44 percent were in the fourth quartile for the former (versus 19 percent for the latter). Second, during the same period, the cross-level interaction between the strength of PID as a predictor of the presidential vote and the degree of competition in congressional elections was statistically significant ($t = 2.05, p < .05$), with a coefficient of .24; in later years, the coefficient was $-.04$ ($t = -.61$).[25] Given the scale of the competitiveness variable, this suggests a difference of about .14 in the effect of PID in a state with no competitive House races compared with a state with the maximum observed during the period (60 percent competitive). But because the overall degree of competition in House races is very low, the typical difference across states in the effect of PID is more on the order of .03—in the expected direction, but of limited substantive importance.

The evidence suggests, therefore, that state-level differences in the role of party identification in influencing the presidential vote may have been associated with the extent of party competition in House races in the first several elections under examination. This finding may reflect state-level differences in the strength of party organizations or other factors affecting party loyalty among voters in elections for lesser offices as well as the presidency. Over time, however, convergence across states in the power of PID suggests that any such state-level differences in party dynamics have declined in importance, at least in presidential elections.

Conclusion

Mounting evidence of growing party strength within the electorate has in recent years inspired a widespread reappraisal among electoral scholars, with previous claims of mass party decline replaced by increasingly confident reports of partisan resurgence. Many students of American politics now acknowledge that the party identification of voters has, in recent national elections, become as powerful as ever in determining vote choice. The once popular account of an electorate largely unmoored from party attachments and prone to widespread defection on the basis of short-term electoral forces has given way to the view that contemporary parties each command the loyalty of large cadres of voters who dependably support their presidential nominees at overwhelming rates.

It is clear that the increased centrality of party identification among the electorate is, in part, a direct response to the ideological polarization of national party elites over the past four decades. As the philosophical divide between the Republican and Democratic officeholders grew, so too did mass perceptions of ideological differences between the parties. Voters who perceive important party differences are—and, throughout the period we studied, always have been—more loyal to their favored party; there are simply more of such voters today than heretofore.

But a distinct phenomenon has been at work as well: what Geoffrey Layman and Thomas Carsey (2002) dubbed "conflict extension" (see also Carmines and Stimson 1989; Brewer 2005). Issues involving race, gender, and morality that arose in the 1960s and 1970s originally cut across party lines, especially within the mass public. The emergence of clear party divisions at the elite level on these formerly crosscutting issues eventually provoked parallel changes in the electorate—increased intraparty homogeneity and interparty heterogeneity on cultural matters. In the short term, these developments contributed to the widespread defections of (especially Democratic) party identifiers that suggested the declining power of mass parties in the Nixon and Reagan eras. Over time, the number of cross-pressured voters declined—especially on cultural issues but also on more traditional, New Deal issues—producing increasing aggregate party loyalty and the resurgence of parties in the electorate.

Because of the nature of the electoral college, the existence of state-level differences in these trends has significant consequences for the conduct of presidential campaigns and the outcome of elections. We find that the national pattern of increasing party strength observed in previous studies did not occur uniformly across the United States. Instead, substantial heterogeneity across states in the power of party identification as a determinant of presidential vote choice in the 1970s and early 1980s has, over time, given way to a growing national convergence. The significant former state-level variation in party strength can be at least partially accounted for by differences across states in the extent to which voters perceived ideological differences between the parties (which is itself in part a consequence of state differences in socioeconomic status), the presence of crosscutting cultural issues prompting high rates of defection in states with large proportions of cross-pressured Democrats, and state variation in partisan competition at the congressional level.

To the extent that conventional accounts allow for geographic variation in these trends, they usually emphasize the southern strategy of Republican candidates and the rise of the Republican presidential vote in the South during the 1960s as a precursor to regional realignment. We have a more complex view. Culturally conservative Democrats were by no means confined to the South in the 1970s and 1980s, nor was exten-

sive party disloyalty merely a southern phenomenon during that period—as is suggested by the success of Nixon and Reagan in winning
states outside the South with a long-standing preponderance of Democratic identifiers, including New York, Illinois, and California, by large
popular margins.

In more recent elections, such widespread defection has almost van-
ished. Party identification has become not only a powerful predictor of
the vote choices of individuals but also a strong indicator of aggregate
statewide results. Democratic states vote habitually for Democratic candidates, and Republicans continue to depend on support from Republican-leaning states. State-level variation in presidential vote outcomes
has increased substantially since the 1970s, as has the stability of state
partisan alignments from one election to the next. The prospect of a candidate winning a coast-to-coast electoral landslide by carrying even the
strongholds of the opposing party seems, in the contemporary political
environment, a near-impossible feat.

With faint hope of success at winning support from voters in the other
party, contemporary presidential candidates face a decreasing incentive
to make appeals across party lines. With little chance of prevailing in
states where the opposing party predominates, they are unlikely to campaign actively there. It is hardly surprising that campaign strategists in
recent elections have placed renewed emphasis on mobilizing the faith-
ful within their own party at the expense of courting voters who identify
with the opposition. Yet these efforts may only reinforce the trends toward greater polarization and conflict extension in the mass electorate.

The implications for representation and democratic governance in a
political world in which the bonds linking voters and officeholders are
primarily partisan, with few crosscutting cleavages, are potentially quite
significant. The party base, whether conceptualized as a group of individual voters or a set of state electorates, becomes a stronger voice as
mobilization outranks persuasion as a strategy of building popular support. Increasingly, the answer to the question of who gets represented
depends on which party holds the reins of power.

Notes

1. See, for example, David S. Broder, "Polar Politics," *Washington Post*, May 6,
   2004, p. A35.
2. The District of Columbia is counted as a state for electoral college purposes.
   Two states, Maine and Nebraska, do not allocate their electoral votes on a
   winner-take-all basis.
3. These eleven states were Colorado, Florida, Indiana, Iowa, Minnesota, Ne-
   vada, New Hampshire, Ohio, Pennsylvania, Virginia, and Wisconsin.
4. Following Marc Hetherington (2001), the hypothesis is that voter loyalty is

spurred when one perceives clearer and starker party differences; as the parties differentiate, the other party becomes less palatable. We take up the additional idea that sharper party differences help people sort themselves into the party that best represents their issue preferences—that is, reduce the percentage of cross-pressured voters. This perspective on the consequences of elite-level polarization leads one to expect variation across states and time in PID effects if the percentage of cross-pressured voters varies.

5. PID distributions might also have become more divergent across states over time. As discussed later, we find no evidence that this is the case.

6. Throughout this text, we speak, for simplicity, of the effect of party identification, but this is a shorthand for the magnitude of the differences in presidential voting that are predicted by party identification. In that sense, PID effects are strong if voters are party loyalists and weak if partisans regularly cast votes for the opposing party's nominee.

7. The presidential vote index averaged reported vote (1 = Republican, 0 = Democratic) and the difference in feeling-thermometer evaluations of the Republican and Democratic presidential candidates (1 = maximum pro-Republican, 0 = maximum pro-Democrat). The two variables were very highly correlated ($r = .78$, aggregating across all cases). Cases missing on both variables were dropped from the analysis. Results found for the index are also found for the vote variable alone, but the continuous index is better suited to the multilevel random effects model that we estimated.

8. The 2008 analysis excluded Michigan, which was a strong outlier despite having a large sample (indeed larger than would be expected at random, given that racial and ethnic minorities were oversampled by the NES in 2008). The Michigan slope averaged .74 from 1972 to 2004, but dropped to .47 in 2008. If Michigan is included in the analysis, the average slope declines by .025 and the standard deviation in the slopes increases by .019.

9. These nine demonstrate no significant linear trend in the PID slope when using either all nine data points or when dropping the most outlying point. For four other states, there is either no trend when all nine points are included but a significant trend when one observation is dropped, or there is a significant trend when all data points are included that turns insignificant when the most outlying point is dropped; these tend to be small states where data in the NES are sparse.

10. Looking at just the eight largest states, we find no increase in the PID coefficient for Texas and Michigan, a modest increase in Florida (post-1984), Ohio, and California, and a substantial increase in New York, Pennsylvania, and Illinois (save for 2008, when favorite son Obama was the Democratic nominee). The coefficient among New Yorkers increased from a low of about .35 in the 1976 election to roughly .80 by 2004. To test the proposition that the rise in PID effects was fueled by the South, we expanded the basic multilevel model that produced figure 4.4 by including a dummy variable for southern states and an interaction between that dummy variable and PID. In no year was the interaction term statistically significant.

11. The mean state-level deviation from the national vote (the measure used in figure 4.1) increased between 1972 and 1980 (three-election average) and between 2000 and 2008 by 4.2 percentage points in the thirteen states with

the flattest PID slopes over time. In the twelve states with a positive slope, the mean increase was 6 points. In other words, the overall growth in state-level variation between the 1970s and 2000s depicted in figure 4.1 occurred disproportionately in states where the PID slope increased over the same period.

12. The intercept variation reflects state differences on the presidential vote index net of PID, regardless of the direction in which PID is scaled.

13. The variation across states is the standard deviation (SD) of the intercepts in a random intercepts model of the presidential index that contains no other predictor. The percentage of variation explained by PID is derived from a comparison of that SD with the smaller SD obtained once PID is added to the model. The analysis was repeated for each year. All models were estimated with RMLE.

14. Because the DW-NOMINATE scores for the 2009 to 2010 Congress were not yet available at press time, we used the scores for the 2007 to 2008 Congress for the 2008 presidential election year.

15. We created a variable subtracting the respondent's placement of the Republican Party on the scale from that of the respondent's placement of the Democrats. Negative scores (where respondents identified the Democrats as more conservative than the Republicans) were recoded to 0. The resulting scale was scaled to range from 0 (no difference between the parties or Democrats more conservative) to 1 (Republicans maximally conservative and Democrats maximally liberal). Respondents unable to place themselves or the parties on the scale were coded at 0.

16. States with delegations from only one party were dropped from the analysis. Small sample sizes within states make this a less than ideal measure of state-level party polarization, which might be responsible for the null findings. The findings quoted were generated by a random-intercepts multilevel regression model estimated with RMLE (with individuals nested within state-years), treating perceptions of ideological differences as the dependent variable, and including the state-level polarization score, the annual polarization score (based on the difference between the parties' overall mean DW-NOMINATE scores in any given year), and the squared value of the annual polarization score. The latter two variables were both substantively and statistically significant ($b = 1.32$ and $t = 3.03$ and $b = -.64$ and $t = -2.17$, respectively).

17. Relatedly, Ellis and Ura (chapter 3, this volume) show overtime differences in the relationship between partisanship and economic and cultural views within different socioeconomic groups.

18. In figure 4.9, the lines shown come from fitting a fourth-order polynomial to each set of state means (regressing the mean ideological difference on year 1, year 2, year 3, and year 4). With the NES data, we fit a cubic polynomial equation, regressing individual-level perceptions of ideological difference on the year, the year squared, and the year cubed, for the states showing a trend in their PID slopes and adding interactions to allow the equation to vary for the states with no PID trend. All of the interactions (on the year, the year squared, and the year cubed) distinguishing the two groups of states were significant at $p < .05$. The equation was estimated with RMLE in

a random-intercepts multilevel framework, with individuals nested within state-years.

19. Perceptions of ideological differences between the parties interact more strongly with liberal-conservative identification in predicting the vote. Thus ideological identification, its consequences for the vote as a function of perceived party differences, its correlation with PID, and its distribution across contexts may all contribute to the observed trend of increased party strength. These interdependencies deserve closer investigation.

20. The index of cultural attitudes toward included seven component variables: aid to blacks, a feeling thermometer toward blacks, women's role, abortion, gay rights, traditional values, and church attendance. Scores on the index were standardized, with the scale running from liberal to conservative. Figure 4.8 shows the average standard score among Democrats and Republicans, excluding leaners. Figure 4.9 shows the percentage of Democrats with standard scores greater than 1 and the percentage of Republicans with standard scores less than –1.

21. In a multilevel random-intercepts framework (allowing for unmodeled state-level variation in Y), we regressed the presidential vote index on PID, the index, and the interaction between the two. Figure 4.10 shows the predicted PID coefficient for liberals (those scoring two standard deviations below the mean on the index) and for conservatives (those scoring two standard deviations above the mean), when the analysis is run for each year separately. The predicted scores in figure 4.11 use the same definition of liberal and conservative; the results, here, are based on running the model for two periods, from 1972 to 1984 (when state-level variation in PID effects was pronounced) and from 1988 on. The interaction between PID and cultural-issue attitudes is significant at $p < .001$ for 1972, 1984, and when the 1972 to 1984 results are pooled. In the 1988 to 2008 results, the interaction is insignificant ($t = .98$). Results are similar if the PID coefficient is also allowed to vary across states.

22. We constructed an economic-issues index based on responses to the NES 7-point scales on government social services and government job assistance, the feeling thermometer toward labor unions, and three forced-choice questions about the size and the scope of government. As with the cultural-issues index, we standardized the scale within each year.

23. As before, to be classified as cross-pressured, a Democrat had to express conservative views that yielded a standard score of less than 1 and a Republican had to express liberal views that yielded a standard score of less than –1.

24. This specification uses closeness of the House races in a given state to measure party competition in the state, asking whether the PID-vote relationship is heightened among individuals living in states with strong party competition. The entire analysis could instead be carried out at the congressional district level. Doing so would shift the question slightly: is the PID–(presidential) vote relationship boosted among those living in congressional districts with highly competitive races? A "yes" answer to this question would then have implications for state-level patterns depending upon the percentage of the state's population residing in competitive districts. This

alternative is worthy of further study; doing so with the NES data would be a challenge as the within-district Ns are frequently very small.

25. The analysis treated individuals as nested in state-years because data over multiple elections was analyzed simultaneously. If we added to the model the predictor variables described earlier as important to understanding state-level variations in PID effects (perceptions of ideological differences alone and in interaction with PID, cultural-issue attitudes alone and in interaction with PID), the coefficient and its significance level grows modestly ($b = .27$, $t = 2.22$).

References

Abramowitz, Alan I., and Kyle L. Saunders. 1998. "Ideological Realignment in the U.S. Electorate." *Journal of Politics* 60(3): 634–52.

———. 2005. "Why Can't We All Just Get Along? The Reality of Polarization in America." *The Forum* 3(2): art. 1.

Ansolabehere, Stephen, Jonathan Rodden, and James M. Snyder Jr. 2006. "Purple America." *Journal of Economic Perspectives* 20(2): 97–118.

Barone, Michael. 2001. "The 49% Nation." In *Almanac of American Politics 2002*, by Michael Barone, with Richard E. Cohen and Grant Ujifusa, 21–45. Washington, D.C.: National Journal.

Bartels, Larry M. 2000. "Partisanship and Voting Behavior, 1952–1996." *American Journal of Political Science* 44(1): 35–50.

Brewer, Mark D. 2005. "The Rise of Partisanship and the Expansion of Partisan Conflict Within the American Electorate." *Political Research Quarterly* 58(2): 219–29.

Brooks, David. 2001. "One Nation, Slightly Divisible." *Atlantic Monthly*, December.

Campbell, Angus, Philip E. Converse, Warren E. Miller, and Donald E. Stokes. 1960. *The American Voter*. New York: John Wiley & Sons.

Carmines, Edward G., and James A. Stimson. 1989. *Issue Evolution: Race and the Transformation of American Politics*. Princeton, N.J.: Princeton University Press.

Doherty, Brendan J. 2006. "The Politics of the Permanent Campaign: Presidents, Fundraising, and the Electoral College." Ph.D. diss., University of California, Berkeley.

Farhi, Paul. 2004. "Elephants Are Red, Donkeys Are Blue." *Washington Post*, November 2, p. C01.

Fenno, Richard F. 1978. *Home Style: House Members in Their Districts*. Boston: Little, Brown.

Fiorina, Morris P., with Samuel J. Abrams and Jeremy C. Pope. 2005. *Culture War? The Myth of a Polarized America*. New York: Pearson Longman.

Gelman, Andrew, David Park, Boris Shor, Joseph Bafumi, and Jeronimo Cortina. 2008. *Red State, Blue State, Rich State, Poor State: Why Americans Vote the Way They Do*. Princeton, N.J.: Princeton University Press.

Green, Donald, Bradley Palmquist, and Eric Schickler. 2002. *Partisan Hearts and Minds*. New Haven, Conn.: Yale University Press.

Hetherington, Marc J. 2001. "Resurgent Mass Partisanship: The Role of Elite Polarization." *American Political Science Review* 95(3): 619–31.

Hillygus, D. Sunshine, and Todd G. Shields. 2008. *The Persuadable Voter: Wedge Issues in Presidential Campaigns*. Princeton, N.J.: Princeton University Press.

Hopkins, David A. 2007. "A Solid North? Social Issues and the Rise of the Democratic Party in Northern Suburbs, 1988–2006." Paper presented at the Annual Meetings of the American Political Science Association. Chicago (August 30, 2007).

———. "The 2008 Election and the Political Geography of the New Democratic Majority." *Polity* 41(3): 368–87.

Keele, Luke, and Jennifer Wolak. 2008. "Contextual Sources of Ambivalence." *Political Psychology* 29(5): 653–73.

Layman, Geoffrey C., and Thomas M. Carsey. 2002. "Party Polarization and 'Conflict Extension' in the American Electorate." *American Journal of Political Science* 46(4): 786–802.

Levendusky, Matthew. 2009. *The Partisan Sort: How Liberals Became Democrats and Conservatives Became Republicans*. Chicago: University of Chicago Press.

Levine, Jeffrey, Edward G. Carmines, and Robert Huckfeldt. 1997. "The Rise of Ideology in the Post–New Deal Party System, 1972–1992." *American Politics Quarterly* 25(1): 19–34.

Mayhew, David R. 1974. *Congress: The Electoral Connection*. New Haven, Conn.: Yale University Press.

———. 1986. *Placing Parties in American Politics*. Princeton, N.J.: Princeton University Press.

National Election Studies. 2010. Cumulative data file. University of Michigan and Stanford University [producers and distributors]. Available at http://www.electionstudies.org (accessed October 13, 2010).

Poole, Keith T., and Howard Rosenthal. 2007. *Ideology and Congress*. New Brunswick, N.J.: Transaction Publishers.

Rohde, David W. 1991. *Parties and Leaders in the Postreform House*. Chicago: University of Chicago Press.

Shafer, Byron E., and William J. M. Claggett. 1995. *The Two Majorities: The Issue Context of Modern American Politics*. Baltimore, Md.: Johns Hopkins University Press.

Steenbergen, Marco R., and Bradford S. Jones. 2002. "Modeling Multilevel Data Structures." *American Journal of Political Science* 46(1): 218–37.

Stoker, Laura, and Jake Bowers. 2002. "Designing Multi-Level Studies: Sampling Voters and Electoral Contexts." In *The Future of Election Studies*, edited by Mark N. Franklin and Christopher Wlezien, 77–109. Amsterdam: Pergamon.

Stoker, Laura, and M. Kent Jennings. 2008. "Of Time and the Development of Partisan Polarization." *American Journal of Political Science* 52(3): 619–35.

Wattenberg, Martin P. 1984. *The Decline of American Political Parties, 1952–1980*. Cambridge, Mass.: Harvard University Press.

Chapter 5

Get Government Out of It: Heterogeneity of Government Skepticism and Its Connection to Economic Interests and Policy Preferences

KATHERINE CRAMER WALSH

O NE OF THE key concerns of contributors to this volume is the extent to which political preferences vary across groups. There are many reasons, for example, to expect that low-income people hold different preferences than upper-income people (see chapter 1, this volume). The editors of this volume, however, through their review of the scholarship and their own analyses, show that the story is more complex.

Unraveling the complexity requires investigating what people of different income levels mean by their survey responses. For example, when a low-income person and a high-income person both report that they believe that the government is spending "about the right amount on health care," do they mean the same thing? Or might one be reporting satisfaction with Medicaid, and the other wishing for no additional government intervention? More fundamentally, what do people of different income levels mean by their skepticism toward government intervention? Within the study of public opinion, there is a need for attention to the processes and interpretations that underlie survey responses. Perhaps especially in the study of inequality, there is a need to use methods that allow us to listen to the perspectives of lower-income people, so that we might minimize the bias we bring to our scholarship as upper-income professionals.

The importance of listening to the people we study hinges on the difference between preferences and perspectives. Surveys capture preferences; they are less adept at capturing the way in which people understand policy, or their perspectives. Moreover, as the previous chapters suggest, it is a range of differences that matter for understanding inequality, such as partisanship, income, education, and race, to name only a few. Understanding how all these aspects of social location—simultaneously—influence the manner in which people interpret policy requires investigating how people weave them together for themselves as they try to make sense of politics.

Recognizing the perspectives people bring to public policy is particularly important for understanding the connections people do—or do not—make between policy and economic interests. For example, what is going on when people who stand to lose (or at least not gain) from tax cuts nevertheless support them (Bartels 2008, chap. 6)? What is going on when white members of the working class are voting for Republicans rather than Democrats, a choice many observers regard as wrong (Frank 2004; but see Bartels 2006; Gelman et al. 2008)?

The link between economic interests and preferences is notoriously weak (Citrin and Green 1990; Stoker 1994). Part of what explains this imperfect link is information. People with greater political knowledge tend to make choices more consistent with their objective economic interests (see, for example, Delli Carpini and Keeter 1996, 238–43). Also, people tend to make decisions that more closely reflect their objective economic interests when they have particular types of information: information that makes it clear which political actors favor a policy (Bartels 2008, 176–81), and information that clearly connects their interests and political choices (Chong, Citrin, and Conley 2001). However, there is more to the story than information, because more information can at times weaken rather than strengthen the connection between interests and preferences, as was the case during the health-care reform debates of the early 1990s (Claassen and Highton 2006).

We know that political predispositions also help account for the way people connect their economic interests and preferences. Partisanship can operate as a lens that prevents people from accepting information that might lead to different policy preferences (Zaller 1992). Orientations toward government can also prevent people from supporting policies that would appear to advance their interests. Referring again to health care, in the years before the passage of the 2010 federal health-care bill, large segments of the public were dissatisfied with heath-care costs, believed that health-care reform should be a major national priority, and considered it the federal government's responsibility to ensure that everyone has adequate health-care coverage.[1] Nevertheless, the public as a whole was deeply ambivalent about whether to expand the government's role in the health-care system (Jacobs, Shapiro, and Schulman 1993).[2] Even though large segments of the public seemed poised to support major government intervention in the health-care system, they opposed it, largely because of their skepticism of big government (Zis, Jacobs, and Shapiro 1996; Jacobs, Shapiro, and Schulman 1993; Popkin 2007).

This chapter uses this insight—that attitudes toward government mediate the effect of economic interests on policy preferences—as its point of departure. It studies how opinions differ across income groups by investigating the perspectives (as in, the frameworks, the lenses, or the viewpoints) that people use to interpret health-care policy. It delves into the questions of what do people mean by the preferences that they report and what do they mean by the skepticism toward government that mediates their attitudes toward health care.

Methods

To examine the linkages between economic circumstances and political preferences, I studied the connections that people make in the course of conversations with people whom they regularly associate with. I used conversational data so that I could see the process of connecting economic interests to health-care preferences, and observe which considerations people brought to bear in articulating these views. Also, I wanted to observe conversations within regular social settings, similar to the way in which the people I studied express opinion in the course of their everyday life and in the physical settings in which they do so.

I chose to focus on conversations about health-care reform because it affects people from a wide variety of economic backgrounds, is an issue on which the public as a whole perceives class conflict (Stoker 1994), and was of prominent public concern at the time of the study. These characteristics meant that the topic was likely to generate sustained conversation in which individuals would talk about their stances in light of their personal economic circumstances.

I chose study sites using a stratified purposeful approach (Miles and Huberman 1994, 28), sampling twenty-three communities across Wisconsin that varied by partisan leaning, median household income, population density, size of community, racial and ethnic heterogeneity, local industry, and agricultural background. To do so, I categorized the counties into eight regions based on these qualities, then selected the city or population center in that region and also randomly chose a smaller municipality. I included several other municipalities to provide additional variation.

To identify the groups I studied, I asked University of Wisconsin Extension offices and local newspaper editors for advice. I sought a group of people who met regularly and casually of their own accord in a gathering place to which I could gain access. The groups my informants suggested were typically informal groups that met in local restaurants, cafés, or gas stations early on weekday mornings, or periodically in a local place of worship (see appendix 5.A for descriptions of these groups and communities). When possible, I spent time with multiple groups in a given municipality, especially to ensure greater socioeconomic and gender variation. I visited each of the groups between one and five times between May 2007 and May 2009.[3] To ensure confidentiality, I use pseudonyms and do not identify the communities by name except for the largest cities of Milwaukee and Madison.

My visits took the following form. The first time I studied a group, I arrived at the location at the time that an informant suggested the members would be meeting. Once I located the group, I greeted the members and asked for permission to sit with them, explaining that I was a public opinion researcher from the University of Wisconsin–Madison traveling around the state to get a sense of the issues people were concerned with and their ideas for ways in which the university could better serve the people of the state. I asked for their permission to record our conversation and passed out "small tokens of my appreciation" for their time—incentives, such as football schedules, donated by the University of Wisconsin Alumni Association. I then asked, "What are the big concerns for people in this community?" and continued with other questions from my protocol (see appendix 5.B), adjusting the order and the number of questions asked when necessary. All conversations were recorded and transcribed, except for two groups, for which I took handwritten notes instead.

I chose to study communities that are all within one state in order to hold constant state current events and state health-care regulations. Also, the demographics of the state provide ample variation across employment status and occupation type.

My sample is obviously not representative of all U.S. adults, or even Wisconsinites. The purpose of the study is not to describe opinions about health-care reform among a general population. Instead, it is to explain the process of connecting economic interests to preferences on health-care reform and to analyze how attitudes about government enter into these processes. Pursuing this type of question is best achieved through intensive study of people who vary on the key independent variable, economic background, rather than through a less in-depth study of a cross section of the entire country.

My strategy for finding groups to study meant that the people I spent time with were predominantly male, non-Hispanic whites of retirement age. Of the thirty-two groups studied, twelve were exclusively male, three exclusively female, and the rest mixed gender but predominantly male. Six of the groups were composed solely of retirees, and five of people currently employed or unemployed. The rest were a mix of retirees and actively working people, though the majority were retirees. Each of the groups was composed of people of a similar occupational and educational background, but almost all showed some variety in that respect (for example, one group of loggers included a local public official and a real estate agent). My strategy resulted in a good deal of socioeconomic variation across groups, from people who were "one step from homelessness" to wealthy business owners. I categorize the groups in this study into lower-income and upper-income based on levels of income inferred from their stated occupations. (Asking group members directly about income in a pilot test not surprisingly was insulting and threatened my chances of gaining access and generating a productive conversation on a return visit.)

My sampling strategy was not intended to provide a representative cross section and resulted in a bias toward local leaders either in politics or in their occupational community—in other words, opinion leaders in their community (Lazarsfeld, Berelson, and Gaudet 1944; Katz and Lazarsfeld 1955). Their perceptions and preferences may not be representative, but they are likely consequential for the way others in their community think about many public issues, including health-care policy. This slice of opinion leaders varied across the municipalities sampled, because I had chosen the communities to vary by key community characteristics, as explained. For example, although the groups often included local business leaders, in some places these people were executives of multinational corporations, and in others, the owners of the businesses on Main Street.

Because this sample includes people who were spending time in groups of their own accord, they may be more attentive to current events, more social, and have larger social networks than the average person. This limits my ability to generalize from this sample to the broader population, but the value of this data is that this information provides a window on the way people interpret the political world and suggests areas of attention for studies using survey data. In addition, if there is a higher level of engagement among these people, they are more likely to vote and thus their processes of understanding are of special interest in the study of representation.

The within-group homogeneity along racial, gender, and socioeconomic lines may have influenced the conversations that I observed. My presence, combined with their relative socioeconomic homogeneity, quite likely led me to perceive more unity in their identities and orientations toward government than individual members might have held. I have chosen to examine public opinion as a social fact, as something that people create together through interpersonal interaction. That is, I am not attempting to describe opinions that solitary individuals might offer pollsters, but rather the way in which people collectively make sense of public affairs. Because my purpose is to compare across groups, this magnification of the central tendencies was useful for discovering patterns. To avoid overstating across-group differences, I am careful to make generalizations only after observing similar patterns across many groups.

Of course, my presence altered these conversations. I intentionally steered the conversations, and the participants likely altered what they said somewhat because of my presence. When I sat in the restaurant, café, or some other venue before asking the group members for permission to join them, I glimpsed what their talk was like when they were not aware I was observing them. Consistent with previous work in this vein (Walsh 2004), my observations found the members of these groups appeared to swear less and talk about public affairs slightly more when they knew I was listening. I have no reason to expect, however, that the manner in which they connected their economic circumstances to their preferences on health-care reform was qualitatively different in my presence.

I designed my interview protocol to generate talk about several topics that prior work on group political conversation suggested were likely to invoke economic considerations and references to social class: tax policy, immigration, higher education, as well as health care (Walsh 2004, 2007a, 2007b). To analyze my data, I used data displays and adjusted my questions as I proceeded to test the conclusions I was reaching (Miles and Huberman 1994). That is, as I collected transcripts from the conversations, I read through them, looking for patterns across groups with respect to the kinds of considerations people brought to bear in talking about health care, the manner in which they connected that stance to their own interests, and whether and how they mentioned social class identity in these conversations. I displayed my data in a matrix in which the rows represented a particular group, and the columns represented different characteristics of the group and their geographic community, and the existence of various patterns. In the cells for the patterns, I inserted exemplar conversations.

As I proceeded, I wrote memos detailing the patterns I perceived (Feldman 1995), analyzing what additional evidence I would need to validate my conclusions, used the visual displays to test whether the patterns were as pervasive as I had first concluded and whether they varied across type of group.[4] For example, after the first round of investigations, it became clear that a key consideration in these discussions was skepticism of the government, and I adjusted the protocol to include questions about perceptions of government. To further verify my conclusions, I considered how the conversations might have been affected by my presence, reexamined conversations that were not consistent with the patterns I identified, considered spurious relations, added additional groups to the study to investigate whether conversations among people of different demographic backgrounds exhibited patterns similar to the groups already in my study, and sent detailed reports of my results to the groups I had visited and gave them brief verbal reports on subsequent visits so that they could comment on the conclusions I was reaching (for these tactics for verifying conclusions, see Miles and Huberman 1994, 262–77).

Results

Skepticism toward government inhibits support for government intervention in health care across a wide range of people. The conversations I observed, however, revealed that what people mean by skepticism toward government varies in important ways across socioeconomic groups. In addition, these attitudes are part of a broader constellation of attitudes toward power in society in general, suggesting that understanding the effect of inequality on political representation requires a broader lens than one focused just on political institutions.

Most groups I visited opposed state-sponsored universal health care, and the members of each of them offered some form of antigovernment attitude to explain their stance. This was often couched in terms of government inefficiency. These sentiments varied by the inferred income of the groups. Those in lower-income occupations expressed a general antigovernment perspective typical of people without access to power, whereas those with more professional occupational backgrounds believed that they could do better if they were in office—a perspective typical of people with access to power.

Opposition to Authority

As political scientists, we tend to treat skepticism of government as a political attitude, but the way it is used by people in practice suggests that it is better understood as one aspect of a perspective on the exercise of power and authority in general. These world views varied by income level. Lower-income groups tended to disdain government intervention in health-care reform from a general antiauthority perspective. By authority or authorities, I mean those institutions and individuals whom people perceive have the capacity to cause them to do something that they otherwise would not do, following Robert Dahl's definition of power (1961). With respect to government, antiauthority attitudes often appeared as distrust. Group members even expressed sentiments similar to standard trust-in-government measures (see Levi and Stoker 2000), for example, that the government is "full of crooks" or is "a bunch of crooks." However, the gist of their comments resembled their sentiments about a wide range of actors. In general, they complained that actors in power pursue interests contrary to their own.

Among the upper-income groups, people were also highly critical of the government. Their opposition, however, was not to authority in general, but rather to particular authorities. Their perspective was that of people closely connected to the exercise of power in business or politics. Their main complaint was that current authorities were doing a bad job, and that they could lead better themselves if they were in power.

To begin demonstrating these patterns among the lower-income groups, I refer to a group of three men who gathered over lunch at a local diner every weekday in a suburb of Milwaukee. One of them, Dan, was middle-aged, on disability for rheumatoid arthritis, and sold vintage magazines with another group member, Don, a home health-care worker for the elderly. The third member, Bob, remodeled and painted houses for a living and described himself as lower class.[5] When I asked, "How about health care? What are your concerns with health care?" they complained that HMOs are building too many facilities and "buying the doctors," do not treat their employees well, and behave as if they are above the law. When I asked, "What are your hopes for the [2008] presidential election?" they expressed the same "they-don't-care-about-people-like-us" attitude that they had when talking about the health-care system.

Bob called the campaign "sickening." Don agreed:

> Don: All they do is chop on each other. Why don't they just get their act together and try to agree on something, and move over? And that's with all of government. They just bitch at each other, and . . . why don't they just get the best, I've always thought, and everybody says, "I guess this is communism." I guess, you get the best scientists, the best mathematicians, the best people in financing, put them all together and try to work together to better the world, better the United States, not all the braggin' and bitchin' at each other, and . . . it's sickening. It's all they do. It's all about them, you know? It's not about us. And they have their agenda. I don't even vote because I think they're all crooks. They all have their ideas about what they're gonna do the minute they get in, they're not gonna do what you wanna do anyways. I've never voted. And that's my prerogative, but I don't, I mean, I don't bitch about it. But I'm just saying that all . . . I mean, I think I'm . . . watch me have the FBI on my doorstep [laughs]. But they all bad-mouth each other, they all backstab.

The three men exchanged a few more comments before Don continued:

Don: But you know, they should make more on the issues, a lot of them. They kind of bad-mouth each other, and not so much the presidents, they do it, too, but all of us, you know.

Bob: It's oil and pharmacies, and that's the payoffs.

Dan: And they're, and they're not big—they're bigger than that, they're international.

Bob: They're monstrous. Just give everyone a pill to keep them dopey.

The men all laughed, then launched into a discussion of a doctor in the state who had recently allegedly killed a mother and her young kids when he hit their car while driving under the influence of drugs. Bob expressed another "they're-above-the-law" sentiment in saying, "If he gets a good lawyer, he might get off in ten years."

This perspective that power operates in favor of the resource-rich but against lower-income people was common across lower-income groups in a variety of communities as well as across groups composed of people of different partisan leanings. The people in the group described above reported that they vote for Democrats. In another Milwaukee suburb, on the northern edge of the Milwaukee metropolitan area, I spent time with a group of retired factory workers and employed construction workers who met every morning at a local restaurant. These men openly called themselves Republican, yet exhibited attitudes toward authority similar to those of Bob, Don, and Dan.

When I brought up the topic of health care in this group,[6] the immediate response from one man was, "The health-care system is completely broken in this country."

Lew: Yeah, don't get me started on that one. We are faced with all these high health-care prices. You go to any doctor's office, and you look at what they're building for hospitals. I mean they are Taj Mahals. I don't need a Taj Mahal because when I am sick I could care less what the hell the decorating is like.

George: Same with schools. They are building all these Taj Mahals as schools, and the facilities don't matter.

Lew: I mean, I am sorry. If this stuff is supposed to be regulated in some way, shape, or form, why do we have to have all the fancy marble and all this stuff to make me feel better? No. When it is all coming out of my pocket and whatnot, forget it.

Skip: Well, there again, the governor wants to tax the hospital. Who's going to pay for that?

Interviewer (KCW): So who do you think the current system benefits?

Skip: The rich.

George: The top.

Skip: The rich.

Lew: It all boils down to everything that is happening costs the middle

class and poor people. The rich people, ah, they just view it as an investment or write-off. They could care less.

They resented the way in which the health-care system, like the government, wasted their money. Despite their perception of stark inequalities in the health-care system, they opposed a universal system run by
the government because they felt that the government, like the HMOs
and hospitals, did not have their interests in mind. On my second visit
with the group, I asked which of several reform alternatives they would
prefer.

> Stan: Well, forcing people to have it, I wouldn't be in favor of that. Then
> you're dependent upon the government for everything. Which I'm not in
> favor of.
> Lew: Keep government out of it. Totally. Those politicians can't sleep
> well at night trying to figure out how to raise our taxes.
> Stan: Yeah.

One might read this exchange as evidence that their stance on health
care is simply a function of their distaste for government spending. But
when viewed in the context of their conversations, that interpretation is
too narrow. It misses the way in which their antigovernment sentiments
are rooted in a broader perspective through which they think about a
range of institutions.

For example, they used the same distance-from-power perspective to
discuss education as they used to discuss health care. As with health
care, conversations about education brought out comments about the
misuse of taxpayer money and the elitism of those in power. Members of
the group viewed professors and university administrators as privileged
people who believe that they are entitled to special treatment and do not
have to play by the same rules as others. I asked, "What do you think the
UW-Madison does well currently, if anything?"

> George: I don't know what they do well. I've just got complaints about
> things that I see happening. . . . One thing I—I wish there were some way
> we could get rid of the tenure system that they have at the university.
> There is far too many professors that they rely on their student aides to do
> their work. They do absolutely nothing, and we're paying their big sala-
> ries, and then you hear of the corruption that goes on with some of the
> sexual things and what not and we can't even get rid of 'em because they
> are tenured in. And then we got county agents that just because they been
> here forever they do whatever they damn well please. Can't get answers
> out of 'em that you need from a county agent, and there is nothing you can
> do to get rid of 'em. I mean the sacred-cow thing that we have with the
> tenure system has gotta be overhauled. Everybody should have to live—

with money being so tight, why can't they?—like in the private sector, if I pissed my boss off, I would be gone today [*chuckles*]. You should have to—just because I been here for ten years, think that we owe you a living? And some of the living that they think that we owe them is just astronomical. Today with money being tight and everything, why do we owe anybody anything?

Not only did they perceive that university professionals wasted their money, and acted from a position of unearned privilege, they also opposed university intervention in their community, just as they opposed government intervention in the health-care system.

> KCW: Are there things that you think UW-Madison should be doing, say in [your city]? Like, can you imagine ways the university could better benefit people who live here? [*Pause*]
> Lew: I think let [our town] be [our town], let Oakville be Oakville, Brighton be Brighton [referring to nearby communities]. We don't need somebody—[7]
> Stan: From Madison—
> Lew: Out of Madison telling us where to plant a tree [*laughs*].

This sense that people in power have a general disregard for the views of common folk was pervasive among the lower-income groups not just in Milwaukee suburbs, but across Wisconsin. In a former mining, now agricultural, community in the southwestern part of the state, a group of men met in a local diner in the morning. One of them who was running for the county board said that he did not want government-run health care, because national-level politicians look down on people like them:

> KCW: When—when you're talking about the "yahoos", you're mostly talking about the federal level?
> Scott: The entrenched. . . . They think that we are idiots and don't have any grasp of *Marbury v. Madison*, *Brown v. Education*, judicial review, anything. They think we're all . . . They underestimate us.

Later that morning, a different member of the group, Steve, also running for a county-board seat, though in a different district, expressed a similar sentiment. He said that he had skills in a certain trade, but that the big companies in that line of work prevented nonunionized workers from getting jobs. His comments were another example of a widespread sentiment that people in power look down on common folks, and that a large part of this imbalance has to do with money. When talking about health care, again the conversation suggested that "the system" is run by the wealthy and that the wealthy do not have the interests of lower-income people in mind.

When I asked people at his end of the counter what types of reforms should be conducted on the health-care system, he suggested eliminating insurance companies altogether. I asked, "Do you think that would go over well?" He shook his head in the negative.

> KCW: And why is that? I mean—
> Steve: People don't do the right thing. They do what's good for their pocket.

He went on to suggest that people working for insurance industries would never choose to eliminate their own jobs, so this kind of reform would never happen.

In another town in the far northwest of the state, an area dominated by logging and tourism, I met with a group of approximately ten men who gathered in the morning at a gas station–grocery store–fishing tackle shop–hardware store. Most of them were loggers on their way to work, though several were retired. One morning in January 2008, I asked the group for their thoughts on the four options for health-care reform. I mentioned a government-sponsored system.

> Louis: How can they do that when, uh, they've got the insurance companies fighting them?
> KCW: Well, they couldn't. That's why they didn't—it didn't work. It didn't pass [recently in the state legislature].
> Louis: Yeah, donate income tax. The insurance companies hold so much power in this state it's—it's pathetic.
> KCW: Say the insurance companies would, I don't know, *not* get their way, do you think that would be a good solution to health-care problems?
> Louis: Well, they're *gonna* get their way. Because they've got all that money, they're just buying everybody off. They're buying Madison. They buy them off. There is no cure to that health-care problem.
> KCW: No cure? Well . . .
> Louis: Well, *you tell me*. Somebody that's working in the—these industries around here that are making eight, nine dollars an hour. With a family of two, how are you going to afford eight hundred dollars a month for health insurance?
> KCW: You can't.
> Louis: On eight dollars an hour?
> KCW: [*quietly*] You can't.
> Louis: Eight, ten dollars an hour? At fifteen—fifteen dollars an hour— how can you afford it?
> KCW: Maybe not, huh? I mean, what is it?
> Louis: Sure.
> KCW: Twelve hundred bucks a month for a family that size?
> Louis: Yeah, sure! To get anything decent. Then you go to the, uh, you go to the cheaper plan where you got the high deductible, okay. Every

time you go to the doctor it costs you a hundred and fifty bucks—you gotta pay for your prescription.

KCW: Just for a doctor visit?

Louis: Oh sure! By the time you get out of there, with the tests and everything. For the doctor call, I think it's a hundred and ten bucks now. Office call?

Steve: A hundred it used to . . .

These comments make it clear that the group felt powerless, that the burdens of the costs of health care were insurmountable, and that the insurance companies would prevent substantial reform, against the interests of people like themselves.

Two visits later, in April 2009, I asked the group to respond to standard questions about trust in government. The sentiment that political power was completely out of line with their interests was so palpable that it seemed almost ridiculous for me to ask them. They spoke so strongly by the third question that I decided not to ask the fourth.

KCW: How much attention to do you feel the government pays to what the people think when it decides what to do? A good deal, some, or not much?

Fred: Zero [laughs]. How about zero?

KCW: When you say "zero," do you have in mind all levels of government, or are some levels better than others?

Fred: All of them.

KCW: All of them?

Sam: All of the above.

Jim: They do what they want to do.

Johnny: That's where it starts.

Fred: Right from the city up.

KCW: Okay. Number two. Would you say the government is pretty much run by a few big interests looking out for themselves, or that it is run for the benefit of all the people?

Johnny: Themselves. They don't care what—

Sam: The insurance companies.

Johnny: Yup.

Sam: The banks.

KCW: Okay. Number three. "People like me don't have any say about what the government does." Do you agree or disagree?

Fred: A hundred percent. They don't care what we think.

Sam: No.

Fred: You can't go right with your DNR [Department of Natural Resources]. They just have meetings around about, you know, the deer herd and everything else. You tell them there ain't no deer around, but they keep telling ya, "Well, there's twelve thousand deer in, uh, [DNR Deer Management] Unit Six." Well, we hunt in Unit Six. You know?

KCW: You don't see them?

Fred: There aren't that many deer there. We tell them that. [But they respond,] "Oh no, well, we're just gonna do what we wanna do."

Conversations in urban areas were nearly identical. Even in Madison, within a short drive from the state capitol, residents felt ignored. I visited a group of retired men and a few women who met every morning in a coffee shop. They were a mix of mainly retired small-business owners and skilled tradesmen and their wives. During each of my five visits, the group members talked about how the university and various levels of government were implementing policies that reflected interests other than their own. Like the others, they argued public officials were motivated by money rather than concern for long-time residents.

Professionals Criticizing Current Authorities, Not Authority in General

In these relatively lower-income groups, antipathy toward government intervention in the health-care system coincided with distrust in government and an antipathy toward powerful people and institutions more generally. In upper-income groups, however, opposition toward government intervention was expressed instead as resentment against current authority or as a feeling that authority was being exercised improperly. Group members indicated that they would make different decisions if they held political power, and that they actually could make different decisions if they took the time to run for office.

The Madison coffee-shop group exhibited a blend of these perspectives. As I noted above, they claimed that various institutions of power in society ignored their concerns. However, at times they spoke as if they used to be close to the exercise of power, or could be if they wanted to get involved. Several groups exhibited this mix of sentiments, and each of them were composed of people representing a range of occupations.

With respect to a group of professionals who clearly conveyed that they believed they could make better decisions if they chose to run for office, I rely on a group that met in a diner in a central Wisconsin city that is both an economic and a residential center. The members consisted of business owners, lawyers, and physicians on their way to work. Their main concerns with health-care reform were with cost containment, and how the system could be reformed so that paying for their employees' benefits would be more feasible. They opposed universal health care and preferred to rely on market mechanisms to reform the system. They resented that state employees see health care as a "God-given right" and resented government overregulation of the system. Their comments, however, did not convey a general distrust of authority as much as a perception that people currently in government were making bad decisions. For example, a lawyer in the group remarked, shortly after I had met him during my first visit, "Statewise, it is a government that is totally in debt. We issue now junk bonds, and only two states issue bonds lower rated than ours—Louisiana and California. We have a budget that is absolutely, um, out of control. And the entire group that [works] in that capitol building, from the governor to every one of those legislators, should be ashamed of themselves."

His reference to "we" when talking about the state government is telling. He distanced himself from the state government because of its poor performance, but not because he felt distance from its networks of power. His group contained leaders in the local and state business community, and several had family members who were local elected officials. Numerous times they mentioned elitists, but, unlike the lower-income groups, used the term for left-leaning academics, not upper-income people. In short, they talked about public policy from the perspective of people who were closely associated with decision-making power.

In a different city, again an economic and residential center, but in the western part of the state, a group of currently working and retired professional men and women (physicians, lawyers, judges, and public school administrators) met each morning in a café. During my initial visit, the first time that someone mentioned health care, several of the people in the group argued that the system was not in crisis. They were critical of the government being overly responsive to members of the public who complained about the health-care system. This conversation took place after I asked what they thought were the main issues of concern in their community.

> Bill: You know, on a statewide level, I'm not sure there are a whole lot of things that people really complain about. You know. Ah, I think that people overemphasize what they think is wrong, like they say, "Oh, our people are running around trying to say what they think is wrong with the health-care system." Well, you know, the health-care system is pretty damn good in this country. Try going someplace else.
> Mike: I think it is pretty good in Wisconsin.
> Bill: It is damn good in Wisconsin. I think they are trying—you know, these people [are] trying to fix things that just aren't broken. I'd rather see government stay out of our lives.

Their conversation suggested that, with respect to health care, they saw current political leaders as being too attentive to ordinary people, a rather stark contrast to comments in the lower-income groups that political leaders routinely ignore the concerns of ordinary people.

This group was composed primarily of self-proclaimed conservatives, but several referred to themselves as "the liberal wing." On my second visit, just these four men had gathered. They expressed open support for substantial government intervention in the health-care system. One man, a doctor, said, "I think you could say that the [John] Edwards plan [proposed while he was running for the Democratic presidential nomination], or the mandated health-care plan, really sort of makes sense. It's sort of a hybrid system saying that everybody's gotta have health insurance, and [for] those who can't afford it [the government provides assistance]."

Another remarked, "I don't think [health care] is a right like freedom of speech—you know, 'It's my right, I insist I have health care.' But I think it is the responsibility of elected legislators to ensure that everyone has it."

Both those who opposed and those who supported government intervention in the health-care system criticized current policymakers and spoke as if they could make better decisions if they were in office. At least one of them had run for local elected office.

They saw themselves as a kind of elite, with more sophisticated views than the ordinary citizen. When I asked the self-described liberal wing whether their group was representative of the surrounding community, they said that they were pretty different from the common person. They referred to their incomes, their levels of education, and their experience working and traveling outside of the community as indicators of their broader view of most public problems than the majority of those in their city.

Another example of this perspective toward authority among the affluent as one of disagreement rather than disempowerment comes from a group of current or retired small-business owners, executives in multinational corporations, newspaper editors, and lawyers in a Minneapolis suburb on the far western edge of Wisconsin. These men met midmorning for a coffee break each weekday in the back room of a local diner. They expressed disagreement with current policies, but never suggested that their concerns were scarcely considered. They held this view about a range of institutions—the state's flagship university, various levels of government, and the institutions that had or currently employed them. When talking about the university, for example, they disagreed with some of its current practices, but also talked about their personal connections to its business school and marching-band director. When talking about politicians, they spoke of the governor's and current president's visits to their community. The only time they mentioned their concerns being ignored was when they discussed the news media that is available to them ignoring local issues because their community is located in the Minneapolis media market rather than a Wisconsin-based one.

They did speak of distrusting government, but not because of a fundamental, persistent imbalance of power that disadvantaged people like themselves. Instead, they felt that current officeholders and candidates were too entrenched, as the following January 2008 conversation about the 2008 presidential election primaries indicates.

KCW: So have you been surprised [by] how the race has gone so far? Like, say start with Iowa. Were you surprised Barack Obama did so well?

Art: No, not really. For the younger generation, he's a very popular candidate, I think.

KCW: Yeah, he is.

Art: Amongst both sides.

Evan: The younger people . . . Now I shouldn't speak for all of them, but for myself I don't trust people that have been entrenched in Washington. Somebody who's been a senator for thirty years—I don't care what side—but if he's been in Washington for thirty years, he won't get my vote. Because look at the mess that's there and you've been a part of it this long. Why would we possibly trust you to now "Oh, I'm going to change things if I get elected?" Yeah, whatever. So people like Barack Obama who haven't been entrenched in Washington very long do well with younger people. Whereas with [Joe] Biden [then a contender in the Democratic primary] and [John] McCain, they don't even make the radar, because they're part of the problem. As far as I'm concerned, the Clintons and the Bidens and the McCains and who . . . I don't even remember who are the long-time Washington people. There are a few other ones, I'm sure.

KCW: So are you hopeful about the next presidential election, or does this seem like the same old thing?

Art: Keep our fingers crossed to any of them.

KCW: So vote, right?

Art: It's a very important election I think. [*Clears throat.*] Very.

John: We like to believe that.

Evan: Well, I would, too, but—

John: I guess I'd like to believe that—everybody thinks the president is such a big job, and it is. I'm not taking that away from him, but Congress still runs the country.

Evan: I would agree, absolutely.

Mike: Yep.

John: What's the difference who's president? Congress runs the country. Be more concerned about your congressional representatives than the president, as far as I'm concerned.

Evan: Yeah.

This exchange about distrust of government went the opposite direction of lower-income group conversations. Rather than devolve into a nobody-pays-attention-to-us lament, it evolved into a discussion about the importance of elections, especially congressional elections.

Groups composed of professionals justified either their support or their opposition to government intervention in the health-care system on the basis of their knowledge of the system or their knowledge of political actors. If they professed distance from political power, it was an expression of geographic distance from the state's or the nation's capital, not the broader sense of alienation that was apparent in the lower-income groups.

Discussion

This chapter has used analysis of conversations among thirty-two groups of people in twenty-three municipalities across Wisconsin to analyze the manner in which people connect their economic interests to their policy preferences. The conversations affirm that attitudes toward government are a key tool in this process and revealed that these attitudes vary significantly by socioeconomic background. Lower-income people tended to make sense of health-care policy through a perspective of attitudes toward authority or power-wielding institutions in general, not just government. Individuals in upper-income groups, namely groups of professionals in this study, tended to speak from the perspective of those in positions of authority and criticized particular actors.

Some groups did support government-funded universal health care. Even in these groups, however, people discussed the possibility while voicing skepticism toward government. These comments mirrored the lower-income versus upper-income distinction observed in the groups opposing greater government intervention. That is, lower-income groups tended to display a general antiauthority perspective, and upper-income groups were critical of specific leaders rather than entire structures of power.

I have argued that the orientations to government expressed among the lower-income people observed in this study are qualitatively different than those expressed by their upper-income counterparts. One might argue that in both cases, people are expressing a perception that they are being ignored by government, and that the more affluent tended to mention particular actors is merely a function of their higher levels of political awareness. However, the difference is not just a matter of how often people discussed specific public officials. Members of the two types of groups brought conceptions of political authority into their conversations about health care in distinctly different ways. Professionals often spoke as if their status was similar to that of the political actors they were criticizing. In contrast, lower-income people often remarked on their lack of power in relation to political actors. They also regularly talked about their lack of power in relation to a wide range of actors and institutions in society, a theme that did not arise among the groups of professionals.

I emphasize these distinctions because though we might find little difference across income groups with respect to preferences on government intervention or health-care policy, the variation in the perspectives through which people determine their choices are important. Among upper-income groups, the opposition to current authorities conveys political efficacy and a basic belief in the system. Among lower-income groups, however, we see a profound alienation that suggests large segments of the public feel as though they are not listened to and have little bearing in the process of representation. These variations in perspectives may affect the types of reforms that people of different income levels will accept, the processes leading to policy change that they will perceive as legitimate, and may even influence their future interactions with government.

That professionals and lower-income people did not exhibit the same type of alienation from government illuminates how the implementation of policy can have different consequences on connections to government for different people. When governments enact policies that go against the grain of public opinion, they might spur action for one group, yet reinforce distance from government (and possibly other institutions) for another. For example, when a presidential administration pushes for health-care reform, upper-income people who disagree with the plan may be agitated enough to contact public officials or donate to candidates or groups. Lower-income people, however, may react by believing even more deeply that no one is listening to their concerns.

This is another part of the story of unequal representation. Whether unequal representation actually exists or not, the evidence of this chapter suggests that the perception of unequal representation perpetuates subsequent perceptions of unequal representation. This aspect of representation is beyond the purview of a focus on correlations between preferences and policy and correlations in preferences across income groups.

The implication for public opinion research is that we need to welcome methodological approaches that analyze the meaning behind the survey responses people offer. Seemingly similar responses may be just the tips of icebergs. Beneath the surface may lie interpretations that more fully explain why members of the public think the way they do about policies and candidates.

This study also serves as a reminder that social identity is a central part of the way people make sense of politics. Policy preferences are not a simple calculation of "Which policy meets my needs?" or even "Which policy meets the needs of people like me?" The calculation also includes perceptions of "What type of people designed this policy?" and "Where do I and the people in my community stand in relation to the networks of power behind it?" This helps explain, in part, the seemingly weak connection between objective economic circumstances and policy preferences.

Looking more closely at the process of political understanding has another pay-off that becomes apparent when probing a paradox in the findings: the conversations within these groups displayed a great deal of distancing from government. However, many of the people I studied were themselves current or former elected public officials in city, town, or county government.

What should we make of this? On the one hand, this seeming hypocrisy is not surprising. Plenty of elected or aspiring politicians on the national level criticize the institutions in which they seek to maintain or gain a seat. On the campaign trail, it is strategically advantageous to make these criticisms, given widespread cynicism toward the federal government. In casual conversation, widespread cynicism often makes it more socially acceptable to express antigovernment rather than progovernment sentiments (Eliasoph 1998, especially chapter 6).

But that their behavior as candidates suggests high internal efficacy and that their comments suggest low external efficacy offers a different insight, a message about the potential for reform. The fact that people who express skepticism toward government are nevertheless behaving as if they value the potential of the government to make a positive difference in their community suggests that opposition to government intervention is not inevitable. The strong strain of liberal individualism in American political culture means that many people believe in the difference individuals can make and believe in the decision making conducted within their own relatively homogeneous communities. The flip side is that they are skeptical of programs and policies enacted in a distant, other realm. As long as people conceptualize government as an "other," the chances of trusting decisions from this out-group are slim (Tanis and Postmes 2005; Wildschut, Insko, and Pinter 2004; but see Brewer 2002).

This suggests that the key to building support for social policy reform is for the policy process to include procedures that actually take the concerns of the public into account, and convey this clearly (see, for example, Harwood 1994). With respect to health-care reform, we could notice the significant gap in understanding on this issue between public officials and members of the public (Schlesinger 2002), appreciate the potential for improved understanding through use of the right policy metaphors (Schlesinger and Lau 2000), and call for better packaging or framing of reform proposals.

However, effective representation is more than good framing or resonating with one's audience. The reform needed to repair the distance between members of the public and their government is a matter of the type of communication, not the type of packaging. More public hearings are not the answer. Public hearings are more useful for providing a stamp of approval for policies that are already decided than for generating dialogue in which members of the public and public officials listen to one another. If we are to create more connections between the public and governments, we need to encourage those in power to go to the people who perceive that they lack power. Officials need to talk to their constit-uents in the settings in which those people are comfortable. Public officials might say that they do this all the time, but the people I studied, low-income and upper-income alike, feel otherwise.

Another undercurrent in this study is the tension between rural and urban interests. Often people associated wealth with urbanicity and poverty with rural areas in their understandings of the balance of power. When people in rural areas who were themselves officeholders spoke about opposition to authority, their comments typically suggested that they opposed any large entity—government, corporate farm, or chain store on Main Street—that had lost touch with local sentiments and values. This overlap between geographic area, perceived wealth, and power was pervasive in these conversations and is an object for further research.

This study has taken an admittedly unorthodox approach to the study of public opinion. Examining opinions as they are expressed in small-group conversation is particularly important when studying representation. Representatives rely a great deal on polling data but, especially at the state and local level, rarely have access to data specific to their geographic constituencies. When they take into account what their constituents think or feel, they are often relying not on polls, but on PBWA, or "polling by walking about," face-to-face conversations within their districts (Walsh 2009; see also Herbst 1998). To better understand representation, we need to make an attempt to understand opinion in the manner that representatives themselves often try to do so.

Appendix

(follows on next page)

Appendix 5.A   Descriptions of Groups Observed and Municipalities in Which They Met

Municipality Description	Group Type	Municipality Population (2000)	Median Household Income, in Dollars (1999)
Central hamlet	Daily morning coffee klatch, local gas station (men)	500	38,000
Northern tourist loation	Weekly breakfast group, local restaurant (women, primarily retired)	500	32,000
North western hamlet	Weekly morning coffee klatch, local church (mixed gender, primarily retirees)	500	35,000
North central village	Group of library volunteers at local library (mixed gender, retirees); also, daily coffee klatch of male local leaders meeting in the local municipal building	500	34,000
North eastern resort village	Group of congregants after a Saturday evening service at Immanuel Lutheran Church (mixed gender)	1,000	41,000
North western village	Daily morning coffee klatch, local gas station (men)	1,000	32,000
Northern American Indian reservation	Group of family members, during a Friday fish fry at a local gas station–restaurant (mixed gender)	1,000	35,000
South central village	Daily morning coffee klatch, local gas station (mixed gender, working and retired)	1,500	31,000
North central village	Daily breakfast group, local diner (men)	2,000	38,000
South central village	Women's weekly morning coffee klatch at local diner; also, group of male professionals, construction workers, and retirees meeting later there	3,000	43,000
Central western village	Two daily morning coffee klatches, one at a local gas station, the other at a local diner (men)	3,000	30,000
Central eastern village	Kiwanis meeting (mixed gender, primarily retirees); also daily morning coffee klatch of male retirees at local fast-food restaurant	3,000	45,000
Western Minneapolis suburb	Daily morning coffee klatch, local diner (male local-business owners, lawyers, retirees)	9,000	51,000

Location	Group observed	Population	Income
South eastern city on northern edge of Milwaukee metropolitan area	Daily morning coffee klatch, local diner (men)	10,000	54,000
South central city	Middle-aged man and woman taking a midmorning break at a local café	10,000	36,000
Central city	Daily morning coffee klatch, local café (middle-aged professionals, mixed gender)	38,000	37,000
East central city	Daily morning coffee klatch, local gas station (retired men)	42,000	41,000
Milwaukee suburb, west of the city	Group of teachers and administrators at local high school (mixed gender); daily lunch group of middle-aged men; mixed-gender breakfast group of retirees	47,000	55,000
Western city	Daily morning coffee klatch, local café (middle-aged professionals, retirees, mixed gender)	52,000	31,000
South eastern city	Weekly breakfast group, local diner (mixed gender, retirees, and currently employed)	82,000	37,000
North eastern city	Daily breakfast group, local diner (men)	100,000	39,000
Madison	Middle-aged female professionals' book club; also, daily morning coffee klatch of male retirees at bakery; female resident volunteers in food pantry in low-income neighborhood	200,000	42,000
North Milwaukee neighborhood	AIDS/HIV activism group meeting after services in a Baptist church (mixed gender)	600,000	32,000
South Milwaukee neighborhood	Group of Mexican immigrants, waiting at a pro bono health clinic (mixed gender)	600,000	32,000

Source: Authors' compilation.
Note: Population and income figures have been rounded to preserve the anonymity of the groups observed.

Appendix 5.B: Listening Investigations Protocol

Initial-Visit Protocol

Most important issues

What do you think are the major issues facing people in [name of municipality] these days? Which of these issues are of special concern to you all personally? [If issues include taxes, health care, or immigration, skip to relevant questions below.]
- What do you think should be done about this?
- Why do you think this has been overlooked?
- Whom does the current policy benefit?

Taxes [if not addressed above]

With respect to property and income taxes, do you think people similar to yourself currently pay a fair share?

Whom do you think benefits from our current tax policies?

Health care [if not addressed above]   Now I would like to talk about health care for a few moments.

Do you feel that you have been able to obtain adequate health care for you and your families?

Are there people in your community who don't/do have adequate health care? Why do you think that is the case?

Immigration [if not addressed above]

Is immigration an issue in this community? How does it affect you? How do you think immigration is affecting life in Wisconsin in general?

Self-description (identity and occupation)

How would you describe the kind of people that are a part of your group to outsiders like me?

Do any of you work outside the home? What kind of work do you do?

Children, activities, and education

Do you have children? How old are they?

What kinds of activities are they involved in after school?

For those of you with kids still in school, do you think they will go on to obtain some kind of post–high school education?

Would you want them to attend the UW-Madison? Why or why not?

Did any of you attend school after high school? Did any of you attend the UW-Madison or another UW-system school? If the latter, which one?

University of Wisconsin–Madison

What, in your opinion, does UW–Madison currently do well?
What, in your opinion, can UW–Madison do better?
What *should* UW-Madison be doing in your community?
Whom do you think the University of Wisconsin–Madison currently benefits?
When you think about the students who attend UW–Madison, and the faculty and staff who work there, what comes to mind?

Financial security

Thinking about your overall situation here in [name of municipality], would you say that you struggle to make ends meet, or do you live comfortably?

Success and deservingness

In America today, some people have better jobs and higher incomes than others do. Why do you think that is—that some Americans have better jobs and higher incomes than others do?
Here are some reasons other folks have stated. How important do you think these reasons are?
  • Because some people have more in-born ability to learn.
  • Because discrimination holds some people back.
  • Because some people don't get a chance to get a good education.
  • Because some people just choose low-paying jobs.
  • Because government policies have helped high-income workers more.
  • Because God made people different from one another.
  • Because some people just don't work as hard.

What does the term "hard work" mean to you?

I'm going to give you a list of occupations. Tell me which of these folks work hard for a living, and why you think that's the case: lawyers, construction workers, waitresses, public school teachers.

Anything else you want to add?
May I come back sometime?

Second-Visit Protocol

During my last round of visits with groups like this around the state, I found that many people were concerned about health care, higher education, and issues related to water. I would like to ask more about your thoughts on these topics.

Health care

What *are* your concerns about health care?

Do you think people here in your community are better or worse off with respect to health care than people in other parts of the state? Why? The country? Why?

In our last Badger Poll, we asked people which of four health-care reform solutions they support. Let me describe these and then ask for your opinions. [Describe four alternatives, based on the wording of the following question.]

A number of proposals have been made about ways to change the health-care system in the state of Wisconsin. I am going to read some of these proposals and for each please tell me whether you strongly oppose it, somewhat oppose it, somewhat favor it, or strongly favor it. [In the Badger Poll, the four questions below were randomized.]

    A. What about consolidating all the money and resources now being spent by employers, individuals, the state government, and insurance companies to operate the current health-insurance system and replace it with a new system, administered entirely by state government and covering all residents of Wisconsin?

    B. How about expanding the eligibility of existing state-government health-insurance programs for low-income people, such as BadgerCare, Medicaid, and Healthy Families, to provide coverage for more people without health insurance?

    C. What about requiring every resident of Wisconsin to have health-insurance, either from their employer or another source, and offer government subsidies to low-income residents to help them pay for it?

    D. How about encouraging individuals to put money into a tax-free health-savings account that they would use to pay for their regular health-care bills and accompany this with a catastrophic-insurance plan that they must also purchase to help pay for major medical bills?

Higher education

In what ways is higher education a big issue for people here in your community?

Is higher education more of a pressing concern for people here than in other parts of the state?

In general, whom do you think the UW-Madison benefits? Whom do you think higher education in general benefits in this country?

Do you have children? Do/did you want your kids to go to college? Why or why not?

Water

Taking care of [name issue related to water mentioned in previous visit] will likely require broad support in the state legislature. Do you think it's possible to get that support? Why or why not?

Is this an issue that all Wisconsinites should be concerned about? How would you sell that to the broader Wisconsin public?

Presidential race

Which of the candidates would be most attentive to the concerns of people here in your community. Why? Most attentive to the concerns of people in Wisconsin? Why?

What are your hopes for this presidential race?

Higher education

[Repeat questions from first round.]

Social class identity

People talk about social classes, such as the poor, the working class, the middle class, the upper-middle class, and the upper class. Which of these classes would you say that you belong to?

Third and Additional Visits Protocol

Most Important Issues

What are the major issues facing people in this community?
- What do you think should be done about this?
- Why do you think this has been overlooked?
- Whom does the current policy benefit?

Power and authority

- How would you describe your group to an outsider like me? How do you think you compare to the rest of the community?
- Who do you think has power in your community? In the state? The nation?
- Do you tend to feel or not feel that most people with power try to take advantage of people like yourself?
- How has this community changed over time?

Political parties

Which party do you feel is more attentive to the concerns of people like you. Why?

Is it fair to say that Republicans are for the rich, and Democrats are for the lower income?

Which party do you trust to handle the economy? Why?

Attitudes toward government

How much attention do you feel the government pays to what the people think when it decides what to do: a good deal, some, or not much?

Would you say that the government is pretty much run by a few big interests looking out for themselves, or that it is run for the benefit of all the people?

[Agree/disagree:] People like me don't have any say about what the government does.

[Agree/disagree:] Public officials don't care much about what people like me think.

News use

Over the past seven days, which of the following have you used to obtain news?

    A. Read a newspaper

    B. Read magazines like *Newsweek, Time,* or *U.S. News and World Report*

    C. Watched the national news on television

    D. Watched the local news on television

    E. Listened to the news on the radio

    F. Read the news on the Internet

Higher education

[Repeat questions from first round.]

Where do you usually get your news about the UW?

This research was funded by an Ira and Ineva Reilly Baldwin Wisconsin Idea Endowment Grant. My sincere thanks to Tim Bagshaw, Valerie Hennings, Tricia Olsen, and Kerry Ratigan for transcribing assistance, and the many people who allowed me to join their conversations for this study. Thank you to two anonymous reviewers, Don Kinder, Nancy Burns, Rosalee Clawson, Elizabeth Rigby, Nathan Kelly, Adam Berinsky, Peter Enns, and Chris Wlezien, and the participants in the Conference on Homogeneity and Heterogeneity in Public Opinion for comments on previous versions of this paper.

Notes

1. See, for example, results regarding health care in the April 22–26, 2009, and September 22–26, 2008, CBS News/*New York Times* polls; the December 3–8, 2008, Pew Research Center for the People and the Press poll; the January and August 2008 World Public Opinion poll; the November 6–10, 2008, Quinnipiac University poll; the October 10–12, 2008, Associated Press/ Knowledge Networks poll; and the June 3, 2008, Kaiser Family Foundation poll.

2. Although support for a government insurance plan has increased steadily since 1996, this support still has not reached a majority of voting-age adults (see "The ANES Guide to Public Opinion and Electoral Behavior," available at http://www.electionstudies.org/nesguide/nesguide.htm).

3. The size of each of the morning coffee klatches varied from day to day, but on the days that I visited with them, most groups ranged between four and ten members.

4. These methods of drawing conclusions are akin to the methods of "counting" and "noting relations between variables," detailed by Matthew Miles and Michael Huberman (1994, chapter 10).

5. In response to a standard social class identity question (see appendix 5.B, Second-Visit Protocol), Bob said, "Lower [class]. There's no middle class anymore. I don't think." John said,"There is, but it's really small. . . . I'm in the lower class, without a doubt. I mean, with what I make? I mean, I work, you know, hand to mouth. That's how I live."

6. One person said "What about health care? I was in northern Wisconsin last week talking to folks up there and—well, you tell me—is it a big issue for folks in [this city]?"

7. This symbol denotes overlapping comments.

References

Bartels, Larry M. 2006. "What's the Matter with *What's the Matter with Kansas?*" *Quarterly Journal of Political Science* 1(2): 201–26.

———. 2008. *Unequal Democracy: The Political Economy of the New Gilded Age.* Princeton, N.J.: Princeton University Press.

Brewer, Marilynn B. 2002. "The Psychology of Prejudice: Ingroup Love and Outgroup Hate?" *Journal of Social Issues* 55(3): 429–44.

Chong, Dennis, Jack Citrin, and Patricia Conley. 2001. "When Self-Interest Matters." *Political Psychology* 22(3): 541–70.

Citrin, Jack, and Donald Phillip Green. 1990. "The Self-Interest Motive in American Public Opinion." *Research in Micropolitics* 3(1): 1–28.

Claassen, Ryan L., and Benjamin Highton. 2006. "Does Policy Debate Reduce Information Effects in Public Opinion? Analyzing the Evolution of Public Opinion on Health Care." *Journal of Politics* 68(2): 410–20.

Dahl, Robert. 1961. *Who Governs? Democracy and Power in an American City.* New Haven, Conn.: Yale University Press.

Delli Carpini, Michael X., and Scott Keeter. 1996. *What Americans Know About Politics and Why It Matters.* New Haven, Conn.: Yale University Press.

Eliasoph, Nina. 1998. *Avoiding Politics: How Americans Produce Apathy in Everyday Life.* Cambridge, Mass.: Cambridge University Press.

Feldman, Martha S. 1995. *Strategies for Interpreting Qualitative Data.* Thousand Oaks, Calif.: Sage Publications.

Frank, Thomas. 2004. *What's the Matter with Kansas? How Conservatives Won the Heart of America.* New York: Metropolitan Books.

Gelman, Andrew, David Park, Boris Shor, Joseph Bafumi, and Jeronimo Cortina. 2008. *Red State, Blue State, Rich State, Poor State: Why Americans Vote the Way They Do.* Princeton, N.J.: Princeton University Press.

Harwood, Richard C. 1994. "Is the Public Ready to Decide?" *Social Policy* 24(3): 13–23.

Herbst, Susan. 1998. *Reading Public Opinion: How Political Actors View the Democratic Process.* Chicago: University of Chicago Press.

Jacobs, Lawrence R., Robert Y. Shapiro, and Eli C. Schulman. 1993. "Medical Care in the United States—An Update." *Public Opinion Quarterly* 57(3): 394–427.

Katz, Elihu, and Paul F. Lazarsfeld. 1955. *Personal Influence: The Part Played by People in the Flow of Mass Communication.* Glencoe, Ill.: Free Press.

Lazarsfeld, Paul F., Bernard Berelson, and Hazel Gaudet. 1944. *The People's Choice: How the Voter Makes Up His Mind in a Presidential Campaign.* New York: Duell, Sloan, and Pierce.

Levi, Margaret, and Laura Stoker. 2000. "Political Trust and Trustworthiness." *Annual Review of Political Science* 3(1): 475–508.

Miles, Matthew B., and A. Michael Huberman. 1994. *Qualitative Data Analysis: An Expanded Sourcebook,* 2nd ed. Thousand Oaks, Calif.: Sage Publications.

Popkin, Samuel. 2007. "Public Opinion and Collective Obligations." *Society* 44(1): 37–44.

Schlesinger, Mark. 2002. "On Values and Democratic Policy Making: The Deceptively Fragile Consensus Around Market-Oriented Medical Care." *Journal of Health Politics, Policy and Law* 27(6): 889–925.

Schlesinger, Mark, and Richard R. Lau. 2000. "The Meaning and Measure of Policy Metaphors." *American Political Science Review* 94(3): 611–26.

Stoker, Laura. 1994. "A Reconsideration of Self-Interest in American Public Opinion." ANES Pilot Study Report, no. 010876. Paper prepared for the Western Political Science Association annual meeting. Albuquerque, N.M. (March 10–12, 1994). Available at ftp://ftp.electionstudies.org/ftp/nes/bibliography/documents/nes010876a.pdf.

Tanis, Martin, and Tom Postmes. 2005. "A Social Identity Approach to Trust: Interpersonal Perception, Group Membership, and Trusting Behaviour." *European Journal of Social Psychology* 35(3): 413–24.

Walsh, Katherine Cramer. 2004. *Talking About Politics: Informal Groups and Social Identity in American Life.* Chicago: University of Chicago Press.

———. 2007a. *Talking About Race: Community Dialogues and the Politics of Difference.* Chicago: University of Chicago Press.

———. 2007b. "Studying the Role of Social Class Identity in Political Understanding: A Proposed Method." Paper prepared for presentation to the annual meetings of the Midwestern Political Science Association. Chicago (April 12–15, 2007).

———. 2009. "Scholars as Citizens: Studying Public Opinion Through Ethnography." In *Political Ethnography*, edited by Ed Schatz, 165–82. Chicago: University of Chicago Press.

Wildschut, Tim, Chester A. Insko, and Brad Pinter. 2004. "The Perception of Outgroup Threat: Content and Activation of the Outgroup Schema." In *The Psychology of Group Perception: Perceived Variability, Entitativity, and Essentialism*, edited by Vincent Yzerby, Charles M. Judd, and Olivier Corneille, 335–39. Philadelphia: Psychology Press.

Zaller, John R. 1992. *The Nature and Origin of Mass Opinion.* Cambridge: Cambridge University Press.

Zis, Michael, Lawrence R. Jacobs, and Robert Y. Shapiro. 1996. "The Elusive Common Ground: The Politics of Public Opinion and Healthcare Reform." *Generations* 20(Summer): 7–12.

Part II

Policy Representation

Part II

Introduction

PETER K. ENNS AND CHRISTOPHER WLEZIEN

IN THE FIRST half of this volume, we have seen repeated evidence that policy preferences often do not align as scholars of representation assume. Together, these chapters combine to offer an important lesson for the study of representation. When asking whose preferences policymakers represent, scholars must first consider what policies different constituent groups prefer. The chapters in part II offer a powerful response to this call. The complexity of group opinions depicted in the first half of the book informs the analytical decisions and the conclusions drawn in the following chapters. The authors pay careful attention to the measurement of group opinions and theorize about when policymakers might pay attention to particular groups and why. The result is an innovative set of chapters that substantially increases our understanding of representation in the United States.

We begin with James N. Druckman and Lawrence R. Jacobs, who show that electoral ambitions provide incentives for politicians to cater to a variety of groups. Specifically, during Ronald Reagan's presidency, the influence of different groups varied across policy areas. On defense, Reagan appears to have catered to his Republican base. On domestic policy, independents and the wealthy were of special interest. On family values, Baptists held the most sway. Druckman and Jacob's theoretical account of political response as a form of constituent coalition building leads them to uncover previously unknown patterns of unequal representation.

The next four chapters combine to offer a substantial revision to how we understand the representation, or the lack thereof, of the different income groups (with the book's concluding chapter offering—at least literally—the final word on this debate). First, Elizabeth Rigby and Gerald C. Wright follow David A. Hopkins and Laura Stoker and consider the implications of state context on representation. Although the preferences of the poor are (predictably) least likely to align with state policy outputs, we see that the implications of this finding are highly contingent on state resources and state-level opinion. We also see that the economic preferences of middle-income individuals tend to correspond with policy outputs as much as or more than the preferences of the rich.

Yosef Bhatti and Robert S. Erikson reexamine Larry Bartels's (2008) study of senatorial responsiveness to different income groups. By paying close attention to the measurement of different income groups' political ideologies, they show that it is not possible to differentiate, at least statistically, between the level of representation of lower-, middle-, and upper-income groups. This finding suggests an important reconsideration of Bartels's conclusions (2008) regarding unequal representation of constituent ideology in the Senate.

Martin Gilens moves from political ideology to individuals' specific policy preferences. We see additional evidence that different income groups often hold similar preferences, but Gilens also shows that when the preferences of the wealthy diverge from those in the middle or those at the bottom of the income distribution, it is the richest 10 percent who see their policy preferences enacted. Furthermore, Gilens's attention to group opinion highlights important and surprising implications of this unequal representation. For example, the differential representation of high- and low-income citizens is often viewed as having a prominent role in rising levels of inequality in the United States (Jacobs and Skocpol 2005). Although his analysis of economic policy offers some support for this assertion, for social welfare policy, which has the greatest potential for mitigating economic inequality, Gilens finds the weakest evidence of differential representation across income groups. We also see that because the affluent are more liberal on moral and religious issues, policymakers' heightened attention to the wealthy in this domain has pushed policies such as birth control more liberal than they would have otherwise been. Gilens's chapter also points to the importance of considering the role of organized interests in the study of representation.

Christopher Wlezien and Stuart N. Soroka also examine policy-specific preferences but emphasize the government response to over-time opinion change. They are interested in seeing who politicians follow as opinion changes, focusing specifically on spending decisions in selected domains. If representation is unequal, politicians will follow the opinions of some groups and not others. In terms of the representation of different income groups, no clear pattern of winners or losers emerges from Wlezien and Soroka's analysis: policymakers appear to be responding about equally to the changing preferences of all income groups. This finding, combined with the previous chapters, suggests that representation is more equal (or more unequal) in some policy areas—and at some levels of policymaking—than others.

The last chapter in this section focuses on partisan representation. In part I, Hopkins and Stoker concluded their chapter by noting, "Increasingly, the answer to who gets represented will depend on which party holds the reins of power." Wesley Hussey and John Zaller's chapter makes this point in striking fashion. Examining roll-call votes, they show that the party affiliation of members of Congress matters at least as much (and usually much more) than constituency preferences. Furthermore, the influence of members's partisanship has increased during the last thirty years. In Hussey and Zaller's view, "parties" might be the most appropriate answer to the question "Who gets represented?"

James A. Stimson's chapter concludes the book. He brings additional data to bear on the question of group opinion analyzed in the first half of the book and develops a view of representation that accommodates the seemingly disparate findings of unequal and equal representation of income groups presented in the second half of this volume. We now move on to part II.

References

Bartels, Larry M. 2008. *Unequal Democracy: The Political Economy of the New Gilded Age*. Princeton, N.J.: Princeton University Press.

Jacobs, Lawrence R., and Theda Skocpol. 2005. "American Democracy in an Era of Rising Inequality." In *Inequality and American Democracy: What We Know and What We Need to Learn*, edited by Lawrence R. Jacobs and Theda Skocpol. New York: Russell Sage Foundation.

Chapter 6

Segmented Representation: The Reagan White House and Disproportionate Responsiveness

JAMES N. DRUCKMAN AND LAWRENCE R. JACOBS

THE RELATIONSHIP BETWEEN the government and the public is commonly used to characterize the nature of a political system. Populist theories of democracy define this relationship as the close association between the wishes and wants of the country's citizens and the substantive policy decisions of elected government officials. Political representation also can be viewed in symbolic terms; kings, for instance, "stand for" the country (Pitkin 1967). American presidents are often said to "speak for the people." Although political representation has been defined in quite different ways, nearly all portrayals share a focus on the government's relationship with its citizenry. For instance, kings or presidents represent the country as a whole, a member of Congress represents all residents within his or her legislative district, and so on.

Empirical research on political representation tends to focus on the nation or other aggregate populations, such as the congressional district or the state. A large body of work has studied the degree of consistency or congruence between the opinions or actions of political elites and the opinions of the public. For example, one body of research studies the dyadic relationship between the actions taken by a member of Congress and the public's attitudes in the member's district or state (for example, Bartels 1991; Erikson, Wright, and McIver 1993; Miller and Stokes 1963). Other work examines collective or systematic political representation—

namely, the relationship between aggregate national public opinion and the decisions of government through collective efforts or separate institutions, such as Congress (Page and Shapiro 1983; Weissberg 1978; see, for review, Manza, Cook, and Page 2002).

Despite significant differences in research design, the dyadic and collective approaches to studying political representation have two similarities. First, they both focus on the government's relationship with largely undifferentiated populations—the attitudes of the public in a congressional district, a state, or the nation. Second, research typically treats the relationship between the public and government officials as one-dimensional—studying aggregated policy rather than variations across distinctive policy domains and focusing either on specific policy preferences or on global liberal or conservative "mood" (but see Wlezien 2004).

The result is that political representation research has become oddly apolitical and neglects inequalities in influence and the calibration of strategy by political elites (also see Bartels 2005, 2008; Gilens 2005). Ample evidence shows that distinct subgroups of citizens, particularly the wealthy and the educated, participate in elections and a range of other political activities at far higher rates than others (Verba, Schlozman, and Brady 1995). Yet few have studied the extent and nature of affluent influence on actual public policy or policymakers' issue positions. Even less attention has been dedicated to better understanding the impact that social and political subgroups not defined by economic advantage—such as religious groups—have on government decision makers. A comprehensive political analysis of representation needs to address not only possible disparities in influence but also the distinct strategies of elites to cultivate and to mobilize segments of the electorate through differentiated appeals based on policy domains. Research on political representation has thus far failed to take into account the changing motivations of government officials, who target specific subgroups and specifically craft public messages to satisfy their interest.

We explore segmented representation across policy domains by studying how President Ronald Reagan responded to a unique dataset—the private public-opinion polling conducted by his White House. Studying segmented representation in presidential behavior cuts across the grain of a long tradition, from the Federalist Papers to contemporary presidents, which emphasizes the chief executive's political and constitutional responsibilities to serve the collective national interest (Jacobs 2005). Yet presidents also often have strategic reasons to attend to the preferences of specific groups to build stronger electoral coalitions.

Archival research demonstrates that the Reagan White House conducted extensive private polling that focused particularly on the interests of specific demographic and political subgroups (Jacobs and Burns 2004). Reagan sought to capitalize on the demise of the Democrats' New

Deal coalition by building a new conservative Republican coalition that appealed to political independents and extended the party's traditional conservative base. The movement targeted those likely to support smaller government, supply-side economics (which accepted higher budget deficits in exchange for lower taxes), social-conservative values, and hawkish military policies. This chapter seeks to systematically determine whether and how Reagan calibrated his public policy statements (and positions) to respond to interests of these particular subgroups.

Studying Segmented Representation

An enduring question in the study of political representation concerns the disproportional influence of economically advantaged citizens. The conclusion that the most advantaged influence government is as old as the United States itself. Charles Beard (1913) argued that the U.S. Constitution was designed by and for the wealthy. C. Wright Mills (1959) argued that a coherent "power elite" directed America's major economic and governmental institutions to serve its interests. Critics of the pluralist account of government point to the influence exerted by economically powerful semiautonomous elites on the political agenda and on decentralized decision making within Congress and the bureaucracy (Bachrach and Baratz 1962; McConnell 1966; Schattschneider 1960). These conclusions, however, have been criticized on the claim that they are based on limited cases rather than systematic evidence.

In this light, a new and growing body of research has begun to supply systematic evidence of the influence of the economically advantaged on government policy. One study of income-weighted preferences and roll-call votes cast by U.S. senators in the late 1980s and early 1990s found that senators are consistently much more responsive to the views of affluent constituents than to the views of the poor (Bartels 2005, 2008). Another study found that the American political system is a great deal more responsive to the preferences of the rich than to the preferences of the poor (Gilens 2005). A third reported that the policy stands of foreign-policy decision makers were most influenced by business leaders, with the general public exerting no significant effect and policy experts largely serving as conduits for the views of other elites, including business (Jacobs and Page 2005).

Virtually no work, however, has explored disproportional influence of noneconomic decisive political forces. The early 1970s was a period of significant change in the electorate and the organization of political parties, with the goal of altering political incentives. In particular, changes in the process for selecting candidates substantially enhanced the influence of single-issue and ideologically extreme party activists. Within the

Republican Party, for instance, social conservatives (especially born-again Protestants and Baptist fundamentalists), economic conservatives (especially supply-side advocates favoring sharp reductions in government taxation), and philosophical conservatives all gained new prominence in candidate selection and thereby in government circles (Aldrich 1995; Edsall and Edsall 1991). Even as ideologically oriented party activists gained more sway, both political parties competed to appeal to the growing ranks of independent voters. As the Democratic Party's New Deal coalition unraveled and stalwart supporters, such as Catholics, drifted from the party, the proportion of voters who described themselves as independent in surveys by the American National Election Studies rose from 23 percent in 1952 to 34 percent by 1980.[1]

These significant changes in the electorate and party organization generated incentives for national political leaders to win over politically critical segments of the electorate. With leaders in both parties maneuvering for advantage, Republican government officials were motivated to construct a new conservative coalition—one that would expand Barry Goldwater's economic libertarianism to include social conservatives, supply-siders who favored sharply lower taxes (even at the risk of higher budget deficits), and more general philosophical conservatives.

Changes in the political incentive structure, along with shifts in the electorate, motivated government officials to devote particular attention to distinct economic and political segments of the electorate. We would expect Republican party-leader policy decisions to be particularly attentive to higher-income groups, social conservatives (namely, fundamental Baptists and Catholics as they defected from the Democratic Party), and political independents (given the nature of the times and attempts to build a conservative coalition). Democratic leaders, meanwhile, gravitated toward social liberals and economic liberals who favored greater government intervention in market distributions, though the pressure to raise campaign contributions also placed a premium on higher-income groups among their supporters (Verba, Schlozman, and Brady 1995).

Another challenge facing research on segmented representation is accounting for variations across policy domains and the public's global and policy-specific attitudes. Previous research suggests that politicians and presidents in particular distinguish between domestic and international issues based on political considerations (Druckman, Jacobs, and Ostermeier 2004; Wildavsky 1994a, 1994b). For instance, bold and aggressive foreign-policy initiatives (such as hawkish defense policy) offer an opportunity to promote a portrait of strength, whereas conciliatory positions on defense issues can project, or be portrayed by their opponents as revealing, a soft, timid, or passive personal character (DeRouen 2000; Foyle 1999; Nincic 1990; Ostrom and Job 1986). In general, domestic issues offer—under normal conditions—an opportunity for government officials to respond to the public's most intense concerns.

In addition, strategic political actors differentiate public attitudes along two distinct dimensions—ideology and policy-specific preferences (Druckman and Jacobs 2006). When the public harbors strong concerns and intense preferences, policymakers tend to behave as "splitters"—they collect and respond to the public's preferences for or against specific policies (see Geer 1991, 1996; Heith 1998, 2003; Monroe 1979, 1998; Page and Shapiro 1983; Soroka and Wlezien 2005; Wlezien 2004).[2] When not facing intense concerns and strong preferences, government officials act like "lumpers" by collecting and using public opinion information to form summary judgments of the liberal or conservative contours of public opinion (Erikson, MacKuen, and Stimson 2002; Kingdon 1984, 68–69, 153). Under normal circumstances, for domestic issues (where the public often forms more intense views given its direct knowledge and experience) government officials are expected to focus on splitting. Conversely, foreign policy is considered more distant and less directly apparent in the public's daily lives and lumping is viewed as a more acceptable practice as a result (Druckman and Jacobs 2006; Wlezien 2004).

Recent research on segmented representation across policy domains and dimensions of public attitudes poses five broad expectations in investigating political leadership and, specifically, President Reagan's positions on key issues. First, we expect political leaders to differentiate their approaches by relying on general ideological data on public attitudes in crafting their foreign policy positions (that is, lumping) and using policy-specific data in fashioning their domestic positions (that is, splitting). Second, we expect that the intense concerns of the affluent regarding specific economic issues will focus the attention of political leaders. Specifically, Republican leaders like President Reagan are expected to be acutely responsive to higher-income groups when fashioning his public position on taxes, government spending, and Social Security (for example, opposition to expanding or even maintaining Social Security). Third, we expect community groups with strong social networks—mainly Baptists and Catholics for Republican leaders—to exert a disproportionately strong influence on Reagan's specific public positions on family values and crime. Fourth, we expect Reagan to be attentive to the domestic issue-specific policy preferences of political independents. Finally, we expect general conservatism to have a strong impact on Reagan's public positions on defense spending (where lumping and ideology play a larger role).

Data and Methods

We test our expectations with a unique body of evidence: President Ronald Reagan's extensive private data on public opinion during his tenure in office, from 1981 to 1989. Although focusing on a single president raises questions about generalizability (that is, from Reagan to politicians more generally), the use of targeted empirical research to generate broader theoretical insights has a distinguished tradition (for example, Conover and Sigelman 1982; Miller and Stokes 1963; Riker 1996). The main advantage of the Reagan White House's polling data is that it provides unparalleled access to actual political decisions about the collection and use of distinct types of public opinion information. Virtually all prior research on public opinion and political action (for example, Cohen 1997; Wlezien 2004), as well as previous analysis of the disproportionate government responsiveness to the economically affluent (Bartels 2005; Gilens 2005; Jacobs and Page 2005), relies on publicly available polls from survey organizations or other secondary sources. This approach lacks direct evidence regarding whether or what kind of public opinion information that government officials actually track or use.

Is there a consistent and systematic relationship between the public policy statements of politicians (Reagan, in our case) and their (that is Reagan's) private polling data on distinct policy domains and electoral subgroups? Research using case studies of various administrations, policy areas, and pressure groups suggests that such a relationship exists (for example, Beard 1913; McConnell 1966; Mills 1959; Schattschneider 1960). Although this work offers valuable insights about the disproportionate influence of distinct groups on government policymaking, case studies cannot detect general patterns of influence. We search for these patterns of influence by studying the relationship of Reagan's White House polling and his specific policy statements. In particular, we use two datasets to investigate the extent and nature of the association between a president's polling information on the core policy concerns of distinct electoral subgroups and the president's public statements on those policy issues; these datasets are Reagan's privately collected polling data and a systematic content analysis of the president's public statements on policy issues.

Public Opinion Data

The Reagan White House developed two distinctive sets of polling questions to track the public's opinions. First, it relied on an item that asked respondents to report their ideological self-identification, producing a percentage who declared themselves conservative. We label this measure the Public's Ideological Identification, with higher scores representing the conservative end of the scale.[3] For example, this measure might report that, at a given point in time, 60 percent of the voters view themselves as ideologically conservative.

The White House's ideological self-identification data provide an appropriate independent variable for the lumper account. While this measure differs from other lumping measures—such as James Stimson's (1991) "public mood" that aggregates over numerous policy areas—the critical point is that archival records show that Reagan treated the data as measuring the public's ideological orientation (see Druckman and Jacobs 2005).

The second set of data from the White House polling measures public opinion toward specific policies (for example, particular positions on Social Security, taxes, defense spending). What we label the Public's Policy Opinions serve as the relevant independent variable for the splitter account. The Public's Policy Opinions items report the percentage of the public holding the conservative position on the given policy proposal (running from 0 percent through 100 percent).[4] For example, this measure might report that 40 percent of voters take a conservative position on taxes. Another of these measures might show that 70 percent report conservative positions on defense spending.

Given our focus on government attention to discrete electoral subgroups, we also used the data on the policy preferences of four distinct segments of voters: party identifiers/nonidentifiers (Democrats, Republicans, and independents who did not identify with either major party), high-income earners,[5] born-again Protestants or fundamental Baptists, and Catholics. (Some of these subgroups—such as Republican identifiers—may reflect the general attitudes associated with conservative mood as described by the lumper account.) These data report the percentage of the particular subgroup taking a conservative position on a given issue—such as 80 percent of Baptists taking a conservative position on crime.

Although the measurement of these subgroup categories is neither consistent nor necessarily comparable with contemporary social science research standards, the White House clearly treated information about these subgroups as valid and politically important (see Druckman and Jacobs 2005). More specifically, we collected the White House's data on the preferences of subgroups toward policy issues that align with its interests and values. For instance, we assembled White House data on the preferences of high-income earners toward lower taxes, less government spending, and Social Security reform.

Politician Behavior Data

We measure behavior by analyzing Reagan's public statements—what we call Presidential Policy Positions.[6] Modern presidents carefully calibrate their public statements to signal their policy positions to congressional committees, interest groups, and voters (Cohen 1997; Riker 1996). In terms of the Reagan White House, the president and his senior advisers crafted the president's public statements to communicate specific messages to the country and to rally public support (see Druckman and Jacobs 2005; Jacobs 2005).

Our specific measure comes from a rigorous content analysis of Reagan's statements on the full range of domestic and foreign policy issues in all news conferences and addresses to the nation as well as a random selection of 50 percent of other oral and written statements.[7] The president's statements were retrieved from the *Public Papers of the Presidents of the United States* and the *Weekly Compilation of Presidential Documents*. Our unit of analysis was each distinct public utterance by the president regarding a specific policy. For each document in the *Public Papers* or the *Weekly Compilation* that we analyzed, we first coded whether Reagan addressed a substantive policy issue (for example, increased defense spending, support for family values, or support for cracking down on crime). We categorized each of Reagan's substantive policy statements as referring to one of 229 particular policy issues, which constitute the universe of distinctive issues that the president addressed throughout his term.

In addition to coding the policy issue that Reagan addressed, we coded the date of the comments and the number of lines of text devoted to the issue. We also coded the ideological direction of each policy statements on a scale of 1 to 5: higher scores indicate increasing conservativeness (that is, policy statements favoring less government responsibility and activity) and lower scores represent liberalism (statements indicating greater government involvement). When necessary, to determine the conservative direction of a proposal, we consulted contemporary accounts in the *New York Times* and the *Washington Post* as well as memoirs and other historical analyses. We carefully assessed the content analysis and found it highly reliable (that is, nearly 75 percent agreement among independent coders).[8]

We collapsed Reagan's statement data by merging the hundreds of distinct issues that the president addressed into a smaller set of aggregated (but substantively related) clusters of ninety-eight policy areas. For some of our analyses, we further aggregated data into domestic issues and foreign policy issues.[9]

Analysis of Public Opinion and Politician Behavior

Our expectation is that the president's policy statements will be significantly and positively related to data on the Public's Ideological Identification, the Public's Policy Opinions, and subgroup policy-specific preferences. To analyze the data, we create monthly aggregated measures of each of the variables. For each month for which data were available, we created measures of Presidential Policy Positions, measures of the Public's Ideological Identification, measures of the Public's Policy Opinions, and the policy preferences of the key subgroups for each of the merged ninety-eight policy areas.[10] As mentioned, we coded all variables so that higher values indicated congruent movements in a conservative direction. Because of the directional nature of the analyses, we exclude issues on which positions could not clearly be classified in a conservative-liberal direction.

We potentially have a substantial number of observations. Reagan could have discussed ninety-eight issues over the course of ninety-seven months from January 1981 to December 1988, which totals 9,506 observations. In practice, however, Reagan did not make a statement on every issue in every month; he made a total of 3,261 statements on different polices in the given months. In addition, Reagan did not collect public opinion data on every issue over time. Our analysis depends on the availability of relevant public-opinion data before the president's statement (that is, we can only analyze the relationship between statements and public opinion data when the public opinion data exist).[11]

We deal with the time-line aspect of our data in several ways. First, in all our analyses, we include a lagged value of our dependent variable, Presidential Policy Positions. We expect a strong positive relationship between prior and present Presidential Policy Positions given the incremental nature of policy movement (Erikson, MacKuen, and Stimson 2002, 285). Including a lagged dependent variable provides a tough test of our models: it serves as a control for various other influences that may have affected the prior position of presidents (for example, interest-group activities).

Second, we use lagged versions of the Public's Ideological Identification, the Public's Policy Opinions data, and the subgroup policy-preference data so as to reflect the White House's operations and decision-making process. This lag captures the time that it took for the survey organizations to enter and analyze their results, and for the White House to weigh the results and incorporate them into presidential activities. White House records and other evidence (such as memoirs and diaries) suggest that Reagan used the previous set of results—even if this meant going back in time. Accordingly, our lagged variables used the most recent data completed at least one month earlier, though most of the data were quite timely.[12] For instance, we related Reagan's policy statements on increasing defense spending in April 1982 to his polling data in March 1982 or, if data were not available in March 1982, in the previous month for which data were available.[13]

Empirical Analyses

Our quantitative analysis proceeds in three steps. First, we begin by examining what types of public opinion data that the Reagan White House collected. Second, we test whether the White House engages in splitting or lumping, with all else constant. Third, we explore whether and how political independents and conservative subgroups impacted his public statements.

Strategic Investments in Information

The White House recognized that space on survey instruments was limited and that collecting and processing data imposed substantial financial and organizational costs on the time and attention of its staff, senior officials, and the president. These costs in conjunction with strategic considerations motivated the White House to calibrate its collection of the Public's Policy Opinions data that required a distinct question for each issue. (This contrasts with the much cheaper Public's Ideological Identification data, which was simply one self-identification ideology question on the survey.) Also, given the potentially large number of demographic, political, and other subgroups, the White House carefully pinpointed certain components of the electorate as especially important strategically and worthy of investment in terms of tracking them.

The White House took a dynamic approach in selecting the domestic and international issues to track in its polling. Rather than asking about the same set of policy issues, Reagan's advisers added and dropped issues in reaction to new events, public concerns, and anticipation of future administration policy and action. Consistent with our earlier expectations about the direct relevance of domestic policy, the White House committed 65 percent of its polling on issues to domestic policy as opposed to foreign policy.[14] Moreover, the attention to individual areas of domestic and foreign policy varied over time, receiving more or less polling depending on events, public concerns, and administration policy development.

The White House devoted particular attention to tracking the reactions of critical segments of the electorate.[15] On domestic issues which presumably have particular relevance to these segments, 71 percent of the White House's polling results broke out the findings for independents, the affluent, Baptists, and Catholics. Specifically, it broke out results for different income groups 46 percent of the time, with 34 percent of these devoted to core economic issues that would be most relevant to income earning—taxes, government spending, and Social Security reform. Of particular interest, the White House concentrated its polling on detecting the views of the highest income earners on these issues: 84 percent of polling on core economic issues, which provided data by income, included specific data from the affluent.

In addition, on domestic issues, the White House broke out results for Baptists and Catholics 53 percent of the time. Fifteen percent of these data were on the social conservative issues of family values and crime that might of particular interest to these subgroups. Finally, across both domestic and foreign policy domains, the White House collected data on the specific views of political-base Republicans 65 percent of the time. In tracking public thinking on defense spending, it broke data down by Republicans 99 percent of the time.

Policy Domain and the Public's Ideological and Policy Attitudes

We now explore how Reagan used these datasets in crafting his policy position statements. In all of the following analyses, we include subgroup opinion data selectively. In part this is due to the methodological reality that, as explained, Reagan did not break out opinion data by subgroup across all issues. Instead, he collected subgroup data only in areas where there was a presumed need to attend to these opinions. Thus, we cannot include many subgroups without substantially reducing the number of our observations. More important, however, substantively it is sensible to include the subgroups that Reagan clearly was prioritizing in certain areas. This is one of the advantages of using private polling data—we know these were the data being used in fashioning responses.

We begin our analyses by looking at the relative impact of the Ideological Identification and the Public's Policy Opinions data on domestic and foreign policy statements. Recall that we earlier suggested that Reagan will rely on Ideological Identification when it comes to foreign policy (which is more distant to the public) and the Public's Policy Opinions on domestic issues. Table 6.1 reports the regression results, for domestic and foreign policy, of Presidential Policy Positions on the Public's Policy Opinions and the Public's Ideological Identification, which the White House possessed. Both variables report the percentage of respondents moving in a conservative direction standardized on scales of 0 to 1. As mentioned, we also include lagged Presidential Policy Positions to capture the incremental nature of policy movement. (The number of cases in all our analyses varies based on the missing lag values for the dependent variable as well as the smaller number of cases for particular policy areas.)[16]

Table 6.1 reveals the predicted domain effect. The Public's Policy Opinions drove Reagan's statements on domestic policy ($p \leq .05$) and exerted no statistically significant effects on his foreign policy comments.[17] In contrast, the Public's Ideological Identification influences Reagan's foreign policy comments ($p \leq .05$) but not his domestic statements. These results seem to suggest that Reagan was playing to his partisan and philosophically conservative base on the Cold War and building a strong defense as the best approach to securing peace. Moreover, the significant and strong effects of the lagged dependent variables suggest that Reagan's foreign and domestic policy positions tended to "lock

Table 6.1   Impact of Public Opinion Data on Domestic or Foreign Policy Positions (Domain Effect Model)

Independent Variables	Dependent Variable: Presidential Policy Positions	
	Domestic Policy	Foreign Policy
Public's Ideological Identification	−.07	3.39**
	(1.08)	(1.55)
Public's Policy Opinions	1.13**	−.16
	(.14)	(.21)
Presidential Policy Positions, $t–1$	.73**	.76**
	(.02)	(.02)
Constant	.44	−1.13
	(.65)	(.93)
R^2	.68	.58
N	1,339	716

Source: Authors' compilation.
Note: OLS coefficients, standard errors in parentheses.
**$p \le .05$, *$p \le .10$, one-tailed test.

in" once he had staked them out publicly. Put simply, he stuck with what he said. In terms of substantive impact, if the public moves 10 percent over the average conservativeness score, Reagan becomes about 8.5 percent more conservative in his statements on foreign policy (as measured by the Clarify program; see King, Tomz, and Wittenberg 2000). By comparison, when the public changes 10 percent over the average Policy Opinions score, Reagan becomes about 4 percent more conservative in his domestic policy statements.

The findings for Reagan suggest a bifurcated approach to how he used his polling information: he turned to disaggregated information on domestic issues on which voters had more knowledge and direct experience, while he relied on aggregated, ideological data on foreign affairs. Political and strategic calculations appear to have conditioned the use of different types of polling information across policy domains: under normal circumstances, electoral risks and rewards are more intense and direct in domestic affairs than in foreign affairs, increasing the political incentives to track and respond to the public's specific policy preference in particular.

The Impact of Subgroups

The next logical question is whether the White House further segmented its responsiveness, particularly on domestic issues that were important to

Table 6.2   Impact of Policy Preferences of Independents on Domestic Policy Positions

Independent Variables	Dependent Variable: Presidential Policy Positions on Domestic Policy
Public's Ideological Identification	−.14
	(1.18)
Public's Policy Opinions	.68**
	(.23)
Policy Opinions of Independents	1.60**
	(.22)
Presidential Policy Positions, $t-1$	.56**
	(.03)
Constant	.49
	(.71)
R^2	.74
N	847

Source: Authors' compilation.
Note: OLS coefficients, standard errors in parentheses.
**$p \leq .05$, *$p \leq .10$, one-tailed test.

subgroups that were targeted as essential to building a new Republican majority. With the erosion of the Democrat's New Deal Coalition and the rise of political independents, Republican leaders paid particular attention to these relatively unattached voters in the hopes of recruiting them. To investigate this, we regressed Presidential Policy Positions regarding domestic issues on the White House's polling data on the Public's Policy Opinions, the Public's Ideological Identification, and the Policy Opinions of Independents (as well Presidential Policy Positions lagged).[18] The Policy Opinions of Independents variable is also measured on a scale of 0 to 1, and reflects the percentage of independents who held a conservative position on a given issue. (In other words, it is the same as the Public's Policy Opinions but includes only independents.)[19]

Our analysis finds evidence of notable effects by political independents on Reagan's domestic positions. Table 6.2 suggests that specific policy preferences are statistically significant, and that the Public's Ideological Identification is not. In particular, the policy preferences of independents were substantially stronger than the policy preferences of the general public—evidence of the White House's attentiveness to this critical segment of the electorate. A key emphasis to note is that the effects of independents emerge even after controlling for the Public's Policy Opinions and the Public's Ideological Identification.

Table 6.3   **Impact of Policy Preferences of High-Income Americans on Economic Policy Positions**

Independent Variables	Dependent Variable: Social Security Reform, Taxes, and Government Spending
Public's Ideological Identification	−.45
	(1.58)
Public's Policy Opinions	.70**
	(.38)
Policy Opinions of Higher Income Americans	4.06**
	(.85)
Presidential Policy Positions, $t-1$	.50**
	(.07)
Constant	−.79
	(1.06)
R^2	.84
N	173

Source: Authors' compilation.
Note: OLS coefficients, standard errors in parentheses.
**$p \leq .05$, *$p \leq .10$, one-tailed test.

The White House devoted particular attention to broadening the Republican Party's conservative coalition. If this effort were systematic, we would expect evidence that the policy preferences of economic, social, and military conservatives had a significant impact on Reagan's statements on issues of particular concern to each of these factions. The affluent have been principal supporters of the modern Republican Party. We would therefore expect the Reagan White House to demonstrate efforts to lock down their continued support. To investigate this possibility, we regressed Presidential Policy Positions on issues of intense interest to high-income Americans (lower taxes, less government spending, and reforming Social Security) on the Public's Policy Opinions, the Public's Ideological Identification, and the Policy Opinions of the affluent (as well a lagged measure of Presidential Policy Positions on core economic issues).[20]

Table 6.3 presents evidence confirming the striking impact of another segment of the electorate—high-income earners. The Public's Ideological Identification is not statistically significant; the White House did not tailor Reagan's public comments on core economic issues to an overriding conservatism among Americans. Instead, Reagan's public statements on core economic policy were driven by the Public's Policy Opinions on these issues but much more strongly by the views of the most

Table 6.4   Impact of the Policy Preferences of Baptists and Catholics on Social-Conservative Policy Positions

Independent Variables	Dependent Variable: Family Values and Crime
Public's Ideological Identification	−.10
	(.53)
Public's Policy Opinions	−.24
	(.20)
Policy Opinions of Baptists	1.38*
	(.85)
Policy Opinions of Catholics	−.27
	(.70)
Presidential Policy Positions, $t-1$	−.11
	(.10)
Constant	4.78**
R^2	.07
N	104

Source: Authors' compilation.
Note: OLS coefficients, standard errors in parentheses.
**$p \leq .05$, *$p \leq .10$, one-tailed test.

affluent. In other words, the impact of the wealthy registered far above whatever impact of the general public's policy preferences and ideological orientations.

One of the most important new groups that the Reagan White House targeted for recruitment to the conservative Republican coalition were social conservatives—namely, Baptists and Catholics who harbored strong views about family values and a law-and-order approach to crime. Table 6.4, which presents regressions on these issues and includes the Policy Opinions of Baptists and Catholics, indicates that Reagan did not systematically tailor his comments on social-conservative policies to Catholics.[21] However, the social-conservative policy preferences of Baptists registered as an important influence on Reagan's statements and were in fact the only statistically significant force in shaping Reagan's public comments on these policy issues. Of particular note, Reagan appeared to be adopting new positions in response to Baptist preferences; the statistical insignificance of the lagged dependent variable suggests that his previous positions did not "lock in" his comments. This evidence demonstrates that Reagan's White House worked hard to update Republican policy stances to target and expand its conservative base.

One of the Reagan administration's most dramatic policy changes was to substantially increase defense spending. Our earlier analysis sug-

Table 6.5   Impact of Policy Preferences of Republicans on Defense-Spending Policy Positions

Independent Variables	Dependent Variable: Increased Defense Spending
Public's Ideological Identification	3.31*
	(2.11)
Public's Policy Opinions	−.32
	(.43)
Policy Opinions of Republicans	5.00**
	(1.74)
Policy Opinions of Independents	−3.88**
	(1.51)
Policy Opinions of Democrats	−2.06*
	(1.29)
Presidential Policy Positions, $t-1$	−.03
	(.10)
Constant	3.15**
	(1.57)
R^2	.15
N	90

Source: Authors' compilation.
Note: OLS coefficients, standard errors in parentheses.
**$p \leq .05$, *$p \leq .10$, one-tailed test.

gests that the White House pursued a lumping approach on matters of foreign policy and national security—namely, that it tended to rely on more general ideological and partisan polling results. Table 6.5 shows that Reagan's comments on defense spending were tailored to the views of Republicans, but not those of independents and Democrats (Reagan moves in a significantly contrary direction to independents and Democrats).[22] The results also show, not surprisingly, that the ideological mood of the electorate continued to influence defense-spending positions. In short, Reagan honed his public statements on defense spending to respond to partisans and conservatives, while in essence turning against other segments of the electorate.

Conclusion

In two significant respects, the findings of this chapter offer a pointed revision of the long-standing treatment of the president as serving the overall national interest. First, the president differentiates how he handles domestic and foreign policy, rather than pursuing a consistent approach based on some objective notion of the country's best interests. In particular, this study and other research (see Druckman and Jacobs 2006; Wlezien 2004) demonstrate that the president treats domestic and foreign policy differently, relying on discrete policy preferences to shape his domestic policy statements and on aggregate public mood in crafting his foreign policy positions.

Second, this chapter extends research on segmented representation by expanding on the set of forces that disproportionately influence government policy. These findings, in conjunction with previous research (Bartels 2005; Gilens 2005; Jacobs and Page 2005), demonstrate that government officials disproportionately respond to the preferences of the highest income earners. This challenges the tendency to associate political representation with strong government responsiveness to the general public (see, for example, Erikson, MacKuen, and Stimson 2002). In some respects, these findings should not be surprising; they are compatible with extensive and long-standing research about the asymmetrical distribution of resources among citizens, organizations, and groups, and the biasing effects that this distribution has on government policy (Beard 1913; McConnell 1966; Mills 1959; Schattschneider 1960). Moreover, this finding is also consistent with a new generation of research that links rising economic inequality with political disparities (American Political Science Association 2004; Bartels 2005, 2008; Gilens 2005; Jacobs and Page 2005; Jacobs and Skocpol 2005).

One of this chapter's key contributions is to identify noneconomic processes that generate disproportionate influence on government policy. In particular, Reagan's public policy positions were particularly shaped by political independents along with religious conservatives and base Republicans. The emergence of these political forces may indirectly or, in interaction with economic groups, serve as pathways by which rising economic inequality impacts government policy. This is an important topic for future research.

The Reagan White House's strategic use of its private polling on electorally significant subgroups played a notable role in reshaping contemporary American politics. Reagan's careful calibration of his public positions to reflect his subgroup polling contributed to the formation of a new and broader conservative coalition—one that widened its appeal from the affluent and philosophical conservatives to political independents and, most strikingly, religious conservatives. The result was a broader and more enduring coalition for future Republican presidential and congressional politicians.

More generally, presidents—like other politicians—attempt to advance their policy objectives (such as by appealing to distinct political subgroups) while minimizing the risk of alienating centrist opinion.

Presidents need to appeal to the median voter to deal with the electoral pressures that come with a national constituency as well as ensure the support of heterogeneous members of Congress. As a result, presidents will also engage, while appealing on particular issues to distinct subgroups, in crafted talk so that their policy proposals resonate with the median voter (Jacobs and Shapiro 2000). In using crafted talk and conveying particular personal images (Druckman, Jacobs, and Ostermeier 2004), presidents appeal to the median voter without touching on policy. Segmented representation combined with determined efforts to base political representation on personal image and crafted presentations raise serious questions about the possibility of the kind of responsive democracy that many accounts of popular sovereignty, including the median-voter theory, both predict and seek (Jacobs and Skocpol 2005).

We thank participants at the Conference on Homogeneity and Heterogeneity in Public Opinion, at Cornell University, and particularly the editors Peter Enns and Chris Wlezien, for helpful advice. We also acknowledge the valuable research assistance of Melanie Burns, Brian Falb, and Lauren Matecki.

Notes

1. The proportion that is independent includes both "independent independents" as well as respondents who indicated after declaring themselves as independent that they were "closer" to one party.
2. Although the "splitter" scholarly tradition shares a common focus on the specific policy preferences of citizens, there are variations in the data sources and the methodological approaches taken (for example, archival-based research of presidents and quantitative analyses that correlate published polls and government policy decisions).
3. The Ideological Identification measure has an overall mean of .60 and variance of .03.
4. The average conservative score for specific issues was .47, with a standard deviation of 0.22, for all issues; .44 for domestic issues with a standard deviation of 0.22; and .52 for foreign affairs, with a standard deviation of .20.
5. Reagan measured income in two ways. Sometimes he asked respondents to classify themselves as low, middle, or upper class. Other times, he asked respondents to report which of three earning categories applied to them (for example, under $15,000 a year). We combined these measures by splitting the three numeric responses into three income-level groups—one below $15,000, one between $15,000 and $30,000, and one above $30,000. This seemed like the most sensible way to reconcile the two measures because each question form offered three response categories. We therefore ordered and combined them from low to high.
6. Although this measure of political activity provides a direct indicator of a

critical strategic form of presidential behavior, it differs from those deployed in some past work (for example, Page and Shapiro 1983; Erikson, MacKuen, and Stimson 2002).

7. Oral statements include bill signings, addresses to the nation, press conferences, and speeches to interest groups, administration officials, state and local government officials, Republican Party leaders, and foreign nations. Written statements include messages to Congress, administration officials, foreign nations, interviews with domestic and foreign news media, proclamations, bill signings and vetoes, and press secretary releases.

8. One coder conducted the content analysis. Accordingly, our reliability analysis focused on external comparisons of lines of text that were coded in common; there was no need to examine intercoder reliability. A second coder who had not been involved in this project analyzed a sample of documents examined by the first coder. A third coder compared the analysis by the first two coders. Comparisons between the first coder and the second showed levels of agreement of 71 percent for identification of the specific policy issue addressed by Reagan. In terms of the directionality of presidential comments, the coders agreed that a policy statement was pro, neutral, or con on 85 percent of the statements by Reagan.

9. The average ideological direction of Reagan's domestic statements was 3.50 (with a standard deviation of 1.80), versus 3.46 (with a standard deviation of 1.80) for his foreign policy statements. The scores are based on a scale of 1 to 5, with $t_{2258} = 9.81$ and $p < .01$, and $t_{1434} = 11.98$ and $p < .01$, respectively. Note that these scores exclude the few issues that could not be classified in an ideological direction, such as position on outer-space exploration.

10. We created monthly aggregated scores by averaging White House polling items on similar issues across geographic areas (state and national) within the same month. Our decision to produce monthly aggregated averages was based on White House memoranda and other evidence in which the president and his aides concentrated on trends and patterns across a number of states and within the nation as a whole. We also took average monthly scores for our Presidential Policy Positions measure; results are generally robust if we instead used weighted averages (that is, weighted by space of the statement).

11. We do not impute missing values in any of our analyses. Our decision was based on an examination of archival evidence suggesting that presidents and their aides did not try to impute missing data, and thus any such imputed data cannot be expected to impact presidential behavior.

12. The interval between presidential statements and prior polling data was generally brief. Details are available from the authors.

13. Our focus on how White House polls influenced subsequent presidential behavior follows how they in fact used the polling data. The White House repeatedly emphasized that the purpose of its polls was to analyze public opinion to form policy and political decisions. In short, they were responding to the polls and not using the polls to systematically measure their effect on public opinion. Although we do not deny the possibility of a reciprocal process (see Hurley and Hill 2003; Druckman and Holmes 2004), it is neither our focus nor how Reagan primarily viewed the polls.

14. All the data reported in this section focus on issues for which an ideological direction could be classified and the availability of data before Reagan actually made a statement. It does not include data collected but not used in fashioning statements. The statistics in this section refer to the most recently available data, which are at least one month old.

15. The number of separate poll results for the subgroups discussed here may differ from the number of observations in later regression analyses; the addition of variables may reduce the number of cases.

16. We do not include policy dummy variables because our Public's Policy Opinions data change over time very slowly or not at all. In this situation, to ensure analysis of between-unit effects, it is preferable not to use policy dummies (see Beck 2001, 285). Also, for all analyses, we checked whether collinearity was a problem; unless otherwise noted, we found it not to be a problem.

17. Because the hypotheses posit directional predictions, we use one-tailed tests (see Blalock 1979, 163).

18. We analyzed the impact of independents on domestic issues generally on the assumption that independents, who typically are less well-informed and interested in politics than partisans and other identifiable political groups, would focus on policies that were closer to their daily lives. Indeed, our findings from analyses of foreign policy reveal no significant impacts by independents.

    Additionally, archival evidence makes it clear that, when it came to domestic issues, Reagan focuses specifically on the opinions of independents, paying scant attention to other subgroups, including Democratic and Republican segments. This also is evident in his decisions regarding data collection (Druckman and Jacobs 2006). Indeed, as mentioned, for much of the data that we analyzed, the segmented opinions of both Democrats and Republicans are not available in the data (that is, Reagan did not provide data on these subsamples). If we nonetheless analyze the subsample of domestic issues for which all types of segmented partisan opinions are available, the opinions of independents continue to exhibit a significant and positive effect. (We can do this in the case of domestic issues because the number of observations remains reasonable; on the other specific issues, however, including additional subgroups would have too dramatic an effect on the number of observations.)

19. Our subgroup measures do not face the scale issues identified in chapter 8 of this volume because we do not multiply our measures by the percentage of respondents in each subgroup. Further, while there is undoubtedly measurement error in the public opinion measures, this is not a problem per se for us insofar as we are interested in how Reagan reacted to the data that he saw (which is what we have).

20. As was the case with the data on domestic issues more generally, archival evidence makes clear that targeted strategic decisions drove data-collections decisions. In the case of the economic issues that we analyze here, little data on middle- and lower-income groups were collected. This reflects the White House's strategic decision to use these economic issues to target the more affluent. It also implies that the White House could not di-

rectly respond to other economic groups since they did not explicitly gauge their opinions.

21. We do not include separate variables for other religious affiliations because Reagan rarely collected such data for other groups, especially in relation to family values and crime, again reflecting the aforementioned strategy to target specific groups.

22. We are able to include separate variables for each partisan group here because Reagan collected such data for all questions on defense spending. (The collection of the data suggests that Reagan was attending to all partisan groups to some extent.) The opinions of the three partisan subgroups do significantly correlate. If we exclude the Democratic variable from the regression, our results stand; however, if we exclude the Republican variable, that impacts of the independents and the Democrats are no longer significant. The most important implication of these results is that our result for Republicans does not change, regardless of which variables we include.

References

Aldrich, John H. 1995. *Why Parties? The Origin and Transformation of Political Parties in America.* Chicago: University of Chicago Press.

American Political Science Association, Task Force on Inequality and American Democracy. 2004. "Governance and Inequality." Available at http://www.apsanet.org/imgtest/governancememo.pdf.

Bachrach, Peter, and Morton Baratz. 1962. "Two Faces of Power." *American Political Science Review* 56(4): 947–52.

Bartels, Larry M. 1991. "Constituency Opinion and Congressional Policy Making: The Reagan Defense Buildup." *American Political Science Review* 85(2): 457–74.

———. 2005. "Economic Inequality and Political Representation." Revised paper presented at the Annual Meeting of the American Political Science Association. Boston. (August 2002).

———. 2008. *Unequal Democracy: The Political Economy of the New Gilded Age.* Princeton, N.J.: Princeton University Press.

Beard, Charles. 1913. *An Economic Interpretation of the Constitution of the United States.* Toronto: Collier-Macmillan Canada.

Beck, Nathaniel. 2001. "Time-Series-Cross Section Data: What Have We Learned in the Past Few Years?" *Annual Review of Political Science* 4:271–93.

Blalock, Hubert M., Jr. 1979. *Social Statistics*, 2nd ed. New York: McGraw-Hill.

Cohen, Jeffrey E. 1997. *Presidential Responsiveness and Public Policy Making.* Ann Arbor: University of Michigan Press.

Conover, Pamela Johnston, and Lee Sigelman. 1982. "Presidential Influence and Public Opinion: The Case of the Iranian Hostage Crisis." *Social Science Quarterly* 63(2): 249–64.

DeRouen, Karl. 2000. "Presidents and the Diversionary Use of Force." *International Studies Quarterly* 44(2): 317–28.

Druckman, James N., and Justin W. Holmes. 2004. "Does Presidential Rhetoric

Matter? Priming and Presidential Approval." *Presidential Studies Quarterly* 34(4): 755–78.

Druckman, James N., and Lawrence R. Jacobs. 2005. "Political Motivations, Information Gains, and Presidential Polling: The Nixon and Reagan White Houses." Paper presented at the sixth annual meeting of the Midwest Political Science Association. Chicago (April 20–23, 2005).

———. 2006. "Lumpers and Splitters: The Public Opinion Information that Politicians Collect and Use." *Public Opinion Quarterly* 70(4): 453–76.

Druckman, James N., Lawrence R. Jacobs, and Eric Ostermeier. 2004. "Candidate Strategies to Prime Issues and Image." *Journal of Politics* 66(4): 1205–27.

Edsall, Thomas Bryne, and Mary D. Edsall. 1991. *Chain Reaction: The Impact of Race, Rights, and Taxes on American Politics*. New York: W. W. Norton

Erikson, Robert S., Michael B. MacKuen, and James A. Stimson. 2002. *The Macro Polity*. New York: Cambridge University Press.

Erikson, Robert S., Gerald C. Wright, and John P. McIver. 1993. *Statehouse Democracy: Public Opinion and Policy in the American States*. New York: Cambridge University Press.

Foyle, Douglas C. 1999. *Counting the Public In*. New York: Columbia University Press.

Geer, John G. 1991. "Critical Realignments and the Public Opinion Poll." *Journal of Politics* 53(2): 434–53.

———. 1996. *From Tea Leaves to Opinion Polls*. New York: Columbia University Press.

Gilens, Martin. 2005. "Inequality and Democratic Responsiveness." *Public Opinion Quarterly* 69(5): 778–96.

Heith, Diane. 1998. "Staffing the White House Public Opinion Apparatus: 1969–1988." *Public Opinion Quarterly* 62(1): 165–89.

———. 2003. *Polling to Govern: Public Opinion and Presidential Leadership*. Palo Alto, Calif.: Stanford University Press.

Hurley, Patricia A., and Kim Quaile Hill. 2003. "Beyond the Demand-Input Model: A Theory of Representational Linkages." *The Journal of Politics* 65(2): 304–26.

Jacobs, Lawrence R. 2005. "Communicating from the White House: From Mass Communications to Specialized Constituencies." In *Presidents and Bureaucrats: The Executive Branch and American Democracy*, edited by Joel Aberbach and Mark Peterson. New York: Oxford University Press.

Jacobs, Lawrence R., and Melanie Burns. 2004. "The Second Face of the Public Presidency: Presidential Polling and the Shift from Policy to Personality Polling." *Presidential Studies Quarterly* 34(3): 536–56.

Jacobs, Lawrence R., and Benjamin I. Page. 2005. "Who Influences U.S. Foreign Policy?" *American Political Science Review* 99(1): 107–23.

Jacobs, Lawrence R., and Robert Y. Shapiro. 2000. *Politicians Don't Pander: Political Manipulation and the Loss of Democratic Responsiveness*. Chicago: University of Chicago Press.

Jacobs, Lawrence R., and Theda Skocpol, eds. 2005. *Inequality and American Democracy: What We Know and What We Need to Learn*. New York: Russell Sage Foundation.

King, Gary, Michael Tomz, and Jason Wittenberg. 2000. "Making the Most of Statistical Analyses: Improving Interpretation and Presentation." *American Journal of Political Science* 44(2): 347–61.

Kingdon, John W. 1984. *Agendas, Alternatives, and Public Policies*. Boston: Little, Brown.

Manza, Jeff, Fay Lomax Cook, and Benjamin Page. 2002. *Navigating Public Opinion: Polls, Policy, and the Future of American Democracy*. New York: Oxford University Press.

McConnell, Grant. 1966. *Private Power and American Democracy*. New York: Alfred A. Knopf.

Miller, Warren E., and Donald E. Stokes. 1963. "Constituency Influence in Congress." *American Political Science Review* 57(1): 45–56.

Mills, C. Wright. 1959. *The Power Elite*. New York: Oxford University Press.

Monroe, Alan D. 1979. "Consistency Between Policy Preferences and National Policy Decisions." *American Politics Quarterly* 7(1): 3–18.

———. 1998. "Public Opinion and Public Policy, 1980–1993." *Public Opinion Quarterly* 62(1): 6–28.

Nincic, Miroslav. 1990. "U.S. Soviet Policy and the Electoral Connection." *World Politics* 42(3): 370–96.

Ostrom, Charles, Jr., and Brian Job. 1986. "The President and the Political Use of Force." *American Political Science Review* 80(2): 541–66.

Page, Benjamin I., and Robert Y. Shapiro. 1983. "Effects of Public Opinion on Policy." *American Political Science Review* 77(1): 175–90.

Pitkin, Hanna F. 1967. *The Concept of Representation*. Berkeley: University of California Press.

Riker, William H. 1996. *The Strategy of Rhetoric: Campaigning for the American Constitution*, edited by Randall L. Calvert, John E. Mueller, and Rick K. Wilson. New Haven, Conn.: Yale University Press.

Schattschneider, Elmer E. 1960. *The Semisovereign People: A Realist's View of Democracy in America*. New York: Holt, Rinehart and Winston.

Soroka, Stuart N., and Christopher Wlezien. 2005. "Opinion-Policy Dynamics: Public Preferences and Public Expenditure in the United Kingdom." *British Journal of Political Science* 35(4): 665–89.

Stimson, James A. 1991. *Public Opinion in America: Moods, Cycles, and Swings*, 2nd ed. Boulder, Colo.: Westview Press.

Verba, Sidney, Kay Lehman Schlozman, and Henry E. Brady. 1995. *Voice and Equality: Civic Voluntarism in American Politics*. Cambridge, Mass.: Harvard University Press.

Weissberg, Robert. 1978. "Collective vs. Dynamic Representation in Congress." *American Political Science Review* 72(2): 535–47.

Wildavsky, Aaron. 1994a. "The Two Presidencies." In *The Beleaguered Presidency*, edited by Aaron Wildavsky. New Brunswick, N.J.: Transaction Press.

———. 1994b. "The Two Presidencies Thesis Revisited." In *The Beleaguered Presidency*, edited by Aaron Wildavsky. New Brunswick, N.J.: Transaction Press.

Wlezien, Christopher. 2004. "Patterns of Representation: Dynamics of Public Preferences and Policy." *Journal of Politics* 66(1): 1–24.

Chapter 7

Whose Statehouse Democracy? Policy Responsiveness to Poor Versus Rich Constituents in Poor Versus Rich States

ELIZABETH RIGBY AND GERALD C. WRIGHT

POLICYMAKING IN A representative democracy requires elected officials to align their policy priorities and choices with the preferences of their constituents. Efforts to test this normative assumption have often identified a strong relationship between average public opinion (or changes in average public opinion) and the political behavior of elected representatives (Erikson, MacKuen, and Stimson 2002; Erikson and Wright 1980, 2005; Erikson, Wright, and McIver 1993; Miller and Stokes 1963; Soroka and Wlezien 2010). Yet, because these studies tend to measure opinion in the aggregate, they do not test another normative foundation of representation: equality of political representation even in the face of differences in resources and other forms of power among constituents (Dahl 1971; Walzer 1983). In other words, most studies fail to ask whether elected officials are as responsive to the opinions of the disadvantaged as to those of the advantaged. The chapters in this book redress this imbalance.

In a society with high rates of income inequality, such as the United States, it is reasonable to be concerned that power imbalances in the economic domain will reproduce themselves within the policymaking process (Jacobs and Skocpol 2005). Recent research has fueled this concern by identifying patterns of differential responsiveness that show the opinions of the wealthy matter more than the opinions of the poor (Bartels 2008; Gilens 2005). For example, Larry Bartels's analysis (2008) of roll-call voting in the U.S. Senate suggests that senators pay more attention to wealthier constituents but ignore the poorest. Similarly, Martin Gilens (2005; see also chapter 9, this volume) has found little correlation between the policy preferences of low-income voters and the policies that Congress enacts. These authors also show that policy is more responsive to those with high incomes than to those in the middle, which is important given the theoretical primacy of the median voter (see also Enns and Wlezien, chapter 1, this volume). If substantiated by further research, these findings pose serious normative challenge to the legitimacy of democracy in this country—at least to the extent that it rests on notions of political equality.

In this chapter, we extend this line of inquiry to the state level—asking whether the differential responsiveness documented at the federal level is mirrored in state politics, as well as whether the level of differential responsiveness varies among states. Despite their important status in American politics, the role of states is often ignored by researchers examining national survey data. The tendency is to treat individual behavior solely as a function of attitudinal and socioeconomic variables, often with little regard to the impact of social or political context. In fact, efforts to account for the geographic location of these individuals most often consist of fixed-effects models to absorb the acknowledged variation across states.

Consistent with Hopkins and Stoke (this volume), we believe that an important part of the story of American politics is lost by ignoring (or absorbing) the varied political contexts of the states in which citizens make decisions. In particular, the differences in both wealth and ideology across states have the potential to structure the class basis of political behavior in ways that influence responsiveness and political equality. In fact, the American Political Science Association Task Force on Inequality and American Democracy highlighted the potential for our system of federalism to "accept and accommodate economic and political inequalities within the separate states rather than challenge these disparities by establishing national uniform standards" (Bartels et al. 2005, 128). Additionally, Andrew Gelman and his colleagues (2007, 2008) identified a key role for state-level income in structuring individual-level vote choice in two distinct areas. First, as expected, in wealthier states, individuals were more likely to vote for the Democratic presidential candidate. But, more surprising, in wealthier states an individual's income had little effect on their vote choice. The opposite was found in poor states, in which individual-level income predicted vote choice much more reliably. Asking "What's the Matter with Connecticut?" these authors concluded that an individual's income matters more in poor states (Gelman et al. 2007). Here, we ask whether this translates into different levels of responsiveness to rich versus poor constituents across rich versus poor states.

In this chapter, we use data from a large national survey to estimate income-based differences in policy priorities—first averaged across states and then situating income groups within their distinct state contexts. Next, we examine the degree to which state policy choices align with the policy preferences of different income groups, as well as whether this varies between rich and poor states. As a result, we are able to address the degree to which patterns of differential responsiveness found at the national level play out in state politics, as well as identify any variation in these patterns across rich and poor states.

Background

Before turning to our empirical examination of policy responsiveness, we review other works examining the degree to which individuals' income shapes policy preferences, as well as how these patterns may vary across types of policy issues. We then discuss why this process may play out differently in poorer versus wealthier states.

Policy Preferences Across Income Groups

Although material resources as well as reliance on distinct types of governmental assistance vary substantially between the rich and the poor (Hacker 2002), there is reason to question the assumption that the rich and the poor want totally different things from government. For example, Yosef Bhatti and Robert Erikson (chapter 8, this volume) question Bartels's (2008) finding of differential responsiveness due to the similarity in ideological self-identification across income groups.[1] And both Joseph Ura and Christopher Ellis (2008) and Stuart Soroka and Christopher Wlezien (2008; chapter 10, this volume), using the General Social Surveys, found a great deal of similarity in preferences for increasing or decreasing spending across income groups. This led Soroka and Wlezien (2008) to conclude that this congruence places a healthy limit on the representation inequality that can occur, because even if the poor are ignored by their elected officials, they will still get what they want—to the degree that their preferences and interests overlap with better represented groups.[2] Bartels (2008) shows a similar congruence in opinion on the estate tax. Gilens (2005) acknowledged the same reality by restricting his analysis to only those policy issues on which the poor and the rich disagree.

Despite these findings, at least as many studies have identified significant differences in the policy preferences of different income groups. Notably, Gilens (2009) addressed the discrepancy between his findings of persistent differences in opinion across income groups and Soroka and Wlezien's (2008) finding of congruence. Through a series of replications and comparisons, he illustrated that the discrepancy is not due to the time period examined, differences in income-group definitions (cut-points), or the different modeling strategy used in each paper. Instead, he showed that the difference is attributable to differences in the range and type of policies considered—differences are much greater for foreign policy, health-care reform, and social or moral policy issues.

Acknowledging the very real difference in opinion between the rich and the poor in many areas is one thing, assessing the substantive significance of this difference is less clear. Plainly, income-based opinion differences do not represent stark class cleavages in which the vast majority of the poor prefer one policy and the vast majority of the rich oppose the same proposal. Yet there are reasons to not dismiss these moderately-sized income differences too quickly. Benjamin Page noted that studies dividing the electorate into a handful (usually three) of income groups are probably touching "only the tip of a very large iceberg [because] the 'rich' citizens in a standard sample survey are not very rich" (2009, 150). Given the rapid growth in income inequality driven by a few Americans at the very top of the income distribution, it is possible that the phenomenon of differential responsiveness to the wealthy is contained among a much more elite group than captured in such analyses of national survey data. In fact, Jeffrey Winters and Page (2008) argue that because the top tenth of 1 percent of wealth holders (fewer than half a million people) hold such concentrated wealth and power, they may have a dramatically disproportionate influence on American politics—so much so that they could be considered an oligarchy.

Income-Group Differences Across Policy Issues

Across studies identifying income-group differences in opinion (using a variety of data sources and analytic methods), a consistent pattern emerges. Specifically, wealthier individuals are less likely to support more liberal redistributive or spending programs (for example, increased spending for schools, reduced differences between rich and poor), but more likely to take liberal stands on social or moral issues, such as abortion, stem cell research, and gay rights (Ansolabehere, Rodden, and Snyder 2006; Bartels 2008; Flavin 2009; Gilens 2005, 2009). Based on the consistent finding that voters of all income groups prioritize economic issues over social issues when casting their votes (Ansolabehere, Rodden, and Snyder 2006; Bartels 2008; Gelman et al. 2008), many authors ignore this crosscutting pattern of policy liberalism. Others have argued that this secondary dimension of social issues still exerts an impact on political behavior (Frank 2004). Without resolving this debate, we can infer that these crosscutting policy preferences may help explain why we see so little differentiation in self-identified ideology between the rich and the poor (see, for example, Bhatti and Erikson, chapter 8, this volume) at the same time that we find substantial differences in their specific policy preferences (Gilens 2009, chapter 9, this volume).

Why State Wealth May Matter

As discussed earlier, Gelman and his colleagues (2007, 2008) have identified a key role for state-level income in structuring individual-level political behavior. Here, we ask whether this translates into different levels of responsiveness to richer versus poorer constituents across richer versus poorer states. State wealth may affect policy responsiveness in either of two distinct ways. First, it may alter the magnitude of differences in opinion across income groups. If individual-level income does not predict vote choice in a wealthy state, like Connecticut, it is also likely that low- and high-income residents of that state may hold similar policy preferences, at least on average. In this context, even highly skewed representation of only the very rich would produce policies congruent with the interests of all income groups. This point is well argued and illustrated (see Soroka and Wlezien 2008; Wlezien and Soroka, chapter 10, this volume; Bhatti and Erikson, chapter 8, this volume; Ura and Ellis 2008). Conversely, if individual-level income strongly predicts presidential voting patterns in poorer states, such as Mississippi, we can deduce that low- versus high-income residents of Mississippi hold distinct policy preferences as well—opening the door for the potential of unequal policy responsiveness. Alternatively, state wealth may not affect the preference gap between rich and poor, but instead could structure the process of representation in ways that heighten or lessen differential responsiveness. For example, in poorer states, income differences may be a more salient cleavage in state politics—serving to sort winners and losers of policy debates along income lines. A third possibility, of course, is that differential policy responsiveness varies across states because states vary on both income-based differences in opinion and income-based differences in representation.

Research Questions

Do income groups vary in economic and social policy preferences? If so, how big are the differences?

Does the magnitude of income-group differences in policy preferences vary with aggregate state income? In other words, does income predict policy liberalism more strongly in wealthy versus poor states?

Are state-level policy outcomes aligned with the interests of the wealthy more than the poor? Is this true for both economic and social policies? Is this true in both rich and poor states?

Data and Measurement

To estimate opinion across income groups, we took advantage of a recent national survey that captures campaign dynamics before each presidential election. The National Annenberg Election Survey (see Romer et al. 2006), which first collected data from 58,373 respondents during the 2000 presidential election, used a similar methodology for the 2004 election, gathering data from 81,422 respondents. The data collected include a large number of survey respondents from the forty-eight continental states, with all but five states having at least five hundred respondents across the two survey years.[3] The limitation of these data is that respondents were interviewed across a series of rolling, cross-sectional surveys in which different sets of (somewhat overlapping) questions were asked of each cross section. To generate measures of policy preferences across these surveys, we pooled the cross-sectional surveys for 2000 into one dataset and those from 2004 into a second dataset. For each of the two, we identified the common policy items in each survey. These included thirty items from the 2000 surveys and twenty-eight from the 2004 surveys—all asking the respondent's position on policy issues across a range of policy areas: economic issues, health and social welfare issues, social and moral issues, energy and environment, campaign finance, and legal and ethical issues. Yet because all respondents were not asked all questions, we imputed the missing data using multiple chained equations (see Royston 2005), which predicts responses based on preferences among questions that they were asked.

Because of this imputation, which maximized similarities in responses across items, these data are best suited to capturing a latent construct (for example, social policy liberalism) rather than precise views on a particular issue (such as the death penalty or abortion). Therefore, for each dataset, we factor analyzed subsets of items to generate two measures: economic policy liberalism and social policy liberalism for each survey (for a total of four scales). The specific items for each scale are shown in table 7.1. For the 2000 dataset, economic policy liberalism was generated from seven items relating to tax policy, health care, and social welfare programs. Similarly, we factor-analyzed six items tapping social policy issues, such as abortion, the death penalty, gay rights, and school prayer. For the 2004 dataset, we used six economic policy items similar to the ones asked in 2000 plus one that asked about funding for K through 12 education. We estimated social policy liberalism using six other items from the 2004 survey that captured views on gay marriage and gun control as well as similar aspects of the abortion and stem cell issues asked about in the 2000 survey.

All four factor models explained the vast majority of the variance among items (at least 97 percent of the variation) in the first factor (eigenvalues ranged from 1.58 to 3.22, with eigenvalues for the second factors remaining below .50).[4] Table 7.2 presents descriptive statistics for the economic and social measures of policy liberalism in 2000 and 2004 for both the individual level of analysis and the state level. Although all four measures are standardized (M = 0, standard deviation = 1), we still find different distributions among the measures at each level. In particular, at the individual level, we find a greater range of opinions on economic policy issues than on social policy issues. Yet when considering averages among the states, we find more variation in social policy issues than in economic policy issues.

To reliably estimate the policy liberalism of different income groups across states, we needed to collapse the nine-category income variable used by the Annenberg survey into fewer categories. To retain large sample sizes within each state, we divided the full sample into three groups: low (those with family incomes of less than $35,000), middle (family incomes between $35,000 and $75,000), and high (above $75,000).[5] We used these income cut-points to estimate the average policy liberalism of low-, middle-, and high-income residents of each state. Table 7.2 also includes descriptive statistics on each of the four opinion measures by sample income terciles.

The other data that we use in this chapter are measures of state policy outcomes on economic and social policies. As much as possible, we identified policy indicators that aligned with the Annenberg survey items that we used to generate each scale. We began by drawing policy indicators from Jason Soren, Fait Muedini, and William Ruger's dataset (2008), which provided statistics on state minimum-wage policies, an index capturing the strength of state mandates for health insurance companies to provide coverage (for the economic policy scale), a gun control index, an abortion restriction index, and a dummy variable indicating whether the state has the death penalty (for the social policy scale). Additional data indicators were also gathered. These included eligibility for healthcare and welfare programs, corporate and capital gains taxes, spending on education (for the economic policy scale), whether the state prohibits discrimination based on sexual orientation, and whether the state requires or allows public schools to set aside time for silent reflection or prayer (for the social policy scale). Table 7.3 lists the specific policy indicators and their sources, the year that they were measured, and descriptive statistics.

From these data, we generated two policy scores—one for economic issues and one for social issues—by factor-analyzing each subset of policy indicators. As shown in table 7.3, the seven economic policy indicators loaded onto one factor, which explained 76 percent of the variance among them (an eigenvalue of 1.77). This scale ranges from −1.57 in South Dakota to 2.15 in New Jersey. The five social policy indicators

Table 7.1   Policy Issue Items Used to Generate Economic and Social Liberalism Scales

			Liberal Position (pre-imput)		
	Raw N	Range	Less Than $10,000	More Than $150,000	F
Economic policy liberalism (2000)					
Inheritance tax should be cut (Q113a & Q113b)	18,292	0 1	63%	75%	14.79
Should spend on health care for uninsured (Q111b)	55,549	0 3	80	61	100.93
Should spend on Medicare (Q111g)	24,501	0 3	81	57	60.09
Favor universal health care for children (Q91d)	29,084	0 1	91	76	54.29
Should spend on Medicaid (Q111h)	24,317	0 3	73	47	67.93
Should reduce income differences (Q136e)	23,758	0 1	69	26	156.76
Should spend on aid to mothers with young children (Q111e)	24,055	0 3	66	43	46.54
Social policy liberalism (2000)					
Favor restricting abortion (Q91b & Q38c)	54,876	0 1	58	78	84.93
Should ban abortion (Q136b)	24,010	0 1	66	88	68.07

Economic policy liberalism (2004)

Favor eliminating estate tax (Q48 & Q74 & Q75)	13,637	0	1	65	70	3.14
Favor spending more on health insurance (Q38)	19,662	0	3	86	65	48.92
Favor health insurance for children (Q62 & Q77)	19,569	0	1	92	75	36.31
Favor health insurance for workers (Q63 & Q78)	18,650	0	1	83	65	41.81
Favor assistance to schools (Q22)	28,317	0	3	79	67	21.98
Should reduce income differences (Q22)	35,149	0	3	48	27	110.58

Social policy liberalism (2004)

Favor banning all abortions (Q20)	56,919	0	3	42	60	101.22
Favor banning all late-term abortions (Q25 & Q26)	22,040	0	3	38	38	4.77
Favor stem cell funding (Q65 & Q66 & Q83 & Q84)	16,076	0	1	67	77	8.88
Favor marriage ammendment (Q17)	55,717	0	3	43	45	18.10
Favor allowing same sex marriage (Q656 & Q657)	17,052	0	3	18	27	37.28
Favor gun control	31,281	0	3	69	62	13.57

Source: Authors' calculations from the 2000 and 2004 Annenberg National Election Surveys (Romer et al. 2006).
Note: Descriptive statistics from datasets prior to imputing for missing values. Income-group responses indicate the percent of each income group selecting the most liberal response option for each item. F statistics drawn from one-way ANOVA tests across all nine income categories. F statistics for each question are significant at $p < .05$

Table 7.2 Economic and Social Policy Liberalism

	Individual Level					State Level				
	N	Mean	SD	Min	Max	N	Mean	SD	Min	Max
All respondents										
Economic (2000)	59,266	0.00	1.00	−5.03	1.86	48	−0.02	0.11	−0.23	0.22
Economic (2004)	72,682	0.00	1.00	−5.70	2.77	48	−0.01	0.10	−0.26	0.21
Social (2000)	59,266	0.00	1.00	−2.05	1.33	48	−0.03	0.21	−0.43	0.44
Social (2004)	72,682	0.00	1.00	−2.99	2.31	48	−0.02	0.19	−0.43	0.40
Low income: less than $35,000										
Economic (2000)	23,992	0.18	0.89	−5.03	1.79	48	0.15	0.13	−0.17	0.42
Economic (2004)	24,130	0.11	0.90	−5.41	2.60	48	0.11	0.09	−0.10	0.25
Social (2000)	23,992	−0.11	1.00	−2.03	1.27	48	−0.10	0.19	−0.47	0.36
Social (2004)	24,130	−0.08	0.99	−2.93	2.31	48	−0.07	0.15	−0.36	0.21
Middle income										
Economic (2000)	22,491	−0.07	1.03	−5.03	1.71	48	−0.10	0.14	−0.51	0.25
Economic (2004)	26,992	0.00	1.00	−5.70	2.77	48	−0.02	0.12	−0.30	0.21
Social (2000)	22,491	0.01	1.01	−2.03	1.28	48	−0.03	0.25	−0.45	0.50
Social (2004)	26,992	−0.02	1.01	−2.99	2.16	48	−0.03	0.20	−0.43	0.43
High income: more than $75,000										
Economic (2000)	12,783	−0.22	1.10	−5.03	1.86	48	−0.25	0.18	−0.72	0.16
Economic (2004)	21,560	−0.12	1.08	−5.59	2.38	48	−0.14	0.18	−0.60	0.30
Social (2000)	12,783	0.19	0.95	−2.05	1.33	48	0.11	0.22	−0.27	0.49
Social (2004)	21,560	0.12	0.99	−2.78	2.22	48	0.03	0.25	−0.60	0.61

Source: Authors' calculations from the 2000 and 2004 Annenberg National Election Surveys (Romer et al. 2006).

loaded onto a single factor as well, which explained 90 percent of the variance (an eigenvalue of 1.49). This scale ranges from -1.05 in Indiana to 1.48 in Vermont. We will use these policy measures later in the chapter to examine differential policy responsiveness to constituents of different income groups, across richer and poorer states.

Findings

Next, we review our findings. We describe the variation in preferences among income groups and examine how these patterns differ in poor versus wealthy states. Then we examine the degree to which states' policies reflect the preferences of each income group.

Income-Group Differences in Policy Liberalism

Before examining income differences in our scaled measures of economic and social policy liberalism, we looked at the income differences in the raw data (before imputing estimates for missing data) used to generate the scales. Table 7.1 also presents a comparison of responses for individuals reporting household incomes of less than $10,000, as well as for those reporting incomes above $150,000. Specifically, we calculated the percentage of each income group selecting the most liberal response category for each policy issue. These two groups differed significantly on every item used in our subscales, though the degree of difference varied substantially (illustrated by the range of F statistics for the one-way analysis of variance across the nine income groups used in the Annenberg survey). Among the items from the 2000 survey, the largest difference by income was seen for the item assessing support for government efforts to reduce income differences between the rich and the poor (supported by 69 percent of those in lowest income group but by only 26 percent of those in the highest). Similarly, those in families with incomes of less than $10,000 a year were also much more likely to express support for providing health care to the uninsured (80 percent versus 61 percent) but were less likely to oppose school prayer (27 percent versus 59 percent). Similarly, in the 2004 survey, the largest income-group differences were seen in the item on reducing income differences (with 48 percent of the lowest income group strongly supporting this action versus 27 percent of the highest income group), followed by differences in support for a ban on all abortions (opposed by 42 percent among the poorest versus 60 percent among the wealthiest).

Yet, for both surveys, we also identified issues with small (though still significant) differences among the income groups. In 2000 the smallest difference was for the item assessing support for allowing gays in the military (favored by 56 percent of the lowest income group versus 66

Table 7.3 Policy Indicators Used to Estimate States' Economic and Social Policy Liberalism

	Data Source	Year	Mean	SD	Range		Factor Loading	Eigen-value	Proportion of Variance
Economic policy indicators									
Eligibility for SCHIP, percent of FPL	(1)	2006	229	62	140	400	.54		
Capital gains tax rate	(2)	2003	4.78	2.86	.00	9.35	.45		
Corporate income tax rate	(2)	2003	6.56	2.65	.00	9.999	.61		
Minimum wage	(3)	2006	5.68	$0.83	$5.15	$7.63	.54		
Per pupil expenditures in K–12	(4)	2006	9,075	$2,016	$5,437	$14,884	.67		
Income eligibility for TANF/welfare	(5)	2006	751	$307	$269	$1,590	.22		
Health insurance mandates index	(3)	2006	.45	.11	.21	.68	.34		
Economic policy score			.00	.86	-1.57	2.15		1.77	.76
Social policy indicators									
Gun control index	(3)	2006	-.5	2.92	-2.50	8.77	.40		
Abortion index	(3)	2006	.10	1.85	-3.53	3.08	-.73		
Has death penalty	(3)	2006	.79	.41	.00	1.00	-.25		
No discrimination for sexual orientation	(6)	2008	.38	.49	.00	1.00	.79		
Requires (2) or allows (1) school prayer	(7)	2008	.98	.76	.00	2.00	-.34		
Social policy score			.00	.86	-1.05	1.48		1.49	.90

Source: Authors' compilation of data from Kaiser Family Foundation (2006); Institute on Taxation and Economic Policy (2003); Soren, Muedini, and Ruger (2008); Education Week (2008); Urban Institute (2006); Human Rights Watch (2008); and Education Commission of the States (2008).
Note: N = 48.

percent of those in the highest income group), followed by the items relating to the inheritance/estate tax, for which the wealthy were more likely to support repeal (75 percent supporting repeal versus 63 percent of poor). In the 2004 survey, the inheritance tax item also identified a small income-group difference (65 percent of the lowest income group favoring elimination versus 70 percent of the highest), followed by the item on banning late-term abortions (favored by approximately 38 percent of both groups).

Next we compared differences in our constructed policy liberalism scales, which include measures with large as well as small variation across income groups. For a means of comparison, we also included a standardized measure of respondents' self-reported ideology ($M = 0$, standard deviation = 1) alongside the economic and social policy liberalism measures for each survey year. Table 7.4 presents the mean on each scale across the nine income categories captured in the Annenberg survey, which range from less than \$10,000 to more than \$150,000.

We find higher levels of self-identified liberalism among the low-income respondents, although as noted by Bhatti and Erikson (chapter 8 this volume) in their analysis of these same data, the income differences are quite small: the poorest group averaged .09 in 2000 and .05 in 2004, in contrast to .00 for the wealthiest group in both years. Although these differences were statistically significant ($F = 8.94$ in 2000, 4.90 in 2004), they represent less than a tenth of a standard deviation difference in ideology. In contrast, in both 2000 and 2004 we find larger differences in our two measures of policy liberalism, which were generated from respondents' stated policy preferences rather than from their self-identification as a liberal, a moderate, or a conservative. As expected, the most pronounced income differences are on economic policy issues, for which the low-income groups are more liberal than their higher-income counterparts. Economic liberalism among each income group ranged from .31 (lowest income) to −.30 (highest) in 2000 ($F = 217.26$), and from .17 (lowest) to −.16 (highest) in 2004 ($F = 91.60$). Also consistent with Gilens (2005) and Stephen Ansolabehere, Jonathan Rodden, and James Snyder (2006), we find that the low incomes are associated with more conservative views on social policy issues, for which our measure of liberalism ranges from −.19 (lowest income group) to .27 (highest income group) in 2000 ($F = 107.33$), and from −.06 (lowest) to .20 (highest) in 2004 ($F = 66.14$). In terms of standard deviation units, these differences range from .26 (social issues in 2004) to .61 (economic issues in 2000) of a standard deviation.

Another way to consider the magnitude of these differences is to compare the gap in opinion between income groups with another well-established gap in opinion: Democrats and Republicans. Figure 7.1 presents the absolute differences in opinion between the two partisan groups versus that between those with the lowest and the highest in-

Table 7.4 Income Differences in Ideology Versus Policy Liberalism Scores

	2000 Annenberg Survey				2004 Annenberg Survey			
	N	Self-ID Liberalism	Economic Policy Liberalism	Social Policy Liberalism	N	Self-ID Liberalism	Economic Policy Liberalism	Social Policy Liberalism
Less than $10K	3,958	0.09	0.31	–0.19	3,728	0.05	0.17	–0.06
$10K to $15K	3,924	0.09	0.25	–0.17	3,939	0.02	0.16	–0.12
$15K to $25K	7,434	0.03	0.17	–0.10	7,515	0.01	0.11	–0.09
$25K to $35K	8,676	0.02	0.10	–0.05	8,948	0.00	0.07	–0.06
$35K to $50K	11,216	0.01	–0.02	–0.01	12,560	–0.03	0.03	–0.04
$50K to $75K	11,275	–0.03	–0.11	0.03	14,432	–0.04	–0.03	–0.01
$75K to $100K	6,277	0.00	–0.19	0.13	9,605	–0.02	–0.09	0.07
$100K to $150K	4,018	0.02	–0.22	0.21	7,138	0.00	–0.15	0.12
More than $150K	2,488	0.00	–0.30	0.27	4,817	0.00	–0.16	0.20
F		8.94	217.26	107.33		4.90	91.60	66.14

Source: Authors' calculations from the 2000 and 2004 Annenberg National Election Surveys (Romer et al. 2006).
Notes: All three measures of liberalism are standardized scores with $M = 0$ and $SD = 1$.

Figure 7.1   Comparison of Partisan Gap Versus Income Gap in Policy Liberalism

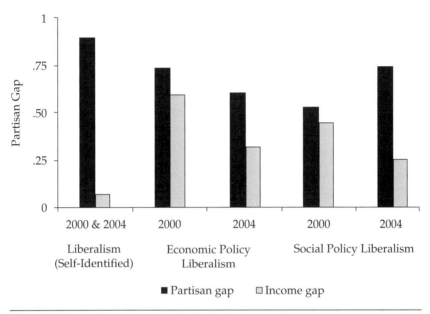

Source: Authors' compilation based on the 2000 and 2004 Annenberg National Election Surveys (Romer et al. 2006).
Note: Bars represent the absolute value of the difference in liberalism scores for Democrats versus Republicans (partisan gap) and those with the lowest (less than $10,000) and highest (more than $150,000) incomes (income gap).

comes. We see that the partisan gap in opinion is larger for both types of policy liberalism and across the two survey years. Yet the income gap nearly reaches the partisan gap for the two 2000 measures, but is about half for the 2004 measures. We attribute the disparity to the different policy issues focused on in each year. Because we do not know which set of items better captures the "true" magnitude of differences, we ran parallel analyses on each set of measures and drew conclusions from results consistent across the two sets of constructed opinion scales. But, across the two survey years, we see again that the magnitude of the income gap in economic issues is somewhat more substantial than that in social issues.

Income Differences in Opinion Across States

As shown in table 7.2, the distribution of economic and social policy liberalism takes a different form when examining the individual- versus state-level values. At the individual level, more variation is seen in economic policy issues (ranging from −5.03 to 1.86 and −5.70 to 2.77) than in social issues (ranging from −2.05 to 1.33 and −2.99 to 2.31). The range of state averages is (as expected) much smaller than that among individuals. Yet what is most notable is that the variation in opinion across states is larger for social issues (ranging from −.43 to .44 and −.43 to .40) than for economic policy issues (ranging from −.23 to .22 and −.26 to .21). In fact, the standard deviation in states' average social policy liberalism is twice that of their average economic policy liberalism. This state-level convergence is also seen in high correlations (.81 and .87 for 2000 and 2004, respectively) between the social policy liberalism of the poor versus the rich. These correlation coefficients are smaller for the state-level economic policy liberalism measures (.38 for 2000 and .63 for 2004).[6]

In the next section we examine variation in the income-opinion relationship between wealthy and poor states. In particular, we are interested in describing the relationship that Gelman and his colleagues (2008) examine, in which individual-level income is much more predictive of presidential vote choice in poor states than in wealthy states. We expect that state-level income may also structure the relationship between individual income and policy liberalism that, in turn, influences vote choice. In order to examine the impact of individual-level income, state-average income, and the interaction between an individual's income and the wealth of his or her state, we estimated multilevel models in which individuals (level 1) are nested within states (level 2). Because our goal is to identify the distribution of opinion across income groups in different states, rather than to explain the sources of this variation, we do not include other control variables that are expected to underlie the income-opinion gradient (that is, race). Instead, we simply regressed individual-level opinion on individual-level income at level 1 in a random-intercept, varying-slope model in which state-level income is used to explain both the state-level intercept (capturing the average policy liberalism in the state) and the slope of the individual income measure (capturing whether the slope is steeper or flatter in wealthier states). The model estimated as follows:

$$Y_{\text{Opinion}} = b_{0j} + B_{1j} * (\text{Individual Income})_{ij} + r$$
$$b_{0j} = y_{00} + y_{01j} * (\text{State Income}) + u_{0j}$$
$$B_{1j} = y_{10} + y_{11j} * (\text{State Income}) + u_{1j}$$

We present the results of these four multilevel models, each regressing one of the two policy liberalism scales for either 2000 or 2004 on the measures of individual-level and state-level income, in figure 7.2. Again, we present these parallel models to assess the robustness of our findings when economic and social issues are captured using different survey

Figure 7.2   Income-Opinion Relationship Across Poor and Wealthy States

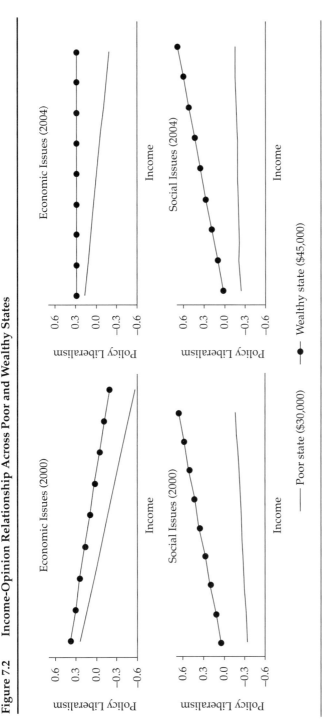

Source: Authors' compilation based on the 2000 and 2004 Annenberg National Election Surveys (Romer et al. 2006).
Notes: Lines represent the predicted policy liberalism for each income group, ranging from less than $10,000 (very left) to more than $150,000 (very right), estimated from multilevel models in which the intercept is estimated as a function of average state income and the slope is estimated as a function of both individual-level income (at level 1) and state-level income (as a cross-level interaction). Solid line presents predicted means for a poor state, such as West Virginia, which is two standard deviations below the mean state income (from Annenberg data), while the line with dots presents predicted means for wealthier states, such as Maryland, whose average state wealth is two standard deviations above the mean.

items; we draw our conclusions from the findings that are consistent across the two sets of measures. Here, we plot predicted levels of policy liberalism by individual-level income, state-level income, and the cross-level interaction of these two income measures. These values are predicted for a prototypical poor state, in which state-level income is set two standard deviations below the mean (most closely matching state wealth among Annenberg survey respondents in West Virginia, approximately $30,000). In addition, we predict values in a state in which wealth is two standard deviations above the mean (most closely matching state wealth in Maryland, approximately $45,000).

The top two boxes present findings for multilevel models estimated for economic policy liberalism. Here, we find little difference in economic policy liberalism among the very poor living in poorer versus wealthier states (the intercept), though the slope that predicts decreasing economic policy liberalism as income increases is much steeper within poor states than in wealthier states. This pattern is somewhat stronger in the 2000 data, but the overall pattern is consistent with the findings of Gelman and his colleagues (2007, 2008) that the income-vote gradient is steeper in poorer states, paired with Ansolabehere, Rodden, and Snyder's (2006) and Bartels's (2008) findings that economic issues are most predictive of individuals' vote choices. We find a different pattern for social policy liberalism, which is presented in the bottom two boxes. For these policy issues, state wealth plays a bigger role in shaping the income-opinion gradient. First, the level of social policy liberalism is significantly higher in wealthier states than in poorer states across the board (illustrated by the gap between the two lines). Second, the positive relationship between an individual's income and social policy liberalism is much stronger in wealthy states than in poorer states, where levels of social policy liberalism are lower overall and quite consistent across income groups. Comparing these findings across policy areas, we find that in wealthier states disagreement between income groups relates to social policy issues. In contrast, in poorer states disagreement is more on economic policy issues. These patterns likely confound efforts to estimate differential responsiveness to each income group or to measure the magnitude of differences in opinion across income groups.

Policy Responsiveness

We now turn our attention to examining the congruence between our measures of state policy liberalism—on both economic and social policy issues—and the policy liberalism of low-, middle-, and high-income constituents. Our normative expectation of equal responsiveness across groups with different resources assumes similar-size groups of constituents. For example, if a state has numerous well-to-do residents, under the notion of equal political representation (one person, one vote), we would expect that the interests of those who are better off (who make up a large proportion of that state's electorate) would be weighed more heavily than those of others. This type of differential responsiveness across income groups does not challenge the norm of political equality among individuals in the same way that differential responsiveness to the rich would if they made up an equal-size or smaller group in the state.

To account for these differences, we construct weighted measures of public opinion by multiplying each group's mean opinion by the proportion of the respondents in the state within that income group. This is the same approach that others use to decompose the average ideology effect into population segments (see, for example, Bartels 2008; Clinton 2006). We regressed state policy liberalism on all three weighted-opinion measures at the same time. In addition, we included two additional variables capturing the proportion of the state population that we classified as poor and the proportion that we classified as rich.[7] From each model we got three coefficients (one for each measure of opinion) that represent measures of how responsive the state policies would be to an entire constituency of each income group (or to a single constituent in each of the three). If policymakers are responsive only to the state's mean ideology, there should be no (or at least little) difference in these coefficients across the three weighted opinion measures because responsiveness to each group is nothing more than a function of responsiveness to the state constituency, consistent with the notion of procedural equality in which each citizen's opinion receives equal weight (Beitz 1990). However, if the coefficient for one group is substantially larger than the others, then policy is more responsive to its interests.

Economic Policy Responsiveness

Table 7.5 presents models for states' economic policies predicted first by the 2000 measures of economic policy (the top panel) and then by the 2004 measures (the bottom panel). In 2000 (the top panel), model 1 establishes the expected relationship between the average economic policy liberalism in the state and the actual economic policies that the state has enacted. Not surprisingly, this coefficient is significant, large, and explains a majority (53 percent) of the variance in states' economic policy liberalism (Erikson, Wright, and McIver 1993). In model 2, we controlled for state wealth to clarify the relationship between individual-level income differences and differences across wealthy and poorer states. This reduces the coefficient slightly, as well as explains an additional 8 percent of variance in state policy. Models 3 and 4 test whether this aggregate relationship differs in poorer states (twenty-four with mean in-

Table 7.5   Economic Policy Responsiveness to Different Income Groups

	All States		Poor	Rich	All States		Poor	Rich
	(1)	(2)	(3)	(4)	(5)	(6)	(7)	(8)
Economic policy liberalism (2000)								
Opinion: average	5.62**	4.49**	3.22**	5.62**				
	(.78)	(.80)	(1.05)	(1.20)				
State wealth		.79**	.88	1.19*		4.26	-1.74	8.94
		(.26)	(.56)	(.53)		(3.09)	(3.36)	(7.09)
Opinion: low					1.62	.51	1.39	5.09
					(1.90)	(2.05)	(2.17)	(5.31)
Opinion: middle					6.98**	8.78**	7.77*	7.44
					(2.12)	(2.47)	(3.14)	(5.04)
Opinion: high					6.36**	4.43+	9.59**	1.64
					(2.21)	(2.60)	(3.25)	(5.70)
Percent low income					-2.84	11.61	-19.69	26.31
					(4.02)	(11.20)	(14.20)	(24.20)
Percent high income					.70	-8.35	-6.29	-16.37
					(4.11)	(7.72)	(8.98)	(18.00)
Constant	.12	-3.88**	-4.30	-6.10*	1.44	-23.32	18.60	-51.22
	(.09)	(1.30)	(2.67)	(2.79)	(2.49)	(18.10)	(20.90)	(40.50)
Observations	48	48	24	24	48	48	24	24
R^2	.53	.61	.36	.67	.65	.67	.66	.69

Economic policy liberalism (2004)

	(1)	(2)	(3)	(4)	(5)	(6)	(7)	(8)
Opinion: average	6.17**	4.81**	3.23*	6.24**				
	(.94)	(.96)	(1.24)	(1.44)				
State wealth		.83	.81	1.28*		4.86+	1.93	7.96
		(.27)	(.59)	(.54)		(2.44)	(2.74)	(6.70)
Opinion: low					-3.84	-4.65	-2.68	-3.18
					(3.23)	(3.14)	(3.30)	(8.19)
Opinion: middle					8.86**	8.88**	8.40*	10.36
					(3.10)	(3.00)	(3.04)	(8.35)
Opinion: high					7.82**	8.60**	7.49+	6.84
					(2.80)	(2.73)	(4.09)	(5.96)
Percent low income					1.54	17.73	-4.71	33.66
					(4.18)	(9.07)	(11.70)	(22.30)
Percent high income					4.87	-5.45	-15.53	-7.13
					(4.04)	(6.48)	(9.11)	(16.80)
Constant	.06	-4.15**	-4.03	-6.64*	-1.29	-29.43*	-3.94	-50.79
	(.09)	(1.36)	(2.81)	(2.87)	(2.51)	(14.30)	(16.90)	(38.10)
Observations	48	48	24	24	48	48	24	24
R^2	.49	.58	.30	.64	.63	.67	.52	.72

Source: Authors' compilation based on analysis of the 2000 and 2004 Annenberg National Election Surveys (Romer et al. 2006), as well as the policy measure presented in table 7.3.
Notes: N = 48 states, excluding Alaska and Hawaii. Coefficients from OLS regression models. Group opinion measures are weighted for the proportion of each grop within each state.

comes below \$35,000) versus wealthier ones. We continued to control for state wealth because it is a significant predictor of policy liberalism, which likely has independent effects on policy beyond its role in structuring group size and opinion. We find a larger relationship between aggregate opinion and economic policies in wealthier states, which is nearly twice the size of the coefficient for the poorer states. Similarly, this model using aggregate opinion explains much more of the variance in wealthy states ($R^2 = .67$) than it does in poorer states ($R^2 = .30$). This indicates that differential responsiveness to income groups is much more important in the poorer states. Models 5 through 8 repeat the first four models but substitute the three weighted measures of income-group opinion for aggregate opinion. Across the models, we find greater responsiveness to the preferences of those with higher incomes (6.36) and middle incomes (6.98), than to those of the lowest income group (1.62). This pattern suggests an underrepresentation of the poor, rather than the heightened responsiveness to the wealthy that Bartels describes (2008). In fact, after controlling for state wealth, we find more responsiveness to the preferences of those in the middle (8.78), and then to those in the high-income group (4.43), and very little to the poor (.51).

Next (models 7 and 8), we divided the sample of states into two groups, poorer and wealthier, to assess whether responsiveness patterns vary by state wealth. Because this approach leaves us with small sample sizes (N = 24 each), we acknowledge that these results are suggestive and more helpful for identifying general patterns than specific dynamics. Yet, even with the small sample size, we identified a clear income gradient in responsiveness in the poor states, for the low-, middle-, and high-income groups (1.39, 7.77, and 9.59, respectively). In contrast, we find no significant gradient among wealthier states. Of course, our earlier analyses indicated that in wealthier states, the income groups hold similar economic policy preferences—at least when compared with the size of income-group differences in poor states. And so variability across the group-specific income measures is less than in poor states.

Another way to assess the substantive differences in responsiveness in wealthy versus poorer states is to compare the R-squared from the models using the aggregate opinion measure (state mean) versus the income-specific opinion measures weighted for each income group. In poorer states, we see a big jump in the R-squared from .36 in model 3 when the relationship between state policy and average opinion is estimated. This R-squared nearly doubles to .66 once we allow for differential responsiveness across income groups. By contrast, in wealthier states, the disaggregated opinion measures do little to explain additional variance (raising the R-squared only .02 from .67 to .69).

The bottom panel of table 7.5 presents parallel models that use the same measure of state economic policy but substitute the aggregate and income-group-specific income measures generated from the 2004 Annenberg survey. Although these measures are based on somewhat different issue items and had smaller magnitudes of income-group differences in economic policy issues, the findings are remarkably similar. In addition, we find a similar effect of disaggregating opinion by income group, which provides more explanation of variance among poorer states (R-squared increased from .30 to .52) than in wealthier states (in which it increased from .64 to .72).

Of course, these findings rely on small sample sizes (N = 24), and so we are limited in our ability to adequately judge the substantive significance of both significant and nonsignificant findings. Therefore we rely more on the general pattern of coefficients across all these models examining responsiveness on economic policy issues. We present the relevant coefficients in figure 7.3. The top panel presents the coefficients for each income group across all states (N = 48), both before and after controlling for state wealth. Here, we see a consistent gradient in which the interests of the poor are underrepresented—with state policy aligning with the preferences of the middle- and high-income residents. The bottom panel presents the coefficients from the model estimated on the subsets of poorer and wealthier states. Poorer states mirror the overall findings—which is not surprising because those states had the largest income-group differences—providing an opportunity for capturing the differential responsiveness that does occur. In the wealthier states, the contrast was not significant, but only differed in form for the 2000 economic policy measure. To sum up our findings for economic policy liberalism, these data suggest that states' economic policies are less responsive to the preferences of the poor than to either middle- or high-income constituents. This is most pronounced in poorer states. In wealthier states we find a similar, but less consistent, pattern of differential responsiveness, which is likely limited by the smaller income gap in economic policy preferences in wealthier states—suggesting that any lack of (significant) differential responsiveness on economic issues in wealthy states stems more from the "natural limit" on political inequality Soroka and Wlezien (2008) describe, in which income-group opinion differences are too small to produce substantial representational inequality even if policymakers only represent the rich or the middle.

Social Policy Responsiveness

Table 7.6 now considers state policy responsiveness on social policy issues, with models estimated using 2000 opinion measures in the top panel and 2004 opinion measures in the bottom panel. Beginning with the 2000 estimates, models 1 through 4 establish the expected relationship between aggregate opinion and states' social policy choices, which

Figure 7.3   States' Economic Policy Responsiveness to Different Income
Groups

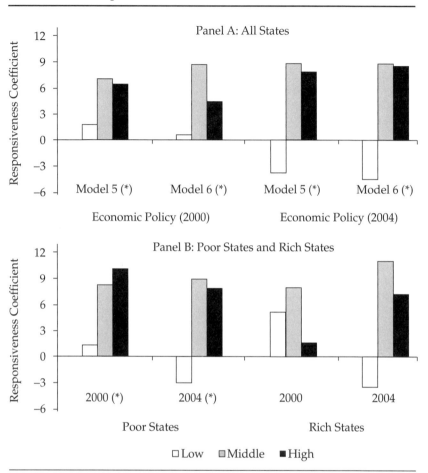

Source: Authors' compilation based on the 2000 and 2004 Annenberg National Election Surveys (Romer et al. 2006), as well as the policy measure presented in table 7.3.
Notes: N = 48 states in panel A, N = 24 poor states and 24 wealthy states in panel B. Bars represent the coefficient for each group's policy liberalism—in panel A, from model 5 (no controls) and model 6 (controlling for state wealth), and in panel B, from model 7 (poor states) and model 8 (rich states) controlling for state wealth.
* $p < .05$, + = $p < .10$

is positive, significant, and explains a large proportion of the variance. When considering aggregate responsiveness in poor and rich states, we find quite similar relationships. For example, the variance explained in the poorer states ($R^2 = .48$) was nearly as large as that in the wealthier states ($R^2 = .61$). This finding contrasts with the opinion-policy relation-

Table 7.6 Social Policy Responsiveness to Different Income Groups

	All States		Poor	Rich	All States		Poor	Rich
	(1)	(2)	(3)	(4)	(5)	(6)	(7)	(8)
Economic policy liberalism (2000)								
Opinion: average	3.09**	3.51**	3.47**	3.79**				
	(.39)	(.55)	(.80)	(.79)				
State wealth		-.36	-1.05	.21		-2.40	-1.21	2.45
		(.33)	(.73)	(.51)		(2.67)	(3.23)	(7.73)
Opinion: low					.78	0.75	-2.12	11.56
					(2.42)	(2.43)	(2.98)	(5.89)
Opinion: middle					4.26+	4.57*	5.52	-.59
					(2.20)	(2.23)	(3.49)	(4.28)
Opinion: high					6.32+	6.34+	8.33	-.38
					(3.68)	(3.69)	(7.46)	(5.19)
Percent low income					.49	-7.25	-7.73	6.88
					(5.16)	(10.10)	(14.20)	(27.50)
Percent high income					-2.21	2.82	-6.34	-1.82
					(5.13)	(7.60)	(12.60)	(16.50)
Constant	.09	1.93	5.23	-1.15	.20	14.02	10.17	-14.37
	(.08)	(1.70)	(3.51)	(2.66)	(3.03)	(15.70)	(19.70)	(45.40)
Observations	48	48	24	24	48	48	24	24
R^2	.58	.59	.48	.61	.61	.62	.59	.65

(Table continues on p. 214.)

Table 7.6 (Continued)

	All States		Poor	Rich	All States		Poor	Rich
	(1)	(2)	(3)	(4)	(5)	(6)	(7)	(8)
Economic policy liberalism (2004)								
Opinion: average	3.49**	3.92**	4.37*	3.79**				
	(.42)	(.59)	(.85)	(.88)				
State wealth		-.34	-.76	.34		-.11	1.06	-.07
		(.32)	(.64)	(.53)		(2.46)	(2.94)	(6.08)
Opinion: low					5.61+	5.61+	.89	10.62+
					(2.90)	(2.93)	(4.41)	(5.78)
Opinion: middle					-3.20	-3.20	2.50	-10.03
					(3.30)	(3.35)	(5.00)	(5.94)
Opinion: high					13.01**	13.03**	12.80*	17.44*
					(3.93)	(4.00)	(5.97)	(6.51)
Percent low income					.13	-.24	5.58	-6.98
					(4.12)	(9.16)	(13.00)	(20.60)
Percent high income					-3.70	-3.48	-7.83	-7.76
					(4.06)	(6.47)	(10.20)	(15.60)
Constant	.08	1.78	3.90	-1.87	.73	1.37	-5.84	4.55
	(.08)	(1.64)	(3.10)	(2.78)	(2.44)	(14.50)	(18.40)	(34.70)
Observations	48	48	24	24	48	48	24	24
R^2	.60	.61	.56	.56	.66	.66	.62	.69

Source: Authors' compilation based on analysis of the 2000 and 2004 Annenberg National Election Surveys (Romer et al. 2006), as well as the policy measure presented in table 7.3.

Notes: N = 48 states, excluding Alaska and Hawaii. Coefficients from OLS regression models. Group opinion measures are weighted for the proportion of each grop within each state.

** $p < .01$, * $p < .05$, + $p < .10$

ship identified for economic issues in which poor states exhibited a much weaker congruence than wealthier states did.

Models 5 through 8 use the 2000 data to replicate these models for the income-group-specific measures of opinion to test our expectation of differential responsiveness. We find evidence of an income gradient in which the coefficient for each group increases as income increases: low (.78), middle (4.26), and high (6.32). Yet, adding these disaggregated opinion measures does little to explain additional variance (raising R^2 by only .03), and the opinion measures are only marginally significant. When examining social policy responsiveness in poor and rich states, we find no significant coefficients, though the pattern of coefficients indicates greater responsiveness to high-income constituents in poor states and to low-income constituents in rich states. The nonsignificance of these findings may be due to the very small sample size, though the limited substantive significance is illustrated by the small increase in the R-squared, which rises from .48 to .59 in poor states and from .61 to .65 in wealthier states. Thus, using either metric, these models provide little evidence of substantial differential responsiveness on social issues.

The bottom panel of table 7.6 presents findings from models using the 2004 measures of social policy liberalism. Unlike the results from the models using 2000 data, model 5 identifies significant differential responsiveness in which states' social policy choices align most closely with the preferences of those with higher incomes (13.01), as well as somewhat less to the preferences of the low-income group (5.61), with the middle-income group's opinions (-3.20) being those overlooked on social policy issues. This is a very different pattern of differential responsiveness than the one seen for economic policy issues, although once we divide the sample into poor and wealthy states, we realize that it is found only among wealthy states. In wealthier states—the states where the income groups varied the most on social policy preferences—we found the distinct pattern of states' social policies being most closely aligned with the preferences of the higher income tercile (17.44), followed by the preferences of the lowest income group (10.62), with the least responsiveness to the middle-income group (-10.03). Yet, in poor states, we find a pattern of skewed responsiveness in which social policy is more responsive to the higher income group with little relative responsiveness to the preferences held by those with lower incomes: low (.89), middle (2.50), and high (12.80).

We present these findings in figure 7.4. The top panel presents the findings for social policy responsiveness across the forty-eight states. Here, we see the difference in results across the two waves of the Annenberg survey data. We do not know whether this stems from differences in measurement across the two surveys or whether it illustrates a valid change in the income-opinion relationship between the two survey

Figure 7.4   States' Social Policy Responsiveness to Different Income Groups

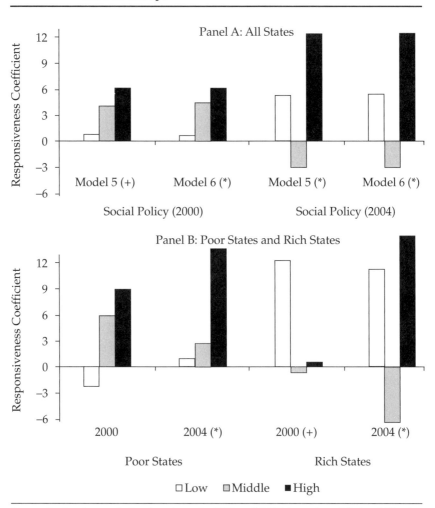

Source: Authors' compilation based on the 2000 and 2004 Annenberg National Election Surveys (Romer et al. 2006), as well as the policy measure presented in table 7.3.
Notes: N = 48 states in panel A, N = 24 poor states and 24 wealthy states in panel B. Bars represent the coefficient for each group's policy liberalism—in panel A, from model 5 (no controls) and model 6 (controlling for state wealth), and in panel B, from model 7 (poor states) and model 8 (rich states) controlling for state wealth.
* $p < .05$, + = $p < .10$

years. Suggesting that this difference is not driven only by some change in the survey (an assumption reinforced by the similarity of earlier findings), we note the more parallel findings across survey years once the sample is broken down into poor versus wealthy state subsamples. The bottom panel of figure 7.4 illustrates the distinct patterns in poor states (for which the underrepresentation of the poor is more consistent with the findings for economic policy responsiveness) compared with wealthier states, which exhibit heightened responsiveness to the poor on social policy issues. What remains distinct across the 2000 and 2004 results is the degree to which the social policy preferences of middle- and high-income constituents are reflected in state policy. Greater responsiveness to the middle-income group is seen using the 2000 measures, and heightened responsiveness to those with higher incomes is most pronounced in the 2004 data. This may reflect the greater inclusion of issues such as gay marriage and stem cell research onto the agenda between these two elections, though without conducting issue-specific analysis we cannot test this possibility.

Conclusion

In this chapter, we situated the question of differential responsiveness of elected officials to the policy opinions of wealthy and poor constituents within the state context. In some ways, our findings echo work focusing on national-level patterns of representation, which identify much greater responsiveness to the wealthy than to the poor. Specifically, we found more responsiveness to those with higher (versus lower) incomes across our social-policy and economic-policy opinion measures in both 2000 and 2004. Differing from previous research, we found policymakers to represent the interests of those with middle and high incomes fairly equally, and much more so than the poorer group, with one exception: the 2004 social policy measure, in which state policies aligned with the interests of the higher-income group, followed by the low-income group, and then the middle-income group.

Further, by taking into consideration differences in state context—in particular state wealth—we identified variation in representation dynamics across states. In particular, we distinguished between the potential for differential responsiveness and its actualization. In poor states, it is economic issues that divide the opinions of the rich and the poor, with much greater agreement on social policy issues across the classes. Therefore, in poor states, policies focused on economic issues contain the greatest potential for representational inequality. In contrast, the general congruence in social policy preferences in these same states places a healthy limit to any inequality in responsiveness that can occur

Table 7.7   Summary of Findings

	More Balanced Responsiveness	More Skewed Responsiveness
Smaller income differences	Economic policymaking in rich states	Social policymaking in poor states
Larger income differences	Social policymaking in rich states	Economic policymaking in poor states

Source: Authors' compilation.

(as argued in Soroka and Wlezien 2008; also see chapter 10, this volume). So even though we find greater responsiveness to the top income group across both opinion measures in poor states, we expect this differential responsiveness to translate into greater representational inequality on economic issues for which the income groups hold more disparate preferences.

In contrast, in wealthier states, the primary income divide is on social policy issues—with more agreement on economic policy issues across income groups. This may help explain the absence of significant differences in responsiveness on economic issues among the wealthier states. Yet, even for social policy issues in which differences are more pronounced, we found substantial responsiveness to the low-income group (in 2000) and jointly for the high- and low-income groups (in 2004), suggesting that in wealthy states, when income groups do differ in opinion, the poor are no less likely to get what they want out of the policymaking process—and may even get better representation. This finding suggests that the distinct patterns of representation in poor versus wealthy states stems from more than just differences in the distribution of opinion across income groups.

Combining these findings, as shown in table 7.7, we see the most unequal representation across income groups within poor states on economic policymaking. Yet our findings do not explain why this would occur. We did consider one potential explanation, that the poor states are simply the southern states. Given the differences in state wealth, as well as generally lower levels of redistributive policy among southern states, this did seem plausible. Yet we soon noticed that among the twenty-four "poorer states" in our analysis, only seven are southern. In fact, the twenty-four "richer states" include four southern states (Florida, Georgia, Texas, and Virginia). Further, when we divided the sample by region and reestimated the responsiveness models, we found a distinct (although nonsignificant with a sample size of eleven) pattern of responsiveness in southern states in which the poor may actually be better represented.

A number of other state-level factors may explain these patterns (for example, the strength of union membership, open versus closed shop rules, and the presence of an enhanced minimum-wage law). A more straightforward explanation, though, may be simple self-interest. Context changes the character of calculations that one makes in deciding whether to support different policies. For the poor, state wealth is unlikely to shift the incentives to support redistribution because the poor are likely to benefit from, rather than pay for, redistributive policies. In contrast, wealthier citizens are more likely to face different costs (in level of taxation) and benefits (in terms of a healthy and educated citizenry) due to redistribution from wealthy states to poorer states. In rich states, a large portion of the population can share in the paying for benefits and so the trade-off of a stronger populace for modestly higher taxes may seem like a good idea. However, in a poor state there are more needy people and fewer rich folks to pay for the benefits they desire. It should not surprise us that, facing a more costly tradeoff for the same stronger populace, the rich in poor states oppose such policies. Because many of the policies in our economic policy measures are paid for by the states, it seems reasonable that the context of state wealth should play a role in self-interested citizens' preferences for policy, which are likely to be conditional by beliefs about who would pay for those policies.

Notes

1. This critique does not extend to Larry Bartels's (2008) policy-specific tests of differential responsiveness.
2. In domains where differences were found across income groups, they were mostly between upper- and middle-income citizens on the one hand and the poor on the other (see also Enns and Wlezien, chapter 1, this volume).
3. Those five states are Wyoming (N = 307), Delaware (N = 344), North Dakota (N = 358), South Dakota (N = 421), and Vermont (N = 437).
4. These strong loadings likely represent a good deal of coherence among respondents' economic or social policy views, though they are likely biased upward due to our missing-data imputation strategy that maximized the similarity among the items and also because of our focus on a small number of items for each subscale.
5. We also reestimated all models using a more relative measure of low-, middle-, and high-income groups. For these measures, we varied the income cut-points for each state to best balance the population into thirds within each state. Use of this relative measurement of income groups did not substantively change our findings.
6. Another way to consider the clustering of opinion within states is to compare the proportion of total variance (in this case, the sum of squared error) explained by the respondents' states of residence. We find that the state of residence accounts for about 1 percent of the variation in economic policy

liberalism, but 3 percent of the variation in social policy liberalism. Although these values of explained variance are small, it is worth noting that a categorical variable capturing whether the respondent is a Democrat, a Republican, or an independent explains only 10 percent of the variation in policy liberalism. Therefore, we conclude that state of residence explains about one-tenth of what party identification explains for economic policy liberalism, but three times that (three-tenths of party identification) for social policy liberalism. Finally, we consider the proportion of variance explained by individual-level income, which accounts for about 3 percent of the variance of the economic policy liberalism scores, and only 1 percent of the variance for the other three policy measures.

7. These variables were included to provide each of the three income groups their own intercept, which is an important amendment to the modeling strategy used by Bartels (2008), as demonstrated by Bhatti and Erikson (chapter 8, this volume).

References

Ansolabehere, Stephen, Jonathan Rodden, and James M. Snyder. 2006. "Purple America." *Journal of Economic Perspectives* 20(2): 97–118.

Bartels, Larry M. 2008. *Unequal Democracy: The Political Economy of the New Gilded Age*. Princeton, N.J.: Princeton University Press.

Bartels, Larry M., Hugh Heclo, Rodney Hero, and Lawrence R. Jacobs, 2005. "Inequalities in Governance." In *Inequality and American Democracy: What We Know and What We Need to Learn*, edited by Lawrence R. Jacobs and Theda Skocpol. New York: Russell Sage Foundation.

Beitz, Charles. 1990. *Political Equality: An Essay in Democratic Theory*. Princeton, N.J.: Princeton University Press.

Clinton, Joshua D. 2006. "Representation in Congress: Constituents and Roll Calls in the 106th House." *The Journal of Politics* 68(2): 397–409.

Dahl, Robert A. 1971. *Polyarchy: Participation and Opposition*. New Haven, Conn.: Yale University Press.

Education Commission of the States. 2008. "School Prayer, Moments of Silence and Other State Policies Toward Religion." Available at http://www.ecs.org/clearinghouse/77/89/7789.pdf (accessed October 13, 2010).

Education Week. 2008. "Quality Counts 2008 Report." Available at http://www.edweek.org/ew/toc/2008/01/10/index.html (accessed October 13, 2010).

Erikson, Robert S., and Gerald C. Wright. 1980. "Policy Representation of Constituency Interests." *Political Behavior* 2(1): 91–106.

———. 2005. "Voters, Issues, and Candidates in Congressional Elections." In *Congress Reconsidered*, 8th ed, edited by Lawrence Dodd and Bruce Oppenheimer. Washington, D.C.: CQ Press.

Erikson, Robert S., Michael B. MacKuen, and James A. Stimson. 2002. *The Macro Polity*. New York: Cambridge University Press.

Erikson, Robert S., Gerald C. Wright, and John P. McIver. 1993. *Statehouse Democracy: Public Opinion and Policy in the American States*. New York: Cambridge University Press.

Flavin, Patrick. 2009. "Differences in Income, Policy Preferences, and Priorities in American Public Opinion." Presented at the 2009 Midwest Political Science Conference. Chicago (April 2, 2009).

Frank, Thomas. 2004. *What's the Matter with Kansas? How Conservatives Won the Heart of America*. New York: Metropolitan Books.

Gelman, Andrew, David Park, Boris Shore, Joseph Bafumi, and Jeronimo Cortina. 2008. *Red State, Blue State, Rich State, Poor State: Why Americans Vote the Way They Do*. Princeton, N.J.: Princeton University Press.

Gelman, Andrew, Boris Shor, Joseph Bafumi, and David Park. 2007. "Rich State, Poor State, Red State, Blue State: What's the Matter with Connecticut?" *Quarterly Journal of Political Science* 2(4): 345–67.

Gilens, Martin. 2005. "Inequality and Democratic Responsiveness." *Public Opinion Quarterly* 69(5): 778–96.

———. 2009. "Preference Gaps and Inequality in Representation." *PS: Political Science & Politics* 42(2): 335–41.

Hacker, Jacob S. 2002. *The Divided Welfare State: The Battle over Public and Private Social Benefits in the United States.* Cambridge: Cambridge University Press.

Human Rights Campaign. 2008. "Employment Discrimination Laws." Available at http://www.hrc.org/issues/workplace/equal_opportunity/equal_opportunity_laws.asp (accessed October 13, 2010).

Institute on Taxation and Economic Policy. 2003. "Who Pays: A Distributional Analysis of the Tax System in All 50 States." Available at http://www.itepnet.org/pdf/wp2003.pdf (accessed October 13, 2010).

Jacobs, Lawrence R., and Theda Skocpol, eds. 2005. *Inequality and American Democracy: What We Know and What We Need to Learn.* New York: Russell Sage Foundation.

Kaiser Family Foundation. 2006. "Income Eligibility Levels for Children's Separate CHIP Programs by Annual Incomes and as a Percent of Federal Poverty Level." Available at http://www.statehealthfacts.org/comparebar.jsp?typ=2&ind=204&cat=4&sub=53&rankbyind=1&o=a (accessed October 13, 2010).

Miller, Warren E., and Donald E. Stokes. 1963. "Constituency Influence in Congress." *American Political Science Review* 57(1): 45–56.

Page, Benjamin I. 2009. "Review Symposium: Perspectives on Lawrence Bartel's Unequal Democracy." *Perspectives on Politics* 7(1): 148–50.

Romer, Daniel, Kate Kenski, Kenneth Winneg, Christopher Adasiewicz, and Kathleen Hall Jamieson. 2006. *Capturing Campaign Dynamics 2000 & 2004*. Philadelphia: University of Pennsylvania Press.

Royston, Patrick. 2005. "Multiple Imputation of Missing Values: Update of Ice." *Stata Journal* 5(4): 527–36.

Soren, Jason, Fait Muedini, and William P. Ruger. 2008. "State and Local Public Policies in the United States." Available at http://www.statepolicyindex.com (accessed October 13, 2010).

Soroka, Stuart N., and Christopher Wlezien. 2008. "On the Limits to Inequality in Representation." *PS: Political Science & Politics* 41(2): 319–27.

———. 2010. *Degrees of Democracy*. Cambridge: Cambridge University Press.

Ura, Joseph Daniel, and Christopher R. Ellis. 2008. "Income, Preferences, and the Dynamics of Policy Responsiveness." *PS: Political Science & Politics* 41(4): 785–94.

Urban Institute. 2006. "Welfare Rules Databook: State TANF Policies as of July 2006." Available at http://www.urban.org/publications/411686.html (accessed October 13, 2010.)

Walzer, Michael. 1983. *Spheres of Justice.* New York: Basic Books.

Winters, Jeffrey A., and Benjamin I. Page. 2008. *"Oligarchy in the United States?"* Unpublished paper. Northwestern University.

Chapter 8

How Poorly Are the Poor Represented in the U.S. Senate?

YOSEF BHATTI AND ROBERT S. ERIKSON

IN HIS WIDELY (and justly) acclaimed book, *Unequal Democracy*, Larry Bartels (2008) presents the case that the rich get more representation than the poor. Among other findings, we learn that Republican administrations serve to advance income inequality rather than to retard it. We also learn that Republicans are capable of fooling voters, though not for the reasons that Thomas Frank (2004) offers in *What's the Matter with Kansas?* Among the most provocative findings is that when it comes to representation in the U.S. Senate (as measured by roll-call voting), the poor—unlike the well-to-do—get virtually no representation. That is, when senators take into account (or respond in some indirect fashion to) public opinion, only the views of the relatively rich—and to a lesser extent middle-income voters—matter. Based on Bartels's statistical analysis, the views of the relatively poor are not visibly represented at all.

In terms of senatorial representation, is political inequality as severe as Bartels makes it out to be? Although one would certainly expect affluence to have something to do with influence over Congress, the degree of inequality reported by Bartels is stronger than one might expect. To entirely neglect the opinions of one-third of the population would be a decidedly risky strategy for legislators seeking reelection. In this chapter we investigate further. We replicate and extend Bartels's analysis, presenting certain methodological hurdles that hinder a decisive verdict. In the end, we do not challenge Bartels's finding of unequal representation

223

as necessarily incorrect. We do, however, offer what we believe to be compelling reasons to interpret the evidence with considerable caution.

Some Theory

In recent years, scholarship has increasingly turned from the study of average opinion representation (for example, Miller and Stokes 1963; Page and Shapiro 1983; Bartels 1991; Erikson, Wright, and McIver 1993; Erikson, MacKuen, and Stimson 2002) to focus on differences in representation among groups (for an extensive review, see chapter 1, this volume). Particular focus has been given to inequalities attributable to income. In line with Bartels, other scholars have shown that the opinions of the rich matter substantially more than the views of the poorest segments of society for federal policy (Gilens 2005; see also Jacobs and Page 2005; Gilens, chapter 9, this volume) as well as for state policy (Rigby and Wright, chapter 7, this volume). Nevertheless, one group of scholars have noted that opinions are not very different across income groups (Ura and Ellis 2008; Page and Jacobs 2009). This limits the unequal responsiveness and means that even if inequalities indeed exist, the poor are substantially represented through the views of the wealthy (Soroka and Wlezien 2008; Wlezien and Soroka, chapter 10, this volume). Hence, the jury is still out on this important research question.

Before turning to Bartels's statistical evidence, it is helpful to review the reasons senatorial representation would be expected to be unequal. That is, why would senators be more responsive to the opinions of the rich than the poor? Bartels mentions several reasons. The rich are more attentive and more likely to vote (see also Verba and Nie 1972; Brady, Verba, and Scholzman 1995). Second, the rich are more likely to contribute to campaigns (see also Verba, Scholzman, and Brady 1995). For these reasons, reelection-seeking senators have reason to pay more attention to rich opinion than to poor opinion—that is, a reelection mechanism (Fiorina 1974; Griffin and Newman 2005). Moreover, senators are themselves from the social strata of the relatively rich. To some extent, they would share the views of the relatively rich and interact with constituents who themselves are relatively rich—that is, a selection and communication mechanism (Miller and Stokes 1963; Erikson 1990; Griffin and Newman 2005). To the extent that the poor are invisible to Senate members, it is unlikely that senators consider the views of the poor.

At the same time, as Bartels acknowledges, these are only relative differences. The statistical analysis suggests that the top third in income gets most of the representation and that the bottom third gets none. Many citizens in the bottom third vote and many in the top third do not. Although the relatively affluent give more to campaigns, it is an elite stratum of the top third in income that gives the most. These considerations make it puzzling that the gap in representation between the moderately rich and moderately poor is as great as Bartels's statistical analysis would suggest.

There is also another consideration. Following the lead of Warren Miller and Donald Stokes's (1963) classic study of congressional representation, political scientists are prone to discuss representation as a phenomenon due solely to the actions of the representatives. When scholars theorize about why legislators represent (or do not represent) constituency opinion, the focus usually is on the supply side—why, deliberately or incidentally, legislators end up following constituency wishes. The demand side should not be ignored. Voters also play a role. At least potentially, they sort candidates into winners and losers in part based on their ideological proximity to the candidates. At a minimum, members of Congress—including senators—behave as if they believe this to be true. Otherwise they would be indifferent to constituency representation. Political scientists—going back to Miller and Stokes's classic work—sometimes write as if legislators overestimate constituency attention to their behavior. Although this is possible, one could also bring forward a "rational expectations" argument that legislators do not make systematic mistakes. That is, given their relative utilities for voting correctly in terms of their personal ideological values and voting to stay elected, representatives weigh the goals correctly in terms of maximizing their long-term welfare.

The implication of this line of theorizing is that legislators know what they are doing. If they respond to public opinion generally (as they seem to do), they respond with good reason rather than with unjustified inflation of their visibility to constituents. But if we take Bartels's finding of differential representation seriously, then legislators rationally ignore the poor. For such behavior to be rational, senators are indeed invisible to the poor but visible enough to the well-to-do to give the well-to-do their attention. To come full circle, for senators to ignore the poor is rational only if the poor ignore the senators.

Based on Bartels's analysis, it is unlikely that senators overestimate the attention they receive from their poorer constituents. But consider the opposite; a world in which senators mistakenly ignore the poor though the poor do pay attention and, just like their affluent counterparts, vote their legislators in or out based on the proximity of candidate positions to their own. The outcome is the positive representation of poor constituents, as the poor have some ability to elect and keep senators who share their views and reject those who do not.

The net result of this theorizing is that for it to make sense for the poor to get no representation of their views in the Senate, the poor must indeed be inattentive to their senators. If Bartels's research is correct, the implication is not only that senators freely ignore the views of the poor, but also that the poor also must ignore the fact that they are not represented.

Bartels's Analysis and Replication

Bartels analyzes the relationship between state opinion and senatorial liberalism for three Congresses following the elections of 1988, 1990, and 1992. These Congresses were chosen because the 1988, 1990, and 1992 elections were the venue for a study of the Senate by the American National Election Study, in which the respondents in larger than usual state samples were interviewed for the purpose of analyzing senatorial representation. The Senate study was designed to provide equal sample sizes in each state, resulting in an average of 185 respondents per state and a range between 151 and 223.[1]

To estimate the degree of Senate representation in general, Bartels modeled senator conservatism (the first dimension of Keith Poole and Howard Rosenthal's W-NOMINATE scores) on party affiliation and the state mean self-identification on a rescaled version of the NES 7-point ideology question (Miller et al. 1993).

As Bartels's analysis makes clear (2008, figure 9.1), state public opinion is a strong predictor of senatorial roll-call ideology, even with the senator's party affiliation controlled. We show this strong relationship in table 8.1, in which both partisanship and state ideology (measured, as Bartels does, from the NES Senate study) are strong predictors of W-nominate first-dimension scores over the three Congresses following the 1988, 1990, and 1992 elections.

That state opinion influences roll-call behavior is not in question. At issue is the equality of the representation process. Do some opinions matter more than others? Specifically, is it mainly the opinions of the affluent that count?

After first demonstrating that state opinion matters for Senate roll-call voting, even with senator party controlled, Bartels turns to the test that is crucial for this discussion. Bartels separates opinion by the lowest third, the middle third, and the highest third on family income, where the thirds are defined by the national division. That is, separate mean ideologies are calculated for each of three income groups in each state. The lowest group is composed of individuals with a family income below $20,000, the middle-income group of those with incomes from $20,000 to $40,000, and the high-income group of those with family incomes above $40,000. Using a methodological principle used elsewhere (for example, Erikson, Wright, and McIver, 1993; Clinton 2006), Bartels decomposes state opinion into three separate variables. The notation is ours.

Table 8.1   **Predicting Senate Roll-Call Ideology from Mean State Ideologies, 101st to 103rd Congresses**

	Mean Ideology = −1 to +1 Scale	Mean Ideology = 1 to 7 Scale
Mean ideology for voting-age population	1.41*** (0.24)	0.47*** (0.08)
Republican senator	0.95*** (0.04)	0.95*** (0.04)
Intercepts	Congress-specific	Congress-specific
Standard error of regression	0.226	0.226
Adjusted R^2	.82	.82
N	303	303

Source: Authors' compilation based on Poole and Rosenthal (1997) and Miller et al. (1993).
Note: Dependent variables in both regressions are senator-specific W-nominates. The coefficients are the unstandardized regression coefficients. Standard errors clustered by senator in parentheses.

Low-income ideology times the proportion in the low-income category,

$$\bar{X}_L P_L,$$

middle-income ideology times the proportion in the middle-income category,

$$\bar{X}_M P_M,$$

high-income ideology times the proportion in the high-income category,

$$\bar{X}_H P_H,$$

where $\bar{X}_G$ = mean ideology among the income group G within the state sample and P_G = the proportion within the sample in income group G. Had Bartels measured senator ideology as a function of the raw mean group ideologies ($\bar{X}_G$), he would have captured senator responsiveness to the actual groups in the population that varies across states. Hence, the purpose in multiplying the proportions (P_G) with the raw mean group ideologies ($\bar{X}_G$) is to take into account the different sizes of the groups in the electorate and thereby to create a common baseline for comparison. Bartels measures ideology by recoding scores on the origi-

Table 8.2   Predicting Senate Roll-Call Ideology from Income-Specific Ideologies, 101st to 103rd Congresses

	Bartels Mean Ideology = −1 to +1 Scale	Replication, Mean Ideology = −1 to +1 Scale	Replication, Mean Ideology = 1 to 7 Scale
Wgt. low-income ideology ($\bar{X}_L P_L$)	−0.33	−0.67	0.50***
	(0.44)	(0.41)	(0.09)
Wgt. middle-income ideology ($\bar{X}_M P_M$)	2.66***	2.52***	0.43***
	(0.60)	(0.53)	(0.13)
Wgt. high-income ideology ($\bar{X}_H P_H$)	4.15***	4.91***	0.50***
	(0.85)	(0.72)	(0.14)
Republican senator dummy	0.95***	0.92***	0.96***
	(0.04)	(0.04)	(0.04)
Intercepts	Congress-specific	Congress-specific	Congress-specific
Standard error of regression	0.207	0.205	.0223
Adjusted R^2	.85	.85	.83
N	303	303	303

Source: Authors' compilation based on Poole and Rosenthal (1997) and Miller et al. (1993).
Note: Dependent variables in all regressions are senator-specific W-nominates. Wgt. low-income ideology, wgt. middle-income ideology, and wgt. high-income ideology are the raw mean ideologies for the respective income groups times the proportion of that group. The coefficients are the unstandardized regression coefficients. Standard errors clustered by senator in parentheses.

nal NES 7-point (from 1 to 7) into a scale from −1 to +1. The original 1 becomes −1; the original 7 becomes +1, and so on. The midpoint shifts from 4 to zero, a seemingly innocuous shift that becomes salient in the discussion that follows.

To sum up, with individual senators as the unit of analysis, Bartels matches the first dimension of the W-nominates (dependent variable) with subgroup constituency ideologies that are weighted by the proportion of the groups in each state. A Republican senator dummy is added to allow for party-specific behavior independent of constituency influence.

We show Bartels's original finding for the pooled 101st to 103rd Congresses in table 8.2, column 1. Senate W-nominate scores are highly responsive to party plus high-income opinion and (to a lesser extent) middle-income opinion. But for the low-income third, the coefficient is non-significant and actually negative in sign. This is the crucial finding that suggests that for poor folks, there is no representation in the upper chamber of Congress.

When we try to replicate Bartels's equation, we come passably close, as shown in column 2 of table 8.2. So this is the starting point of our investigation. Would further analysis lead to the discovery of anything different? The first step of our investigation was a seemingly innocuous variation. We repeated the model with the only change being a rescaling of the key independent variables on the original scale of 1 to 7 instead of our scale of −1 to +1. The results are in column 3 of table 8.2.

One's first thought is that the equations in columns two and three should be identical except for the matter of scale since scores on the scale of −1 to +1 correlate perfectly with the scores on the scale of 1 to 7. One can refer back to table 8.1 to see that this is true about total opinion. When the scale range is stretched by a factor of three from 2 points (−1 to +1) to 6 points (1 to 7), the coefficients are identical except for the proportional shrinkage of the opinion coefficient by one-third.

But when opinion is measured separately by income group, as in table 8.2, scale matters. Observe first that by replacing the −1 to +1 scale with the scale of 1 to 7, the explained variance (adjusted R^2) actually declines slightly from .85 to .83. The relative sizes and significance levels of the three components of state opinion also changed. Taking the equation in column 3 at face value, opinion is about equally influential among low-income, middle-income, and high-income families. Moreover, the coefficients are statistically significant at the .001 level for all three income groups. Thus by measuring ideology on a 7-point scale instead of a 2-point scale, we have transformed our result into one approaching a utopia of equal and strong ideological representation.

Clearly something is amiss. The problem lies in the algebra with which the independent variables in table 8.1 are constructed. Recall that our three opinion variables are each a multiplicative term, with the within-group state mean multiplied by the proportion of the state sample within the group category. When we modify the original measures of a state's income-category mean opinion by adding or subtracting a constant for all values, the initial coefficients for ideology effects (depicted as betas [β]) change to represent the composite weighted contribution of group ideology plus the proportion in the group (depicted as gammas [γ]).

Let us examine algebraically what happens when we add an arbitrary constant (k) to the state mean and thus replace the original set of estimates of relative state opinion effects (the βs) with the new ones (the γs).

For low-income ideology,

$$\beta_L \bar{X}_L P_L \text{ is replaced by } \gamma_L\, (\bar{X}_L + k)P_L = \gamma_L (\bar{X}_L P_L + kP_L).$$

For middle-income ideology,

$$\beta_M \bar{X}_M P_M \text{ is replaced by } \gamma_M\, (\bar{X}_M + k)P_M = \gamma_M (\bar{X}_M P_M + kP_M).$$

And, similarly, for high-income ideology,

$$\beta_H \bar{X}_H P_H \text{ is replaced by } \gamma_H (\bar{X}_H + k) P_H = \gamma_H (\bar{X}_H P_H + k P_H).$$

As long as the $P_L, P_M,$ and P_H "effects" are zero, adding the constant makes no difference. But they will not be zero, because these effects are the accounting mechanisms that anchor the equation when the state mean and proportion within the income category are zero. By arbitrarily adding or subtracting a constant k, one can change the order and the signs of the relative effects of ideology within the three income categories. We have already seen this when we shift from a −1 to +1 range for ideology to a 1 to 7 range. The culprit is not the expansion of the range from 2 to 6 points, but rather the shift of the midpoint from zero to four.

The problem is readily solved, however, by simply incorporating the proportions in the categories as additional variables. With three categories, adding the proportion low-income and the proportion high-income are sufficient because they perfectly define the proportion in the middle as the portion left over from 100 percent. With this step, adding an arbitrary constant will not affect the estimate of the relative contributions of income categories. The relative effects of the $\bar{X}_G P_G$s become scale invariant. The relative effects of the P_Gs however will indeed vary, as they remain conditional on the (arbitrary) choice of zero point. Thus any substantive interpretation of the relative P_G coefficients must be conditional on the location of the zero points on the $\bar{X}_G P_G$ scales.

We see the result of adding coefficients for the P_Gs in table 8.3. The new table appears to validate Bartels's original finding. With proportions in the low-income and high-income category controlled, the relative impact of ideology within the state appears to be highest for high-income voters, next highest for middle-income voters, and nonexistent (actually negative) for low-income voters. The two sets of estimates are now equivalent, with the 1 to 7 estimates being exactly three times those of the −1 to +1 scale.[2]

We have also replicated Bartels's separate analyses of Democrats and of Republicans, adding as independent variables the proportion high-income and the proportion low-income. As before, the estimated impact of high-income opinion is positive and significant; the estimated impact of middle-income opinion is also but less so; and the estimated impact of low-income opinion is trivial and actually negative. So, like Bartels, our replication finds that even Democratic senators appear unresponsive to low-income opinion. We also performed separate analyses, one of which excluded the South, and another that excluded the South separately by party of the senator. In each case, the essential findings are unmoved.

So far, our analysis supports Bartels. Analyzing the same NES Senate data as he did, we find considerable evidence for public opinion influ-

Table 8.3   Predicting Senate Roll-Call Ideology from Income-Specific Ideologies, 101st to 103rd Congresses

	Replication, Mean Ideology = −1 to +1 Scale	Replication, Mean Ideology = 1 to 7 Scale
Wgt. low-income ideology ($\bar{X}_L P_L$)	−1.06** (0.39)	−0.35** (0.13)
Wgt. middle-income ideology ($\bar{X}_M P_M$)	2.26*** (0.56)	0.75*** (0.19)
Wgt. high-income ideology ($\bar{X}_H P_H$)	4.58*** (0.75)	1.52*** (0.25)
Republican senator dummy	0.92*** (0.04)	0.92*** (0.04)
Proportion low-income (P_L)	0.75 (0.39)	5.18*** (1.03)
Proportion high-income (P_H)	0.14 (0.35)	−2.97* (1.35)
Intercepts	Congress-specific	Congress-specific
Standard error of regression	0.202	0.202
Adjusted R^2	.86	.86
N	303	303

Source: Authors' compilation based on Poole and Rosenthal (1997) and Miller et al. (1993).
Note: Replicated results with proportions added. Dependent variables in both regressions are senator-specific W-nominates. Wgt. low-income ideology, wgt. middle-income ideology, and wgt. high-income ideology are the raw mean ideologies for the respective groups times the proportion of that group. Proportion low-income and proportion high-income denotes the proportions entered separately. The coefficients are the unstandardized regression coefficients. Standard errors clustered by senator in parentheses.
*** $p < .001$, ** $.001 < p < .01$, * $.01 < p < .05$

encing roll-call behavior, but only for citizens with sufficiently high incomes. We should not lose sight of the fact that opinion generally seems influential (table 8.1); some opinions simply count more than others.

For further understanding, we replicated a step that Bartels reports in a footnote. Instead of dividing state samples into three groups based on the national income division, we divided each state into thirds based on income within the state, allotting each group (low income, middle income, and high income) as close to one-third of the sample of opinion holders as possible. Then we ran a simple regression predicting roll-call W-nominate scores from senator party affiliation plus mean scores in each state's lowest, middle, and highest thirds in terms of family income. The advantage is that these results require no correction by proportion since each state's subsamples are designed to be roughly equal in size.

Table 8.4   Predicting Senate Roll-Call Ideology from Income-Specific Ideologies, Defined Statewise, 101st to 103rd Congresses

	Mean ideology = −1 to +1 scale	Mean ideology = 1 to 7 scale
Low-income ideology ($\bar{X}_L$)	−0.21	−0.07
	(0.17)	(0.06)
Middle-income ideology ($\bar{X}_M$)	0.57*	0.19*
	(0.26)	(0.10)
High-income ideology ($\bar{X}_H$)	1.24***	0.41***
	(0.22)	(0.07)
Republican senator dummy	0.94***	0.94***
	(0.04)	(0.04)
Intercepts	Congress-specific	Congress-specific
Standard error of regression	0.214	0.214
Adjusted R^2	.84	.84
N	303	303

Source: Authors' compilation based on Poole and Rosenthal (1997) and Miller et al. (1993).
Note: Dependent variables in both regressions are senator-specific W-nominates. Low-income ideology, middle-income ideology, and high-income ideology are the mean ideologies for each group where the group is defined statewise (one-third in each state), not nationally. The coefficients are the unstandardized regression coefficients. Standard errors clustered by senator in parentheses.
*** $p < .001$, ** $.001 < p < .01$, * $.01 < p < .05$

Table 8.4 shows the results. The first and second columns show an equation predicting W-nominate scores from the senator's party plus the mean ideology of each of the three income groups in the NES sample. We see once again that high-income respondents appear to matter but not low-income respondents. The difference is that this time respondents' placement in their income category is based on their income relative to that of other families in their home state rather than their classification in the national income breakdown.

An important issue when using survey-generated means to predict legislative behavior is the measurement error in the ideology variables (Achen 1978; Erikson 1978). As large as the samples are for the NES Senate study, their use produces wobbly estimates when the data is sliced by income groups. The mean Ns for the low-income, medium income, and high-income samples are, respectively, only forty-eight, sixty-eight, and fifty-four cases per state. We draw on sampling theory to estimate the measurement error and reliability of the three sets of ideology scores based on states' Ns and within-state variances and the observed between-state variances. Reliability estimates for these data suggest that more than half the variance of the three income-group means is actually sampling error rather than variance in true state means—more specifically, the reliabilities are .41, .48, and .50 for the low-income, middle-income, and high-income groups, respectively.[3]

This assessment represents both bad news and good news. The bad is that estimates of the effects should be taken as more uncertain than the coefficients in tables 8.1 through 8.4 would suggest. The good news is that, in general, the measurement error attenuates the relationships so that the error must tilt in the direction of underestimation of the magnitudes of state opinion effects. In short, we should expect even more representation generally than reported so far.

The reliabilities are in this case unfortunately too small to run errors-in-variables regression. This calls for further examination, using datasets with larger sample sizes with the purpose of obtaining higher reliabilities. Thus, in the next section we examine Bartels's findings using two large recent datasets, the Annenberg surveys of 2000 and 2004 and exit poll data from the 2004 election.

New Data I: Annenberg 2000 and 2004

We replicated the findings from the Senate study by pooling the Annenberg surveys from 2000 and 2004 (Romer et al. 2006). The advantage of the Annenberg surveys over the Senate study is that they provide us with extremely high sample sizes and hence less measurement error in the main independent variables (Clinton 2006). When the 2000 and 2004 surveys are pooled, a total of 155,000 respondents are available. This is a substantial improvement over the 9,253 respondents available to Bartels. Thus, with this new dataset we can expect the income-specific mean ideology scores to be estimated with a much higher reliability. Furthermore, using the Annenberg surveys allows us to test Bartels's findings across time (1999 through 2005 versus 1989 through 1995). The downside of this new dataset is that it was sampled nationally and not statewise, as the NES Senate study was, resulting in notably unequal sample sizes across states.[4]

As in the previous analysis, we recode the original 5-point measure to range between –1 and 1. In the interest of space, only the recoded measure will be presented. For comparison with Bartels, the dependent variable is still the first dimension of W-nominates. As with the NES Senate data, using the Annenberg data results in a strong effect of state opinion on roll calls (see table 8.5).[5] It is the equality of opinion that is at issue.

In table 8.6, we have applied the methodology from Bartels (2008) to the Annenberg surveys. At first sight, the results seem to verify the findings from table 8.3. Statistical evidence indicates that senators are representative of high-income ideology, while the coefficient for the poorest third is insignificant. However, a Wald test for the difference between low-income representation and high-income representation fails the .05

Table 8.5   Predicting Senate Roll-Call Ideology from Mean State Ideologies, 106th to 108th Congresses (Annenberg Study Data)

Mean ideology for voting-age population	1.99***
(−1 to +1 scale)	(.35)
Republican senator	1.31***
	(.04)
Intercepts	Congress-specific
Standard error of regression	.196
Adjusted R^2	.93
N	291

Source: Authors' compilation based on Poole and Rosenthal (1997) and Romer et al. (2006).
Note: Dependent variables are both senator-specific W-nominates. The coefficients are the unstandardized regression coefficients. Standard errors clustered by senator in parentheses.
*** $p < .001$, ** $.001 < p < .01$, * $.01 < p < .05$

Table 8.6   Predicting Senate Roll-Call Ideology from Income-Specific Ideologies, 106th to 108th Congresses, Defined Nationally (Annenberg Study Data)

	Mean Ideology = −1 to +1 Scale
Wgt. low-income ideology ($\bar{X}_L P_L$)	1.02
	(1.14)
Wgt. middle-income ideology ($\bar{X}_M P_M$)	2.06
	(1.99)
Wgt. high-income ideology ($\bar{X}_H P_H$)	3.72*
	(1.57)
Republican senator dummy	1.30***
	(.05)
Proportion low-income (P_L)	.02
	(.79)
Proportion high-income (P_H)	−.56
	(.82)
Intercepts	Congress-specific
Standard error of regression	.194
Adjusted R^2	.93
N	291

Source: Authors' compilation based on Poole and Rosenthal (1997) and Romer et al. (2006).
Note: Dependent variables are senator-specific W-nominates. Wgt. low-income ideology, wgt. middle-income ideology, and wgt. high-income ideology are the raw mean ideologies for the respective income groups times the proportion of that group. The groups are defined nationally. Proportion low-income and proportion high-income denotes the proportions entered separately. The coefficients are the unstandardized regression coefficients. Standard errors clustered by senator in parentheses.
*** $p < .001$, ** $.001 < p < .01$, * $.01 < p < .05$

Table 8.7   Predicting Senate Roll-Call Ideology from Income-Specific Ideologies, 106th to 108th Congresses, Defined Statewise (Annenberg Study Data)

	Mean Ideology = −1 to +1 Scale	− Mean Ideology = −1 to +1 Scale EIVREG
Low-income ideology ($\overline{X}_L$)	.59	1.16
	(.41)	(0.76)
Middle-income ideology ($\overline{X}_M$)	.04	−.95
	(.62)	(.96)
High-income ideology ($\overline{X}_H$)	1.14*	1.58*
	(.50)	(.71)
Republican senator dummy	1.31***	1.30***
	(.04)	(.04)
Intercepts	Congress-specific	Congress-specific
Standard error of regression	.196	.193
Adjusted R^2	.93	.93
N	291	291

Source: Authors' compilation based on Poole and Rosenthal (1997) and Romer et al. (2006).
Note: Dependent variables are senator-specific W-nominates. Low-income ideology, middle-income ideology, and high-income ideology are the mean ideologies for each group where the group is defined state-wise (one-third in each state), not nationally. The coefficients are the unstandardized regression coefficients. Standard errors in parentheses are clustered by senator in column 1. Because the Eivreg procedure in STATA does not allow for clustering, we also estimated the model in column 2 with only one observation per senator/cluster. That is, the dataset was collapsed at the individual senator level to preclude statistical dependence due to senators holding office in multiple sessions. This did not alter the results substantively.
*** $p < .001$, ** $.001 < p < .01$, * $.01 < p < .05$

threshold. That is, we cannot find statistical evidence for a difference between the low-income and high-income groups.

Now, why is that? If we compare the Annenberg results with the Senate study, two main differences emerge. First, though still insignificant, the low-income ideology now has a positive coefficient. Second, and most important, the standard errors of the coefficients are more than twice the magnitude of the 1989 to 1995 results. This can be ascribed to the fact that the income categories are much more internally correlated in the Annenberg data (low-middle .64, low-high .67, and middle-high .86) than in the Senate study (low-middle .31, low-high .31, and middle-high .33).[6] This results in higher multicollinearity and thus higher standard errors.

The results are substantively equivalent when we base the income groups on state-specific definitions (table 8.7, column 1). High-income ideology is the only significant ideology variable but it is not significant differently from low-income ideology. As in table 8.4, we exclude the proportions, because each group includes approximately one-third of the respondents in each state.

An advantage of the Annenberg data over the NES Senate study is the higher reliabilities that allow us to run errors-in-variables regression (table 8.7, column 2). Using sampling theory, reliabilities of .70 (low income), .88 (middle income), and .95 (high income) are obtained. The differences in the reliabilities are mainly due to lower true variance in the low-income group than in the two other groups. The lower reliability for low-income could mean that it is differentially attenuated, that is, that part of the tendency toward a larger high-income coefficient is a statistical artefact.

When errors-in-variables regression is applied (table 8.7, column 2), the coefficients increase somewhat in magnitude, and the relative difference between low-income and high-income decreases further. Additionally, multicollinearity becomes even more severe as the error-corrected correlations between the income groups are as high as .82 (low-middle), .82 (low-high), and .94 (middle-high). This adds to the impression that the income groups are too closely related to statistically separate their individual impact and that robust statistical evidence for uneven representation therefore cannot be found in the Annenberg data.

New Data II: The 2004 Exit Polls

As a further dataset, we replicate the Senate study findings using the 2004 state exit polls. For this part of the analysis, we also experiment with different dependent variables to check the robustness of the results across policy dimensions. More specifically, we use three measures of senator ideology in the 109th Congress: Poole and Rosenthal's DW-nominate scores on dimension 1, DW-nominate scores on dimension 2, and a composite, weighing the second dimension .35 of the first (.74 times dimension 1 and .26 times dimension 2).

The advantage of the exit poll dataset is that the large state samples allow an expansion of the state Ns to an average of 1350 (summed across income categories) and a minimum of 584. Thus most Ns per income category are in the multiple hundreds, an advantage over the Annenberg study with its more uneven set of Ns per state. One obvious difference from both the NES Senate data and the Annenberg data is that exit polls are limited to voters only. Also, the exit-poll mean ideology scores are based on a 3-point scale, on which respondents are allowed to declare themselves only as liberals, moderates, or conservatives. As in the previous part, we calibrate this ideology scale to range from −1 to 1.

Table 8.8 displays the estimated effects for dependent variables, using the national income categories[7] and weighting within-category means by their proportions. Relating Senate ideology to opinion within income

Table 8.8   **Predicting Senate Roll-Call Ideology from Income-Specific Ideologies, Defined Nationally (2004 Exit Poll Data)**

	1st Dimension of DW-Nominates	2nd Dimension of DW-Nominates	Composite Measure
Wgt. low-income ideology	2.32*	4.03	2.77**
$(\bar{X}_L P_L)$	(.99)	(2.08)	(1.02)
Wgt. middle-income ideology $(\bar{X}_M P_M)$	1.61*	1.07	1.47*
	(.62)	(1.31)	(.65)
Wgt. high-income ideology	−.47	1.59	.06
$(\bar{X}_H P_H)$	(.61)	(1.29)	(.64)
Republican senator	.79***	−.55***	.44***
dummy	(.04)	(.07)	(.04)
Proportion low-income $(\bar{P}_L)$	.22	1.04	.43
	(.63)	(1.33)	(.66)
Proportion high-income	.40	−.43	.18
$(\bar{P}_H)$	(.50)	(1.06)	(.52)
Intercept	−.68*	−.08	.35
	(.30)	(.64)	(.71)
Standard error of regression	.150	.307	.155
Adjusted R^2	.90	.45	.82
N	101	101	101

Source: Authors' compilation based on Poole and Rosenthal (2007) and Edison Mitofsky Research (2004).
Note: Dependent variables are different versions of senator-specific DW-nominates. The composite measure is .74 times the 1st dimension score plus .26 times the 2nd dimension score. Wgt. low-income ideology, wgt. middle-income ideology, and wgt. high-income ideology are the raw mean ideologies for the respective income groups times the proportion of that group. The groups are defined nationally. Proportion low-income and proportion high-income denotes the proportions entered separately. The coefficients are the unstandardized regression coefficients. Standard errors in parentheses.
*** $p < .001$, ** $.001 < p < .01$, * $.01 < p < .05$

groups in the 2004 exit polls, we find some pattern of senatorial responsiveness to opinion. However, although the coefficients for all three groups for all three versions of the dependent variable are positive, they are most positive for low-income opinion. This is an outcome that does not seem right and will be challenged below. One possibility is that breaking down exit poll opinion by income group adds virtually nothing to the prediction of senator behavior.

Consider that if we substitute ideological means for the entire state sample (see table 8.9), we obtain not only highly significant coefficients but also virtually the same explained variance as when parsing by income. When each of the three dependent variables of table 8.8 is pre-

Table 8.9   Influence of General Opinion on Three Versions of DW-Nominates (2004 Exit Poll Data)

	1st Dimension of DW-Nominates	2nd Dimension of DW-Nominates	Composite Measure
Mean ideology	.79***	2.36***	1.33***
	(.14)	(.32)	(.16)
Republican senator dummy	.78***	−.51***	.42***
	(.03)	(.07)	(.04)
Intercept	−.46***	−.08	−.39***
	(.02)	(.05)	(.03)
Standard error of regression	.153	.318	.155
Adjusted R^2	.90	.41	.81
N	101	101	101

Source: Authors' compilation based on Poole and Rosenthal (2007) and Edison Mitofsky Research (2004).
Note: Dependent variables are different versions of senator-specific DW-nominates. The composite measure is .74 times the 1st-dimension score plus .26 times 2nd-dimension score. The coefficients are the unstandardized regression coefficients. Standard errors in parentheses.
*** $p < .001$, ** $.001 < p < .01$, * $.01 < p < .05$

dicted from party and net state ideology alone, the adjusted R^2 is within a point or two of those shown in the more elaborate model.

As for Annenberg, the main problem with the Senate exit poll data is that mean ideology scores for the three income categories were highly correlated (.85 low-middle, .75 low-high, and .90 middle-high). That is, the three income groups move together. If a state is liberal, all three groups are relatively liberal; if it is conservative, all three groups are relatively conservative. This extreme multicollinearity rendered problematical any attempt to separate the effects of opinion across income groups. The problem is even slightly worse when measurement error is taken into account.[8]

A different but also odd verdict arises when exit poll respondents are classified by thirds of income within their state. For this exercise, we divide the state exit poll electorate into precise thirds for the division into low-, medium-, and high-income respondents. We do so in a slightly more refined way than previously. When voters in an income category span the percentile threshold between the first and second thirds of the income categories or the second and final thirds, their group identity is assigned proportionally. For instance when voters in an income category are between the 27.3 and 35.3 percentile, they are assigned 75 percent to

Table 8.10　Predicting Roll-Call Ideology from Ideology of State Income Groups, Defined Statewise (2004 Exit Poll Data)

	1st Dimension of DW-Nominates	2nd Dimension of DW-Nominates	Composite Measure
Low-income ideology	1.00	−1.23	.45
	(.86)	(1.79)	(.89)
Middle-income ideology	1.70	2.34	1.86
	(1.04)	(2.17)	(1.08)
High-income ideology	.40	4.78**	1.54
	(.76)	(1.59)	(.79)
Republican senator dummy	.77***	−.60***	.41***
	(.04)	(.07)	(.04)
Intercept	−.50***	−.12*	−.40***
	(.03)	(.06)	(.03)
Standard error of regression	.149	.312	.155
Adjusted R^2	.90	.44	.81
N	101	101	101

Source: Authors' compilation based on Poole and Rosenthal (2007) and Edison Mitofsky Research (2004).
Note: Dependent variables are different versions of senator-specific DW-nominates. .The composite measure is .74 times the 1st-dimension score plus .26 times the 2nd-dimension score. Low-income ideology, middle-income ideology, and high-income ideology are the ideologies of voters in the state's lowest, middle, and highest third of family income respectively. The coefficients are the unstandardized regression coefficients. Standard errors in parentheses.
*** $p < .001$, ** $.001 < p < .01$, * $.01 < p < .05$

the low-income group and 25 percent to the middle-income group. The advantage of doing it this way is that the proportions within each group by construction become exactly .333. The correlations of state ideology across these three groups remain high—between .83 and .91.

The least influential group from table 8.10 is low-income voters. On the presumably most salient first dimension, middle-income ideology appears as most influential, but the positive coefficient is not statistically significant. High-income voters have a particularly positive (and significant) coefficient on the second dimension, as if this dimension—dealing with issues such as civil rights and civil liberties—has special significance to high-income voters.[9]

We should not, however, put much weight on the results of either table 8.8 or table 8.10. In only one of the six equations are the three ideology variables significantly different from each other. Oddly, that is for the composite measure of roll-call ideology in table 8.8. In general, the coefficients vary widely but with large standard errors that dampen confidence in the estimates. The collinearity makes it difficult for the researcher to distinguish among the effects of ideology for the different income groups. Perhaps this challenge is also true for senators. The evidence just examined would suggest that senators see the same relative differences across states whether they observe the opinions of high- or of low-income voters.

Based on the exit poll data, senators are highly responsive to state opinion, as much if not more so than circa 1990, the time of the Senate study. What has changed is that in 2004, ideology within income categories tended to move together because the states tended to be uniformly liberal or conservative across income categories, unlike for the period circa 1990, when the mean ideology scores for the three income groups were relatively uncorrelated.[10]

An Important Note on Mean Scores

From the focus on the influence of state opinion by income group, one might think that the question is whether a liberal underclass is getting its proper representation relative to a conservative middle class or perhaps a reactionary economic elite. At least when opinion is measured by self-identified ideology, this framing is not correct. Ideological identification does not necessarily correlate one might expect with income (for similar points, see also Soroka and Wlezien 2008; Page and Jacobs 2009; Wlezien and Soroka; chapter 1, this volume; chapter 10, this volume).[11] In addition, in the Senate study data, the three income groups were essentially tied in terms of mean ideological identification and with the poor actually being the slightly most conservative group. The Annenberg data has the groups in their "correct" order (poor = liberal, and so on) but only by a slim margin (see also Rigby and Wright, chapter 7, this volume). Only in the 2004 exit poll data does one find that the mean self-identification of the three groups decidedly follow in a stereotypical pattern of conservatism increasing with income (see tables 8.A1 through 8.A6 in the appendix).

This set of facts should help put the findings of this chapter in perspective. Perhaps we get the expected order among exit poll voters because among voters, ideology follows the rich versus poor gradient, but among nonvoters, it does not. In any case, for those seeking evidence of class-based opinion structure, ideological identification is not the place to look. Indeed, one might argue that in terms of ideological identification, ignoring the views of the poor is not a problem, because states' views tend to be systematically shared by rich and poor. As a question for further research, it might be worthwhile to explore differential representation, not on self-described ideology, but rather on some concrete domestic policy issues, such as differences between the rich and poor in terms of taxing and spending (Gilens 2009).

Conclusions

When Larry Bartels in *Unequal Democracy* (2008) examined inequality in representation, his finding was unambiguous: the richest third of the population is substantially better represented than their poorest counterparts. In fact, the poorest third is not even represented in the voting behavior of U.S. senators. Our reinvestigation is not directly contradictory to Bartels's findings, but suggests that assessing the degree of inequality in representation is more complicated than it might seem.

First, the results are not scale invariant when proportions are added to the raw mean scores, as done in the existing literature. We found two ways of dealing with this challenge. First, one can add the proportions to the equations to make the relative results insensitive to zero point. Second, and perhaps more elegantly achieved, the definition of the groups can be changed to thirds in each state instead of nationally. This is exactly what the proportions were intended to correct for. Although the corrections ultimately turned out not to challenge Bartels's results, they are important in a broader perspective because the scale variant weights are commonly used in the existing literature.

To limit the measurement error, we also reexamined Bartels's findings using two newer datasets with much higher sample sizes than the original NES Senate study. Conclusive statistical evidence could not be found in favor of the differential representation hypothesis. For the Annenberg data, high-income ideology was the only significant variable in all regressions, but it was not statistically different from low-income ideology. For the exit poll data, the expected unevenness in favor of the high-income group was only present for the second dimension of the DW-nominates, and only when the breakdown of income groups was done on a state basis. This is peculiar, because both datasets could be expected to be superior to the original NES Senate study, given the much larger sample sizes for each group.

We suspect the reason for our failure to confirm Bartels's results in the newer datasets was multicollinearity, and hence the higher standard errors compared to those in the NES Senate study. This multicollinearity was caused by much higher correlations between the income-group ideologies than in the original study. In fact, in the two newer surveys we did not find any error-corrected correlations between the income groups below .80. That the income-group average ideologies are similar and covary closely across states when reliable surveys are used indicates that the stakes are not particularly high when examining differential representation on the basis of general ideology. In this perspective, it might be worthwhile for future research to look more into detail on differences between rich and poor on concrete domestic policy issues.

Appendix

Table 8.A1   Descriptive Statistics for NES Senate Study (−1 to +1 Scale)

Variable	Mean	Std. Dev.	Min	Max	N
W-nominate 1st dimension	−.19	.54	−1	.99	303
Low-income ideology	.14	.11	−.09	.33	303
Middle-income ideology	.15	.09	−.03	.37	303
High-income ideology	.13	.09	−.10	.32	303
Overall mean ideology	.14	.07	.03	.31	303
Republican senator	.44	.50	0	1	303

Source: Authors' compilation based on Miller et al. (1993) and Poole and Rosenthal (1997).
Note: Income groups are defined nationally.

Table 8.A2   Correlation Matrix for NES Senate Study (−1 to +1 Scale)

	WN	LII	MII	HIO	OMI	RS
W-nominate 1st dimension (WN)	—					
Low-income ideology (LII)	.01	—				
Middle-income ideology (MII)	.17	.31	—			
High-income ideology (HIO)	.31	.30	.33	—		
Overall mean ideology (OMI)	.23	.71	.78	.69	—	
Republican senator (RS)	.89	−.04	.00	.09	.04	—

Source: Authors' compilation based on Miller et al. (1993) and Poole and Rosenthal (1997).
Note: The coefficients are the pair-wise correlations. Income groups are defined nationally.

Table 8.A3   Descriptive Statistics for the Annenberg 2000 and 2004 (−1 to +1 Scale)

Variable	Mean	Std. Dev.	Min	Max	N
W-nominate 1st dimension	−.02	.73	−1	1	291
Low-income ideology	.06	.06	−.06	.16	291
Middle-income ideology	.10	.06	−.02	.22	291
High-income ideology	.12	.08	−.06	.33	291
Overall mean ideology	.10	.06	−.03	.19	291
Republican senator	.52	.50	0	1	291

Source: Authors' compilation based on Romer et al. (2006) and Poole and Rosenthal (1997).
Note: Income groups are defined nationally.

Table 8.A4 Correlation Matrix for the Annenberg, 2000 and 2004 (−1 to +1 Scale)

	WN	LII	MII	HIO	OMI	RS
W-nominate 1st dimension (WN)	—					
Low-income ideology (LII)	.33	—				
Middle-income ideology (MII)	.42	.63	—			
High-income ideology (HIO)	.50	.69	.85	—		
Overall mean ideology (OMI)	.48	.81	.93	.95	—	
Republican senator (RS)	.95	.22	.30	.37	.35	—

Source: Authors' compilation based on Romer et al. (2006) and Poole and Rosenthal (1997).
Note: The coefficients are the pair-wise correlations. Income groups are defined nationally.

Table 8.A5 Descriptive Statistics for Exit Poll Data (−1 to +1 Scale)

Variable	Mean	Std. dev.	Min	Max	N
DW-nominate 1st dimension	.02	.46	−.60	.48	101
Low-income ideology	.06	.11	−.16	.28	101
Middle-income ideology	.15	.12	−.18	.34	101
High-income ideology	.20	.15	−.09	.49	101
Overall mean ideology	.14	.12	−.12	.34	101
Republican senator	.48	.50	0	1	101

Source: Authors' compilation based on Edison Mitofsky Research (2004) and Poole and Rosenthal (1997).

Table 8.A6 Correlation Matrix for the Exit Poll Data

	WN	LII	MII	HIO	OMI	RS
DW-nominate 1st dimension (WN)	—					
Low-income ideology (LII)	.48	—				
Middle-income ideology (MII)	.65	.75	—			
High-income ideology (HIO)	.64	.80	.90	—		
Overall mean ideology (OMI)	.65	.86	.96	.96	—	
Republican senator (RS)	.93	.35	.51	.51	.52	—

Source: Authors' compilation based on Edison Mitofsky Research (2004) and Poole and Rosenthal (1997).
Note: The coefficients are the pair-wise correlations.

Notes

1. The numbers drop slightly when we take into account nonrespondents to the ideology question and its follow-up. Thus, an average of 171 valid respondents could be used in the analysis, ranging from 138 to 209.
2. One might ask why, given that we incorporate the proportions in the income categories as additive right-hand-side variables, we do not also include the ideology scores for the three income groups. The proportions are necessary in the equation to maintain coefficients that are independent of the choice of zero-point. The proportion coefficients have no interpretation other than necessary algebraic bookkeeping. The coefficients for the ideology scores, however, are zero by theory. When an income group consists of 0 percent of a state's citizens, by theory it has no impact beyond what is represented by the coefficient for the product of the group's ideology score and its proportion of the sample. Moreover, should we decide otherwise and include the additive terms for income-group ideology, the result is a fierce level of multicollinearity that prevents meaningful analysis.
3. We calculated the reliability for the three groups using the following formula based on sampling theory: reliability = (total variance − error variance)/total variance. The total variance is simply the observed between-state variance, that is, the variance of state ideology means of the group in question across states. The error variance is the within-state variance. It is obtained by first taking the variance for the group in question in each state and dividing by the number of valid observations for that group in the states. The mean is then taken of these state-specific within-state variances. The intuition is the greater variance between states compared to the (within-state) error variance, the higher reliability.
4. The state-level sample sizes varied between 344 (Wyoming) and 15,419 (California) in the Annenberg pooled file, and between 151 (New York) and 223 (Idaho) in the Senate study.
5. We examine the 106th to 108th Congresses instead of the 107th to 109th because W-nominate scores are not at presstime available for the 109th Congress. This should be inconsequential for the results.
6. When corrected for reliability, the correlations among the ideology scores for the income groups in the Senate study are approximately twice as high as was observed.
7. Low-income voters are defined as those with under $30,000 in family income (22 percent). High-income voters are defined as those with $75,000 or more in family income (33 percent). The remainder who revealed their income were coded as middle-income voters (45 percent). We used the $30,000 threshold to distinguish low-income voters from middle-income voters even though it reduces the low-income percentage to barely over one-fifth because the next highest income category in the questionnaire ($30,000 to $50,000) contains 22 percent of all voters.
8. The error-corrected pair-wise correlations are .95 (high-middle), 92 (middle-low), and .80 (high-low). In the interest of space, we do not present eivreg results, which only amplify our conclusions.
9. This would be in line with the argument that Christopher Ellis and Joseph

Daniel Ura made in chapter 3 this volume on the relative importance of economic versus cultural issues across income and education groups

10. Note again, however, that part of the explanation for the difference is likely to be the low reliability of the NES Senate study, which roughly halves the correlation between the income groups.

11. Although the focus of the present chapter is cross-sectional, other work indicates that the opinion time series for income groups are also remarkably parallel (see, for example, Ura and Ellis 2008; Soroka and Wlezien 2008; Enns and Wlezien, chapter 1, this volume; Wlezien and Soroka, chapter 10, this volume; for similar conclusions for knowledge-sophistication groups, see Enns 2006; Enns and Kellstedt 2008; for the more general point of "parallel publics," see Page and Shapiro 1992).

References

Achen, Christopher H. 1978. "Measuring Representation." *American Journal of Political Science* 22(3): 475–510.

Bartels, Larry M. 1991. "Constituency Opinion and Congressional Policy Making: The Reagan Defense Buildup." *American Political Science Review* 85(2): 456–74.

———. 2008. *Unequal Democracy: The Political Economy of the New Gilded Age.* Princeton, N.J.: Princeton University Press.

Brady, Henry E., Sidney Verba, and Kay Lehman Schlozman. 1995. "Beyond SES: A Resource Model of Political Participation." *American Political Science Review* 89(2): 271–94.

Clinton, Joshua D. 2006. "Representation in Congress: Constituents and Roll Calls in the 106th House." *The Journal of Politics* 68(2): 397–409.

Edison Mitofsky Research. 2004. *National Election Pool General Election Exit Polls.* Sommerville, N.J.: Edison Media Research. Available through the Interuniversity consortium for Political and Social Research, University of Michigan, Ann Arbor.

Enns, Peter K. 2006. "The Uniform Nature of Opinion Change." Paper presented at the Annual Meeting of the American Political Science Association. Philadelphia (September 2006).

Enns, Peter K., and Paul M. Kellstedt. 2008. "Policy Mood and Political Sophistication: Why Everybody Moves Mood." *British Journal of Political Science* 38(3): 433–54.

Erikson, Robert S. 1978. "Constituency Opinion and Congressional Behavior: Re-Examination of Miller-Stokes Representation Data." *American Journal of Political Science* 22(3): 511–35.

———. 1990. "Roll Calls, Reputations, and Representation in the United States Senate." *Legislative Studies Quarterly* 15(4): 623–42.

Erikson, Robert S., Michael B. MacKuen, and James A. Stimson. 2002. *The Macro Polity.* Cambridge: Cambridge University Press.

Erikson, Robert S., Gerald C. Wright, and John P. McIver. 1993. *Statehouse Democracy: Public Opinion and Policy in the American States.* Cambridge: Cambridge University Press.

Fiorina, Morris P. 1974. *Representatives, Roll Calls, and Constituencies*. Lanham, Md.: Lexington Books.

Frank, Thomas. 2004. *What's the Matter with Kansas? How Conservatives Won the Heart of America*. New York: Metropolitan Books.

Gilens, Martin. 2005. "Inequality and Democratic Responsiveness." *Public Opinion Quarterly* 69(5): 778–96.

———. 2009. "Preference Gaps and Inequality in Representation." *PS: Political Science and Politics* 42(2): 335–41.

Griffin, John D., and Brian Newman. 2005. "Are Voters Better Represented?" *Journal of Politics* 67(4): 1206–27.

Jacobs, Lawrence R., and Benjamin I. Page. 2005. "Who Influences U.S. Foreign Policy?" *American Political Science Review* 99(1): 107–23.

Miller, Warren E., Donald R. Kinder, Steven J. Rosentone, and the National Election Studies. 1993. *American National Election Study: Pooled Senate Election Study, 1988, 1990, 1992*. Ann Arbor: University of Michigan. Available at http://www.electionstudies.org (accessed August 20, 2010).

Miller, Warren E., and Donald E. Stokes. 1963. "Constituency Influence in Congress." *American Political Science Review* 57(1): 45–56.

Page, Benjamin I., and Lawrence R. Jacobs. 2009. *Class War? What Americans Really Think About Economic Inequality*. Chicago: University of Chicago Press.

Page, Benjamin I., and Robert Y. Shapiro. 1983. "Effects of Public-Opinion on Policy." *American Political Science Review* 77(1): 175–90.

———. 1992. *The Rational Public: Fifty Years of Trends in Americans' Policy Preferences*. Chicago: University of Chicago Press.

Poole, Keith T., and Howard L. Rosenthal. 1997. *Congress: A Political-Economic History of Roll Call Voting*. New York: Oxford University Press. Data available at http://www.voteview.com (accessed August 18, 2010).

———. 2007. *Ideology and Congress*, Piscataway, N.J.: Transaction Press. Data available at http://www.voteview.com (accessed August 18, 2010).

Romer, Daniel, Kate Kenski, Kenneth Winneg, Christopher Adasiewicz, and Kathleen Hall Jamieson. 2006. *Capturing Campaign Dynamics 2000 and 2004*. Philadelphia: University of Pennsylvania Press.

Soroka, Stuart N., and Christopher Wlezien. 2008. "On the Limits to Inequality in Representation." *PS: Political Science and Politics* 41(2): 319–27.

Ura, Joseph Daniel, and Christopher R. Ellis. 2008. "Income, Preferences, and the Dynamics of Policy Responsiveness." *PS: Political Science and Politics* 41(4): 785–94.

Verba, Sidney, and Norman H. Nie. 1972. *Participation in America*. New York: Harper and Row.

Verba, Sidney, Kay Lehman Schlozman, and Henry E. Brady. 1995. *Voice and Equality: Civic Voluntarism in American Politics*. Cambridge, Mass.: Harvard University Press.

Chapter 9

Policy Consequences of Representational Inequality

MARTIN GILENS

OBSERVERS OF AMERICAN government have long disagreed over how much influence citizens have over public policy. Some view American democracy as little more than a sham in which elections provide legitimacy for a government ruled by a small elite. Others see elected officials as acutely responsive to the changing preferences of their constituents. But even the most sanguine observers acknowledge that not all citizens have equal sway over government policy.

Recently, empirical studies have sought to appraise the extent of inequality in the link between public preferences and government policy. Not surprisingly, these studies find that affluent Americans are considerably more likely to find their policy preferences reflected in government policy than those who are less well-off (Bartels 2008; Gilens 2005, n.d.; Jacobs and Page 2005). In this chapter, I establish the extent of the inequality in the preference-policy link across income levels and explore how this inequality varies across substantive issue domains. My goals are to shed light on the specific policies that contribute to inequalities in representation; to identify the ways in which government policy would differ if representation across income levels were more equal; and to use variation across (and within) issue domains to understand the bases of unequal responsiveness to public preferences.

My central findings can be summarized as follows. First, I show that government policy reflects the preferences of the most affluent Americans but appears to be virtually unaffected by the preferences of either the poor or the middle class. Second, I find that this representational inequality is spread broadly across issues domains and is just as great on moral and religious values issues as it is on economic and tax policy, or foreign policy and national security. This pattern is inconsistent with accounts of U.S. politics that view conservative policies on moral issues, like abortion and gay rights, as the payoff that working-class "values voters" receive in return for ceding economic policy to business interests and the affluent (see Thomas Frank's *What's the Matter With Kansas?* [2004] and subsequent critiques by Bartels [2006, 2008] and Gelman et al. [2008]). The consistent inequality across multiple issue domains also means that income-based representational inequality sometimes pushes policies in a conservative direction (for example, on economic, tax, and trade policy), and sometimes in a liberal direction (for example, on abortion and civil rights). This representational inequality, in other words, seems genuinely rooted in economic inequality and cannot be reduced to a partisan or ideological bias.

Finally, I do find somewhat greater representational equality in the domain of social welfare policy. I argue that those cases in the social welfare domain, for which government policy adheres more closely to the preferences of the less advantaged, typically reflect a correspondence between the preferences of the less well-off and those of organized interest groups active in Washington. Within the social welfare domain, for example, interest groups, such as the National Education Association, the AARP, the pharmaceutical industry, and the National Governors' Association, align with less well-off Americans in opposition to school vouchers and in support of Social Security, Medicare, and public works spending. I conclude that though interest groups do push government policy on these issues in a direction favored by the less advantaged, this process does not primarily reflect the influence of these citizens but the "happy coincidence" (from their point of view) that powerful groups happen to share their preferences on this subset of social welfare policies.

In these pages, I follow a long tradition of research in democratic representation by analyzing the association between public preferences and government policy. The absence of a link between preferences and policies implies that constituents lack influence over what the government does. But the presence of a link is not, in itself, proof that the public shapes policymaking. Government policy and the preferences of the public (or of a subgroup of the public, such as the affluent) might align because they are both shaped by powerful interest groups, or because citizens are persuaded by government policymakers to support their preferred course of action. In this chapter, I interpret the link between public preferences and government policy as representing, at least to some substantial degree, the influence of preferences on policy. In other work, I bring a variety of evidence to bear on this question (Gilens 2005, n.d.; see also Bartels 2008; Page and Shapiro 1983; Page 2002; Erikson, MacKuen, and Stimson 2002; Burstein 2003).

Data

My dataset consists of 1,935 survey questions asked of national samples of the U.S. population between 1981 and 2002 (for more details on the data, analysis, and findings from this project, see Gilens 2005, 2009, n.d.). Each survey question asks whether respondents support or oppose some proposed change in U.S. government policy: raising the minimum wage, sending U.S. troops to Haiti, requiring employers to provide health insurance, allowing gays to serve in the military, and so on.[1] The survey question is the unit of analysis in the dataset, with variables indicating the proportion of respondents answering "favor," "oppose," or "don't know" within each income category and a code indicating whether the proposed policy change occurred.

The data for this project were collected from the iPOLL database (maintained by the Roper Center at the University of Connecticut), from the Public Opinion Poll Question database (maintained by the Odum Institute at the University of North Carolina), and, for periods where these databases lacked enough appropriate questions with demographic breakdowns, raw survey data supplied by a variety of sources.[2] In all cases, questions were identified using keyword searches for *oppose* in the question text or response categories and then manually sifting through the results to find appropriate questions. After identifying appropriate questions, research assistants used historical information sources to identify whether the proposed policy change occurred, and if so, whether fully or only partially and within what period from the date that the survey question was asked.[3] After eliminating proposed policy changes that would require a constitutional amendment or a Supreme Court ruling, proposed changes that were partially but not fully adopted, and questions that lack income breakdowns, 1,781 questions remain for the analyses reported below.

Because the surveys were conducted by different organizations at different times, the income categories use different break points in different surveys. To create consistent measures of preferences comparable across surveys and across years, I used the following procedure.

For each survey, respondents in each income category were assigned an income score equal to the percentile midpoint for their income group based on the income distribution from their survey. For example, if on a given survey 10 percent of the respondents fell into the bottom income category and 30 percent into the second category, those in the bottom group would be assigned a score of .05 and those in the second group a score of .25 (the midpoint between .10 and .40, which are the bottom and top percentiles for the second group).

After rescoring income for each survey, predicted preferences for specific income percentiles were estimated using a quadratic function. That is, for each survey question, income and income-squared (measured in percentiles) were used as predictors of policy preference for that question (resulting in 1,781 separate logistic regressions, each with two predictors). The coefficients from these analyses were then used to impute policy preferences for respondents at the desired percentiles.

In the final stage of the analysis, the imputed preferences for respondents at a given income percentile were used as predictors of the policy outcomes across the available survey questions (that is, separate regressions for each desired income percentile each with one predictor and an N of 1,781). This approach has the double advantage of allowing comparisons across survey questions with different raw income categories and smoothing out some of the noise inherent in estimating preferences for population subgroups with limited numbers of respondents (for robustness analyses of the imputation procedure described, see Gilens 2005, 2009).

The Link Between Preferences and Policy Outcomes

Many of the policies in my dataset generate similar levels of support across the income distribution and others shows substantial differences between more and less well-off Americans (for details, see Gilens 2009). For policy questions that generate comparable levels of support across different income groups, the preference-policy link is necessarily the same irrespective of income. But what does the link between preferences and policy outcomes look like as the preference gap across income levels increases? Table 9.1 shows the relationship between government policy and the imputed preferences of respondents at the 10th, 50th, and 90th income percentiles for questions that generated different size preference gaps between income levels. To the extent that government policy reflects the preferences of all income levels equally, the preference-policy link should decline for all groups as the preference gap increases. This is clearly not the case. The first two columns of table 9.1 show that the association of preferences and policy outcomes for the poor declines dramatically as the preference gap between rich and poor grows from less than 5 to more than 10 percentage points (declining from .56 to .09) but does not change at all for the affluent (declining from .55 to .54; full results in the appendix table 9.A1). The top panel of figure 9.1 shows the preference-policy link when preferences between the 10th and 90th income percentiles diverge by more than 10 percentage points (row 3 of

Table 9.1   **Strength of the Preference-Policy Link by Size of Preference Gap Across Income Percentiles**

Size of Preference	10th vs. 90th Income Percentiles		50th vs. 90th Income Percentiles	
	10th	90th	50th	90th
Gap between income percentiles				
Less than 5 points	.56 (.09) ***	.55 (.09) ***	.49 (.07) ***	.52 (.07) ***
Between 5 and 10 points	.42 (.11) ***	.53 (.11) ***	.36 (.10) ***	.54 (.12) ***
Greater than 10 points	.09 (.09)	.54 (.10) ***	.13 (.14)	.58 (.19) ***
All policy questions	.34 (.05) ***	.53 (.06) ***	.41 (.05) ***	.53 (.06) ***

Source: Author's calculations.
Note: Table shows regression coefficients (with standard errors in parentheses) from 16 bivariate logistic analyses. The dependent variable is the policy outcome, coded 1 if the proposed policy change took place within four years of the survey date and coded 0 if it did not. The predictors are the logits of the imputed percentage of respondents at a given income percentile favoring the proposed policy change. N = 1779 for all policy questions (in the bottom row) and from 322 to 936 for analyses in the first three rows. See appendix table 9.A1 for full results.
*** $p < .001$

table 9.1), conveying the fairly steep relationship between preferences and policy outcomes for the well-off and the virtually flat relationship for the poor.

The virtual lack of government responsiveness to the preferences of the poor is disturbing and seems consistent only with the most cynical views of American politics. But these results could be compatible with an egalitarian and majoritarian polity if poor people held attitudes that consistently differ from those held not only by the affluent but by the middle class as well. If the preferences of the poor are systematically at variance with the majority of Americans, the lack of responsiveness to their preferences might actually reflect a well-functioning democracy. Middle-income respondents better reflect the preferences of the median voter on most issues, so the responsiveness of government policymakers to the preferences of the middle class might therefore serve as a more appropriate test of biases in representation.

The right two columns of table 9.1 and the bottom panel of figure 9.1 show that median-income Americans fare little better than the poor when their policy preferences diverge from those of the well-off. For those proposed policy changes on which middle- and high-income respondents' preferences diverge by at least 10 percentage points, the pref-

Figure 9.1   Preference-Policy Link When Preferences Across Income Groups Diverge

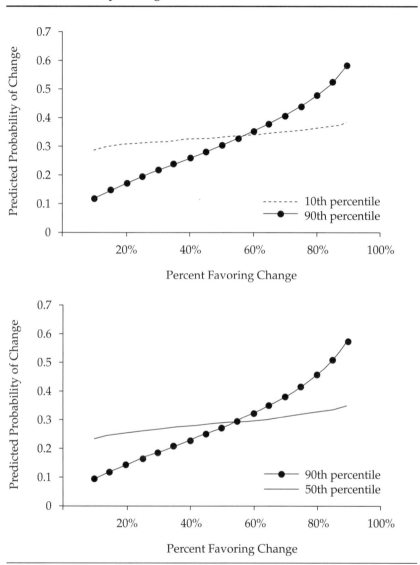

Source: Author's calculations. Predicted probabilities based on the logistic regressions reported in row 3 of table 9.1.

Figure 9.2   Strength of Preference-Policy Link When Preferences Diverge from Income Percentiles

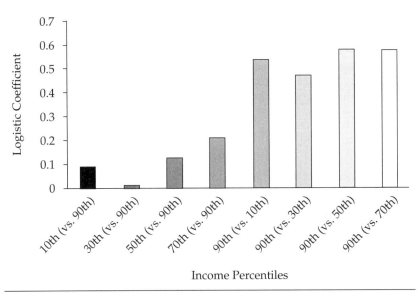

Source: Author's calculations based on the logistic regressions reported in appendix table 9.A2.

erence-policy link for the 90th income percentile remains strong but is weak (and not significantly different from zero) for the 50th percentile.

To provide a more complete picture of the relative influence of different economic groups, figure 9.2 repeats the analyses shown in row 3 of table 9.1 for the 10th, 30th, 50th, and 70th income percentiles for those proposed policy changes where the preference gap with the 90th percentile is larger than 10 percentage points (the numeric results of these analyses are in appendix table 9.A2).[4] This figure makes clear the dramatically greater influence of the affluent when their preferences diverge from those of less well-off Americans. The four left-most columns in figure 9.2 show the modestly greater responsiveness to the preferences of the 50th and 70th income percentiles compared with the 10th and 30th (when the preferences of each are pitted against those of the 90th percentile). But none of these estimated associations are statistically distinguishable from each other or from zero.

In stark contrast, responsiveness to the preferences of the 90th percentile are equally strong whether their preferences diverge from the poor, from the middle-class, or even from respondents at the 70th income percentile. Of course, the number of proposed policy changes that elicit divergent preferences is greatest between groups farthest apart on the income distribution—in this case, the 10th and 90th percentiles. Nevertheless, when preferences did diverge from the affluent, Americans at the 70th income percentile appear as powerless to shape government policy as their less well-off fellow Americans.

In short, figure 9.2 suggests that for Americans below the top of the income distribution, any association between preferences and policy outcomes is likely to reflect the extent to which their preferences coincide with those of the affluent. Although responsiveness to the preferences of the affluent is far from perfect, responsiveness to less well-off Americans is virtually nonexistent, at least based on the full set of proposed policy changes in my dataset.

The lack of responsiveness to the preferences of the 10th and 50th income percentiles illustrated in figure 9.1 does not mean that those groups never get what they want from government or that high-income Americans always see their preferences enacted in government policy. On the policy questions on which low- and middle-income respondents have the same preferences as their high-income counterparts, they are, of course, just as likely as high-income Americans to get what they want. In addition, the strong status quo bias evident in figure 9.1 means that even proposed policy changes with strong support among the affluent often fail. Finally, many policies that disproportionately benefit the poor or the middle class nevertheless receive strong support among high-income Americans. The minimum wage, the Earned Income Tax Credit, federal aid to education, child care and job training for welfare recipients, and employer health insurance mandates, for example, are all strongly favored by the affluent (even if some of these policies receive greater support still from the less well-off). Clearly some government policies do benefit the less advantaged at the expense of the more advantaged. The findings reported, however, suggest that such policies are not adopted in response to the influence of the poor or the middle class. When the preferences of the less well-off diverge from those of more affluent Americans, government policy appears to be fairly responsive to the well-off and virtually unrelated to the desires of low- and middle-income citizens.

Heterogeneity in Responsiveness Across Policy Domains

In the remainder of this chapter, I look at the specific policies that account for the differential responsiveness across income groups in order to understand what policies contribute to the observed inequality and how national policy would differ if responsiveness were more egalitarian. In addition, the variation in responsiveness, and in inequality in responsiveness, across different issue domains may provide clues to the causes of unequal responsiveness and insights into the strategies that might make public policies more reflective of the preferences of all Americans.

The policy questions in my 1981 to 2002 dataset contain proposals for changes in dozens of different policy areas, from taxes, to gun control, to abortion policy, to foreign military engagements. Three-quarters of these questions fall into four major domains of government policy: foreign policy–national security, social welfare, economic policy, and issues with strong moral or religious components (for illustrations of the major sets of policy issues contained in each domain, see tables 9.3 to 9.6).

In most other respects, the issues within the different domains are quite similar. For example, the proposed policy changes were, on average, about equally popular across the four domains, with 52 percent of respondents favoring the proposed changes in foreign policy and 57 percent favoring the proposed changes in each of the other three domains. Similarly, the proportion of proposed changes that generated lopsided preferences for the public as a whole was similar across policy domains, ranging from 30 percent to 37 percent. (Lopsided issues are those for which at least two-thirds of the respondents who expressed a preference were on one side of the issue or the other.) Finally, the percentage of proposed changes with large preference gaps across income groups was similar in the four domains: the proportion of policy changes generating preference gaps of more than 10 points between the 10th and 90th income percentiles ranged from 40 percent (for foreign policy issues) to 45 percent (for economic policy issues). The one characteristic of these proposed policy changes that does clearly differ across the domains is the number of changes adopted, which is highest for foreign policy (at 54 percent), and lowest for social welfare and religious values issues (at 22 percent and 24 percent, respectively). The reasons for these differences are discussed shortly.

In short, the characteristics of proposed policy changes do not differ substantially across the four issue domains in most respects. Although one might expect the dynamics of agenda formation and policy change to be different in areas as diverse as foreign policy and religious values issues, the findings outlined suggest that there may be more commonalities than differences across these four substantive domains.

Of central interest here, however, are variations in inequalities of responsiveness to the preferences of lower- and higher-income Americans across these domains. These patterns are shown in table 9.2 and figure 9.3, which reveal the decline in responsiveness to the preferences of each income level as the preference gaps across income levels grow (with the full logistic regression results shown in appendix table 9.A4). Because the number of policy questions in each domain is limited, I don't divide

Table 9.2   Decline in Preference-Policy Link as Preferences Across Income Groups Diverge

	N	10th		50th		90th	
				Income Percentile			
Foreign policy	428	−.62 **	(.22)	−.42 *	(.22)	−.06	(.21)
Social welfare	399	−.26 *	(.14)	−.13	(.14)	−.03	(.16)
Economic and tax policy	389	−.43 *	(.24)	−.45 *	(.23)	−.16	(.24)
Religious values issues	161	−.79 *	(.38)	−.46 +	(.33)	−.27	(.34)
Four domains combined	1,377	−.28 ***	(.09)	−.19 *	(.09)	−.02	(.09)

Source: Author's calculations.
Note: Shows interaction coefficients (with standard errors in parentheses) from fifteen logistic analyses. The dependent variable is the policy outcome, coded 1 if the proposed policy change took place within four years of the survey date and coded 0 if it did not. Predictors are policy preferences at a given income level, preference divergence across income levels, and the interaction of the two. Policy preference is measured by the log of the odds ratio of the imputed percentage supporting the proposed policy change at each income level. Preference divergence is measured by the log of the mean absolute difference between the 10th and 50th income percentiles and the 50th and 90th income percentiles. Negative signs reflect a decline in the strength of the preference-policy link for a given income level as the preference gap across income levels grows. Full regression results in appendix table 9.A4.
$+ p < .10, * p < .05, ** p < .01, *** p < .001$ (one-tailed tests)

the proposed policy changes into categories as in table 9.1. Instead, I use the interaction between the preferences at a given income level and the size of the preference gap across income levels as an indicator of the degree to which the preference-policy link declines depending on the size of the preference gap.

For those at the 10th income percentile, this decline is significant for all four policy domains but smallest for social welfare and largest for religious values issues (table 9.2). For median-income Americans, declines in the preference-policy link is quite small and nonsignificant for social welfare and about equal for the other three domains. For those at the top of the income distribution, there are no statistically significant declines in the association of preferences and outcomes as the preference gap across income groups increase. Figure 9.3 shows these twelve relationships in graphical form.

Foreign Policy, Defense, and Terrorism

In the domain of foreign policy and national security, the drop-off in responsiveness to low- and middle-income Americans is strong as their preferences diverge from those of the affluent (table 9.2 and figure 9.3).

Figure 9.3   Decline in Preference-Policy Link as Preferences Across Income Groups Diverge

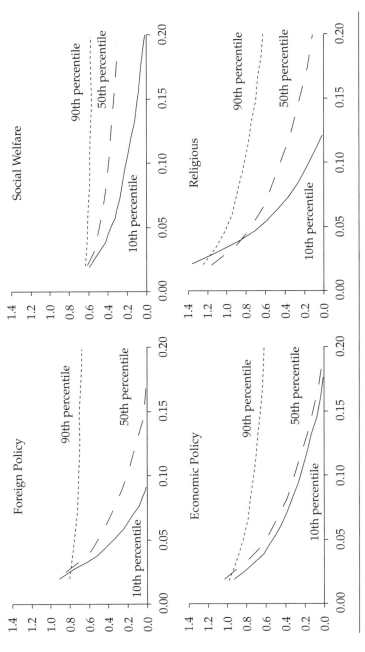

Source: Author's calculations.
Note: Based on logistic regressions reported in table 9.2 and appendix table 9.A4. Y-axis represents the strength of the preference-policy link. X-axis represents preference divergence across income groups. See note to appendix table 9.A4 for details.

The substantive policy issues that underlie these patterns are clarified in table 9.3, which presents the policy preferences for the 10th, 50th, and 90th income percentiles for those proposed changes that attracted the greatest attention from pollsters or that resulted in the largest preference divergence across income levels. To make the data in table 9.3 and the subsequent tables for the other policy domains easier to absorb, I rescored preferences from percentages to a 11-point scale in which –5 represents strong opposition, +5 strong support, and 0 an approximately equal division of support and opposition. The notes section of these tables contains the legend, which shows the relationship between percentage favorable and the 11-point scale.

The first section of table 9.3 shows U.S. involvement in foreign military engagements (either directly or indirectly), including Latin America in the 1980s, the former Yugoslavia in the 1990s, and Afghanistan and Iraq starting in 2001 and 2003. Public support for these various foreign interventions varied considerably, with the invasion of Afghanistan in the aftermath of the 9/11 terrorist attacks receiving the strongest support and aid to anticommunist forces in Latin America during the 1980s the strongest opposition. With the exceptions of Afghanistan and (to a lesser degree) Iraq, the public has been ambivalent toward or opposed to the various proposed military interventions that survey organizations have asked about. When queried in advance, majorities expressed opposition to most of the direct foreign military operations that the United States did engage in (including Panama in 1989, Haiti in the early 1990s, and the former Yugoslavia in the mid-1990s) as well as possible operations that the United States did not engage in (taking military action against Iran, invading Libya, invading Nicaragua).

Consistent with previous research (see, for example, Kull and Destler 1999; Page and Bouton 2006), public support was strongest when risks to American lives appeared lowest, when the United States acted as part of an international force rather than unilaterally, and in response to an attack on Americans. In sum, U.S. military policy was sometimes consistent with public preferences (invading Iraq and Afghanistan but not Iran, Libya, or Nicaragua) and sometimes not (invading Panama, sending troops to Haiti and Bosnia, supporting anticommunist forces in Central America). As the last column in table 9.3 shows, preferences on issues of military engagement tended to be quite similar across income groups.

The preferences of high- and low-income Americans also coincided on most aspects of nuclear weapons policy. In the mid-1980s, for example, support was strong across the board for a nuclear-freeze agreement between the United States and the Soviet Union. Despite the popularity of the nuclear freeze among the public, the policy ran strongly counter to

Table 9.3   Policy Preferences on Foreign Policy and National Security, by Income Percentile

	Income Percentiles			Difference
	10th	50th	90th	(90th–10th)
Foreign military engagements				
Invade Afghanistan	+4	+4	+5	+ 1
Invade Iraq	+2	+2	+1	− 1
Use air power against Serbia	0	0	0	0
Send U.S. ground troops to Serbia	−3	−2	−2	+ 1
U.S. troops in international peace-keeping force in Bosnia	−1	0	0	+ 1
Send U.S. troops to Haiti	−1	−2	−2	− 1
Give military aid to El Salvador or Sandinistas	−3	−2	−2	+ 1
Nuclear weapons				
Negotiate a nuclear freeze with U.S.S.R.	+4	+4	+4	0
Build the MX missile	−3	−1	+1	+ 4
Build a missile defense system	+3	+4	+4	+ 1
War on terrorism				
Restrict Americans' freedom of speech	−1	−2	−4	− 3
Relax legal protections (e.g., habeas corpus)	+3	+4	+5	+ 2
Monitor Americans' phone calls, etc.	+1	0	0	− 1
Torture known terrorists	0	0	−1	− 1
Attack nations that harbor terrorists	+3	+4	+5	+ 2
Foreign economic policy				
Development aid generally	0	+1	+2	+ 2
Development aid to former Soviet Union	−2	0	+2	+ 4
GATT, NAFTA, free trade	−1	0	+1	+ 2
Mexico loan guarantees	−4	−4	−3	+ 1

Source: Author's calculations.
Legend:
between 45% and 55%	0
over 55% or under 45%	+/− 1
over 60% or under 40%	+/− 2
over 65% or under 35%	+/− 3
over 75% or under 25%	+/− 4
over 85% or under 15%	+/− 5

the hard line the Reagan administration had adopted against the Soviet Union.[5]

Americans at all income levels also expressed strong support for antimissile defense. Reagan's 1983 Strategic Defense Initiative vastly increased the resources devoted to developing a defense against nuclear attack. Despite continued doubts about the technical feasibility of such a system, funding remained relatively steady throughout the 1980s and 1990s and increased dramatically under George W. Bush (U.S. Department of Defense 2006).

Preferences of high- and low-income Americans did diverge on one aspect of nuclear weapons policy. The development of the MX missile in the 1980s was strongly opposed by those with low incomes but weakly favored by the affluent. Intended to enhance the ability of the U.S. nuclear arsenal to survive a Soviet attack, the MX became mired in controversy over how it was to be based. Alternative strategies were proposed and rejected, but development of the missile itself proceeded. The drawn-out compromise and the funding that the missile received over the years despite the continuing uncertainty about its basing was more consistent with the mild support of the well-off than the strong opposition of poor Americans.

Larger differences of opinion across income groups sometimes emerged concerning the war on terrorism, though it would be hard to characterize either the poor or the affluent as consistently more hard-line in the policies they support. For example, well-off respondents were more likely to oppose restrictions on Americans' freedom of speech, but more supportive of proposals to relax legal protections, such as habeas corpus, and more willing to attack nations that harbor terrorists. For most aspects of antiterrorism policy, however, differences in preferences across income groups were minor.

In general, war-on-terror policies have been fairly consistent with public preferences. Policies with strong public support have been adopted (for example, attacking nations that harbor terrorists, relaxing detainees' legal protections, assassinating terrorists in foreign countries) and policies with strong opposition have not (for example, restricting speech that might incite terrorism).

The most consistent divergence in preferences across income groups in the realm of foreign policy and national security concerns trade policy and foreign aid. Affluent Americans tended to be at least somewhat supportive of free-trade policies, such as NAFTA and GATT, and somewhat supportive of nonmilitary aid to developing countries, including the former Soviet Union. Low-income Americans tend to be somewhat opposed to all these aspects of foreign policy. U.S. policy on tariffs and trade during the past few decades has clearly been more consistent with the preferences of the affluent and has become more so over time as trade barriers have fallen (U.S. International Trade Commission 2006). On the other hand, U.S. foreign aid in general and development aid in particular declined somewhat during the 1980s and 1990s (a trend more congenial to lower-income than higher-income Americans) before increasing sharply beginning in 2002 (U.S. Census Bureau 2008).

In sum, table 9.3 reveals that the weak overall preference-policy link in the domain of foreign affairs and national security reflects both a large number of issues on which public opinion is split and the many aspects of military engagement and weapons policy on which public preferences and government policy diverged. In contrast, the drop-off in responsiveness to middle- and low-income Americans as their preferences diverge from the affluent is accounted for primarily by policies concerning the war on terror and (especially) aid and trade. Affluent Americans' greater opposition to restricting freedom of speech and greater support for relaxing the legal rights of detainees, as well as their greater support for both free trade and aid to the states of the former Soviet Union, all contributed to inequality across economic groups in responsiveness to preferences in this domain.

The politics of policymaking in the foreign policy domain are somewhat distinct in that the president is more frequently able to set the agenda and make policy decisions independently of Congress than is the case in other domains. This independence may account, at least in part, for the higher proportion of proposed policy changes adopted in the foreign policy domain. If the president is more likely to set the agenda in foreign policy and less constrained by Congress in foreign-policy decision making, policies that are opposed by the administration are less likely to make it onto the national agenda and those that do are more likely to have the support of the political actors needed to implement the proposed changes.

Previous research has documented large gaps between the general public's preferences in foreign policy and the preferences of elites (Page and Barabas 2000; Page and Bouton 2006; Jacobs and Page 2005; Kull and Destler 1999). The findings presented show that preference gaps also exist between less and more affluent Americans. If foreign policy had more equally reflected the preferences of all Americans over the past decades, we would have seen even lower levels of foreign aid than we did, especially for Russia and the states of the former Soviet Union, and a more protectionist trade policy.

Religious Values Issues

A wide range of policy issues—from taxes to health care to terrorism—may involve moral or religiously based considerations, but such considerations typically play a more direct or more dominant role in most people's preferences on issues like abortion, school prayer, and gay rights. As figure 9.3 shows, the preference-policy link for religious values issues is strong on policies where agreement across income groups is high. But when preferences across income groups diverge, responsiveness to lower- and middle-income Americans falls sharply. Responsiveness to high-income Americans also appears somewhat lower on issues with divergent preferences, though this decline is not statistically significant (table 9.2). When preferences across income levels diverge, affluent Americans consistently express more liberal views than those with low or middle incomes.

Table 9.4 shows that affluent Americans were significantly more liberal on abortion policy, school prayer, stem cell research, and mandatory AIDS testing (a highly moralized policy debate when these questions about AIDS were asked in the mid-1980s). The affluent were also slightly more liberal on gay rights than low- and middle-income Americans, though on this set of issues the differences across income groups tended to be smaller.[6]

On other religious values issues, preferences were shared across income groups. Majorities at all income levels opposed gay marriage, supported George W. Bush's faith-based social services initiative, favored strengthening laws restricting sex and violence on television, and favored intensifying the fight against illegal drug use and teenage smoking. On most of these issues, federal policy was consistent with majority opinion. Consequently, as figure 9.3 shows, when income groups agreed on religious values issues, the association of preferences and government policy was strong.

George W. Bush established his faith-based initiative by executive order shortly after coming into office in January 2001 and expanded its scope in subsequent years (White House 2008). Also consistent with public preferences, federal policy throughout the 1980s and 1990s moved toward greater regulation of sex and violence on television. Actual restrictions on content were struck down by the Supreme Court, but Congress did succeed in mandating a new rating system, requiring television manufactures to install V-chips in new televisions that enable parents to block objectionable shows, and increasing fines for broadcasting indecent material (Cohen 2006; Smith 2002).

Americans at all income levels expressed similar, and typically strong, opinions on federal policy toward recreational drugs. The poor and the well-off alike strongly favored strengthening the fight against drugs and teenage smoking and encouraging mandatory drug testing in the workplace. Similarly strong majorities opposed legalizing marijuana for personal use, but, perhaps surprisingly, strong majorities at all income levels favored allowing use of marijuana for medical reasons with a doctor's prescription.

Table 9.4   **Policy Preferences on Religious–Moral Values Issues, by Income Percentile**

	Income Percentiles			Difference
	10th	50th	90th	(90th–10th)
Abortion and birth control				
Approve RU-486	−1	0	+2	+3
Constitutional ban on abortion	−2	−3	−4	−2
Federal funding for abortions	−2	−2	0	+2
Ban partial-birth abortion procedure	+2	+2	+1	−1
Require biological father's consent or notification for abortion	+3	+3	0	−3
Require parental consent for birth control assistance for teens	0	0	−2	−2
Gay rights				
Gays, extend legal protection	+1	+3	+3	+2
Gay marriage	−2	−2	−1	+1
Gay civil unions	−1	0	0	+1
Gays in the military	0	0	+1	+1
Recreational drugs and teen smoking				
Strengthen fight against drugs and teenage smoking	+4	+4	+4	0
Legalize marijuana for medical use with doctor's prescription	+4	+4	+4	0
Legalize marijuana for personal use	−3	−3	−3	0
Encourage mandatory drug testing in workplace	+4	+3	+3	−1
Misc. moral-religion issues				
Constitutional amendment to permit school prayer	+4	+3	+1	−3
Stem cell research: source unspecified	+1	+1	+3	+2
From discarded embryos	0	+1	+3	+3
From newly created embryos	−2	−1	+1	+3
Mandatory AIDS testing of all citizens (mid-1980s)	+3	+2	0	−3
G.W. Bush's faith-based initiative	+3	+3	+2	−1
Strengthen TV rating system or time restrictions; require V-chip	+4	+5	+4	0

Source: Author's calculations.
Legend:
between 45% and 55%	0
over 55% or under 45%	+/− 1
over 60% or under 40%	+/− 2
over 65% or under 35%	+/− 3
over 75% or under 25%	+/− 4
over 85% or under 15%	+/− 5

Federal policy during these decades reflected public support for fighting recreational drug use, with spending on antidrug efforts increasing six-fold (in inflation-adjusted dollars) between 1981 and 2004 (White House 2006; U.S. Department of Justice 2003). In addition, workplace drug testing expanded greatly between the mid-1980s and the early 1990s (U.S. Department of Labor 2003). The clearest exception to the consistency of federal policy and majority preferences on religious values issues concerns medical marijuana. Federal policy never reflected the strong public support for legalizing medical marijuana, and to the contrary both the Clinton and G. W. Bush administrations tried to shut down growers and distributors of medical marijuana in states that had legalized marijuana for medical use (Eddy 2005).

Although federal policy on consensual issues in the religious-values domain generally reflected public preferences, policy on nonconsensual issues fell largely in line with the preference of the affluent. The issue in this area that got the greatest attention from survey organizations (and the media) in the decades under study was reproductive policy. High-income Americans opposed laws that would have required parental consent for teenagers to receive birth control assistance from federally financed clinics (low-income Americans were split on this). Despite repeated efforts by Republican legislators to require parental notification for federally funded contraception services to minors, federal law continues to guarantee the confidentiality of such services, regardless of age (Jones and Boonstra 2004).

Opinions also differed on approving the abortion pill RU-486, which the affluent supported and the poor opposed. FDA approval of RU-486 was delayed for a few years by President G. H. W. Bush, but eventually gained approval under President Clinton (Hogan 2000). Because few survey questions concerning RU-486 were asked until the late 1990s, coded outcomes (reflecting final approval of RU-486 in 2000) were consistent with the more liberal preferences of the well-off on this issue for most of the questions in my dataset.

One aspect of abortion law that has clearly favored the stronger anti-abortion sentiments of low-income Americans is—perhaps ironically—the prohibition on federal funding of abortion services for low-income Americans. Although the specific exceptions (for example, in cases of rape or danger to the life of the woman) have changed over the years, the exclusion of abortion services from Medicaid and other federal government health programs has been in effect continuously since 1976 (Fried 2000).

The highly moralized debate about AIDS in the mid-1980s also reflected very different attitudes among less and more affluent Americans. During the early stages of the AIDS epidemic, some called for compulsory universal AIDS testing of American citizens.[7] Affluent Americans were split on this policy, but it was strongly favored by the poor and somewhat less strongly favored by the middle class. Public health officials unanimously rejected such large-scale compulsory testing and this policy was never adopted (Johnson and Smith 1988).

Federal policy in the religious values domain did not always reflect the preferences of the affluent. High-income Americans were strongly supportive of efforts during the Clinton years to expand the scope of civil rights laws to include sexual orientation while low-income Americans were only mildly supportive. Despite this favorable public opinion, no new federal legislation of this kind was adopted.

Finally, federal funding for stem cell research was arguably more consistent with the preferences of lower- and middle-income Americans, although the degree of support among all groups varied depending on the source of the stem cells in question. During the 1990s, federal funding of stem cell research was limited. Under G. W. Bush, funding became available for work with cells that came from embryos that had already been destroyed, but not for cells extracted from additional embryos. On the whole, the strict conditions on federal funding for stem cell research was more consistent with the split opinions of low-income Americans than the generally strong support of the well-off (Shimabukuro 2007).

Of the four major policy domains examined, moral and religious values policies stand out as being the least impacted by logistical or economic factors and the least influenced by the economic interests of organized groups or identifiable classes of citizens. In addition, the moral and religious values policies in table 9.4 do not impose significant economic costs on government. Extending legal protections, restricting abortion procedures, or permitting federal research dollars to be used on one or another source of stem cells does not require significant government expenditures the way many social and economic policies do. Consequently, politicians are freer to follow the public's preferences in this domain, a pattern reflected in the higher estimated responsiveness of policy to preferences shown in figure 9.3 and in appendix table 9.A4.

Economic Policy

Unlike foreign policy or religious values issues, economic policies tend to have clear and distinct consequences for Americans at different income levels. Yet, as reported, preferences across income groups do not differ more in the domain of economic policy than they do on religious values issues. This attests both to the important role of non–interest-based considerations in shaping Americans' policy views (Citrin and Green 1990; Sears and Funk 1991) and to the substantial number of economic issues on which low- and high-income Americans agree. As table 9.5 shows, for example, Americans of all incomes opposed proposals for

Table 9.5   Policy Preferences on Economic Issues, by Income Percentile

	Income Percentiles			Difference
	10th	50th	90th	(90th–10th)
Income taxes				
Cut personal income tax (across the board)	+3	+3	+3	0
Cut income tax rates for low and/or middle income earners	+4	+4	+3	−1
Raise income tax rates to reduce the deficit (1980s)	−3	−3	−3	0
Raise taxes on very high income earners	+4	+4	+3	−1
Cut top marginal tax rate	0	+1	+2	+2
Flat tax	−1	0	+1	+2
Other taxes				
Support a federal sales or consumption tax	−2	−2	−2	0
Cut capital gains taxes	0	+1	+3	+3
Cut/eliminate inheritance tax	+1	+2	+3	+2
Raise gas/energy taxes	−2	−1	0	+2
Other economic issues				
Unpaid family leave law	+3	+3	+3	0
Reform corporate accounting rules (post-Enron)	+3	+3	+3	0
Raise minimum wage	+5	+4	+3	−2
Extend/increase unemployment benefits	+2	+1	−1	−3
Increase gov't regulation of oil/gas industry	+1	+1	−2	−3
Increase misc. corporate regulation	+3	+2	+1	−2

Source: Author's calculations.
Legend:

between 45% and 55%	0
over 55% or under 45%	+/− 1
over 60% or under 40%	+/− 2
over 65% or under 35%	+/− 3
over 75% or under 25%	+/− 4
over 85% or under 15%	+/− 5

a federal sales tax, opposed across-the-board increases in income tax, favored across-the-board income-tax cuts, and favored unpaid family leave laws. Americans at all income levels also strongly supported corporate accounting reform in the wake of the Enron scandal and differed only modestly on cutting taxes for low- and middle-income taxpayers and increasing taxes on extremely high earners.[8]

Federal government policy on many of these "consensual" economic issues did reflect the predominant preferences of the public. A federal sales (or consumption or value-added) tax has never been seriously considered by lawmakers and the marginal income-tax rate for the average taxpayer fell from about 31 percent in 1981 to about 24 percent in 2002 (National Bureau of Economic Research 2006). Also consistent with public preferences, a national family and medical leave law was adopted in 1993, requiring employers to grant up to twelve weeks of unpaid leave per year. The 2002 Sarbanes-Oxley Act strengthened corporate accounting rules in the wake of the Enron, Tyco, and other corporate scandals, again reflecting strong public support. In contrast, changes in income tax rates for very high earners did not consistently reflect the consensus for increases expressed by Americans at the 10th through 90th income percentiles. Effective (average) income taxes on the top 1 percent of earners fell during the Reagan years but rose under Clinton, ending slightly higher in 2002 than in 1981 (Congressional Budget Office 2005).

On many other economic policies, preferences across income groups did diverge, reflecting the differing interests at stake for lower- and higher-income Americans. In these cases, there was little decline in policy responsiveness to affluent Americans, but substantial decline in responsiveness to both the middle class and the poor (table 9.2 and figure 9.3). Poor people were evenly split on cutting both the top income tax rate and the capital-gains tax rate, for example, while the affluent strongly supported both ideas. During the period under study, the top tax rates for both capital gains and ordinary income fell during the Reagan administration and rose under Clinton, the net effect being a decline from 24 percent to 15 percent for the top capital gains rate and from 70 percent to 35 percent in the top income tax rate (Congressional Budget Office 1988; Burman and Kobes 2004; U.S. Department of the Treasury 2006). These shifts in capital-gains taxes and top income-tax rates clearly reflect the differing ideological orientations of the Democratic and Republican administrations, the changing revenue needs of the federal government, and a general trend toward lower and less progressive taxes consistent with the preferences of the well-off.

Cutting or eliminating the inheritance tax was also quite popular among the affluent, but even poor respondents were, on balance, in favor of it. The period since the early 1980s was marked by repeated weakening of the estate tax, consistent with the preferences of higher-income Americans (Luckey 2003; Bartels 2008; Graetz and Shapiro 2005).

The only proposal to raise taxes that did not generate opposition across all income groups concerns federal gasoline or energy taxes. Although poor people, who are hit hardest by gas (and most other excise or consumption) taxes, were solidly opposed, the affluent were evenly split. During the years under study, the federal gas tax increased substantially: from only 4 cents per gallon in 1981 to about 18 cents beginning in 1993, though this is, of course, still very low by international standards (Jackson 2006).

On most tax proposals that generated significant differences in preference across income groups, then, policy was more consistent with high-
income preferences (cutting capital gains taxes, cutting the estate tax,
cutting the top marginal income-tax rate, and increasing gasoline taxes).
The exceptions are proposals for replacing the graduated income tax
with a flat tax that would eliminate deductions and apply a single rate to
all taxpayers. Across the decades examined, the flat tax was favored by
modest majorities of well-off Americans and opposed by modest majorities of the poor, with median-income Americans evenly split. The failure
of flat tax proposals to gain traction in Washington is a consequence of
ideological opposition among lawmakers (primarily Democrats) who
favor progressive taxes on equity grounds and powerful interests that
benefit from exemptions in the current tax system that would be lost
under most flat tax proposals.

Nontax policies that generate preference gaps between low- and high-
income Americans often reflect the greater attraction to the free market
among the affluent (who, arguably, benefit most from the relative lack of
government regulation in the United States). The well-off generally opposed proposals to increase government regulation of the oil and gas
industry, opposed increases in unemployment benefits, and were only
modestly supportive of efforts to increase corporate regulation outside
of the post-Enron period. Poor Americans were considerably more en-
thusiastic toward government regulation and tended to favor expansion
of unemployment benefits. Americans at all income levels strongly favored raising the minimum wage, but, unlike the affluent, the poor were
nearly unanimous on this question.

In sum, we would expect a more egalitarian responsiveness of economic policy to the preferences of all Americans to result in a higher
minimum wage, more generous unemployment benefits, stricter corporate regulation (including the oil and gas industries in particular), and a
more progressive personal-tax regime in general. Some of these policies
are favored by a majority of Americans at the 90th income percentile as
well, but not with sufficient enthusiasm to overcome opposition from
business and other interests. (I return to the role of interest groups in
shaping policy outcomes shortly.)

Social Welfare

Patterns of responsiveness in the social welfare domain are somewhat
distinct from the other three policy domains examined, especially for
middle- and low-income Americans. As figure 9.3 shows, the preference-
policy link on issues with similar preferences across income groups is
the weakest of the four domains. Moreover, social welfare policy is the
only policy area in which the decline in responsiveness to middle-in-

come Americans, as their preferences diverge from those of the affluent, is negligible. As shown in table 9.2, the interaction of policy preference and preference divergence for the 50th income percentile ranges from −.42 to −.46 for the other three domains but is only −.13 (and not significantly different from zero) for social welfare policies. A similar pattern is evident for the 10th income percentile, where the decline in responsiveness as preferences across income groups diverge is also far weaker than in the other three policy domains.

Social welfare policy during the decades under study was most consistent with public preferences on Medicare and Social Security, which were enhanced or sustained despite budgetary pressures, and the Clinton administration's welfare reforms. In contrast, substantial public support for health-care reform was not reflected in government policy. Perhaps surprisingly, preferences across income groups differed more on the "universal" policies of Medicare and Social Security (as well as health care) than on welfare per se (that is, the means-tested cash assistance programs TANF and its predecessor AFDC), programs strongly tied to income.

The top section of table 9.6 shows that most welfare policy preferences do not in fact differ much across income groups. Americans of all income levels strongly support work requirements for welfare recipients and favor increasing job training opportunities and child care resources for people on welfare. Americans across the income spectrum shared similar (split) opinions on the question of ending additional payments to women who have additional children while on welfare. Middle- and upper-income respondents did express more support for time limits on welfare receipt and were more inclined to want overall welfare spending cut than were low-income respondents. In sum, preferences on welfare reform display a surprising degree of consensus across income groups, a consensus that has characterized public attitudes toward welfare for many decades (Gilens 1999).

In contrast to the clearly redistributive means-tested welfare programs referenced in the top section of table 9.6, preferences on universal programs, like national health insurance, Social Security, and Medicare, show larger preference gaps across income levels. As the second section in table 9.6 shows, the poor strongly support federal government involvement in health care, whether in the form of a tax-funded national health plan, employer mandates, or the Clinton health-reform proposal, whereas the affluent support involvement only weakly. Despite the strong support from low- and middle-income Americans and the strenuous efforts of the Clinton administration in 1993 and 1994, these sorts of broad expansions of the federal government's role in health care were not adopted during the decades under study. Studies have pointed to numerous obstacles to health-care reform in the United States, including

Table 9.6   Policy Preferences on Social Welfare Issues, by Income Percentile

	Income Percentiles			Difference
	10th	50th	90th	(90th–10th)
Welfare reform				
Work requirements	+4	+4	+3	−1
Job training for welfare recipients	+5	+5	+5	0
Child care for welfare recipients who work	+5	+5	+5	0
Time limits	+1	+3	+3	+2
No extra money for extra kids	0	0	+1	+1
Cut total spending on welfare	+1	+3	+4	+3
Health care				
Tax funded national health care	+3	+3	+1	−2
Employer mandates	+4	+3	+2	−2
Clinton Plan	+3	+2	+1	−2
Medical savings accounts	−3	−2	0	+3
Social Security reform				
Gov't invest Soc. Sec. money in stocks	−3	−2	0	+3
Individuals control own stock accounts	0	+2	+3	+3
Change Soc. Sec. rules to discourage early retirement	−2	0	+1	+3
Medicare reform				
Encourage recipients to move to HMOs	−1	+1	+1	+2
Raise premiums/deductibles for Medicare beneficiaries	−3	−1	0	+3
Cut overall Medicare spending	−4	−3	−2	+2
Add a prescription drug benefit to Medicare	+5	+5	+4	−1
Education				
Federal grants and loans to college students	+4	+4	+4	0
School vouchers	−1	0	+1	+2
Other social welfare issues				
Federal unpaid family-leave law	+3	+3	+3	0
Cut public works spending (mass transit, highways, sewage)	−2	0	+1	+3

Source: Author's calculations.
Legend:
between 45% and 55%   0
over 55% or under 45%   +/− 1
over 60% or under 40%   +/− 2
over 65% or under 35%   +/− 3
over 75% or under 25%   +/− 4
over 85% or under 15%   +/− 5

doctors and hospitals, insurance companies, unions, employers, and political gridlock (Skocpol 1997; Quadagno 2005; Gottschalk 2000; Hacker 2008). To this list we can add a lack of enthusiasm among affluent Americans.

Social Security and Medicare are the two most expensive social programs in the United States, accounting for over half of all federal social spending (U.S. Census Bureau 2008). As table 9.6 shows, affluent Americans are more supportive of market-oriented reforms to both Social Security and Medicare, such as shifting Social Security toward individual stock accounts and encouraging Medicare beneficiaries to join HMOs. The affluent are also more willing to consider changes in these programs that would reduce the benefits that they provide, such as raising the age at which full Social Security benefits are available or raising premiums and deductibles for Medicare recipients.

Despite the growing costs of Social Security and Medicare, changes to both programs since the early 1980s have been fairly modest. The Social Security reform bill of 1983 increased the retirement age for full benefits from sixty-five to sixty-seven, to be phased in over the first two decades of the twenty-first century, and made a portion of Social Security benefits subject to income tax for higher-income beneficiaries, about 10 percent of all Social Security beneficiaries at the time (Kollmann 2000). Cost savings in Medicare have come primarily at the expense of health-care providers, though these savings may translate into poorer service for Medicare beneficiaries, with the most substantial cuts occurring in the early 1980s and late 1990s (Chaikind et al. 2001).

In economic terms, the most significant change to the Medicare program over the past few decades was not a cutback but rather the addition of a prescription drug benefit (Medicare Part D) in 2003. Although the legislation was criticized by many as a giveaway to pharmaceutical companies and a bad deal for American taxpayers, the principle of government-provided prescription drug coverage for Medicare recipients was quite popular across all income levels, though slightly less so for the most affluent Americans.

In sum, the lack of significant change in the core middle-class social welfare programs—Social Security and Medicare—is consistent with the strong support for these programs among lower- and middle-income Americans. Small changes to the Social Security retirement age and efforts to encourage Medicare beneficiaries to join HMOs were more consistent with the preferences of the well-off. But the failure of Social Security privatization, the increase in overall Medicare spending, the addition of drug benefits for Medicare recipients, and the lack of change in the portion of Medicare costs paid by the government[9] are all consistent with the preferences of lower- and middle-income Americans. This pattern of policy responsiveness on Medicare and Social Security, along with other policy issues discussed below, contributes to the distinctive nature of the social welfare domain illustrated in table 9.2 and figure 9.3.

The majority of questions on education policy in my dataset concern either school vouchers for K–12 education or federal financial assistance to college students.[10] College assistance was uniformly popular across income levels, but school vouchers, which would help parents pay for private school education, were opposed by the poor and favored by the affluent. Although it is hard to identify the exact mix of considerations that accounts for the greater support for school vouchers among the well-off, this preference is consistent with the greater appeal of market solutions to high-income Americans across a range of policies. School vouchers, like many market-oriented social policies, are likely to be most beneficial to those with the financial and informational resources to take advantage of them. Similarly, poor Americans may be more likely to oppose vouchers because they are most concerned about the negative impact such programs might have on existing public schools. Despite numerous proposals over the years and support from affluent Americans, the only federal voucher program Congress ever passed is an extremely limited experiment available to fewer than two thousand students in Washington, D.C.

Finally, government spending on public works, like bridges, roads, water, and sewage is more popular among middle-income than high-income Americans. After a brief drop between 1981 and 1983, federal spending for such projects rose about 40 percent in constant (inflation-adjusted) dollars over the next two decades (Congressional Budget Office 2007).

Social Welfare Policy and Inequality in Responsiveness to the Public

Social welfare is the only policy domain examined in which the divergence of preferences across income groups does not lead to a substantial decline in responsiveness to the preferences of lower- and middle-income Americans (table 9.2 and figure 9.3). The account that was just given of social welfare policy identified four well-represented sets of policy questions on which lower-income Americans' preferences were most likely to prevail: Social Security, Medicare, school vouchers, and public works spending. More specifically, compared with the affluent, lower-income Americans are stronger opponents of cuts to Social Security and Medicare benefits, tax increases, and privatization proposals, stronger supporters of prescription drug benefits for Medicare recipients, stronger opponents of school vouchers (especially vouchers that could be used to help pay for private schooling), and stronger support-ers of public spending for highways, sewer systems, and so on.

What unites these different policies, and sets them apart from most policies on which lower- and higher-income preferences diverge, is that poor and middle-income Americans have powerful allies that tend to share their preferences on these issues. The AARP, widely viewed as one of the most powerful lobbies in Washington, has been a strong supporter of Social Security and Medicare (Morris 1996). In addition to support from the AARP, the Medicare prescription drug benefit, which President Bush signed into law in 2003, also had the backing of the pharmaceutical companies and their well-funded lobbyists.[11] The public education lobby, led by the American Federation of Teachers and the National Edu-cation Association, was allied with lower-income Americans in oppos-ing school vouchers. Finally, government spending on public works like bridges and roads, which is more popular among lower- than higher-income Americans, is backed by developers and the construction indus-try. Just as important, public works can provide a highly visible form of pork barrel benefits for individual states or districts, and members of Congress frequently tout their ability to secure such funding in their re-election campaigns.[12]

Powerful interest groups happen to share the preferences of lower-income Americans on these prominent social welfare issues. But the less well-off lack allies on other issues within this domain. For example, lower-income Americans are more supportive of both taxpayer-funded national health care and mandates requiring employers to provide health insurance for their employees. Lower-income Americans also ex-press more support for proposals to expand unemployment benefits (for example, to cover part-time workers) and to increase federal support for public schools in poor neighborhoods.

Of the 399 policy questions in the social welfare domain, about half concern the four issues on which the preferences of the less well-off are more aligned with powerful interest groups than those of the affluent: Social Security, Medicare, school vouchers, and public works spending. For these issues, there is no evidence that the middle class or the poor lose out when their views diverge from the well-off. The interactions of preferences and preference divergence (analogous to those in table 9.2) are $-.08$ and $.08$ for the 10th and 50th income percentiles, respectively ($p = .34$ and $.35$, respectively; see appendix table 9.A5 for full regression results). But for the remaining issues in the social welfare domain, where the less well-off lack strong allies, the estimated decline in the influence of the poor and the middle class is substantial and comparable to the declines in other issue domains shown in table 9.2 ($b = -.53$ and $-.39$ for the 10th and 50th income percentiles, respectively; $p = .02$ and $.05$, re-spectively).

Conclusion

Previous research has found a high degree of inequality in government responsiveness to the preferences of more and less affluent segments of the American public. This chapter shows that these representational inequalities extend broadly but not uniformly across policy domains. For the most part, the patterns of inequality evident in the overall analysis of the preference-policy link were replicated in each of the issue domains examined, but social welfare issues did constitute a partial exception to this pattern. In particular, the subset of social welfare issues on which the most significant interest groups were aligned with the preferences of lower- rather than upper-income Americans were immune from the inequalities evident with other issues.

Even if exceptional, the alignment of interest groups with the preferences of the less affluent raises the question of why this alignment takes place on these issues and whether such alignments can be fostered more broadly. In most cases, the confluence of preferences between interest groups and less well-off Americans results from a happy coincidence and not from any actual influence exerted by the poor or the middle class. The pharmaceutical lobby and the National Educational Association, for example, pursue policies that benefit their members and happen to coincide with the preferences of the less advantaged. The AARP, however, as a mass membership organization, might actually be considered a conduit through which the influence of less well-off Americans flows. Yet studies of interest group politics suggest that even those organizations that advocate on behalf of less advantaged citizens tend to favor their more advantaged subconstituencies (Strolovitch 2006), and the AARP has come under increasing fire for favoring the interests and preferences of its most advantaged members (Dreyfuss 2004).

This rather bleak conclusion about the ability of less well-off Americans to influence the course of government policymaking cannot help but give one pause. If democracy, in Robert Dahl's formulation, consists of "the continuing responsiveness of the government to the preferences of its citizens, considered as political equals," then our society has far to go to before we can fully claim the designation "American democracy."

Appendix

Table 9.A1   Policy Preference as a Predictor of Policy Outcome, by Income Percentile

Size of Preference Gap	10th Versus 90th Income Percentiles		50th Versus 90th Income Percentiles	
	10th	90th	50th	90th
Less than 5 points				
Logit coefficient	.56 (.09)	.55 (.09)	.49 (.07)	.52 (.07)
Intercept	−1.02 (.11)	−1.03 (.11)	−.94 (.08)	−.96 (.08)
N	600	600	936	936
Log likelihood	715	714	1,136	1,130
Likelihood ratio χ^2	$\chi^2(1) = 42$	$\chi^2(1) = 43$	$\chi^2(1) = 58$	$\chi^2(1) = 64$
	$p = .001$	$p = .001$	$p = .001$	$p = .001$
Between 5 and 10 points				
Logit coefficient	.42 (.11)	.53 (.11)	.36 (.10)	.54 (.12)
Intercept	−.94 (.11)	−1.00 (.12)	−.81 (.10)	−.87 (.10)
N	456	456	521	521
Log likelihood	549	538	648	638
Likelihood ratio χ^2	$\chi^2(1) = 17$	$\chi^2(1) = 28$	$\chi^2(1) = 13$	$\chi^2(1) = 23$
	$p = .001$	$p = .001$	$p = .001$	$p = .001$
Greater than 10 points				
Logit coefficient	.09 (.09)	.54 (.10)	.13 (.14)	.58 (.19)
Intercept	−.69 (.08)	−.83 (.09)	−.90 (.12)	−.98 (.13)
N	723	723	322	322
Log likelihood	922	892	388	379
Likelihood ratio χ^2	$\chi^2(1) = 1$	$\chi^2(1) = 31$	$\chi^2(1) = 1$	$\chi^2(1) = 10$
	$p = .15$	$p = .001$	$p = .18$	$p = .001$
All policy questions				
Logit coefficient	.34 (.05)	.53 (.06)	.41 (.05)	.53 (.06)
Intercept	−.83 (.05)	−.94 (.06)	−.88 (.05)	−.94 (.06)
N	1,779	1,779	1,779	1,779
Log likelihood	2,200	2,142	2,175	2,142
Likelihood ratio χ^2	$\chi^2(1) = 45$	$\chi^2(1) = 102$	$\chi^2(1) = 70$	$\chi^2(1) = 102$
	$p = .001$	$p = .001$	$p = .001$	$p = .001$

Source: Author's calculation.
Note: Shows full results for table 9.1 and figure 9.1. Standard errors in parentheses.

Table 9.A2   Policy Preference as a Predictor of Policy Outcome, by Income Percentile When Preferences Across Income Groups Differ

	10th and 90th Income Percentiles Diverge		30th and 90th Income Percentiles Diverge		50th and 90th Income Percentiles Diverge		70th and 90th Income Percentiles Diverge	
	10th	90th	30th	90th	50th	90th	70th	90th
Logit coefficient	.09	.54***	.01	.47***	.13	.58**	.21	.58*
(standard error)	(.09)	(.10)	(.11)	(.14)	(.14)	(.19)	(.22)	(.30)
Intercept	-.69	-.83	-.84	-.93	-.90	-.98	-.95	-1.00
N	723	723	481	481	322	322	165	165
-2 Log likelihood	922	892	589	577	388	379	196	193
Likelihood ratio χ^2	$\chi^2(1) = 1.1$	$\chi^2(1) = 31$	$\chi^2(1) = 0.0$	$\chi^2(1) = 12$	$\chi^2(1) = 0.8$	$\chi^2(1) = 10$	$\chi^2(1) = 0.9$	$\chi^2(1) = 3.9$
	$p = .15$	$p = .001$	$p = .47$	$p = .001$	$p = .18$	$p = .001$	$p = .17$	$p = .03$

Source: Author's calculations.

Note: Shows full results for figure 9.2. Results above are from four pairs of logistic regressions in which the sample of survey questions is restricted to those for which preferences between the specified income percentiles differ by at least 10 percentage points. To provide enough number of policy questions with divergent preferences, however, the analysis of the 70th v-ersus the 90th income percentiles includes questions on which preferences differ by at least 8 percentage points.

* $p < .05$, ** $p < .01$, *** $p < .001$

Table 9.A3   Policy Preference as a Predictor of Policy Outcome, by Policy Domain

	Foreign Policy/ National Security	Social Welfare	Economic Policy	Religious Issues
Logit coefficient	.59	.51	.66	.93
(standard error)	(.12)	(.12)	(.13)	(.26)
Intercept	.12	−1.50	−.84	−1.61
N	428	399	389	161
Log likelihood	562	403	482	161
Likelihood ratio χ^2	$\chi^2(1) = 28$	$\chi^2(1) = 20$	$\chi^2(1) = 27$	$\chi^2(1) = 15$
	$p = < .001$	$p < .001$	$p < .001$	$p < .001$

Source: Author's calculations.
Note: Cases consist of survey questions about proposed policy changes asked between 1981 and 2002. The dependent variable is policy outcome, coded 1 if the proposed policy change took place within four years of the survey date and coded 0 if it did not. The predictors are the logits of the percentage of respondents favoring the proposed policy change.

Table 9.A4   Interaction of Preference-Policy Link and Preference Gap across Income Levels

	Income Percentile					
	10th		50th		90th	
Foreign policy (N = 428)						
Income group's preference	−1.51 *	(.65)	−.76	(.66)	.59	(.66)
Preference gap across income groups	.03	(.18)	.04	(.18)	.01	(.18)
Interaction	−.62 **	(.22)	−.42 *	(.22)	−.06	(.21)
Constant	.18	(.54)	.22	(.54)	.12	(.55)
Likelihood ratio χ² (3)	21.7, p < .001		30.7, p < .001		48.1, p < .001	
Social welfare (N = 399)						
Income group's preference	−.41	(.45)	.08	(.47)	.52	(.54)
Preference gap across income groups	.27	(.22)	.22	(.22)	.14	(.22)
Interaction	−.26 *	(.14)	−.13	(.14)	−.03	(.16)
Constant	−.67	(.61)	−.88 +	(.64)	−1.18 *	(.65)
Likelihood ratio χ² (3)	17.5, p < .001		22, p < .001		23.2, p < .001	
Economic policy (N = 389)						
Income group's preference	−.74	(.69)	−.75	(.66)	.36	(.72)
Preference gap across income groups	.09	(.21)	.10	(.22)	.01	(.21)
Interaction	−.43 *	(.24)	−.45*	(.23)	−.16	(.24)
Constant	−.48	(.60)	−.55	(.64)	−.87 +	(.63)
Likelihood ratio χ² (3)	21.7, p < .001		27.2, p < .001		42.3, p < .001	
Religious issues (N = 161)						
Income group's preference	−1.70 +	(1.16)	−.61	(1.06)	.22	(1.09)
Preference gap across income groups	.53	(.44)	.34	(.40)	.30	(.41)
Interaction	−.79 *	(.38)	−.46 +	(.33)	−.27	(.34)
Constant	−.01	(1.26)	−.58	(1.15)	.77	(1.19)
Likelihood ratio χ² (3)	16.3, p < .001		15.8, p < .001		19.7, p < .001	
Four domains combined (N = 1,377)						
Income group's preference	−.52 *	(.28)	−.16	(.27)	.54 *	(.30)
Preference gap across income groups	.10	(.10)	.07	(.10)	.02	(.10)
Interaction	−.28***	(.09)	−.19 *	(.09)	−.02	(.09)
Constant	−.40	(.29)	−.50	(.29)	−.70	(.30)
Likelihood ratio χ² (3)	46.4, p < .001		61.5, p < .001		90.8, p < .001	

Source: Author's calculations.
Notes: Shows full logistic regression results for table 9.2 and figure 9.3. Table shows logistic regression coefficients (with standard errors in parentheses) indicating the interaction of policy preference at each income level with preference divergence across income levels. Policy preference measured by the log of the odds ratio of the imputed percentage supporting the proposed policy change at each income level. Divergence measured by the log of the mean absolute difference between the 10th and 50th and the 50th and 90th income percentiles.
+ p < .10, * p < .05, ** p < .01, *** p < .001 (one-tailed tests)

Table 9.A5   Interaction of Preference-Policy Link and Preference Gap across Income Levels for Social Welfare Issues

	Income Percentile					
	10th		50th		90th	
Interest group allies (N = 184)						
Income group's preference	.28	(.64)	.82	(.66)	1.54	(.88)
Preference gap across income groups	.49	(.33)	.39	(.32)	.27	(.32)
Interaction	−.08	(.20)	.08	(.19)	.25	(.24)
Constant	−.11	(.91)	−.43	(.90)	−.85	(.90)
Likelihood ratio χ^2 (3)	11.1, $p < .01$		12.9, $p < .005$		13.1, $p < .004$	
No interest group allies (N = 215)						
Income group's preference	−1.44 *	(.77)	−.82	(.79)	−.15	(.79)
Preference gap across income groups	.24	(.31)	.26	(.34)	.12	(.33)
Interaction	−.53 *	(.23)	−.39 *	(.24)	−.22	(.23)
Constant	−.60	(.89)	−.67	(1.00)	−1.17	(.98)
Likelihood ratio χ^2 (3)	9.8, $p < .02$		11.7, $p < .009$		12.0, $p < .008$	

Source: Author's compilation.
Note: The top half of the table shows analyses of policy questions on which interest groups align more closely with the preferences of less affluent Americans (Social Security, Medicare, school vouchers, and public works); the bottom half shows all other policy questions in the social welfare domain. The table shows logistic regression coefficients (with standard errors in parentheses) indicating the interaction of policy preference at each income level with preference divergence across income levels. Policy preference measured by the log of the odds ratio of the imputed percentage supporting the proposed policy change at each income level. Divergence measured by the log of the mean absolute difference between the 10th and 50th and the 50th and 90th income percentiles.
* $p < .05$ (one-tailed tests)

Notes

1. Most policy debates involve more than a single alternative to the status quo and cannot therefore be fully captured by dichotomous measures of public support or opposition. However, many policy debates generate more than a single measure in my dataset and therefore allow me to take some of these nuances into account. For example, although there were survey questions that simply asked whether respondents favored or opposed the Clinton administration's health-care reform proposal, many other questions asked about specific elements of health-care policy, such as employer mandates, health insurance portability, parity of coverage for mental health, and so on.

2. Survey data were obtained from the Inter-University Consortium for Political and Social Research, the Institute for Social Science Research at UCLA, the Kaiser Family Foundation, the Pew Research Center for the People and the Press, and the Roper Center.

3. Alan Monroe (1998) looked for policy changes over a long period and reports that 88 percent of the policy changes that occurred did so within two years of the date of the survey questions he examined. For my project, coders looked for policy change within a four-year window following each survey question. If no change consistent with the survey question occurred within that period, the outcome was coded as "no change." If change did occur within that period, the year the change took place was recorded. In coding outcomes for survey questions with specific quantified proposals (for example, raising the minimum wage to $6 an hour), coders considered a change to have occurred if it represented at least 80 percent of the change proposed in the survey question. If the actual policy change represented less than 80 percent but more than 20 percent, the outcome was given a "partial change" code. Relatively few outcomes were coded as partial changes, and in the analysis here, only "full changes" occurring within the four-year window are coded as policy change. Intercoder agreement for policy outcome (whether the proposed change occurred within four years of the survey question) was 91 percent; intercoder agreement on the year the change occurred for those occasions where both coders agreed change had occurred was 93 percent.

4. To provide enough policy questions with divergent preferences, the analysis of the 70th versus the 90th income percentiles includes questions on which preferences differ by at least 8 percentage points rather than the 10 percentage point cutoff used for the other comparisons. We would expect this more inclusive criterion for the 70th percentile analysis in figure 9.2 to slightly increase the estimated impact of the preferences of respondents at the 70th income percentile relative to the other analyses in the figure.

5. After Mikhail Gorbachev came to office and introduced far-reaching reforms to the Soviet system in 1986, Reagan administration policy on nuclear arms began to change, and the Strategic Arms Reduction Treaty (START) was eventually signed in 1991. The signing of the START treaty, however, cannot be considered a positive example of government response to public preferences, both because of the long delay and because of appar-

ently critical role of altered conditions in bringing about change in U.S. government policy.

6. As explained, the attitudes on constitutional amendments to ban abortion or permit school prayer shown in table 9.4 are not included in the quantitative analyses.

7. William Buckley Jr., "Crucial Steps in Combating the Aids Epidemic; Identify All the Carriers," *New York Times*, March 18, 1986, p. A27.

8. The group targeted for tax increases in these proposals was considerably better off than the 90th income percentile that I use to represent high-income Americans. The relevant questions in my dataset were asked during the early 1990s and referred to families with incomes above $180,000 or $200,000 at a time when the 90th percentile of household income was about $75,000.

9. The most significant cost increases to Medicare beneficiaries between 1981 and 2004 were deductibles for inpatient hospital care, which increased from $204 to $876 (roughly equal to the medical inflation rate and about twice the overall rate of inflation), and monthly premiums for Medicare Part B, which increased from $11 to $66 (about 1.5 times the rate of medical inflation). In contrast, deductibles for Part B rose only 67 percent across these decades—considerably less than inflation—and Part B coinsurance remained at 20 percent (U.S. Social Security Administration 2006).

10. The No Child Left Behind Act was passed by Congress in 2001, but the first survey question to ask explicitly about this legislation in the Roper Center's iPOLL database is from January 2003 (beyond my December 2002 cutoff for survey questions).

11. Although the AARP had initially opposed many of the bill's provisions (like forbidding Medicare to negotiate for lower drug prices), it eventually came round to supporting the legislation, creating a powerful alliance (Dreyfuss 2004).

12. District pork-barrel projects and the interest of developers and construction companies frequently come together when these projects benefit specific developers or other commercial interests within a district that then increase their support for their incumbent representative. That is, the benefit of pork barrel projects may be less in their direct appeal to voters and more in their appeal to district businesses.

References

Bartels, Larry M. 2006. "What's the Matter with *What's the Matter with Kansas?*" *Quarterly Journal of Political Science* 1(2): 201–26.
———. 2008. *Unequal Democracy: The Political Economy of the New Gilded Age*. Princeton, N.J.: Princeton University Press.
Burman, Leonard, and Deborah Kobes. 2004. "Preferential Capital Gains Tax Rates." *Tax Notes* (January 19). Available at http://www.taxpolicycenter.org/UploadedPDF/1000588_TaxFacts_011904.pdf (accessed October 25, 2010).
Burstein, Paul. 2003. "The Impact of Public Opinion on Public Policy: A Review and an Agenda." *Political Research Quarterly* 56(1): 29–40.

Chaikind, Hinda Ripps, Sibyl Tilson, Jennifer O'Sullivan, Carolyn Merck, and Madeleine Smith. 2001. "Medicare Provisions in the Medicare, Medicaid, and SCHIP Benefits Improvement and Protection Act of 2000 (BIPA, PL 106–554)." CRS Report RL30707. Washington: Congressional Research Service.

Citrin, Jack, and Donald Philip Green. 1990. "The Self-Interest Motive in American Public Opinion." *Research in Micropolitics* 3(1): 1–28.

Cohen, Henry. 2006. "Regulation of Broadcast Indecency: Background and Legal Analysis." CRS Report RL 32222. Washington D.C.: Congressional Research Service.

Congressional Budget Office. 1988. *How Capital Gains Tax Rates Affect Revenues: The Historical Evidence*. Washington: Government Printing Office. Available at http://www.cbo.gov/ftpdocs/84xx/doc8449/88-CBO-007.pdf (accessed October 25, 2010).

———. 2005. "Historical Effective Federal Tax Rates:1979 to 2003." Washington: Government Printing Office. Available at http://www.cbo.gov/ftpdocs/88xx/doc8885/12-11-HistoricalTaxRates.pdf (accessed October 25, 2010).

———. 2007. "Trends in Public Spending on Transportation and Water Infrastructure, 1956 to 2004." Washington: Government Printing Office. Available at http://www.cbo.gov/ftpdocs/85xx/doc8517/08-08-Infrastructure.pdf (accessed October 25, 2010).

Dreyfuss, Barbara T. 2004. "The Shocking Story of How AARP Backed the Medicare Bill." *The American Prospect* (May 12). Available at http. Available at http://www.prospect.org/cs/articles?articleId=7702 (accessed October 25, 2010).

Eddy, Mark. 2005. "Medical Marijuana: Review and Analysis of Federal and State Policies." CRS Report RL33211. Washington: Congressional Research Service.

Erikson, Robert S., Michael B. MacKuen, and James A. Stimson. 2002. *The Macro Polity*. New York: Cambridge University Press.

Frank, Thomas. 2004. *What's the Matter with Kansas? How Conservatives Won the Heart of America*. New York: Metropolitan Books.

Fried, Marlene Gerber. 2000. "Abortion in the United States: Barriers to Access." *Health and Human Rights* 4(2): 174–94.

Gelman, Andrew, David Park, Boris Shor, Joseph Bafumi, and Jeronimo Cortina. 2008. *Red State, Blue State, Rich State, Poor State: Why Americans Vote the Way They Do*. Princeton, N.J.: Princeton University Press.

Gilens, Martin. 1999. *Why Americans Hate Welfare: Race, Media, and the Politics of Antipoverty Policy*. Chicago: University of Chicago Press.

———. 2005. "Inequality and Democratic Responsiveness." *Public Opinion Quarterly* 69(5): 778–96.

———. 2009. "Preference Gaps and Inequality in Representation." *PS: Political Science & Politics* 42(2): 335–41.

———. n.d. "Paying the Piper: Economic Inequality and Democratic Responsiveness in the United States." Unpublished manuscript. Princeton University.

Gottschalk, Marie. 2000. *The Shadow Welfare State: Labor, Business, and the Politics of Health Care in the United States*. Ithaca, N.Y.: ILR Press.

Graetz, Michael J., and Ian Shapiro. 2005. *Death by a Thousand Cuts: The Fight over Taxing Inherited Wealth*. Princeton, N.J.: Princeton University Press.

Hacker, Jacob S. 2008. *Health at Risk: America's Ailing Health System—And How to Heal It.* New York: Columbia University Press.

Hogan, Julie A. 2000. "The Life of the Abortion Pill in the United States." Harvard Law School, Legal Electronic Document Archive. Available at http://leda.law.harvard.edu/leda/data/247/Hogan,_Julie.html (accessed October 25, 2010).

Jackson, Pamela J. 2006. "The Federal Excise Tax on Gasoline and the Highway Trust Fund: A Short History." CRS Report RL30304. Washington: Congressional Research Service.

Jacobs, Lawrence R., and Benjamin I. Page. 2005. "Who Influences U.S. Foreign Policy?" *American Political Science Review* 99(1): 107–23.

Johnson, Judith A., and Pamela W. Smith. 1988. "AIDS: An Overview of Issues." Washington: Congressional Research Service.

Jones, Rachel K., and Heather Boonstra. 2004. "Confidential Reproductive Health Services for Minors: The Potential Impact of Mandated Parental Involvement for Contraception." *Perspectives on Sexual and Reproductive Health* 36(5): 182–91.

Kollmann, Geoffrey. 2000. "Social Security: Raising the Retirement Age Background and Issues." CRS Report 94-622. Washington: Congressional Research Service.

Kull, Steven, and I. M. Destler. 1999. *Misreading the Public: The Myth of a New Isolationism.* Washington, D.C.: Brookings Institution Press.

Luckey, John R. 2003. "A History of Federal Estate, Gift, and Generation-Skipping Taxes." CRS Report 95-444. Washington: Congressional Research Service.

Morris, Charles R. 1996. *The AARP: America's Most Powerful Lobby and the Clash of Generations.* New York: Times Books.

Monroe, Alan D. 1998. "Public Opinion and Public Policy, 1980–1993." *Public Opinion Quarterly* 62(1): 6–28.

National Bureau of Economic Research. 2006. "Summary Measures of the U.S. Income Tax System, 1960–2005." Cambridge, Mass.: National Bureau of Economic Research. Available at http://www.nber.org/~taxsim/ally/fixed-ally.html (accessed October 25, 2010).

Page, Benjamin I. 2002. "The Semi-Sovereign Public." In *Navigating Public Opinion*, edited by Jeff Manza, Fay Lomax Cook, and Benjamin I. Page. Oxford: Oxford University Press.

Page, Benjamin I., and Jason Barabas. 2000. "Foreign Policy Gaps Between Citizens and Leaders." *International Studies Quarterly* 44(3): 339–64.

Page, Benjamin I., and Marshall M. Bouton. 2006. *The Foreign Policy Disconnect: What Americans Want from Our Leaders But Don't Get.* Chicago: University of Chicago Press.

Page, Benjamin I., and Robert Y. Shapiro. 1983. "Effects of Public Opinion on Policy." *American Political Science Review* 77(1): 175–90.

Quadagno, Jill S. 2005. *One Nation, Uninsured: Why the U.S. Has No National Health Insurance.* New York: Oxford University Press.

Sears, David O., and Carolyn L. Funk. 1991. "The Role of Self-Interest in Social and Political Attitudes." *Advances in Experimental Social Psychology* 24(1): 1–91.

Shimabukuro, Jon O. 2007. "Background and Legal Issues Related to Stem Cell Research." CRS Report RS21044. Washington: Congressional Research Service.

Skocpol, Theda. 1997. *Boomerang: Health Care Reform and the Turn Against Government*. New York: W. W. Norton.

Smith, Marcia. 2002. "V-Chip and TV Ratings: Helping Parents Supervise Their Children's Television Viewing." CRS Report 97-43SPR. Washington: Congressional Research Service.

Strolovitch, Dara Z. 2006. "Do Interest Groups Represent the Disadvantaged? Advocacy at the Intersections of Race, Class, and Gender." *Journal of Politics* 68(4): 894–910.

U.S. Census Bureau. 2008. *The 2008 Statistical Abstract*. "U.S. Foreign Economic and Military Aid Programs: 1980 to 2005." Table 1270. Available at http://www.census.gov/compendia/statab/2008/tables/08s1270.pdf (accessed October 25, 2010).

U.S. Department of Defense. Military Defense Agency. 2006. "Historical Funding for MDA FY85–10." Available at http://www.mda.mil/global/documents/pdf/histfunds.pdf (accessed October 25, 2010).

U.S. Department of Justice. Office of the Inspector General. 2003. *Drug Demand Reduction Activities*. Report No. 03–12. Washington: Government Printing Office. Available at http://www.justice.gov/oig/reports/plus/a0312 (accessed October 25, 2010).

U.S. Department of Labor. 2003. "Workplace-Related Policies, Programs and Laws." Paper presented at the Drug-Free Workforce Conference. Washington, D.C. (July 10–13, 2003).

U.S. Department of the Treasury. 2006. "U.S. Individual Income Tax: Personal Exemptions and Lowest and Highest Bracket Tax Rates, and Tax Base for Regular Tax, Tax Years 1913–2006." Available at http://www.irs.gov/taxstats/article/0,,id=175910,00.html (accessed November 8, 2010).

U.S. International Trade Commission. Statistical Services Division, Office of Operations. 2006. *Value of U.S. Imports for Consumption, Duties Collected, and Ratio of Duties to Values 1891–2005*. Washington: Government Printing Office.

U.S. Social Security Administration. 2006. "Annual Statistical Supplement, 2006: History of SSI, Medicare, and Medicaid Provisions." Table 2.c1. Available at http://www.socialsecurity.gov/policy/docs/statcomps/supplement/2006/2b-2c.pdf (accessed October 25, 2010).

White House. 2006. *National Drug Control Strategy, FY 2007 Budget Summary*. Washington: Executive Office of the President. Available at http://www.ncjrs.gov/pdffiles1/ondcp/212977.pdf (accessed October 25, 2010).

———. 2008. *The Quiet Revolution: The President's Faith-Based and Community Initiative: A Seven-Year Progress Report*. Washington: Executive Office of the President.

Chapter 10

Inequality in Policy Responsiveness?

CHRISTOPHER WLEZIEN AND STUART N. SOROKA

A LARGE BODY of empirical work demonstrates a correspondence between public opinion and policy behavior, in the United States and elsewhere.[1] The research almost exclusively presumes that policymakers represent the average person. That is, scholars typically produce some measure of the central tendency of opinion in a population and assess whether the average opinion and policy behavior match up at particular points in time, or whether they change together over time.

This previous research is important but may not accurately depict the process. That is, it may be that politicians do not represent the average person. A long line of theory and scholarship (beginning with Downs 1957) highlights the importance of the median voter to politicians. The average citizen and the median voter are not one and the same, and the differences can be meaningful (Griffin and Newman 2005; McCarty, Poole, and Rosenthal 2006). It also may be that voters themselves do not have equal weight in the policymaking process—that is, it may be that the preferences of some people matter more than others. This is an old idea, but one that has been the subject of some recent and important empirical work. Much of this work addresses the representation of income groups; among the most notable of which are works by Larry Bartels (2005, 2008) and Martin Gilens (2005).

Bartels (2005, 2008) relates constituency opinion, measured using average scores on the National Election Study (NES) ideology question as well as on some policy-specific items, to U.S. senators' roll-call votes. In doing so, he finds that senatorial roll-call voting records are better accounted for by variation in the ideological orientations of upper-income citizens (across states) than by the dispositions of middle- or lower-income citizens. Gilens (2005, 2004) examines the association between levels of public support for policy change—imputed for different income categories—and actual (binary) policy change (or stasis) within the following four years. His results for a very large number of policy domains are similar to those of Bartels: policy change is better explained by variation in higher-income citizens' support for policy change than by variation in support from lower-income citizens.

Lawrence Jacobs and Benjamin Page (2005) explore a different though related theme. They do not look specifically at the effects of public preferences across income categories, but examine the varying associations between U.S. foreign policy officials and those of business leaders, experts, labor leaders, or the general public. More so than others, however, they directly examine opinion dynamics, and find that the change in policy support among U.S. foreign policy officials most closely matches the change in the preferences of business leaders and experts, not the public per se. This provides further—albeit indirect—evidence of a representational bias toward upper-income citizens.[2]

Although this work all provides evidence that policy in the United States is related principally to the preferences of the wealthiest citizens, recent research suggests quite the opposite. Joseph Ura and Christopher Ellis (2008) examine how general tendencies in U.S. congressional roll-call voting over time relate to the general opinions of low-, middle-, and high-income citizens. They find that the House of Representatives is responsive to the opinions of all groups and not particularly those making high incomes—if anything, the House is more responsive to the poor. They find that the Senate, by contrast, is not responsive to public opinion, let alone to any particular group. The set of results raises more questions than it resolves. Are policymakers more responsive to the rich, to the poor, or not at all?

We effectively pick up where Ura and Ellis leave off, though our approach differs in a number of ways. First, we focus on actual policy, namely, government spending, and not roll-call votes. Although roll calls are important, policy matters most. Second, we examine representation across various domains. Although global activity is important, it may conceal what is happening in particular policy areas. Third, we explore both public responsiveness to policy and policy representation of opinion. Although representation is especially important, assessing inequality of representation without taking account of public opinion inputs is difficult, as we will see.

The empirical analyses focus on a set of spending domains of recurring political importance in the United States, about which we have identical question wording over time, and in which governments have tended to be quite responsive to public opinion (Wlezien 1996, 2004). To begin with, we focus on preferences across income levels. Building on our previous research (Soroka and Wlezien 2008, 2010; also see the introductory chapter to this volume), we find that preferences for different groups move together over time but that preferences also vary independently. Analysis of preferences reveals pervasive "thermostatic" public responsiveness to policy, though this varies somewhat across subgroups and domains. Analysis of spending reveals pervasive representation as well, and this also varies across groups and domains. The net effect of these differences is strikingly the same, however—differences in representation of income groups remain, but the rich do not consistently fare better than the middle class or the poor. The results suggest that concerns about the inequalities in the representation of different income groups may be overstated.

On Studying Inequality in Policy Responsiveness

As we have seen in previous chapters, the study of inequality in representation largely depends on the existence of differences in preferences across groups. If people had the same preferences, policy would end up in the same place—after all, we could not tell who is getting represented. If different groups want different amounts of policy, we can ask, who wins? This is an easy question to answer, at least in theory. We simply measure the different groups' preferences and see where policy ends up. It is much trickier in practice, however.

One fundamental problem with analyzing unequal representation is measuring public preferences. It is difficult to measure what people really want. First, simple, precise options do not exist in most policy domains. Most policy objectives are not adequately captured by categorical items, but rather by ranges of support or opposition. Second, policy will often be far too complex for individuals to prefer—independent of current policy—a specific level of policy. Not surprisingly, survey organizations usually do not ask people about their preferred level of policy. They more typically ask whether people want more or less—their relative preferences. This is understandable. Consider asking people how much health spending they want. Even when measuring relative preferences, it is not clear that we actually can tap whether people really want more or less policy in a particular area. The language used in survey questions can make a big difference. For instance, asking about "assistance to the poor" instead of "welfare" produces fundamentally different results (see Weaver, Shapiro, and Jacobs 1995). Do people want less or more spending? We simply cannot tell (for a more complete discussion of various measurement issues, see Soroka and Wlezien 2010).

Measurement is important because it limits what kinds of analyses we can do with the data. Consider the problems with conducting consistency analyses, which involve matching policy changes with expressed preferences for policy change (Monroe 1979; Page and Shapiro 1983; Gilens 2005).[3] If minor alterations in question wording can dramatically alter measured levels of policy support, how can we match a policy change with observed preferences?[4] We still can assess differences across space, such as states, as others in this volume have done (see Rigby and Wright, chapter 7, this volume). Specifically, scholars can assess whether policies in different states better correspond with variation in the opinions of the rich vis-à-vis variation in the opinions of those in the middle, for instance. It also is possible to examine responsiveness over time. That is, we can see who politicians follow as preferences of different groups change. This affords an especially powerful test and is the focus of the analyses that follow.

Just as with studying inequality in representation at a particular point in time, differences in preferences are critical to assessing differential responsiveness over time. Here, we are less interested in differences in the levels of preferences, however. That is, consistently different levels of support across groups matter not at all to the longitudinal relationship between preferences and policy. So long as the preferences of different groups move in parallel over time, public responsiveness and policy representation will for these groups be indistinguishable—just as one group's preferences are increasing or decreasing, so too are the others. (Of course, differences in levels of support across groups may matter a good deal for levels of policy, but this is a different subject, one that was raised in the first chapter of this book and to which we will return at the end of this chapter.)

To effectively assess whether politicians follow one group or another over time, it is necessary that preferences of different groups evolve differently over time. Figure 10.1 presents a hypothetical case, in which preferences for three income groups move perfectly in parallel until 1987 and then diverge. At this point, politicians are offered a choice. They can follow those in the middle and raise policy by a little. Or they can follow the rich and raise policy by a lot. Who do politicians follow? If Bartels and Gilens are right, then politicians follow the rich. Whether they do can be tested directly.

Inequality in Spending Preferences?

Our focus is on public preferences for government spending. Data are the same as those used in the introductory chapter and are based on

Figure 10.1   Time-Serial Roots of Unequal Representation

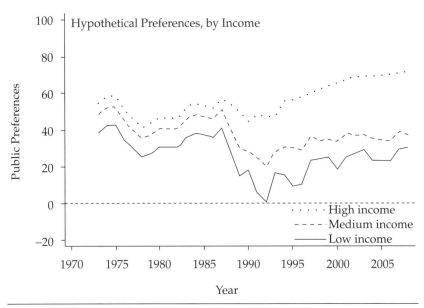

Source: Authors' figure.

responses to the following question from the General Social Surveys (GSS):

> We are faced with many problems in this country, none of which can be solved easily or inexpensively. I'm going to name some of these problems, and for each one I'd like you to tell me whether you think we're spending too much money on it, too little money, or about the right amount. Do you think the government is spending too much, too little, or about the right amount on [health care]?

Notice that the question asks about people's relative preferences—their preference for policy change—not their absolute preferences. Respondents are asked consistently about spending in other categories besides health care in the GSS in almost every year from 1973 to 1994 and then in alternate years until 2008, twenty-seven years in total. Using the responses to these questions, when question wording is identical over time and across domains, allows us to assess whether and to what extent differences are truly systematic and not unique to particular times and domains. We focus here on defense, the major social domains (welfare, health, and education), the environment, and crime.[5]

Figure 10.2   Spending Preferences for Different Programs, by Income Level

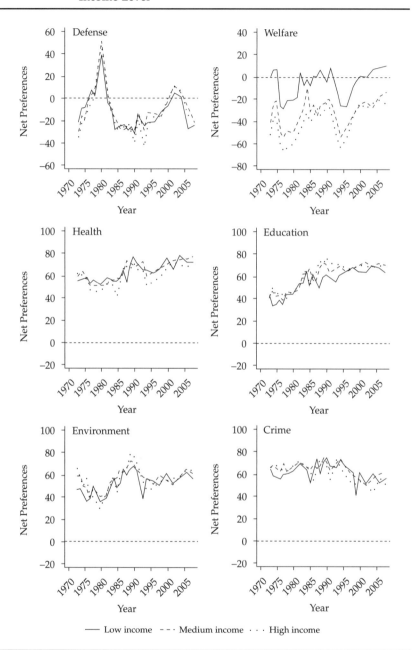

Source: Authors' compilation based on the General Social Surveys (Davis, Smith, and Marsdsen 1973–2008).

Table 10.1   ANOVA Results, U.S. Spending Preferences by Year and Income Level, 1973 to 2008

	Year	Group
Defense	91.3	.4
Welfare	38.8	54.8
Health	74.4	3.9
Education	80.9	5
Environment	72.8	3.7
Crime	52.9	2.4
Mean	68.5	11.7

Source: Authors' compilation based on the General Social Surveys (Davis, Smith, and Marsdsen 1973–2008).
Note: Table shows the percent of total variance in preferences across time and groups explained by year and group dummy variables.

From the responses, we generate a standard summary measure—what we refer to as net support—for each domain across years. The measure is the percentage of people who think we are spending "too little" minus the percentage of those who think we are spending "too much" in each domain.[6] Net support is calculated separately for income terciles, based on the income levels reported in the GSS.[7] The resulting series are plotted in figure 10.2. There, we see relatively little difference in preferences across income levels in all spending domains but welfare—the basic patterns already were described in the introductory chapter (also see Soroka and Wlezien 2008).[8] Regardless of differences in levels, preferences across income groups in each domain track one another over time, implying that people tend to respond to many of the same things in similar ways (also see Page and Shapiro 1992; Wlezien 1995; Enns 2006; Soroka and Wlezien 2008; Enns and Kellstedt 2008; Ura and Ellis 2008).

Temporal movement almost always matters much more than group differences. This is clear from table 10.1, which shows analysis of variance (ANOVA) results for the different spending domains and subgroups. The results are the percentages of variance due to time and group differences.[9] For instance, at the top of the first two columns we see that approximately 90 percent of the total variance in defense spending preferences across years and income terciles is due to parallel temporal movement and only .4 percent is due to differences across the groups. The impact of income groups on preferences in other domains is larger, but only substantially so for welfare, where they account for just over half of the variance in welfare preferences. This is an important result, for it reveals that, where income matters most, the common temporal movement matters almost as much. In the other five domains, income accounts for only 3.1 percent of the total variance in spending preferences on average.

Assessing the True Variance in Spending Preferences

Although evidence of parallelism in spending preferences across income groups is strong, we need to determine whether there also is group-specific movement. Consider the case of health preferences across income levels, where 74.4 percent of the variance is common and 3.9 percent of the variance is group-specific. What of the remaining 21.7 percent? Part of this is sampling error, but part is unique variance. It is possible to estimate the former and, thus, the latter, at least to some extent.

Toward this end, table 10.2 decomposes the variance of spending preferences across income groups into different components. The first column shows the average variance in preferences across income groups and years for each domain. The second column shows the amount of that variance that is due to systematic differences across groups. The third column then shows the remaining other (the total minus the group) variance, which is of special interest to us. We want to see how much of this is due to temporal movement, and whether there is any remaining true variance that is unique to each group, that is, when preferences for the different income groups vary independently over time. We begin by subtracting out the common temporal movement—the variance accounted for by the year (fourth column)—leaving the residual variance (fifth column). This is exactly the amount left unexplained from the corresponding income ANOVA results in table 10.1.

Some of this residual variance is mere sampling error. Given the frequencies and sample sizes of the actual polls, the amount of observed variance that is due to sampling error is relatively easy to compute (following Heise 1969).[10] The resulting error estimates are shown in the sixth column of the table. Producing the true unique variance for each group does not follow perfectly, however. The reason is that we cannot simply take the residual from table 10.2 and subtract the estimated error variance. This is because the error is shared in some unknown way between the common temporal component and the residual. For instance, in overrepresenting the northeastern part of the country at one point in time, the preferences across all income groups would tend to become more liberal (see, for example, Gelman et al. 2008). We cannot provide exact numbers of how much true preferences in the different groups vary independently over time, then. But we can provide lower- and upper-bound estimates by subtracting all the error variance from the residual, and then subtracting none. The penultimate column of table 10.2 gives this range of unique variance for each domain.

Table 10.2   A Decomposition of the Variance of Spending Preferences Across Income Groups, 1973 to 2008

				Variance Components				
	Total	Group	Other	Year	Residual	Error	Unique	% Unique[a]
Defense	306.3	1.2	305.1	279.7	25.4	10.5	14.9–25.4	4.9–8.3
Welfare	397.2	217.7	179.5	154.1	25.4	16.2	9.2–25.4	5.1–14.2
Health	74.2	2.9	71.3	55.2	16.1	13.3	2.8–16.1	3.9–22.6
Education	133.9	6.7	127.2	108.3	18.9	12.3	6.6–18.9	5.2–14.9
Environment	104.0	3.8	100.2	75.7	24.5	10.9	13.6–24.5	13.6–24.5
Crime	46.2	1.1	45.1	24.4	20.7	14.5	6.2–20.7	13.7–45.9

Source: Authors' compilation based on the General Social Surveys (Davis, Smith, and Marsdsen 1973–2008).
[a] Calculated as a percentage of the Other variance.

Assuming the median estimate, the true unique variance for each subgroup is just less than 16 percentage points on average across the six domains. A standard deviation of about 4 points implies real unique movement of plus or minus 8 points around the common trend—for example, when those with high incomes become a lot more favorable toward spending while those with middle incomes become a little more favorable and those with low incomes do not change.[11] The final column expresses the numbers as percentages of the other variance (in the third column of the table). Clearly, preferences across income groups are much more similar over time than different, but there are differences and some of the differences are real—15 percent on average assuming the median estimate. This is important because it means that there is an opportunity for differential policy responsiveness, when politicians follow the preferences of some income groups more than others. Before turning to that analysis, however, we first want to see whether thermostatic public responsiveness to policy itself varies across income groups.

Public Responsiveness

The thermostatic model of opinion is a basic one (Wlezien 1995). In the model, the public's preference for more or less policy—its relative preference, R—represents the difference between the public's preferred level of policy (P^*) and policy (P) itself:

$$R_t = P_t^* - P_t. \qquad (1)$$

Thus, R can change because either P^* or P changes; a change in P^* positively influences R and a change in P negatively influences R.

This theoretical model does not translate directly into practice. Most important, we typically do not observe P^*. Survey organizations rarely ask people how much policy they want. Instead, as we have noted, these organizations usually ask about relative preferences—whether we are spending too little, whether spending should be increased, or whether we should do more. This, presumably, is how people think about most policies. (Imagine being asked about your preferred level of health or education spending.) The public preference, however defined, also is necessarily relative. This is quite convenient, as we can measure the thermostatic signal that the public sends to policymakers.

We know that the thermostatic model works well in certain spending domains in the United States (Wlezien 1995, 1996).[12] That is, the public adjusts its preferences in response to policy, other things being equal: when policy increases, relative preferences decrease; when policy decreases, relative preferences increase. We are only beginning to explore how pervasive the tendency is (Soroka and Wlezien 2010). Do different segments of the public respond to policy in similar ways? Or do the na-tional-level patterns conceal the responsiveness of a portion of the broader public?

To answer these questions, we estimate models of feedback across the different subaggregates. The model that we estimate is a slightly revised version of equation 1, as follows:

$$R_t = a + \beta_1 P_t + \beta_2 W_t + e_t, \tag{2}$$

where a and e_t represent the intercept and the error term, respectively, and W designates the instruments for the public's preferred level of pol-icy (P^*). In practice, these instruments are relatively hard to come by. For defense, following Wlezien (1996), we include a survey measure of American dislike of Russia to indicate variation security threat;[13] we also include a measure for the post–9/11 period, equal to 0 until 2001 and 1 thereafter. For the major social domains, following Wlezien (1995), we include a linear counter to account for the gradual increase in the under-lying preferred level of spending over time.[14] Models also include a lagged value of the dependent variable (at $t - 1$).[15]

Our measures of policy (P_t) rely on outlays drawn directly from the historical tables in the 2009 federal budget. The specific definitions of the functions used are described in Wlezien (2004). We create real-dollar val-ued measures using a deflator based on the GDP (chained) price index, also from the historical tables. Following equation (1), levels of relative preferences are expected to be associated with current levels of spend-ing; if the thermostatic model applies, the coefficient (β_1) that relates the two is expected to be less than 0. Equation (2) is estimated for each sub-group. Within each domain, then, there are three separate estimations to account for the three income groups. We do not present the full models here and show just the feedback coefficients (β_1).[16] If there are systematic differences in the responsiveness of different subaggregates, it will be apparent in these estimates.

Table 10.3 displays the results for the different income groups. What is most noteworthy from this table is that every one of the spending coef-ficients is negative and almost every one is significantly different from 0—specifically, fifteen of the eighteen coefficients are significant. This is an important finding, for it indicates that people with different circum-stances respond in much the same way to changes in policy, on average. Most groups receive and accept basic information about the true direc-tion and magnitude of policy change. The responsiveness of all the groups clearly does differ across domains, however: a $1 billion increase (decrease) in defense spending leads to about a .27 point decrease (increase) in preferences for more spending (looking across all three groups), while an identical change in environmental spending has eight

Table 10.3   Public Responsiveness, by Income Level, 1973 to 2008

	Low	Middle	High
Defense	−.243**	−.274**	−.290**
Welfare	−.659**	−.692**	−.615**
Health	−.045	−.122	−.178*
Education	−.200	−.310**	−.269**
Environment	−1.677**	−2.208**	−2.456**
Crime	−.542**	−.542**	−.414**

Source: Authors' compilation based on the General Social Surveys (Davis, Smith, and Marsdsen 1973–2008).
Note: Table values are OLS coefficients.
* $p < .10$, ** $p < .05$

times that effect on preferences (roughly 2.1 points on average). The varying magnitude of feedback coefficients illustrates differences in the spending preference metric across domains, where, for instance, 1 point "means" a lot more in spending on defense—about $4 billion—than it does in spending on the environment—about $.5 billion. This has implications for representation, as we will see.

There also are differences in responsiveness across subgroups within particular domains. Consider the first row of table 10.3, which shows defense coefficients for the three income groupings—from low income in the first column to high income in the third column. Here, we can see that the magnitude of responsiveness increases as income increases, though the differences are not statistically significant. The pattern is similar in the domestic domains, and here, some of the differences are significant—that is, people with middle and high incomes are more responsive to health and education spending than those with low incomes. Although there is substantial parallelism across these subgroups, there are some differences.[17] Now let us consider whether they matter for policy itself.

Policy Responsiveness

Is there inequality in representation? Descriptive statistics suggest that there is not much difference over time in the preferences of different groups. Even if policymakers represent one group more than another, the resulting pattern of policy change would be pretty much as we would predict using the preferences of other groups. Still, as we have seen, there are differences in the flow of groups' preferences, and these at least partly reflect differences in public responsiveness to policy. This is important, for it provides a possible basis for differential representation. Let us see what policymakers do.

The model of representation follows our earlier work (see Wlezien 1996, 2004; Soroka and Wlezien 2004, 2005). In the model, policy change (ΔP_t) is a function of public preferences for policy change (R_{t-1}), and the partisan control of government (G_{t-1}) during the previous fiscal year. The lag serves to reflect preferences and party control when the current year's budget is made. The equation is

$$\Delta P_t = \rho + \gamma_1 R_{t-1} + \gamma_2 G_{t-1} + \mu_t, \qquad (3),$$

where ρ and μ_t represent the intercept and the error term, respectively. This model captures both indirect and direct representation: the former—representation through election results and subsequent government partisanship—is captured by γ_2, and the latter—annual adjustments to policy reflecting shifts in preferences—is captured by γ_1.

The coefficient γ_1 is the most critical for our purposes. It captures policy responsiveness, the kind of dynamic representation that we expect to differing degrees across policy domains. A positive coefficient need not mean that politicians literally respond to changing public preferences, as it may be that both they and the public respond to something else—for example, changes in the need for more spending. All we can say for sure is that γ_1 captures policy responsiveness in a statistical sense: the extent to which policy change is systematically related to public preferences, other things being equal.[18]

Of course, we are interested here in the extent to which representation differs across subgroups. The most straightforward way to do this is to enter measures of preferences for different groups together in the same equation, as follows:

$$\Delta P_t = \rho + \gamma_{1A} R_{At-1} + \gamma_{1B} R_{Bt-1} + \gamma_{1C} R_{Ct-1} + \gamma_2 G_{t-1} + \mu_t, \qquad (4)$$

where policy change is now modeled as a function of the relative preferences for three different groupings (A, B, and C), say, of income. We would want to see whether the coefficients differ and, in particular, whether policymakers are more responsive to those with higher incomes. Actually estimating such an equation does not work very well in practice, however, because of the strong similarities in preferences over time. Consider table 10.4, which shows results of regressing spending in each domain on preferences for spending by income tercile.

In table 10.4, eleven of the eighteen coefficients are positive and only three are statistically significant—low-income preferences for health spending, middle-income preferences for welfare, and high-income preferences for the environment. At the same time, the joint significance of the three preference variables in each equation is very high, with p values

Table 10.4 Policy Representation, All Income Subgroups Included, 1973 to 2008 (Billions of 2002 Dollars)

	Defense	Welfare	Health	Education	Environment	Crime	Mean
Low income	-.524	.052	.277*	-.181	-.061	.232	-.034
	(.455)	(.214)	(.156)	(.254)	(.048)	(.143)	
Middle income	.257	.436*	.087	.387	-.015	-.386	.128
	(.589)	(.246)	(.199)	(.339)	(.067)	(.261)	
High income	.848	-.135	.170	-.081	.110**	.207	.187
	(.509)	(.192)	(.189)	(.274)	(.052)	(.164)	

Source: Authors' compilation based on the General Social Surveys (Davis, Smith, and Marsdsen 1973–2008).
Note: Table values are OLS coefficients, with standard errors in parentheses.
* $p < .10$, ** $p < .05$

Table 10.5   **Policy Representation by Income Group, 1973 to 2008 (Billions of 2002 Dollars)**

	Low	Middle	High
Defense	.803**	.773**	.694**
Welfare	.248*	.331**	.176*
Health	.493**	.453**	.448**
Education	.094	.166	.118**
Environment	.021	.049	.059
Crime	.124	.020	.069

Source: Authors' compilation based on the General Social Surveys (Davis, Smith, and Marsdsen 1973–2008).
Note: Table values are OLS coefficients.
* $p < .10$, ** $p < .05$

of well below .01. These two results tell us that public opinion matters but that it is difficult to distinguish responsiveness to particular groups.

An alternative approach to capturing potential inequality is to directly model spending change as a function of preferences for each of the different subgroups taken separately, as follows:

$$\Delta P_t = \rho_A + \gamma_{1A} R_{At-1} + \gamma_{2A} G_{t-1} + \mu_{At},$$
$$\Delta P_t = \rho_B + \gamma_{1B} R_{Bt-1} + \gamma_{2B} G_{t-1} + \mu_{Bt},$$
$$\Delta P_t = \rho_C + \gamma_{1C} R_{Ct-1} + \gamma_{2C} G_{t-1} + \mu_{Ct}. \qquad (5)$$

We want to see whether the effect of preferences differs or is the same ($\gamma_{1A} = \gamma_{1B} = \gamma_{1C}$): put more substantively, whether policy responds more to the preferences of some groups than others. (Note that, though we allow the other coefficients in the models to differ across equations, we do not expect them to differ meaningfully, and in no case are the differences statistically significant.)

The results are summarized in table 10.5. The table shows just the representation coefficients (γ_1).[19] Note first that there is substantial evidence of representation: every one of the opinion coefficients is positive, and many (ten of the eighteen) are statistically significant. Clearly, policy, at least in certain domains—defense, welfare, and health, moves with the highly parallel flow of opinion across various groups. In other domains, namely the environment and crime, spending does not reliably follow opinion for any groups, for example, policymakers are equally nonresponsive.

Are policymakers more responsive to the opinions of some groups than others? The coefficients suggest that they may pay more attention to the preferences of people with low and middling income levels; that is, the coefficients for these groups tend to be higher than for those with high income. Comparing the raw coefficients across groups is, however, complicated by the fact that the variance in preferences is in some cases quite different from one group to another. Take, for instance, defense preferences. The variance in preferences for the high-income group is roughly 370.1 points and for the low-income group only 245.8, approximately 33 percent lower. Thus, the "average" change in high-income preferences would be proportionately larger than that in low-income preferences. These raw coefficients do not take these differences into account and so may overstate the representation of the poor and the middle. One thing we can do is compare standardized coefficients. Doing so for defense produces estimates, for low income to high, of .69, .72, and .73. Taking into account the variance in preferences, the apparent difference in raw defense coefficients across income levels essentially disappears. This also is true for some of the other domains, though some differences do remain.

A more direct way to calibrate the level of representation is to examine the net effect of estimated public responsiveness and policy representation. This tells us how effectively policymakers represent public opinion given public responsiveness—the degree to which the magnitude of representation is indexed to that of responsiveness.[20] It may be that responsiveness and representation are positively related across certain subgroups in some domains—that is, that representation is greater where public responsiveness itself is greater. This would parallel what we observe across policy domains (Soroka and Wlezien 2010). Alternatively, it may be that representation is lower for those with high-income levels because their responsiveness to spending is greater—that is, that the one effectively balances out the other. This would be true if there is no real difference in representation across groups, and that the apparent differences merely reflect difference in calibration.[21] The point is that inferring from the representation coefficients alone can be deceiving. The results in table 10.5 may understate the influence of the rich in government spending, for example.

To produce the net effect statistics, we simply multiply the feedback and representation coefficients for each group in each domain from tables 10.3 and 10.5.[22] Table 10.6 shows the results. Generally, these suggest that the net effect of representation and feedback is quite similar across sets of subgroups. This is no great surprise when there was little difference in representation and feedback in the first place, such as for welfare across income levels. For other domains and subgroups, apparent differences in feedback and representation effectively net out. Consider defense. In table 10.3 the largest responsiveness coefficient is for those with high income, and in table 10.5 the largest representation coefficient is for those with low income. The net effects of public responsiveness and policy representation in table 10.6 are virtually identical across the groups.

Table 10.6   **Net Effects of Responsiveness and Representation, by Income Group, 1973 to 2008**

	Low	Middle	High
Defense	−.195	−.212	−.202
Welfare	−.164	−.229	−.108
Health	−.022	−.055	−.080
Education	−.019	−.051	−.032
Environment	−.035	−.109	−.146
Crime	−.067	−.011	−.028
Mean	−.084	−.111	−.099

Source: Authors' compilation based on the General Social Surveys (Davis, Smith, and Marsdsen 1973–2008).

Net effects do not entirely erase the differences apparent in table 10.5. Real differences in responsiveness do remain across income levels for spending on the environment and crime—and the corresponding patterns are even more pronounced in table 10.6. In some cases, new differences emerge. Consider the coefficients for spending on health. In table 10.5, representation appears relatively similar across groups, but in table 10.6, when taking into account public responsiveness, representation appears slightly greater for the middle and the rich. There is no clear tendency in table 10.6 to represent one group or another across domains, however. For defense, there is substantial equality; for welfare, there is a hint that those in the middle are best represented. The biggest differences are in education, where spending best tracks the preferences of those with middling incomes, and the environment, where spending most closely follows high-income preferences, and crime, where the low-income group is the best represented. Even where there is inequality in representation, therefore, the well-to-do do not matter consistently more than others. They tend to matter more than the poor, but overall our results indicate that policymakers are guided at least as much by those with middling incomes.

Discussion and Conclusions

Is there inequality in policy representation across income subgroups in the United States? We began here by looking at whether there were differences in public preferences in the first place. Overall, our data indicate that, with the exception of welfare, there is a great degree of identity in preferences for spending across income groups at particular points in time. In all domains, there also is substantial parallelism over time. This parallelism implies substantial homogeneity in the structure of preferences, when citizens respond to much of the same information and in similar ways. For instance, people with different income levels adjust their preferences in response to changes in actual spending over time. This finding challenges the conventional wisdom about the level and the consequences of heterogeneity in information (see also Soroka and Wlezien 2010). Preferences are not perfectly parallel, however. People with middle and higher incomes tend to be more responsive to policy changes in certain areas than those with low incomes. This has possible implications for representation.[23]

That said, we also observe extensive representation. Policy change is associated with preferences of all income groups, and in the most salient domains—defense and welfare—the differences are marginal. Even to the extent that the independent drift in preferences across groups in these domains registers with policymakers, it simply does not matter for what they do, at least when taken as a whole. There are real differences in other areas—namely, health, education, the environment, and crime. But policymakers are not consistently more responsive to the rich; indeed, they appear to be guided as much by the median voter as anyone else. This is about all that we would expect if people had equal weight in the policy-making process. There is little basis in democratic theory or practical politics, after all, for representing the lower third of the income distribution—the group does not contain the average person, let alone the average voter, and it does not have the power of money or organization.

Our analyses address the relationship between preferences and policy over time; they do not directly address the relationship between levels of preferences and policy at any particular point in time. To the extent that policymakers represent the preferences of certain groups at each point in time, however, they should be more responsive to those groups' preferences over time as well (recall figure 10.1). That we have not observed systematic differences in longitudinal representation does therefore raise doubts about the likelihood of differences in representation cross-sectionally in most spending domains. Of course, it may be that such differences are difficult to detect over time because preference change across groups is a relatively small portion of the movement that we do observe—that is, we do not see differences in representation because policymakers do not distinguish subtle changes in the preferences of different groups over time. It also may be that our analysis overstates the amount of true over-time movement that is unique to different income groups.[24]

Even to the extent that there is real inequality in the representation of the levels of preferences, it makes a difference only in the welfare spending domain. In the other domains, the mean preference across income groups is indistinguishable, so substituting the preferences of one income group for another makes little difference—policy would end up in essentially the same place. Even in the welfare domain, there is relatively little difference in the preferences of people with middle and upper incomes, and even this has have declined over time (see chapter 1, this volume).[25] Of course, representing public opinion is not all that policymakers do, and we know that the party control of government matters for policy in important ways (Wlezien 1996, 2004; Erikson, MacKuen, and Stimson 2002; Soroka and Wlezien 2010; see Hussey and Zaller, chapter 11, this volume). As Bingham Powell (2000) has argued, the effects of party control may not enhance the representation of the median voter in majoritarian systems like the United States—that is, it tends to bring policy off to the left or to the right.[26]

Our findings contrast with what Gilens (2005) has shown across a range of policy areas, including many more specific ones. His approach is different to ours in a number of ways, some of which were noted in the text, and it may be that these differences produce the differences in our results. Then again we may both be right. It may be that there is a lot of equality in representation of preferences for spending in comparison with other types of policy.[27] It also may be that there is more equality at highly aggregated levels of policy, like the ones in our analysis. They are salient to many citizens, at least more so than specific programs and policy decisions, and it may be on the latter that the well-to-do and other special interests have more say. This would not surprise us given what we know about the legislative process in the United States (Kingdon 1973). It nevertheless remains to be seen.

Earlier versions of this paper were presented at the Conference on Homogeneity and Heterogeneity in Public Opinion, at Cornell University, Ithaca, N.Y., October 2008; the 67th Annual National Conference of the Midwest Political Science Association, Chicago, April 2009; and at Nuffield College, Oxford University, March 2009. Related work was presented at the 2008 Meeting of the Elections, Public Opinion, and Parties (EPOP) subgroup of the Political Studies Association, Manchester, UK; the 2007 Meeting of the American Political Science Association (APSA), Chicago; the 2007 Meeting of the Midwest Political Science Association, Chicago; the 2006 Meeting of the APSA, Philadelphia; and the 2006 Meeting of EPOP, Nottingham, UK. For helpful comments, we thank Peter Enns, Geoff Evans, Steve Fisher, Michael Hagen, Armen Hakhverdian, Sara Hobolt, Jeff Manza, Mark Pickup, G. Bingham Powell, Guy Whitten, John Zaller, and the two anonymous reviewers.

Notes

1.   The U.S. literature is vast (see, for example, Miller and Stokes 1963; Weissberg 1978; McCrone and Kuklinski 1979; Monroe 1979; Bartels 1991; Page

and Shapiro 1992; Hartley and Russett 1992; Erikson, Wright, and McIver 1993; Goggin and Wlezien 1993; Jacobs 1993; Stimson, MacKuen, and Erikson 1995; Wlezien 1996; Wood and Hinton-Anderson 1998; Hill and Hurley 1998; Smith 1999; Sharpe 1999; Erikson, MacKuen, and Stimson 2002; Soroka 2003; Wlezien 2004). The literature on other countries is vast as well (see, for example, Petry 1999; Eichenberg and Stoll 2003; Soroka and Wlezien 2004, 2005, 2010; Stimson 2005; Brooks and Manza 2006; Hobolt and Klemmensen 2008). Reviews of the literature are also extensive (see Weakliem 2003; Burstein 2003; Brooks 2006; Wlezien and Soroka 2007).

2. Research by James Druckman and Lawrence Jacobs in chapter 6 of this volume also shows that changes in President Ronald Reagan's positions on economic policy tended to more closely follow the opinion of the rich. Interestingly, his positions on other issues tended to follow other types of subgroups; for example, defense spending proposals were more responsive to the opinions of self-identified Republicans.

3. The "consistency" designation comes from Alan Monroe (1979, 1998). Note that the approach should be distinguished from what Benjamin Page and Robert Shapiro (1983) and Monroe (1998) call "congruence" analyses, looking at whether policy change is associated with changes in preferences. Recent work on the dynamic relationship between opinion and policy is an advanced form of such congruence analyses (for example, Wlezien 1995; Erikson, MacKuen, and Stimson 2002; Soroka and Wlezien 2010; for a more extended discussion, see Wlezien and Soroka 2007).

4. Things are further complicated by the level of thermostatic public responsiveness itself in different domains. Where the public does not notice and respond to policy change, for example, measured preferences contain no information about whether the public really wants more or less.

5. Results for the other areas for which questions have been asked on a recurring basis, including cities, crime, foreign aid, and space in the United States, as well as transportation, present a similar story. Much the same is true for Canada. These results are available upon request.

6. Using the mean response, which takes into account the "about right" responses, makes no difference to any of the analyses that follow.

7. Using terciles from the GSS has the advantage of keeping our three categories equal in size—that is, the number of respondents in each category is the same, and no one category is more (or less) susceptible to measurement error. (For income categories, and others, the total sample size is about 1,050 on average. Approximately 5 percent of respondents do not answer the income question, leaving an average N of just less than 1,000, or 333 in each income category.) Given that the income distribution reported to the GSS always is lower than what we see in census data, we also calculated using terciles from the U.S. Census Bureau. This makes virtually no difference to any of the results—specifically, using the census distribution slightly expands the range of differences. To determine preferences by income tercile, we begin with preferences aggregated by income response categories in the individual-level survey file. We then collapse these into income terciles. When survey response categories overlap the divide between two income terciles, the respondents in this category are assigned the mean score

(in the category) and allocated to the two income terciles proportionally, based on where the tercile division lies.

8.   To the extent that one takes the zero-points (or neutral points) in the measures seriously, preferences rarely differ at all across income groups. That is, the "direction" of support for spending is almost always the same. For the six domains, preferences among the low- and high-income terciles are on different sides of zero (where one group favors "more" spending on balance and the other "less") fewer than 8 percent of the time (34 percent of the time for welfare). The percentage drops to 7 percent for the low- and middle-income terciles and below 1 percent for the middle- and high-income terciles. For health, education, the environment, and crime, the direction of preference for the three groups never differs and is always in support of more spending. Where preferences do differ most—for welfare—the difference is always between the poor on the one hand the middle and the rich on the other, and the preferences of low-income citizens are closest to zero, suggesting that the median voter in this group is actually happiest with the policy status quo. (Indeed, separate analyses show that the median low-income person almost always—in twenty-one of twenty-four years—thinks that spending is "about right." By contrast, the median middle-income person gives this response in only fifteen of the twenty-four years; for the high-income voter, in nine.) The same is true for taxes, as we saw in the introductory chapter (also see Soroka and Wlezien 2008). The problem with all this analysis, however, as we have already discussed, is that it is not clear what the zero point represents.

9.   The percentages are adjusted for the number of degrees of freedom—that is, the residual variance is equal to the mean squared error.

10. To estimate the error variance, it was necessary to transform net support into a proportions measure, specifically, the number of people saying that we are spending too little divided by the number (N) of people saying that we are spending either too little or too much. The estimated error variance for this measure is the average yearly error variance, which is equal to $p(1-p)/N$. The corresponding error variance for net support shown in table 10.2 is simply the proportionate amount of the total variance—for example, when error variance is 2.5 percent of the total variance in the proportions measure, the estimated error variance for net support is 2.5 percent of the total variance in net support.

11. Note that this is a conservative estimate, because income group effects are usually not significant but we subtract that variance. It also may be that there is more sampling error in the common component than in the residual.

12. It also works very well in Canada and the United Kingdom (Soroka and Wlezien 2004, 2005; see also see Jennings 2009).

13. The measure represents the percentage of Americans who dislike Russia less the percentage who do like the country. The data are drawn from the GSS; for years when the GSS was not in the field—1979, 1981, and 1995—we interpolate using data from adjacent years. After the collapse of the Soviet bloc, we take the 1989 value and simply project it forward. That is, net dislike varies until 1989 and is constant afterward.

14. Defense spending preferences show no such trend. The underlying over-time increase in welfare and health-care preferences is nonlinear, and so we use quadratic versions of the counter in those domains. Note that various economic variables were included in the different models to little effect.

15. For the regression analyses, we fill in the six (never consecutive) missing values in the preference series using linear interpolation. Doing so makes only a minor difference to results, though it does naturally tend to increase the coefficient on the lagged dependent variable. Note also that spending preferences are, both in theory and in practice, stationary. As expected, the spending series are all integrated.

16. The full results are available on request.

17. Separate analyses reveal that a similar pattern is evident across education groups. In each case, the coefficient is largest for those with high education, particularly for health and education spending domains. The extent to which these results parallel those for income suggests a possibly common source—for example, that it is education that drives the differences across income groups. That the differences across education levels are more pronounced underscores the point.

18. Note that different economic variables—unemployment, inflation and business expectations—were included in the model though to little effect.

19. The full results are available on request. Note that for all the representation models, we tested the significance of the lagged spending level as a control variable, following Soroka and Wlezien (2010). The variable is not significant in any of the domains but education, and including it reveals greater representation for all groups but especially for people with middling and low incomes. For the sake of consistency, the tables present results using the same basic model without lagged spending, but it is important to recognize that this tilts in the direction of finding greater representational inequality. These results also are available upon request.

20. Indeed, it provides an estimate of efficiency—how effectively a shock to preferences is converted into policy (Wlezien 1996; Soroka and Wlezien 2010).

21. In other words, if public responsiveness is greater for one group, then a one-unit change in that group's preferences will represent a smaller amount of money than a one-unit change in another group's preferences. For instance, if a $1 billion increase in spending leads to a .5 point drop in preferences for the rich and a .25 drop for other groups, then it takes $2 billion to produce a one-unit shift in the preferences of the rich, and $4 billion for other groups. The units of preferences are, in short, worth different amounts. If policymakers are equally representative of each group's preferred spending change, therefore, the opinion representation coefficient for the rich will (in this hypothetical case) be half that of the other groups—that is, the net effect of public responsiveness and policy representation would be the same.

22. This approach may not seem quite right because the preference equations (in table 10.3) capture policy feedback on levels of public support and the representation equations (in table 10.5) capture opinion effects on changes in policy. That is, the equations taken together do not describe the long-

term effect of a shock in preferences, which requires estimates of policy change on first differences of public preferences. It is not possible to produce such estimates given missing data (see note 15), and so we rely on coefficients from the analyses of levels. Our analysis of net effects thus assumes that the effects of changes and the lagged levels of policy change are essentially the same. This assumption is not highly controversial. Even if it is in fact incorrect, it presumably applies to all groups and so should not affect our cross-group comparisons.

23. Note that the differences in public responsiveness across income groups may not be due to income per se, and ultimately may reflect differences in education, for instance.

24. Our analysis has controlled for sampling error, but it is far from the only source of measurement error (see, for example, Groves 1989).

25. The differences in levels of welfare support across groups may matter for the levels of welfare spending—for example, whether we have a large welfare state or a modest one. In table 10.1 we saw a sizable gap between low-income people on the one hand and middle- and high-income people on the other. There is a gap, albeit smaller, between the middle- and high-income groups as well, which may be more important. Let us assume that policymakers represent high-income preferences, so then we might ask: what difference would it make if the rich had the preferences of those with middling incomes? To determine this, we calculate how much additional spending is necessary to drive preferences down—95 percent of the way—to the mean level that we observe for high-income respondents. The answer is an almost 20 percent net increase in spending. (This is a liberal estimate, as it assumes that the equilibrium level of preferences would not change—that is, it would not increase.) The effect of representing low-income preferences could have a considerably greater effect in spending over the long term, up to a 50 percent increase. This is a substantial difference. Although important as an indicator of the extent of inequality, it is not a realistic estimate of what we might expect in policy were people to have equal weight in the policymaking process. That is, as we have noted in the text, the lower third of the income distribution does not include the average person or the average voter.

26. Of course, the extent to which this is true will depend partly on the degree to which parties (and partisans) differ.

27. Note that in these other domains, the rich tend to be much more liberal than the poor (Gilens 2009).

References

Bartels, Larry M. 1991. "Constituency Opinion and Congressional Policy Making: The Reagan Defense Build Up." *American Political Science Review* 85(2): 457–74.

———. 2005. "Economic Inequality and Political Representation." Unpublished manuscript. Princeton University.

———. 2008. *Unequal Democracy: The Political Economy of the New Gilded Age.* Princeton, N.J.: Princeton University Press.

Brooks, Clem. 2006. "Voters, Satisficing and Public Policymaking: Recent Directions in the Study of Electoral Politics." *Annual Review of Sociology* 32:191–211.

Brooks, Clem, and Jeff Manza. 2006. *Why Welfare States Persist: The Importance of Public Opinion in Democracies.* Chicago: University of Chicago Press.

Burstein, Paul. 2003. "The Impact of Public Opinion on Public Policy: A Review and an Agenda." *Political Research Quarterly* 56(1): 29–40.

Davis, James A., Tom W. Smith, and Peter V. Marsden. 1973–2008. "General Social Surveys, 1972–2008" [cumulative file] [computer file]. ICPSR25962-v2. Storrs, Conn.: Roper Center for Public Opinion Resarch, University of Connecticut/Ann Arbor, Mich.: Inter-University Consortium for Political and Social Research [distributors], 2010-02-08. doi:10.3886/ICPSR25962.

Downs, Anthony. 1957. *An Economic Theory of Democracy.* New York: Harper and Row.

Eichenberg, Richard, and Richard Stoll. 2003. "Representing Defense: Democratic Control of the Defense Budget in the United States and Western Europe." *Journal of Conflict Resolution* 47(4): 399–423.

Enns, Peter K. 2006. "The Uniform Nature of Opinion Change." Paper presented at the Annual Meeting of the American Political Science Association. Philadelphia (September 2006).

Enns, Peter K., and Paul M. Kellstedt. 2008. "Policy Mood and Political Sophistication: Why Everybody Moves Mood." *British Journal of Political Science* 38(3): 433–54.

Erikson, Robert S., Michael B. MacKuen, and James A. Stimson. 2002. *The Macro Polity.* Cambridge: Cambridge University Press.

Erikson, Robert S., Gerald C. Wright, and John P. McIver. 1993. *Statehouse Democracy: Public Opinion and Policy in the American States.* Cambridge: Cambridge University Press.

Gelman, Andrew, David Park, Boris Shor, Joseph Bafumi, and Jeronimo Cortina. 2008. *Red State, Blue State, Rich State, Poor State: Why Americans Vote the Way They Do.* Princeton, N.J.: Princeton University Press.

Gilens, Martin. 2004. "Public Opinion and Democratic Responsiveness: Who Gets What They Want from Government?" Social Inequality working paper. New York: Russell Sage Foundation.

———. 2005. "Inequality and Democratic Responsiveness." *Public Opinion Quarterly* 69(5): 778–96.

———. 2009. "Preference Gaps and Inequality in Representation." *PS: Political Science & Politics* 42(2): 335–41.

Goggin, Malcolm L., and Christopher Wlezien. 1993. "Abortion Opinion and Policy in the American States." In *Understanding the New Politics of Abortion,* edited by Malcolm L. Goggin. Newbury Park, Calif.: Sage Publications.

Griffin, John D., and Brian Newman. 2005. "Are Voters Better Represented?" *Journal of Politics* 67(4): 1206–27.

Groves, Robert M. 1989. *Survey Errors and Survey Costs.* New York: John Wiley & Sons.

Hartley, Thomas, and Bruce Russett. 1992. "Public Opinion and the Common Defence: Who Governs Military Spending in the United States?" *American Political Science Review* 86: 905–15.

Heise, David R. 1969. "Separating Reliability and Stability in Test-Retest Correlations." *American Sociological Review* 34(1): 93–101.

Hill, Kim Quaile, and Patricia A. Hurley. 1998. "Dyadic Representation Reappraised." *American Journal of Political Science* 43(1): 109–37.

Hobolt, Sara B., and Robert Klemmensen. 2008. "Responsive Government? Public Opinion and Policy Preferences in Britain and Denmark." *Political Studies* 53: 379–402.

Jacobs, Lawrence R. 1993. *The Health of Nations: Public Opinion and the Making of Health Policy in the U.S. and Britain*. Ithaca, N.Y.: Cornell University Press.

Jacobs, Lawrence R., and Benjamin I. Page. 2005. "Who Influences U.S. Foreign Policy?" *American Political Science Review* 99(1): 107–23.

Jennings, Will. 2009. "The Public Thermostat, Political Responsiveness, and Error Correction: Border Control and Asylum in Britain, 1974–2007." *British Journal of Political Science* 39(4): 847–70.

Kingdon, John W. 1973. *Congressmen's Voting Decisions*. New York: Harper & Row.

McCarty, Nolan, Keith T. Poole, and Howard Rosenthal. 2006. *Polarized America: The Dance of Ideology and Unequal Riches*. Cambridge, Mass.: MIT Press.

McCrone, Donald J., and James H. Kuklinski. 1979. "The Delegate Theory of Representation." *American Journal of Political Science* 23: 278–300.

Miller, Warren E., and Donald E. Stokes. 1963. "Constituency Influence in Congress." *American Political Science Review* 57(1): 45–56.

Monroe, Alan. 1979. "Consistency Between Constituency Preferences and National Policy Decisions." *American Politics Quarterly* 12(1): 3–19.

———. 1998. "Public Opinion and Public Policy, 1980–1993." *Public Opinion Quarterly* 62: 6–28.

Page, Benjamin I., and Robert Y. Shapiro. 1983. "Effects of Public Opinion on Policy." *American Political Science Review* 77: 175–90.

———. 1992. *The Rational Public: Fifty Years of Trends in Americans' Policy Preferences*. Chicago: University of Chicago Press.

Petry, Francois. 1999. "The Opinion-Policy Relationship in Canada." *Journal of Politics* 61: 540–50.

Powell, G. Bingham. 2000. *Elections as Instruments of Democracy: Majoritarian and Proportional Visions*. New Haven, Conn.: Yale University Press.

Sharpe, Elaine. 1999. *The Sometime Connection: Public Opinion and Social Policy*. Albany: SUNY Press.

Smith, Mark A. 1999. "Public Opinion, Elections, and Representation Within a Market Economy: Does the Structural Power of Business Undermine Popular Sovereignty?" *American Journal of Political Science* 43: 842–63.

Soroka, Stuart N. 2003. "Media, Public Opinion, and Foreign Policy." *Harvard International Journal of Press and Politics* 8(1): 27–48.

Soroka, Stuart N., and Christopher Wlezien. 2004. "Opinion Representation and Policy Feedback: Canada in Comparative Perspective." *Canadian Journal of Political Science* 37(3): 531–59.

———. 2005. "Opinion-Policy Dynamics: Public Preferences and Public Expenditure in the United Kingdom." *British Journal of Political Science* 35(4): 665–89.

———. 2008. "On the Limits to Inequality in Representation." *PS: Political Science & Politics* 41(2): 319–27.

————. 2010. *Degrees of Democracy*. Cambridge: Cambridge University Press.

Stimson, James A. 2005. *Tides of Consent: How Public Opinion Shapes American Politics*. New York: Cambridge University Press.

Stimson, James A., Michael B. MacKuen, and Robert S. Erikson. 1995. "Dynamic Representation." *American Political Science Review* 89: 543–65.

Ura, Joseph Daniel, and Christopher R. Ellis. 2008. "Income, Preferences, and the Dynamics of Policy Responsiveness." *PS: Political Science & Politics* 41(4): 785–94.

Weakliem, David. 2003. "Public Opinion Research and Political Sociology." *Research in Political Sociology* 12: 49–80.

Weaver, R. Kent, Robert Y. Shapiro, and Lawrence R. Jacobs. 1995. "Trends: Welfare." *Public Opinion Quarterly* 59(4): 606–27.

Weissberg, Robert. 1978. "Collective vs. Dyadic Representation in Congress." *American Political Science Review* 72: 535–47.

Wlezien, Christopher. 1995. "The Public as Thermostat: Dynamics of Preferences for Spending." *American Journal of Political Science* 39(4): 981–1000.

————. 1996. "Dynamics of Representation: The Case of U.S. Spending on Defense." *British Journal of Political Science* 26(1): 81–103.

————. 2004. "Patterns of Representation: Dynamics of Public Preferences and Policy." *Journal of Politics* 66(1): 1–24.

Wlezien, Christopher, and Stuart Soroka. 2007. "The Relationship Between Public Opinion and Policy." In *Oxford Handbook of Political Behavior*, edited by Russell Dalton and Hans-Deiter Klingemann. Oxford: Oxford University Press.

Wood, B. Dan, and Angela Hinton-Anderson. 1998. "The Dynamics of Senatorial Represenation, 1952–1991." *American Journal of Political Science* 60: 705–36.

Chapter 11

Who Do Parties Represent?

WESLEY HUSSEY AND JOHN ZALLER

POLITICAL PARTIES ARE the unwanted stepchild of American democracy. The Founding Fathers feared them and designed the Constitution to defeat "the mischiefs of faction." Generations of reformers have passed laws aimed at hobbling them. Americans regularly express disapproval of them in polls. Yet parties thrive. They develop their own agendas, nominate candidates loyal to these agendas, and dominate the outcomes of state and federal elections. By these means, parties make themselves central players in the process of political representation.

This chapter aims to show how parties behave in this role. We argue that parties are more responsive to their own agendas than to the public. Even when they claim to follow public opinion, it is often a cover for what they want to do anyway. Nonetheless, parties still facilitate a degree of genuine government responsiveness to public opinion. How much, and under what circumstances, are the focus of this chapter.

Our main evidence comes from the relationship between the roll-call votes of members of Congress (MCs) and the partisanship of their constituents. Other scholars have examined this evidence and found only modest responsiveness by MCs to constituent opinion (Ansolabehere, Snyder, and Stewart 2001; McCarty, Poole, and Rosenthal 2006, 2009). We find much the same, but delve further into the relationship.

Most studies of representation give parties rather short shrift. They may use party as a control variable in regressions, or test the effect of party performance, but few pay more than passing attention to the independent importance of party agendas. Yet, evidence indicates that party agendas have a large and independent impact on government policy and are therefore more an imposition on public opinion than a response to it. We undertake to incorporate this widely known, but often overlooked, evidence into a fuller picture of how representation works in the United States.

Introduction to Political Parties

If students of American politics want to know what a congress is, they can turn to the Constitution. There they will find information about how members are chosen, an enumeration of powers, and other key features. Nothing about parties is as clear. Parties developed outside the Constitution and remain to a large extent outside the law. They shun transparency, making it difficult for outsiders to observe them.

Political scientists have nonetheless managed some agreement on what a party is. One classic definition holds that it is "a team of men seeking to control the governing apparatus by gaining office in a duly constituted election" (Downs 1957, 25). Another is that a party is "a coalition of elites to capture and use office" (Aldrich 1995, 283–84). These definitions embody two notable features: that a party consists of diverse actors working together toward a common goal, and that the goal is controlling government. The reader should note that's one heck of a goal, and that it makes parties especially important for scholars of representation.

Political scientists also agree on the character of the political elites—no longer mainly men—who make up the party.[1] They include not only the politicians who run for office, but also a large supporting cast of interest groups, ideological activists, and other "policy demanders." Prominent among the Democratic Party's policy demanders are labor unions; advocates of civil rights for blacks, women, gays, and others; environmentalists; trial lawyers; and liberal and left-wing ideologues. Within the Republican Party are policy demanders for business; traditional religious values; gun rights; and conservative and right-wing ideology. The demands of these and other activist groups are the basis of each party's agenda. Parties seek the support of the centrist voter, but aim above all to advance their own activist-driven agendas.

It is often said that "democracy is unthinkable save for parties" (Schattschneider 1942, 1). This is no doubt true. Parties offer voters clear choices between competing agendas. But it doesn't follow that the choices offered are the choices most voters want. For one thing, parties may, in catering to their policy demanding groups, offer alternatives that are more extreme than most voters want. They may also organize those choices in arbitrary ways. This last point requires elaboration.

The United States has dozens of important issues but only two important parties. If these parties are to offer choices on all of the issues about which Americans care, they must therefore bundle them into multiple-issue agendas. How this bundling occurs is critical for representation, because issues that are not on any party's agenda are likely to be neglected by government.

So what determines what issues get bundled into a party agenda? Perhaps the main factor is how well interest groups and other policy demanders get along. For example, unions and civil rights groups both often clash with business, which brings them and their preferred policies together in the Democratic Party. Some alliances, however, may have less natural basis. For example, the alliance of religious traditionalists and antitax activists in the Republican Party seems a marriage of convenience: the groups may have little in common except the need for the other as an ally. Still, that both are in the Republican Party means that their issue preferences get bundled in that party's agenda.

One of the most striking features of the American party system is how groups that initially have nothing in common later come to be seen as natural allies. Another poorly understood but important phenomenon—ideology—may be responsible for this. The diverse groups within the Republican Party have come to be seen as sharing conservative principles, even though these principles are never fully articulated. On the basis of similarly ill-defined principles, the diverse groups associated with the Democratic Party have come to be seen as liberal.

The widespread use of ideological labels is a central feature of representation. The terms *liberal* and *conservative* define an idealized policy dimension that runs from far left to far right. In the contemporary United States, these terms are closely associated with the Democratic and Republican parties. Thus, voters who view themselves as conservative tend to seek representation through the Republican Party. In so doing, they can be confident they are supporting groups that support the causes they care about. Likewise for liberals and the Democratic Party. The central importance of left-right ideology in our party system is the basis of our analysis in the pages that follow.

Party Representation in Congress

In this section we consider more concretely the role of parties and voter opinion in congressional representation. The analysis is based on three measurable variables: whether a member of the House of Representatives affiliates with the Republican or the Democratic Party; how strongly voters in the representative's district support the Democratic or Republican candidate for president; and the degree to which the representative votes liberal or conservative on House roll calls. We take the effect of party to be strong if MCs support their party's agenda no matter how the voters in their district feel about it. We take the effect of district opinion to be strong if MCs tend to follow district opinion regardless of which party they are in.

We begin by explaining what exactly each variable measures. An

MC's party affiliation is straightforward. Nearly all MCs compete for office as the official nominee of one of the two major parties. This means they have been vetted by some kind of formal party process, usually a party primary. Many also receive help from their party in the general election. Once elected, they join their party's congressional caucus, from which they receive their committee assignments. Parties have little formal power to compel MCs to vote yes or no on a particular vote, but the role of party activists in nominations tends to produce uniformity of outlook. Hence, the extent to which party members in the House of Representatives vote together on a range of diverse issues we view as *party influence*.

Our second variable is a congressional district's vote for the Republican presidential candidate. We take presidential vote as a measure of general partisan attitudes.[2] This makes sense because presidential candidates are usually good representatives of their party tradition and are well-known to voters.[3] Over the period from 1876 to 2006, congressional districts vary from 0 to 93 percent Republican in their presidential vote. About half of all cases, however, fall between 40 and 60 percent Republican and about 95 percent fall between 15 and 70 percent Republican. The average is 48.6 percent.

Our variable measuring liberal-conservative voting on House roll calls requires a bit more explanation. When members of Congress vote on a bill, they do not announce themselves to be voting liberal or conservative or even Democrat or Republican. They simply vote yea or nay. However, observers watching hundreds of such votes can assign meaningful ideological labels to MCs. One such observer is the American Conservative Union (ACU), a conservative interest group. Each year, it rates each MC on a scale running from 0 percent conservative to 100 percent conservative. Many other groups do so as well.

One shortcoming of these ratings is that they exist only for recent decades. Two political scientists, Keith Poole and Howard Rosenthal (1984, 1997), however, have developed a statistical model for assigning ideology scores that overcomes this problem. Their ratings, called NOMINATE scores, correlate highly with the ACU and other ratings for the recent period in which several measures exist, but NOMINATE can be calculated back to the first Congress in 1789. Our analysis will rely on NOMINATE, as is common among political scientists. NOMINATE scores run from −1, which indicates very liberal voting, to +1, which indicates very conservative voting.

Because NOMINATE scores play a central role in this analysis, we must say a little more about what they measure. From Poole and Rosenthal's work (1997), two points are key. First, over 220 years of congressional voting, NOMINATE scores seem to be most clearly associated with disagreement over economic issues—taxes, tariffs, trade, banks, unions, and redistribution of wealth. By the latter, we mean the extent to which the government taxes the rich to fund social and other public services. For more than a century, the Democratic Party has tended to favor redistributive measures and the Republican Party to oppose them. Congress obviously votes on many noneconomic issues, but the striking finding from Poole and Rosenthal's work is that MCs who vote together on economic issues usually vote together on other issues too. Thus, congressional voting seems to be dominated by a strong, fairly general left-right dimension in which economic issues are especially important. The existence of this dominant left-right dimension through most of American history is the second point.

At two periods, centering on the 1850s and the 1950s, Poole and Rosenthal (1997) find evidence of a second dimension: race. In saying that race is a second dimension, they mean that congressional voting on race does not correlate with voting on most other issues, as captured by the first NOMINATE dimension. We shall see evidence of the independent importance of civil rights in our analysis of congressional representation, which is why we raise it in these introductory comments.

We turn now to the question of what, given the three variables just described, political representation might look like in these data.

One possibility is that MCs, regardless of their party, become more conservative on NOMINATE as their constituents vote more strongly Republican for president. Panel A of figure 11.1 illustrates this idea with simulated data. Each point on the graph stands for one member of Congress, Democrat (D) or Republican (R). As the district's presidential vote becomes more Republican (as shown on the horizontal axis), the MC's voting record (as shown on the vertical axis) becomes more conservative. The party of the MC has no independent importance in this example: Republican MCs tend to be more conservative than Democratic MCs, but only because they come from districts that vote more strongly Republican. Panel A shows a pure case of responsiveness to district preferences, independent of party.[4]

Panel B, by contrast, is all-party influence. MCs do not become more conservative as their districts become more Republican (as indicated by the flat trend lines). Party differences, however, are large (as indicated by the gap between Democratic and Republican MCs). This is a pure case of responsiveness to party agendas: the partisanship of a district affects whether a Republican or Democratic MC is elected, but has no further effect. MCs, once elected, respond to their party's agenda, not their district's preferences. Thus, for example, a Democrat who wins election to Congress from a district that leans Republican in presidential voting will be as liberal as a Democrat from an overwhelmingly Democratic district.

Panel C is a mixed case. MCs are responsive to district opinion (as captured by the sloped line), and they are also responsive to party agen-

Figure 11.1   Three Possible Models of Responsiveness

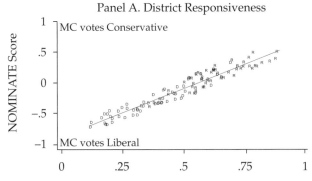

Panel A. District Responsiveness

NOMINATE Score

MC votes Conservative

MC votes Liberal

District Support for Republican Presidential
Candidate in Last Election

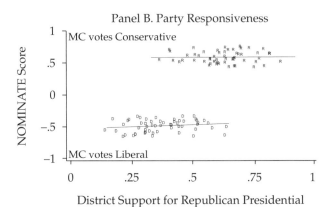

Panel B. Party Responsiveness

NOMINATE Score

MC votes Conservative

MC votes Liberal

District Support for Republican Presidential
Candidate in Last Election

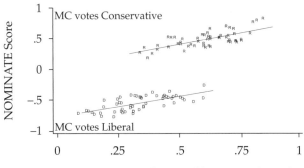

Panel C. District and Party Responsiveness

NOMINATE Score

MC votes Conservative

MC votes Liberal

District Support for Republican Presidential
Candidate in Last Election

Source: Authors' compilation.
Note: Democratic members of Congress (MCs) shown as D; Republican shown as R.

das (as captured by the gap between lines). Note, however, that the gap between the parties is large and the slope of the trend lines is small. This suggests that responsiveness to party agendas is greater than responsiveness to district opinion.

With these theoretical possibilities in mind, we turn to actual data on political responsiveness. The roll-call data are DW1 NOMINATE scores downloaded from Keith Poole's website. These particular NOMINATE scores are designed to be comparable across legislative sessions of Congress.

The data on presidential voting in congressional districts were provided by James Snyder of the Massachusetts Institute of Technology. For the period before 1952, the data were created by painstakingly mapping presidential vote by county and ward onto congressional districts. A small percent of cases is missing, mainly in urban areas in the nineteenth century. These district-level data are the same that Stephen Ansolabehere, James Snyder, and Charles Stewart (2001) use.

The design of our study differs from that of Ansolabehere and his colleagues in an important way. They examine data from pairs of candidates who oppose each other in the same election, but their data are available only for cases in which both candidates eventually serve in Congress. Most of these are cases in which a challenger defeats an incumbent. Over the period 1876 to 1996, Ansolabehere and his colleagues have about 1,800 candidate pairs. Our data are from almost all MCs in our period, whether the opponent makes it to Congress or not. MC roll-call records in our study are therefore not paired against those of another MC from the same district; rather, through multiple regression, they are paired with the records of MCs whose districts are comparably Democratic or Republican in basic partisanship. The design of Ansolabehere and his colleague is superior for analyzing candidate positions in elections, which is its purpose; for studying responsiveness, which is our purpose, our design seems equally valid.[5]

We turn now to a preliminary look at the data in figure 11.2. Panel A at the top shows roll calls in the Congress elected in 1906. The speaker of the House for that Congress was Joseph Cannon, a Republican from Illinois, one of the most powerful speakers in history. Cannon personally controlled the content of major legislation and insisted on unwavering support from his party's MCs. The result is evident in the data: a huge gulf between the NOMINATE scores of Democratic and Republican MCs, and scant evidence of responsiveness to district opinion. Cannon's House is an example of responsiveness to party agendas.

Speaker Nancy Pelosi's House, based on the elections of 2006, is on the bottom. The gap in NOMINATE scores between Democratic and Republican MCs is large, which indicates a high level of partisan voting. However, the gap is not quite as big as in Cannon's day. And Pelosi's

Figure 11.2   Political Representation in Three Eras

Panel A. Speaker Joe Cannon's House (1906)

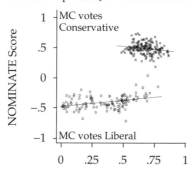

District Vote for Republican Presidential
Candidate in Last Election

Panel B. Speaker Sam Rayburn's House (1956)

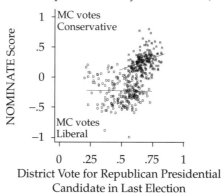

District Vote for Republican Presidential
Candidate in Last Election

Panel C. Speaker Nancy Pelosi's House (2006)

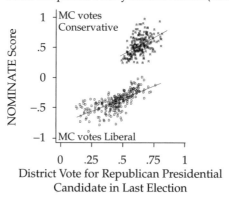

District Vote for Republican Presidential
Candidate in Last Election

Source: Authors' compilation. Presidential vote data from Ansolabehere, Snyder, and Stewart (2001); NOMINATE data from Poole (n.d., http://voteview.com).

House differs greatly in terms of responsiveness: within both parties, there is a tendency for MCs to move to vote more conservatively as their constituents become less Democratic and more Republican. The case thus exemplifies our mixed pattern: MCs respond both to their party's agenda and to voters in their districts.

The pattern from Speaker Sam Rayburn's House, based on the 1956 election, fits none of our three scenarios. The gap between parties is small, and Democratic MCs from Democratic strongholds are slightly more conservative than Democratic legislators from Republican-leaning districts.

If the pattern in the 1950s seems disorganized, it is because the party system was unstable in the 1950s. Civil rights for African Americans had become an issue, which undermined the old patterns of partisanship. In looking more closely at the 1956 pattern, we can learn a good deal about how party representation works, as we shall do in a moment. Before concluding this section, however, we note that none of these examples is consistent with a pattern of full responsiveness to voters, as depicted in panel A of figure 11.1. In fact, we have found no case of this pattern in our data, which go back to 1876. Party agendas always matter in our data, and sometimes they are the only things that matter.

Race and the Party System

We noted earlier that an issue that is not part of either party's agenda might be neglected by the political system. From the 1870s to the 1940s, civil rights for African Americans were such an issue. The Republican Party paid increasingly little attention to the reassertion of white dominance in the South after Reconstruction. Meanwhile, the Democratic Party, anchored by white voters in the South, fiercely opposed equal treatment of blacks. The result was that, even where African Americans were allowed to vote, they had no party for which to cast a pro–civil rights vote.

This began to change in the early decades of the twentieth century. Self-described progressive intellectuals—soon to call themselves liberal—argued in books, journals, and newspapers that treatment of blacks in the United States was unconscionable (Noel 2006). In so writing, these progressive pundits bundled racial concerns with other progressive issues. Their readers, often activists aligned with the Democratic Party, followed up by pressing for equal rights amendments to many northern state constitutions (Feinstein and Schickler 2008). Also in the early decades of the twentieth century, many African Americans migrated to northern cities, where they joined the urban political machines of the Democratic Party. A new generation of black leaders gave up on the "Party of Lincoln" and turned to the Democratic Party for redress. In a pivotal party event, a group of liberal ideologues calling themselves Americans for Democratic Action allied with the bosses of these machines to enact a strong civil rights plank at the 1948 Democratic Convention. This compelled many white southerners to bolt from the convention and mount a third-party presidential campaign in favor of segregation. But the 1948 convention sent a clear message: the activist base of the Democratic Party was committed to racial equality. Among the ambitious politicians who got this message was Lyndon Johnson of Texas. To establish credibility with the activists and group leaders who controlled his party's presidential nominations, he prodded the Senate to pass the first modern civil rights act in 1957 and later, as president, led the party to historic civil rights laws (for further analysis, see Cohen et al. 2008, chapter 5).

This thumbnail sketch does only rough justice to the myriad forces that led the Democratic Party to embrace civil rights after a century of defending southern racism. It suffices, however, to illustrate the role of parties as vehicles of political representation. African Americans, a group too small to win battles on their own, got policies that they deeply wanted only after those policies were incorporated into a party agenda. At the same time, southern segregationists, after losing their influence within the party that had been their champion, lost out in national politics as well.

In light of this as background, figure 11.3 provides considerable insight into the nature of party representation. It shows the same data as figure 11.2 does, except separately for states of the South and North.[6] Note first the huge regional difference in support for the two parties in the North and the South in 1906. The North, having fought and won the Civil War under the Republican Party, is still overwhelmingly Republican; the South, embittered by its loss to the Republican-led North, is equally firm in its commitment to the Democratic Party.[7] Although not visible in the data, the white South used its position of strength in the Democratic Party to make it a vehicle of opposition to racial equality.

When the Democratic Party changed to support racial equality, white voters in southern states began to leave. This drift can been seen in two ways in the middle left panel of figure 11.3. First, the NOMINATE scores of southern Democratic MCs are distinctly higher (more conservative) in 1956 than in 2006. This shows that southern Democratic MCs are no longer supporting their party agenda in Congress. Second, southern voters are becoming more Republican in presidential elections, as can be seen in the fact that districts are more toward the right of the x-axis in figure 11.3.

Most notable about 1956, however, is the sharp contrast between the South and the rest of the country. In the northern states, we see the expected pattern of difference in the NOMINATE scores of Democratic

Figure 11.3   Party Alignment in North and South, 1906 to 2006

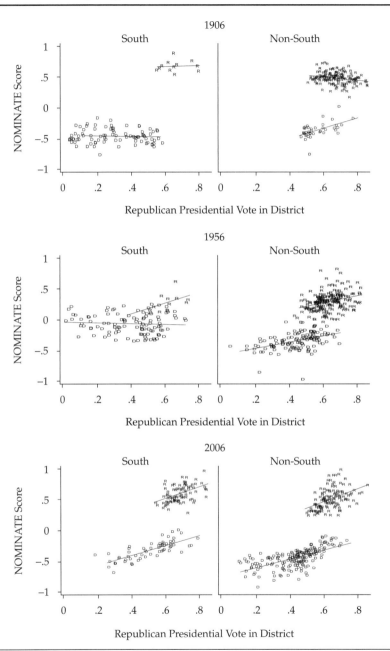

Source: Authors' compilation. Presidential vote data from Ansolabehere, Snyder, and Stewart (2001); NOMINATE data from Poole (n.d., http://voteview.com).

and Republican MCs. This shows that the party system was not losing its shape in 1956, as it appeared to be in figure 11.2. Only the South was in turmoil—and for reasons that make sense from the standpoint of political representation: when the Democratic Party changed where it stood on an issue of great importance to the white South, the white South turned away from the Democratic Party.

Now look at the bottom panel of figure 11.3. The key point here is the stark similarity of patterns in the North and the South. Party differences between MCs are about the same in each region, and the degree of responsiveness to district opinion (as indicated by the slant of the trend lines) is also about the same. Party divisions have lost most of their regional accent and become national.

The point here is not that the North and the South support the two parties equally. In fact, the South leans Republican in both presidential and congressional voting, as can be seen by close examination of figure 11.3. The point, rather, is that partisanship is linked to representation in the same way in both areas. Thus, a southern district that votes Democratic for president and elects a Democratic MC will get the same representation from that MC as will a comparable northern district. This was not so in 1956.[8]

Closely related is a parallel change in what the NOMINATE measure of congressional voting captures. As we explained earlier, House votes on civil rights in the 1950s were only weakly correlated with votes on the first NOMINATE dimension. Thus, an MC could be liberal on race but conservative on the economic issues that dominate this NOMINATE measure. By 2000, this was no longer so: an economic liberal on NOMINATE was also a racial liberal, and an economic conservative was also a racial conservative. Thus, race became bundled within the general agenda of each party. This development cannot be seen in the simple data we report, but it is the reason the party system operates similarly in both regions.

Our analysis so far has made three points. One is that sharp differences in party agendas are the rule rather than the exception in American politics, as was first noted by Poole and Rosenthal (1984). Only in periods of party change do MCs from each party fail to vote for distinctly different partisan policy agendas. The second point is that when differences exist in the roll-call votes of Democratic and Republican MCs, they cannot usually be explained by the proclivities of the district voters that elect them. Differences in NOMINATE scores are to a large extent independent from what MCs' local voters appear to want. This point, first demonstrated by Ansolabehere and his colleagues (2001), is indicated by the gap between NOMINATE scores elected from comparably partisan districts. The third point, in partial contradiction of the second, is that parties may now be somewhat more responsive to district opinion than they were at the turn of the century. This is indicated by the steeper slant in trend lines in 1956 and especially in 2006 than in 1906. Analysis of all cases from 1874 to 2006 in the next section confirms these points.

The account of racial politics in this section underscores the limited interest of parties in representing voter opinion. When a majority of Democratic activists came to favor racial equality, the party abandoned white southern voters, historically the party's most loyal supporters. Democratic activists wanted the votes of the South, but they wanted even more to take what they considered a just stand on race. Later generations of party activists have felt similarly about issues like abortion, gay rights, gun control, war, global warming, and taxes, among others. Winning elections is important to parties, but winning elections on behalf of causes considered just by their activist groups is more important. The commitment of parties to causes and interests they consider important is the main reason the gaps between party MCs in our graphs are typically large, as well as the reason the slopes indicating responsiveness to local voters are often shallow.

Knowing what parties stand for, voters can use them as vehicles for the expression of their preferences. The support of the white South for the Democratic Party when it championed segregation, and its movement away from the party when it began to favor racial equality, illustrate this point. But southern voters were responding to the position of the Democratic Party on race more than it was responding to theirs. We turn now to a more systematic presentation of evidence on the three points above.

Who Gets More Representation—
Parties or Voters?

We ask the representation question in a precise and narrow way: which better predicts an MC's votes, party affiliation or the partisanship of the district? The analysis is closely tied to panel C of figure 11.1, which we reproduce as figure 11.4, along with annotation to clarify our method.

The effect of an MC's party, as illustrated in this figure, is the difference in NOMINATE scores between the average Democrat and the average Republican. This difference looks to be about .8 points, which is the difference between an MC who mostly votes conservative and an MC who mostly votes liberal.

The district effect, also illustrated, is the difference in NOMINATE scores between an MC from a party stronghold and an MC of the same party from a district leaning to the other party in presidential voting. The effect appears to be about .3 NOMINATE units, or roughly the difference between always voting on the same ideological side in Congress

Figure 11.4   The Mixed Model of Political Representation

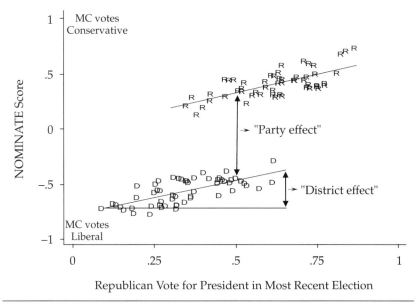

Source: Authors' compilation.

and usually voting on the same side. We take this difference to be the effect of pressure on MCs from moderate voters in swing districts. As the numbers .3 and .8 suggest, voter pressure in our example is less than half the effect of pressure from the party agenda.

Using this general method, we have estimated the effect of party and district for every House of Representatives from 1876 to 2006 (for details of the estimation procedure, see the appendix). A graphical summary of the results is presented in figure 11.5. Each point on the graph represents either the effect of party agenda in a given year (upper set of Xs) or the pressure of district partisanship (lower set of solid dots). The smooth lines running through the points summarize the trend in the data.

The overall pattern of results is consistent with the sample graphs presented earlier. The effect of party agendas was large around the turn of the twentieth century, the heyday of Speaker Joe Cannon; lower at mid-century when Sam Rayburn held sway; and high again at the end of the twentieth century, when Nancy Pelosi led the House. Responsiveness to district opinion was initially low, but rose and is presently an important but secondary factor in political representation. Its effect appears to be about half that of party agendas in the current period. These results are in line with what other scholars, using different methods and

Figure 11.5   Effect of Party and District Partisanship on MC's Roll-Call Votes

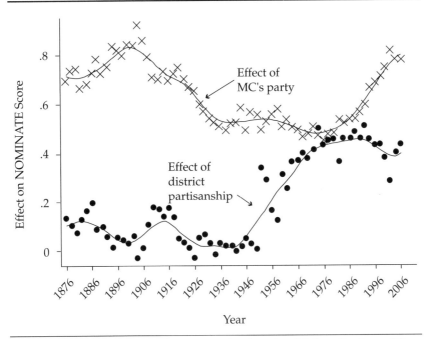

Source: Authors' compilation. Presidential vote data from Ansolabehere, Snyder, and Stewart (2001); NOMINATE data from Poole (n.d., http://voteview.com).

time periods, have also found (Ansolabehere, Snyder, and Stewart 2001; McCarty, Poole, Rosenthal 2006, 2009).[9]

Based on these results, it seems fair to say that contemporary American parties respond both to district opinion and to their own agendas, but more so to the latter. The remaining question is what exactly this pattern of responsiveness means in practice. To answer, we take a detailed look at the enactment of two major policies.

Party Politics in Action

We examine both a series of big tax cuts in 2001 and 2003 and a new federal program to pay the cost of prescription drugs for seniors. Both were proposed by Republican President George W. Bush, opposed by most Democratic members of Congress, and passed by majorities of Republican MCs.

The section has three parts. In the first, we review survey data to gauge popular demand for the tax cuts and aid to the elderly. Because President Bush's support for tax cuts and a senior drug benefit was a major factor in their enactment, we examine the role of these issues in his election to the presidency in 2000. Last, we describe congressional enactment of the policies. Our claim, as in the earlier part of the essay, will be that parties play the dominant role in political representation, but responsiveness to public demand is also important.

Trends in Public Opinion on Taxes and the Elderly

"To speak with precision about public opinion," wrote V. O. Key, "is a task not unlike coming to grips with the Holy Ghost" (1961, 8). The vast amount of polling done today often only magnifies the problem, since more polls often mean more conflicting results.

We shall try to cut through the morass of available data with two time series that we consider roughly representative. Figure 11.6 shows, first, trends in support for the view that taxes are too high or too low. As can be seen, there is a fairly stable majority that taxes are too high, creating continuous pressure on public officials to cut them. Pressure appeared, however, to rise slightly through the 1990s. It also fell in 2002, which was just after Republican-sponsored tax cuts went into effect.

Figure 11.7 shows trends in attitudes toward Social Security spending. On this issue, stable majorities exist that spending is either about right or should be higher, with a small uptick in support for spending in the 1990s. We view these data as roughly typical of the public's generally positive attitude toward spending on the elderly, which is the biggest category of domestic federal spending.

Thus, the public solidly favored both lower taxes and more spending on the elderly, with both attitudes probably gaining strength as the 2000 election approached.[10]

Election of George W. Bush

The 2000 election took place in the shadow of an unusual circumstance: a $230 billion federal budget surplus. Experts projected, moreover, that surpluses would continue at the rate of $100 billion a year for the next ten years, or 5 percent of all spending in that period (Congressional Budget Office 2000). Amidst public debate on how to use the surplus, ABC News reported the following poll results on the question of which four items that respondents thought should be the top priority for any surplus money in the federal budget: cut federal income taxes (14 percent), put the surplus toward reducing the national debt (19 percent), strengthen the Social Security system (36 percent), or increase spending

Figure 11.6   Trends in Public Opinion on Taxes

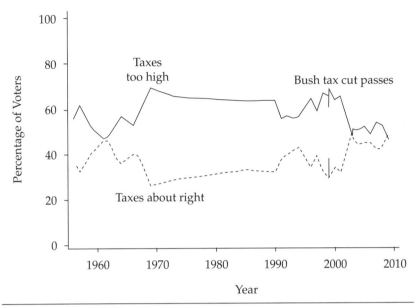

Source: Authors' compilation based on Gallup (2010).

on other domestic programs, such as education or health care (29 percent).[11]

In the presidential debate shortly afterward, Bush made the surplus the centerpiece of his opening remarks: "I want to take one-half of the surplus and dedicate it to Social Security. One-quarter of the surplus for important projects, and I want to send one-quarter of the surplus back to the people who pay the bills."[12]

This position is quite consistent with public preferences and, in this sense, responsive to public opinion. However, the dollar value of Bush's proposed tax cut was $1.3 trillion over ten years.[13] This was 1.3 times greater than the entire estimated surplus in that period, and thus more than the public appeared to want in tax cuts. When we say that parties often use responsiveness as a cover for what they want to do anyway, this is the kind of thing we that have in mind.

Bush also pledged in the debates to provide a prescription drug benefit for seniors. Democrats, he said, had promised this benefit in 1992 but failed to deliver: "Let me make sure the seniors hear me loud and clear. . . . All seniors will be covered, all seniors will have their prescription drugs paid for, and in the [time needed to enact the program], we'll have a plan to help poor seniors."[14]

Figure 11.7   Trends in Public Opinion on Social Security Spending

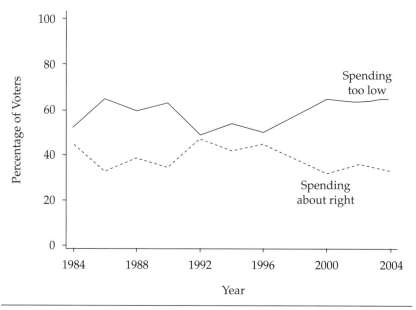

Source: Authors' compilation based on data from the National Election Studies (NES, various years).

Did pledges to slash taxes and provide a drug benefit to seniors help Bush win the election? Political scientists cannot usually provide reliable answers to such questions, but we shall do our best.

The 2000 Democratic candidate, Al Gore, also promised large tax cuts and a senior drug benefit, but Gore's tax break was smaller than Bush's and his drug benefit bigger,[15] a package that was probably better aligned with the public's preferences in polls. Gore also pummeled Bush's tax plan as a giveaway to the rich: "[Bush] spends more money for tax cuts for the wealthiest 1% than all of his new spending proposals for health care, prescription drug, education and national defense all combined. I agree that the surplus is the American people's money, it's your money. That's why I don't think we should give nearly half of it to the wealthiest 1%, because the other 99% have had an awful lot to do with building the surplus in our prosperity."[16]

Gore repeated this charge, which was roughly true, several times, but Bush responded, also probably correctly, that Gore's "targeted tax cuts" gave nothing to 50 million Americans. "I want everybody who pays taxes to have their tax rates cut," Bush said.[17] In the blizzard of statistics the two men threw at each other, we think neither gained much on the tax issue. The claims were huge, but the numbers were probably daunting for many voters.

The drug benefit, however, probably did matter. Gore outbid Bush in his attempt to woo the elderly by promising a program that was about 50 percent bigger.[18] But the key fact is that Bush offered a drug benefit. Since at least the 1930s, the Republican Party had largely opposed such social welfare programs. More Republican than Democratic MCs voted against Social Security in 1935 and Medicare in 1965.[19] That Bush even pledged to create a new social welfare program in 2000 was most likely because he felt that he needed to do so to win. And he was probably right. The 2000 election came down to one state, Florida, which happens to have the nation's largest concentration of senior voters. Bush strategists recognized that Florida could be pivotal and made extraordinary efforts to carry it. As it turned out, Bush won Florida by 537 votes of almost 6 million cast. Had Gore offered a drug benefit and Bush offered nothing, it is a good bet the Florida outcome—and the outcome of the election itself—would have been different.[20]

Bush's promise of a senior drug benefit thus seems an example of responsiveness to public opinion. Note, however, that the response was not to opinion in general, but to a key voting block. In our account, parties are not in the business of representing voters; they are in the business of attracting votes as necessary to win elections and gain control of government, which is what Bush and the Republicans did in 2000.

Parties in Congress: Tax Cuts

In his fifth year as speaker of the House of Representatives, Republican Dennis Hastert listed the principles that guided his work. One was "to please a majority of the majority."[21] Though stated blandly, this principle has enormous importance in today's House. What it means is that members of the majority party first decide among themselves what they want, and then use parliamentary control of the House to get it. By closing ranks, the majority party can rule without any votes from the minority. Indeed, the majority party often does not even consult the minority party. Since the 1980s, when Democrats revived the practice of party government, leaders of both parties have increasingly followed the principle of pleasing a majority of the majority.

When the same party controls both Congress and the presidency, congressional leaders also close ranks with the president, thus raising the importance of party considerations in legislation. In such cases, as Thomas Mann and Norman Ornstein write, "leaders of Congress . . . see themselves as field lieutenants in the president's army far more than they do as members of a separate and independent branch of government" (2006, 155).

These principles were in full operation in the House's enactment of the Bush tax cuts. Following guidance from the White House, the bill was written without Democratic input and passed on an almost perfect party-line vote. Democrats offered substitute bills proposing smaller tax cuts (to preserve revenue for popular programs), but their amendments were brushed aside, also on mostly party-line votes.[22] On final passage of the 2001 tax cuts, Republican MCs voted 211 to 0 in favor; Democrats voted 153 to 28 in opposition. The Democrats who supported the Republican bill were mainly from Republican-leaning districts, such that votes to cut taxes would appear in our earlier graphs as evidence of responsiveness to district opinion.[23] This responsiveness, however, made no discernible difference in the content of the final bill, which was drafted solely by Republicans.

Because of tradition and the smaller size of the Senate, party control is weaker in that chamber. The party balance, moreover, was 51 to 50, with the deciding vote coming from Republican Vice President Dick Cheney. Under these circumstances, party control actually faltered and district responsiveness made an important difference. President Bush asked Congress to cut taxes by $1.6 trillion, which was somewhat more than he promised in the election, but the Republican leadership was unable to round up enough votes.[24] Hence it reluctantly negotiated with a set of four senators from states in which responsiveness to moderate opinion was essential for reelection.[25] The figure they arrived at was $1.35 trillion, tilted somewhat more toward middle-income taxpayers than Bush's original request.[26] Having made this compromise, Republican leadership kept control of other elements in the bill, mainly by convincing conservatives this was the best deal they would get. The Democratic minority in the Senate, like its House counterpart, was largely cut out of the process. The best Democrats could manage was a press conference at which the star attractions were a $46,000 Lexus and a low-end replacement muffler. The former, said Democratic leaders, was what the rich could buy with their Bush tax cut, the latter what working Americans could get.[27] President Bush, however, hailed the bill as a victory for the overtaxed American worker.

Public support for tax cuts dipped after passage of the Bush tax bill, as shown earlier in figure 11.6, but the president pressed in 2003 for $674 billion in additional cuts.[28] The story of this proposal was almost the same as for the first. The disciplined Republican majority in the House wrote the bill the president wanted, beat back Democratic attempts to weaken it, and passed it with mainly Republican votes. The Senate process was more precarious, with Vice President Cheney again casting the decisive vote—this time for a bill that delivered only about half of what the president requested, some $330 billion in tax reductions.[29] Again, moderate senators responsive to centrist electorates reduced the ability of party leaders to produce the bill that they and the president wanted. Media reports indicated that pivotal senators were paid off in increased federal aid for their home states.[30]

From this evidence, we ask the same questions we asked earlier in our quantitative analysis: how much did the Bush tax cuts reflect the Republican Party agenda, and how much did it reflect responsiveness to district opinion? With some patient arithmetic, we can provide plausible answers to these questions. Gore's original tax proposal was for $50 billion per year; what Bush proposed to Congress totaled about $230 billion per year. This is a difference of $180 billion per year.[31] How big a difference is that?

One benchmark is the cost of the Iraq War, which was about $100 billion per year over its first seven years.[32] Another is the annual cost of President Obama's health-care reform measure as passed by the Senate in January 2010, which was about $90 billion.[33] By these benchmarks, the $180 billion party difference on tax cuts was huge—enough to fund two historically important government endeavors.[34] It is notable that the vast majority of legislators in both the House and the Senate supported their party's line on these vastly different tax policies. In this sense, legislator responsiveness to district opinion was slight.

A handful of centrists nonetheless forced the Republicans into compromise. How much compromise? The midway point between Gore's $50 billion and Bush's $230 billion is $140 billion. What actually passed was $170 billion. Translating these numbers into verbal labels as best we can, we conclude that the $170 billion tax cuts were much larger than the $50 billion that Democrats wanted and moderately smaller than the $230 billion that Republicans wanted. Party control, thus, made a large difference, and pressure to compromise by legislators from centrist electorates made a moderate difference.

Whether the $170 billion amount of the tax cuts was bigger or smaller than the public wanted is difficult to say. Polls at the time of the 2000 election suggested that voters wanted only a moderate tax cut in order to maintain revenues for health, education, and retirement programs. But it is possible that, having been offered a large tax cut by President Bush, voters decided that they wanted a big cut after all (see Bartels 2005; Lupia et al. 2007; Bartels 2007). However this may be, polls from 2010 indicate that most voters are upset about federal deficits that are due in significant part to the Bush-era tax cuts, and yet blame President Obama and the Democrats for the problem. This can be taken as further success for the Republican Party's antitax agenda.

Parties in Congress: Prescription Drugs for the Elderly

The Republican president promised a drug benefit as part of his campaign to win the 2000 election; to win the 2004 election, his party would have to deliver. If it didn't, said one Republican leader, "the American people will say, 'You had the House, you had the Senate, why don't we have a prescription drug benefit?" Leading the congressional fight was Republican House Speaker Hastert, whose press spokesman said, "This is the thing he thinks will keep us in the majority for a while."[35]

But some of the party's most reliable officeholders—conservative MCs from staunchly Republican districts—balked at the drug benefit plan President Bush proposed. They were concerned not only about the party's principled commitment to small government but also the rising cost of the program as the population aged and expensive new drugs came on the market. "[Senior citizens] will be back, year after year, petitioning Congress to massively expand this already oversized new entitlement," said Dick Armey, the party's former majority leader in the House.[36] "I worry that the drug program will grow the same way that Medicare and Medicaid have grown since 1965," said a Republican MC.[37] "I trust and love my president," another Republican MC explained. "But I have tremendous concern about creating what I am confident will become one of the largest, most expensive entitlements in the nation's history."[38]

The drug benefit legislation was, like the Republican tax cuts of 2001 and 2003, written almost exclusively by the Bush administration and the Republican leadership in Congress, and it was passed by mostly Republican votes. The main difference from the tax cut bills was that, because the Republicans couldn't hold the support of some of their most conservative legislators, they had to work harder to fashion a bill that could pass a narrowly divided Congress.

Some of the partisan maneuvering used to pass the bill raised charges of ethics violations. One Republican MC who opposed the bill charged that leaders had threatened to withhold party support from his son, who was campaigning to take over his retiring father's seat. A senior official in the executive branch also charged publicly that he had been threatened with firing unless he withheld from Congress the true cost of the drug program.[39] The actual voting process was handled in a highly controversial way: when the drug benefit came up two votes short of passage at the end of the regular voting period in the House, party leaders held the balloting open for nearly three hours while they rounded up additional votes, quite possibly on the basis of undisclosed side payments.[40] Any such side payments were on top of the $25 billion for rural health care that moderate Democrats had earlier extracted as their cost for supporting the bill. Note that $25 billion is one-fourth of the annual cost of the Iraq War, a large benefit to the rather small group of swing-state voters who received it.

An important point in this narrative is that some or possibly most of the Democratic votes needed to pass the bill, which could show up in a statistical analysis as MC responsiveness to district pressures for moderation, did not actually cause the plan to be more moderate. Rather, the Republican leadership brought particular swing MCs on board without forcing significant compromise in core features of the party-designed bill.

What were these core features? And how did they differ from Democratic ideas?

Disagreement centered mainly on the role of government. Republicans were inclined to oppose any subsidy to drug costs, but if they had to pass a drug plan, they wanted the role of government to be as limited as possible. Republicans therefore sought to channel money for the drug benefit to private insurance companies, who would use it as a subsidy for low-cost drug insurance plans. The insurance companies would in theory compete with one another, leading to more efficient service. Democrats, for their part, wanted the federal bureaucracy to administer the drug benefit on the model of Medicare, whereby seniors choose a doctor and the government pays the cost of treatment. Democrats saw this approach as more efficient because it cut out profits by private insurance.[41]

Republicans also sought to use the new drug benefit as a vehicle for increasing the role of private insurance companies in Medicare. Specifically, Republicans proposed to channel public money to insurance companies so they would offer low-cost general health plans, thus drawing patients away from government-run Medicare. As with the drug benefit, Republicans argued this would lower costs in the long run. But Democrats attacked the idea as a wasteful giveaway to insurance companies. Democrats also feared that a private option could stigmatize Medicare as welfare for those who stayed on it.[42]

Republicans got most of what they wanted in the final bill. Private insurance companies rather than Medicare administered the new drug benefit, and insurance companies received some new tax funds to sweeten their health-care packages. A major fight occurred on whether the private insurance would receive enough government support to offer more generous insurance than Medicare. On this point, Democrats held ranks and defeated the Republicans.[43]

We turn now to the key question of this case study: how much of what happened in this policy area was due to party agendas, and how much to public pressure?

In our analysis of the tax plans, which centered on the dollar value of tax cuts, it was easier to say exactly how much the parties differed and which side won. For prescription drug coverage, in which the advantages claimed by each side were based more on ideological theory than actual knowledge, the problem is more difficult. We shall score the outcome as best we can.

We begin with money, where evaluation remains easy. Republicans proposed to spend $40 billion per year and the Democrats $80 billion.[44] This works out to about $1,000 per year per senior under the Republican plan versus $2,000 under the Democratic one. For seniors, many of whom have low incomes, this is a large difference.[45] Polls cited above indicate that both seniors and the general public preferred more rather than less spending on seniors. We therefore conclude that, although Republicans were responsive to public opinion, their response was significantly tempered by the party's low-tax and antigovernment agenda.

At least as large as the monetary difference was another ideological difference—whether to funnel tax dollars through insurance companies or to administer them through the Medicare bureaucracy. We are aware of no evidence that the public was pressing for privately administered eldercare. In fact, public opposition was so strongly against the president's proposal to turn Social Security toward private management that the Republican leadership did not even bring it to a vote.[46] In the case of the drug benefit, however, Republicans were able to enact a substantial amount of private management—another important success for the party agenda.

Yet the triumph of party agenda was less than total. As noted earlier, because several conservatives opposed the plan, the Republican leadership needed Democratic votes to pass it. Much of this support came, also as noted earlier, from a group of Democratic MCs in moderate and rural districts, who provided their votes in exchange for purely local benefits.[47] Yet these same Democrats refused to go along with Republican plans for a stronger private insurance option. Democrats from swing districts thus managed both to moderate the Republican bill and to obtain special payoffs for their rural constituents—a striking case of how MC responsiveness to district concerns can be extremely important.

Overall, we see the drug benefit as a case in which a party was quite responsive to public pressure: Republicans spent a large amount of money on a program on which they would have preferred to spend little or nothing. The party could shape drug spending to its principles and try to limit the amount, but could not avoid a big bow to electoral pressure. Even worse from the party's point of view, the drug benefit established a new entitlement that was likely to grow much larger over time.

One should not, however, conclude that parties are always so responsive. As we maintain, Republicans responded to the wishes of the elderly for a drug benefit because the elderly were a pivotal group in a pivotal state in the electoral college for two presidential elections in a row. A number of rural voters in certain Democratic districts were similarly pivotal and similarly rewarded. But not all groups can be pivotal. What this case illustrates is that parties will be as responsive as they need to be to win pivotal voters, not that they are generally responsive to voters.

Discussion

Taken together, the tax and drug benefit case studies show that both party agendas and public opinion affect what Congress does. In the case of the drug benefit, public opinion probably mattered more than the party agenda. This is a different result than we obtained in our statistical analysis, which found responsiveness important but party agendas more so.

Although we cannot be sure without additional case studies, we believe that results from the statistical analysis are more valid. First, the statistical analysis is based on, literally, tens of thousands of policy decisions and the case study analysis on only two. Second, the tax-cut and drug-benefit policies were probably the two most hotly debated and heavily publicized domestic issues of the eight-year presidency of George W. Bush, and there is ample reason to believe that Congress is more responsive to public opinion when the public is watching than when it is not (Arnold 1990).

In an important wrinkle on the nature of congressional responsiveness, Robert van Houweling, of the University of California, Berkeley has developed a thesis on how seemingly centrist MCs take devious advantage of the public's limited attentiveness (see van Houweling, n.d.).[48] Many centrist MCs who push for compromise on high-profile roll-call votes are, he argues, "closet extremists" who secretly favor the agendas of their parties but make a show of seeming to favor compromise. They do so by voting both for obscure procedural devices that ensure the ultimate defeat of moderate proposals, and for moderating amendments to major legislation. In an analysis similar in form to ours, van Houweling shows that party responsiveness to district opinion is nil for procedural votes, but robust for moderating amendments. Some or perhaps most of what appears to be responsiveness in NOMINATE scores, which count all contested roll calls, may therefore be fake responsiveness (our term, not van Houweling's).

More work is obviously necessary to pin down the degree to which congressional parties are responsive to public opinion versus their own agendas. There can be little doubt, however, that what parties want and do is to a substantial degree independent of what voters want.

Who Do Parties Represent?

We began with the theoretical premise that parties primarily represent the views of interest groups and ideologues that we call intense policy demanders. We cannot demonstrate this view of parties in this paper, but we do attempt to demonstrate an implication of this view—namely, that parties will attempt to get their way with policies they care about rather than attempt to represent the preferences of the people who vote for them. We found evidence for this implication in our statistical analysis of the roll-call votes of MCs. Between 1876 and 1940, MCs were almost exclusively responsive to the agendas of their parties, regardless of the partisanship of the districts that elected them. Since the 1940s, MCs may have become more responsive to the partisanship of their voters, but still appear to give more allegiance to party agendas than voter preferences.

In examining two recent policy enactments, we found qualitative evidence generally consistent with this analysis. In the case study of Republican-led tax cuts, we found that, in service of its ideological commitments, the party gave voters bigger tax cuts than the majority of voters probably wanted. Party leaders would, moreover, have provided even larger cuts except that senators vulnerable to centrist voters refused to go along. In the case of the drug benefit program, Republicans were probably more tightly tethered to public opinion, but it was the opinion of a group of pivotal voters rather than the public as a whole. The kind of responsiveness revealed in our two case studies is, in our view, typical of both parties: their focus is not on what voters want, but how much of the party agenda they can enact and still be elected and reelected to office. Although our analysis has focused on two Republican-led policy innovations, we could demonstrate similar behavior by Democrats.

To this view, we add one clarification and one caveat. The clarification involves ethics. Parties do, as suggested by our study of the drug benefit, sometimes behave unethically or even illegally. Obviously we condemn such behavior. But we view effort and organization as the main reason for party success. And, provided parties stay within correct legal and ethical limits, we find it hard to argue that they are wrong to organize and fight for policies that voters often do not want. Who, for example, could tell opponents of racial segregation they should give up their struggle because most voters are indifferent to segregation? Who could tell conservative activists that redistribution of wealth from rich to poor is fine if most voters want it, or tell liberal activists that children growing up without medical care is acceptable if most voters accept it? Parties are made up of people with strong views about what America should be, and they have every right to fight for those views—and to do so even if most voters disagree. Some of what we observe in Congress, where narrow majorities try to do what they believe in regardless of what centrist voters may want, is unsavory, but we do not criticize the organizational efforts that enable them to succeed.

The caveat is that, even in a polarized system in which neither party cares about popular representation as an end in itself, some representation still occurs. One major reason is that parties tend to rotate in office, each getting a turn to press voters to accept its view of good policy. While in power, and seeking to win it, parties must be attentive to what pivotal (or centrist) voters think. We saw this most clearly in the Republican Party's offer, against all of the party's traditions, of a drug benefit to senior voters.

Scholars need, however, to take care not to exaggerate the democratic qualities of this representation. Parties may give the public the outward appearance of what it wants while taking great liberties with major details. Individual legislators, offering what is sometimes fake representation, may do the same. Parties and legislators are also most attuned to the representation of pivotal voters, who may not want what most voters want and often get paid off in purely local benefits (see Bishin 2009).

To be sure, pivotal voters sometimes want what most other voters want. When they do, parties are likely to represent majority opinion. But when they don't, and when party leaders aim to please only a majority of the majority party, parties represent their own views of good public policy. These views are defined by the various business, union, religious, civil rights, and other ideological groups that constitute the parties' activist base. Parties' representation of their own views of good public policy may be the most common and important form of political representation in the United States today.

Appendix: Estimation of Effects

In this appendix, we discuss estimation of what we identify in figure 11.4 as the District Effect and the Party Effect. Estimation is based on the following equation:

$$\text{NOMINATE} = b_O + b_1[\text{Republican Presidential Vote}] + b_2[\text{Republican MC}] + b_3[\text{South}][49]$$

In this model, b_1 captures the former and b_2 captures the latter. We cannot, however, straightforwardly compare the coefficients because they apply to variables that have different ranges. The party variable takes only two values, 0 and 1; Republican Vote for President has a theoretical range that runs from 0 to 1, but values in most congressional districts fall in between.

The usual way to estimate the effect of a variable is to multiply its coefficient by the spread of the variable. We might, then, estimate the District Effect as $b_1 \times .93$, because the lowest value of Republican Presidential Vote in any congressional district is 0 percent Republican and the highest value is 93 percent Republican. But several problems arise. One is that 0 and .93 are both extreme values and unrepresentative of the vast bulk of the data. So, rather than use the full range of the data, we could take plus or minus 2 SDs of Republican Presidential Vote as the spread of this variable. This value is .64 (that is, $.16 \times 4$) in the whole dataset, but the SD varies significantly by year, from about .4 to more than .85. The SD of Republican Presidential Vote is greatest early in the period, when the South was solidly Democratic and the North solidly Republican, and smallest around mid-twentieth century. We do not want our estimates of MC responsiveness (that is, the District Effect) to be affected by changes in the spread of the vote in different election years. Our solution is to use .5 as the spread of Republican Presidential Vote in all years. This corresponds to the difference between a Democratic stronghold in which Republican Presidential Vote is 25 percent and a Republican stronghold in which it is 75 percent. This range seems both reasonable and intuitively easy to grasp. If anything, the value of .5 seems a fairly high value, which makes all of our estimates of responsiveness to district opinion a bit high. But given the emphasis in our paper on lack of party responsiveness, this bias is conservative. Readers who believe the value of .5 is too high or too low can make a mental adjustment in viewing figure 11.5, in which the value of .5 has been used in all calculations of the District Effect.

To summarize, we estimate the District Effect as $.5 \times b_1$, and the Party Effect as $1 \times b_2$. Figure 11.5 reports these values for each election from 1876 to 2006.[50] We used two other approaches to the estimation of the District Effect and Party Effect to verify that the above method does not produce misleading results. We shall now describe these two approaches to statistical estimation.

A large literature in statistics considers the problem of estimating "treatment effects" from observational data. In our analysis, one might view the party of the MC as a dichotomous treatment that districts either receive or do not receive. The estimation of such treatment effects is often improved by matching cases on their propensity to receive the treatment. The recommended method is to drop cases outside the range of values in which variation in treatment occurs, and to estimate effects within that range.

Consider the data from the House elected in 2006, as shown in figure 11.8. Districts in which Republican Presidential Vote is below about 45 percent are quite unlikely to receive the treatment of Republican MC. Districts with Republican presidential vote above about 65 percent are, on the other hand, very likely to receive the treatment. Given this, esti-

Figure 11.8   Trimming Extreme Values from Pelosi's House

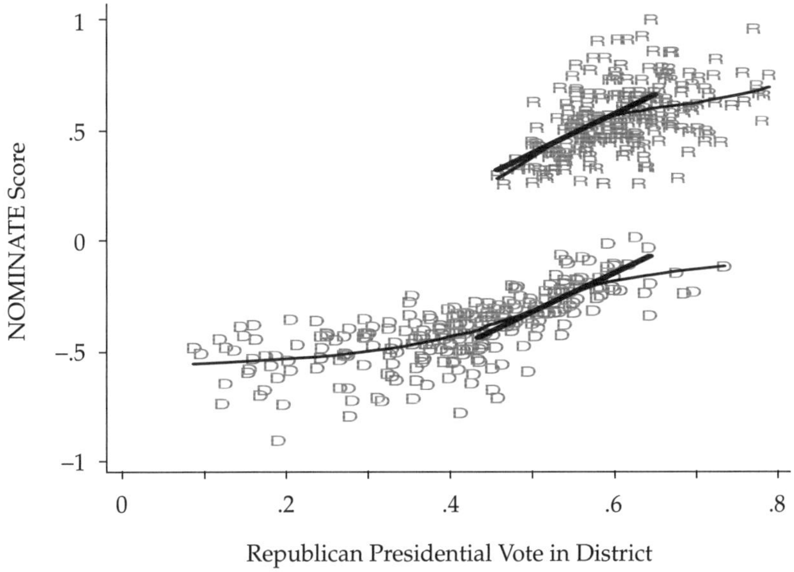

Source: Authors' compilation. Presidential vote data from Ansolabehere, Snyder, and Stewart (2001); NOMINATE data from Poole (n.d., http://voteview.com).

mating the effect of the treatment Republican MC on the full range of cases could be misleading. There is no necessary bias in using the full range of cases, but nonlinearity in the data, of the kind shown by the lowest trend lines in figure 11.8 introduces inefficiency. The most reliable method, as methodologists recommend, is to base estimates on data within the range in which variation in treatment actually occurs. The OLS lines in figure 11.8 provide estimates within the treatment range.

In this example, the difference in estimates of the party effect is not great. Controlling for district partisanship, the estimated effect of party (a 0–1 variable) on the NOMINATE score is .78 when all cases are used, and .74 when only cases within the treatment range (as shown by the OLS lines above) are used. But in some years restricting the range makes a more important difference.

Estimates of the District Effect vary more, but remain similar. The estimate for b_1 in the full data is .86; the estimate of the District Effect is then $.5 \times .83 = .43$. The estimate of b_1 for values of Presidential Vote from .44 to .65 (which are the cutoffs for .1 and .9 probability of treatment) is 1.58; the estimate of the district effect is then $.21 \times 1.58 = .33$.

A reestimation of figure 11.5 based on the latter method produces a pattern that is substantively equivalent to the results in the text of this chapter. Stata commands to generate this alternative figure are included in our replication materials.[51]

Another alternative is to estimate the above equation on the full data, and to calculate the district effect as $b_1 \times 4$SDs of the Republican Vote in the given year. This method also produces results that are substantively equivalent to the published figure 11.5, as can be confirmed in our replication materials.

We thank James Snyder for providing the primary data on which the paper is based, Congressional district-level vote for president for the period 1876 to 2006. We also thank David Pedersen, Kathy Scott, the editors of this volume, Peter Enns and Chris Wlezien, and two anonymous reviewers for helpful comments.

Notes

1. By political elite, we mean someone who is unusually active in politics.
2. More specifically, we use the Republican percentage of the two-party presidential vote.
3. Another possibility for measuring voter attitudes would be the popular vote for the MC in the district. However, many congressional elections are low-key events in which neither party campaigns hard because everyone expects the incumbent to win, making the vote tally a poor measure of general voter attitudes in the district.
4. Our argument here depends on the idea that median partisanship in a district increases as a roughly linear function of presidential vote in the district. This assumption would not be reasonable if, for example, partisanship were bimodally distributed in the population. We have found from survey data, however, that mass preferences usually, though not always, have a single-peaked distribution within a given geographical area, which makes our assumption reasonable.
5. In a study spanning a shorter period, from 1974 to 2002, Nolan McCarty, Keith Poole, and Howard Rosenthal (2006) use a design similar to ours to examine representation.
6. The South consists of the eleven Confederate states plus Kentucky and West Virginia.
7. Most Republican MCs from the South in 1906 are from border-state regions that opposed secession. Many northern Democrats in 1906 were elected by recent immigrants.
8. In a regression with DW1 as the dependent variable, and district vote for president, MC party, and the South as independent variables, the South gets a statistically significant coefficient in 2006 of about .04. In 1956, this coefficient was .25.

9. More specifically, our results agree closely with those of Ansolabehere and his colleagues for the period from 1874 to 1996, except for the 1990s, in which they find a decline in responsiveness to almost pre-1930 levels (Ansolabehere, Snyder, and Stewart 2001, 151). However, in a separate analysis focusing on 1996 alone, they find results similar to ours (see figure 11.1). McCarty, Poole, and Rosenthal (2006, 2009) examined the period since 1970 and get results that are consistent with ours.

10. Public support for defense spending, the second largest category of spending, also rose at the end of the 1990s.

11. ABC News.com Poll, *Surplus Priorities*, August 27, 2000, available at http://abcnews.go.com/images/pdf/796a48TaxCut.pdf

12. Richard Stevenson, "Sorting It Out: Tax Cuts and Spending," *New York Times*, October 6, 2000.

13. Alison Mitchell, "Spate of Numerical Sparring Highlights the Fiscal Focus of the Presidential Race," *New York Times*, May 3, 2000.

14. John T. Woolley and Gerhard Peters, "Presidential Candidates Debates: Presidential Debate in Boston, October 3, 2000," *The American Presidency Project*, available at http://www.presidency.ucsb.edu/ws/?pid=29418.

15. Alison Mitchell, "Gore and Bush Agree on Basics, But Differ Sharply on the Details," *New York Times*, July 4, 2000.

16. Woolley and Peters, "Presidential Candidates Debates."

17. Ibid.

18. Estimated to cost $198 to $338 billion. See Kevin Sack, "Differences on Medicare Take Center Stage in Gore Campaign," *New York Times*, September 25, 2000.

19. Social Security, available at http://www.ssa.gov/history/tally.html; Medicare, http://www.ssa.gov/history/tally65.html.

20. The *Washington Post* wrote during the campaign, "The winning formula [in Florida], leading Republicans believe, begins with a hard-sell on Bush's plans for Medicare drug coverage and Social Security" (David Von Drehle, "In Florida, Not Where Bush Wanted to Be," September 26, 2000, p. A10; see also James Gerstenzang and Matea Gold, "Gore, Lieberman Stress Prescription Costs; Campaign: As vice president spotlights four Florida seniors who can't afford all their drugs, Bush pledges to reveal his own aid plan next week," *Los Angeles Times*, August 29, 2000, p. A14; Federal Election Commission, *2000 Official Presidential General Election Results*, available at http://www.fec.gov/pubrec/2000presgeresults.htm).

21. Charles Babington, "Hastert Launches a Partisan Policy," *Washington Post*, November 27, 2004.

22. "Congress Cuts Deal on Taxes," *CQ Almanac 2001*.

23. Ibid.

24. Ibid.

25. These were Senators Chaffee (R-RI), Jeffords (R later turned Independent–VT), Baucus (D-MT), Breaux (D-LA).

26. "Congress Cuts Deal on Taxes," *CQ Almanac 2001*.

27. Douglas Waller, "What Is That Oink, Oink?" *Time*, February 11, 2001.

28. "Bush Scores Win on Tax Cuts," *CQ Almanac 2003*.

29. Ibid.
30. David Firestone, "With Plan for State Aid, Senate Republicans Gain Crucial Democratic Vote on Tax Cut," *New York Times*, May 15, 2003.
31. In the course of enacting the tax bills, Democratic leaders proposed higher cuts, but we take their proposals as attempts—and failed attempts at that—to attract swing voters to their position. Hence, we stick with Gore's campaign pledge as the Democrats' sincere preference.
32. "Cost of Iraq War to Surpass Vietnam's," *Los Angeles Times*, April 11, 2009.
33. "Obama's Health Bill Plan Largely Follows Senate Version," *New York Times*, February 22, 2010.
34. As, noted earlier, the Republican bill was tilted toward wealthy taxpayers, with about half of its benefits going to the top 2 percent of income earners, but Democrats managed to pass an amendment that gave bigger breaks to lower income persons. Because it is difficult to calculate the size of this party difference, we omit it from our summary of party differences, but it may have been fairly large.
35. Robin Toner, "An Imperfect Compromise," *New York Times*, November 25, 2003.
36. Dick Armey, "Say 'No' to the Medicare Bill," *Wall Street Journal*, November 21, 2003.
37. "President Leads the Roundup for Votes to Add Drug Benefits to Medicare," *New York Times*, June 26, 2003.
38. Ibid.
39. Sheryl Gay Stolberg, "Senate Democrats Claim Medicare Chief Broke Law," *New York Times*, March 19, 2004.
40. "Sharply Split, House Passes Broad Medicare Overhaul; Forceful Lobbying by Bush," *New York Times*, November 23, 2003.
41. "Medicare Revamp Cuts It Close," *CQ Almanac 2003*.
42. Ibid.
43. Ibid.
44. Ibid.
45. Because, as noted, the Bush administration understated the true cost of the drug benefit, the party difference might be smaller than this; yet it is a fair bet that the Democratic proposal, if enacted, would also have cost more than advertised.
46. One typical poll from this period showed the public against Bush's Social Security plan 37 to 55 percent ("Bush's Social Security Plan is Tough Sell President's Job Approval Steady, But Most Americans Don't Like His Social Security Plans," *ABC News*, March 14, 2005).
47. Regarding initial passage in the House, "Collin C. Peterson, D-Minn., said he and other conservative Democrats, as well as lawmakers from both parties representing rural areas, would vote for the bill because it contained $28 billion for hospitals, physicians and other providers in rural areas, the largest such package the House had passed." The conference committee later tweaked the amount to $25 billion "in additional funds for doctors, hospitals and other rural providers" ("Medicare Revamp Cuts It Close," *CQ Almanac 2003*).

48. Evidence that partisanship matters more on final passage than on procedural votes is also found in "The Two Faces of Congressional Roll-Call Voting" (Jessee and Theriault, n.d.).
49. Use of South as a control variable stabilizes the results without affecting the overall pattern in figure 11.5.
50. A Stata data file and do file to replicate these results have been posted at www.sscnet.ucla.edu/polisci/faculty/zaller.
51. In a portion of their analysis that is similar to ours, Nolan McCarty, Keith Poole, and Howard Rosenthal (2009) used interactions among mean-centered controls to assure the integrity of their estimate of the effect of party on NOMINATE scores. Implementation of these controls did not importantly affect our results and so we follow a rule of simplicity and leave them out. This can be verified in our replication materials.

References

Aldrich, John H. 1995. *Why Parties? The Origin and Transformation of Political Parties in America.* Chicago: Chicago University Press.

Ansolabehere, Stephen, James M. Snyder Jr., and Charles Stewart III. 2001. "Candidate Positioning in U.S. House Elections." *American Journal of Political Science* 45(1): 136–59.

Arnold, R. Douglas. 1990. *The Logic of Congressional Action.* New Haven, Conn.: Yale University Press.

Bartels, Larry M. 2005. "Homer Gets a Tax Cut: Inequality and Public Policy in the American Mind." *Perspectives on Politics* 3(1): 15–31.

———. 2007. "Homer Gets a Warm Hug: A Note on Ignorance and Extenuation." *Perspectives on Politics* 5(4): 785–90.

Bishin, Ben. 2009. *Tyranny of the Minority: The Subconstituency Politics Theory of Representation.* Philadelphia: Temple University Press.

Cohen, Marty, David Karol, Hans Noel, and John Zaller. 2008. *The Party Decides.* Chicago: University of Chicago Press.

Congressional Budget Office. 2000. *The Budget and Economic Outlook: Fiscal Years 2001–2010.* Washington: Government Printing Office. Available at http://www.cbo.gov/ftpdocs/18xx/doc1820/eb0100.pdf (accessed November 9, 2010).

Downs, Anthony. 1957. *An Economic Theory of Democracy.* New York: Harper and Row.

Feinstein, Bruce, and Eric Schickler. 2008. "Platforms and Partners: The Civil Rights Realignment Reconsidered." *Studies in American Political Development* 22(1): 1–31.

Gallup. 2010. "Taxes and Tax Cuts: Gallup's Pulse of Democracy." Available at http://www.gallup.com/poll/1714/taxes.aspx (accessed August 20, 2010).

Jessee, Stephen, and Sean Theriault. N.d. "The Two Faces of Congressional Roll Call Voting." Unpublished manuscript. University of Texas, Austin.

Key, Valdimer Orlando, Jr. 1961. *Public Opinion and American Democracy.* New York: Alfred A. Knopf.

Lupia, Arthur, Adam Seth Levine, Jesse O. Menning, and Gisela Sin. 2007. "Were Bush Tax-Cut Supporters 'Simply Ignorant'?" *Perspectives on Politics* 5(4): 773–84.

Mann, Thomas, and Norman Ornstein. 2006. *The Broken Branch*. New York: Oxford University Press.

McCarty, Nolan, Keith Poole, and Howard Rosenthal. 2006. *Polarized America: The Dance of Ideology and Unequal Riches*. Cambridge, Mass.: MIT Press.

———. 2009. "Does Gerrymandering Cause Polarization?" *American Journal of Political Science* 53(3): 666–80.

National Election Studies (NES). Various years. Available at: http://www.elec tionstudies.org (accessed August 20, 2010).

Noel, Hans. 2006. "The Coalition Merchants: How Ideologues Shape Parties in American Politics." Ph.D. diss., University of California, Los Angeles.

Poole, Keith T. n.d. *Voteview*. Available at: http://www.voteview.com (accessed August 23, 2010).

Poole, Keith T., and Howard L. Rosenthal. 1984. "U.S. Presidential Elections 1968–1980: A Spatial Analysis." *American Journal of Political Science* 28(May): 282–312.

———. 1997. *Congress: A Political-Economic History of Roll Call Voting*. New York: Oxford University Press.

Schattschneider, Elmer E. 1942. *Party Government*. New York: Holt, Rinehart and Winston.

Van Houweling, Robert. N.d. "Legislators' Personal Policy Preferences and Legislative Organization." Unpublished manuscript. University of California, Berkeley.

Part III

On Inequality in Political Representation

Chapter 12

The Issues in Representation

JAMES A. STIMSON

W HO GETS REPRESENTED? This volume, like the volleys in a tennis match, has seen that issue swatted back and forth in a series of chapters that never stray far from asking the central question. Is representation pretty much equal? Or do some Americans—often richer Americans—command more than their fair share of attention in the policy process? No one asserts a third alternative, like the antiunion rhetoric of an earlier era, that the poor command more attention than they proportionally deserve. But between the two primary positions it is hard to imagine that objective research could produce such discrepant conclusions. It is my assigned duty in this chapter to make some sense of the conflict.

The Debate About Representation

With roots as far back as Benjamin Page and Robert Shapiro's 1992 argument about "parallel publics," but coming to the fore in Peter Enns and Paul Kellstedt's 2008 article in the *British Journal*, is the theory from opinion dynamics that groups defined by various indicators of political sophistication change their preferences in tandem. That means that if governing officials respond to net movements in opinion—and we know that they do (see Stimson, MacKuen, and Erikson 1995; Erikson, MacKuen, and Stimson 2002)—all groups are effectively being represented, and pretty much equally. Because income class is a correlate of education and other sophistication criteria, the argument extends also to groups defined by income. The finding of parallel response could lead to only two conclusions: that all are being represented by government or that none are. It logically excludes the possibility that some groups see their changing preferences mirrored in government policy and that others do not.

At about the same time, a stream of research best exemplified by Larry Bartels's book *Unequal Democracy* (2008) reaches the opposite conclusion. Bartels finds that the preferences of the relatively rich are well reflected in government policy choices, that middle-income preferences are less well represented, and that the preferences of the poorest third of Americans are not represented at all. This is part of a larger argument that the growth of inequality in America reflects political biases and conscious policy choices. If only the preferences of the rich are well represented in politics, then it follows that government choices will systematically tend to favor the interests of the rich over others. Government itself becomes the engine of inequality.

That view is forcefully argued by Martin Gilens (chapter 9, this volume), who, using an altogether different research design, concludes that only those at the very top of the income distribution appear to have their views well represented in government policy. Focusing on policy issues where the preferences of those with low and high incomes diverge the most, he finds that policy reflects the views of upper-income respondents and not lower-income respondents.

And so the debate is joined. There is enough difference in the research designs and assumptions of each set of scholars that both might be valid products. But the conclusions drawn seem squarely in conflict. Both, it would seem, cannot be right. Some of the chapters in this volume add to this debate in one way or another. Sorting through the research, assumptions, and conclusions of authors on both sides of this divide is the task I set for myself in this concluding chapter.

Models of Representation

Who gets represented is partly a matter of fact. But, like much scholarship, the answer to this question depends in part on the models of the process that are entertained. I reflect on three of these: two cross-sectional (naive and sophisticated) and one dynamic.

Naive Cross-Sectional Models

In thinking of representation, American political science usually begins with—and pretty often ends with—geography. That is, the unit of representation is the constituency and the constituency is defined by its legally constituted geographical boundaries. The idea is both empirical (representatives *do* represent constituencies) and normative (representatives *should* represent constituencies). (For an intriguing exception on the normative side, see Mansbridge 2003.) The idea is part of American culture, at least as old as the nation itself.

The essential idea, either empirical or normative, is that constituencies have a dominant preference on policy issues and representatives either do or should mirror it in their acts. What makes this idea naive is that the implicit behavior of representatives—in effect, that members somehow assess that dominant opinion and vote that way—ignores most of what we believe about representative behavior. We think representatives are moved by their own preferences, by party, by ideology, and often by strategic considerations, all of which violate the simple geographical idea.

Richard Fenno's (1978) insights about representation from the member point of view are also much more sophisticated than the geographical constituency, which is at the bottom of the list of political forces in representation. Fenno's representatives see first a personal constituency, peopled by trusted friends and associates whose support is unconditional. Then they think of a primary constituency, of supporters from their party whose support can be counted on in an internal contest, such as a primary election. Beyond that is the reelection constituency, made up of party members and others whose support is critical in putting together a plurality in general elections. Last is the geographical constituency.

From the point of view of the electoral career, members should pay close attention to representing the views of the primary and reelection constituencies because of the twin threats of primary and general election defeats. Implicitly, that means ignoring the views of personal (because its support is unconditional) and geographical constituencies (because it is the wrong set of voters and nonvoters). Typical evidence for this view is the usually large differences in voting patterns between Senators of opposite parties who represent the same state. Having the same legal constituency does not promote uniformity—or often even similarity—in their votes.

I call these naive cross-sectional models, because they ignore most of what we know about representative behavior. But naive is not stupid. In part because of its cultural dominance, the geographical idea remains an empirical and normative standard against which we can judge observed behavior. It is the implied standard of Bartels (2008) when he observes that senators' votes reflect the views of upper- and middle-income voters, but not those of lower-income voters. That senators should represent all three classes requires an assumption that the geographical constituency (to which all income classes contribute about equally) is the relevant standard.

Sophisticated Cross-Sectional Models

If faithfully following the dominant views of the geographical constituency is not how a rational reelection-seeking politician would behave, what then should we expect? If electoral ambition is the glue that makes representation work, as is the common view of political theory, then we can begin to move one step away from the geographical constituency to the voters. If representatives are capable of discerning differences in views between typical voters and typical nonvoters, and electoral ambition is the connection between public opinion and representative behavior, then it follows that representatives should heed seriously the views of typical voters and ignore those of typical nonvoters.

With a further assumption that income class is associated with voter turnout, that then yields a part of the Gilens and Bartels results. If the lowest economic class is the least likely to vote in the aggregate, then its views should have the least influence. This view finds empirical support in the work of Jan Leighley and Jonathan Nagler (2008). They find, contrary to a long tradition of asserting that voters well represent the views of their constituencies, that on certain issues, voters are noticeably different from nonvoters. The issues that tend to produce differences between voters and nonvoters are issues of provision of government welfare benefits and services of various types, where nonvoters are decidedly more supportive than voters are. (This is paralleled in my analysis of issues along economic class lines.) Thus the views of voters are more conservative than the norm for the districts where they live. And if representatives are choosing to follow the views of potential voters, rather than the geographically defined set of eligible voters, then a conservative bias (relative to the geographical constituency) will be found in their behaviors.

On the standard issues of the New Deal party system, upper-income voters have more conservative views than their low-income counterparts. Thus an upper-income bias in representation is a conservative bias, essential to the Bartels argument about the role of government in producing growing income inequality. But it is not automatic that we can equate upper income with conservative. On the electorally important abortion controversy, upper-income respondents, we shall see, tilt toward the pro-choice side of the controversy.

A second, and critical, aspect of adding sophistication to our story of representation is building in a role for parties. Hussey and Zaller do just that in chapter 11, reminding us that a two-party system produces huge departures from majoritarian governance. With a party system in the mix, who wins and who loses comes to depend on what bedfellows the various factions have chosen rather than their simple numbers. They cite the telling case of African Americans, ignored for a century, as we would have expected from the tiny size of their voting block, who went on to triumph on the crucial issue of civil rights because they allied themselves—with labor and white intellectual liberals—into a winning coalition that became dominant in the 1960s.

All this logic changes, though, when we think of representation as a dynamic phenomenon: changes of public opinion producing changes of representative behavior.

Dynamic Models

The static rule for representative behavior is "find out what is the dominant view of the constituency (however defined) and follow it." The dynamic rule is "find out in what direction public opinion is moving and change behavior to move in the same direction." There is no inherent reason why the two rules should produce a different outcome. But here is where the parallel publics finding becomes critical (see Enns and Kellstedt 2008; Enns and Wlezien, chapter 1, this volume).

The views of various groups might track through time responding to different or even opposite cues and produce between group variation over time. In a world of nonattitudes (Converse 1964) or of "conflicting considerations" (Zaller 1992), we would expect sophisticated respondents to be much more responsive to the context of politics and show much more varied response over time than would be seen among the unsophisticated, who are paying little attention and not understanding much of the information flow they do witness. The now common finding of scholarship on opinion dynamics is that they do not, that different groups defined, for example, by measures of political sophistication, respond strongly in parallel over time. That leads to the conclusion that the same stimuli must be moving all.

That sophistication of various kinds is related to economic class sustains an argument that politicians, seeing all classes move in tandem, will move with all of them equally. And so dynamic representation comes to mean equal representation.[1] This would predict a result similar to what Wlezien and Soroka (chapter 10, this volume) find; when responsiveness by income group is assessed dynamically, the result is mixed and inconsistent across policy areas. There is no income class which is dominant across policies.

So the conflict is squarely framed. It will help to look at some evidence of differences in policy preferences by income class.

Some Empirical Questions in Representation

It is helpful to think about the actual distribution of opinions in America. An assertion that the views of the rich carry greater weight in represen-

Figure 12.1   Preferences for Spending Between Categories of Spending by Income Groups

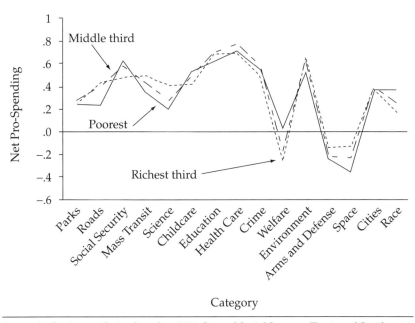

Source: Author's compilation based on 2008 General Social Surveys (Davis and Smith, various years).

tation has one kind of consequence when the views of rich and poor conflict and quite another outcome when they are generally similar. Similarly, Gilens's finding that the rich tend to win when rich and poor disagree is much more striking if such disagreement is typical than if it is atypical. We have seen in the first half of this volume that group opinions often do not reflect group interest in obvious ways.

A brief review of the data is in order.

Are Policy Preferences Aligned with Economic Class?

I begin by constructing low, medium, and high income groups from the 2008 General Social Survey. Using the most recent update of the family income question (INCOME06), I divide the various reported incomes into low (less than $30,000), medium ($30,000 to $75,000), and high (over $75,000) groups of roughly equal size.[2]

I first examine attitudes toward spending and priorities. Each of the main spending questions is scored -1 for "too much," 0 for "about right," and 1 for "too little." A net pro-spending index for each is just the average value. Figure 12.1 then displays these averages across categories of federal spending broken down by income groups. Of the two types of effect, category of spending matters a great deal, as we would expect, and the income breakdown is much less important. But our question is not its relative size but whether income class even matters.

The answer is that it does, for some issues, but never very much. Welfare spending is the strongest case, as noted by several authors in this volume (for example, Enns and Wlezien, and Wlezien and Soroka). Low-income respondents favor more (just barely) than their middle- and upper-income counterparts, who favor less (just barely). It seems reasonable to speculate that low-income respondents are more likely to be receiving, or have received, or have family or friends receiving welfare, currently or in the past, and to be familiar with the usual causes: divorce, layoffs, child care problems, and so forth. With a better safety net, middle- and upper-income respondents, in lieu of knowing real people, seem more likely to subscribe to the negative stereotypes of welfare recipients. One could also argue for a complementary self-interest explanation. Low-income respondents lack the income cushion that would prevent them from needing welfare assistance in the event of layoff, health problems, or some other difficulty. However much they might prefer work to welfare, they would find it reassuring that welfare exists should they need it. Middle- and upper-income respondents would have savings or family to fall back on and would not see welfare as a likely prospect.

Two other categories produce transitive—and therefore probably meaningful—income effects. Upper-income respondents are more likely to support spending for science and for space exploration. These would appear to be education effects. Having nothing to do with self-interest, the well-educated are more likely to be concerned about these domains. And so the income effect is probably spurious. Race is a similar case. The significant difference between income groups disappears when one looks only at white respondents. This is accidental covariation.

So, on balance, the income effects are usually too small to observe. The R^2 predicting attitude from income group is .02 for the strongest case of welfare and goes down from there. A few cases cross the border into significance, when most do not. One has to wonder whether even for the strongest case a representative could correctly perceive such small differences to act on them.

To get an idea about the income-class structure of opinion items more generally, similar breakdowns are reported in table 12.1. The items are Party Identification, which uses the usual 0 to 6 scale for Strong Democrat to Strong Republican; ideological self-identification, ranging from

Very Liberal (1) to Very Conservative (7); a New Deal additive scale based upon GSS items HELPPOOR, HELPSICK, HELPBLK, and HELP-NOT, each scaled 1 to 5 in the conservative direction; an abortion scale in the pro-choice direction combining yes/no responses to seven standard items that probe whether abortion should be legal under particular conditions (ABANY, ABSINGLE, ABNOMORE, ABHLTH, ABRAPE, AB-POOR, ABDEFECT); and a single item on redistribution (whether government should reduce income differentials, GOVEQINC). There is to be sure much more in the GSS, but this is a pretty broad selection of what is generally believed to be important.

In each case, the means by income group are transformed into a standard scale from 0 to 1—with direction determined by the original items—to permit comparisons of the size of differences across issue domains. For a crude indicator of how important income class is in shaping response, I report a R^2 in each case for a regression in which the three-category income scale is independent.

The items in table 12.1 show generally stronger associations with income class than was the case for spending variables. The party identification result simply documents an uncontested fact of American politics, that the poor are more likely to identify as Democrats, and the rich as Republicans. Income differences in ideological self-identification are statistically significant (with a large sample), but thoroughly unimpressive. This case, the foundation of the Bartels (2008) analysis, shows a plainly trivial separation by income level. This is not wholly unexpected. The phenomenon of "conflicted conservatives" (Stimson 2004) predicts such a result. Almost one-fourth of all Americans misidentify themselves as conservative when their views are plainly left of center. Because this misclassification is related to education level, it becomes also related to income class. The poorest Americans are liberal by the measure of their expressed policy preferences, but not by their own self-classification—which is very often a misclassification.

The four-item New Deal issues scale, by contrast, is at least relatively robustly related to income class, a stronger association than already seen in the welfare spending case. Liberalism and conservatism as measured by policy preferences capture the association with income when self-identification largely fails.

Redistribution of income is the classic issue of income class, an issue that pits the poor against the rich, based on conflicting self-interests. Respondents are asked whether government should do more to equalize incomes. It is plainly in the self-interest of the poor to favor such action and in the interest of the rich to oppose it. That is what we see to a substantial degree.[3]

I have asked, "Are policy preferences aligned with economic class?" The answer clearly is yes. At least some of the time they are. The align-

Table 12.1   Selected Important GSS 2008 Opinion Items, by Income Level

Income	Party Identification (Republican)	Self-Identification (Conservative)	New Deal Scale (Conservative)	Abortion (Pro-Choice)	Redistribution (Oppose)
Low	.37	.49	.41	.58	.43
Medium	.43	.53	.48	.62	.52
High	.52	.53	.55	.70	.62
R^2	.029	.004	.057	.018	.062

Source: Author's compilation based on 2008 General Social Surveys (Davis and Smith, various years).
Note: R^2 in each case is from a regression with the three-category income variable independent. All variables are rescaled to have minima and maxima of 0 and 1.

ment is never striking. And sometimes it doesn't exist at all. But sometimes it does. And when it does, it leads us to ask whether those differing views get translated into public policy.

Do Class-Aligned Differences Get Translated into Policy?

Across a variety of designs and approaches, several accounts in this volume say that the system of representation in American politics differentially translates public views into policies.

Wesley Hussey and John Zaller (chapter 11) find that party is implicated in everything and show in multiple cases—two Bush tax cuts and the addition of a pharmacy benefit to Medicare—that the translation of loose ideas and support for them into law requires a disciplined party apparatus.

Martin Gilens (chapter 9) focuses on the question of translation and finds repeated evidence that the views of the relatively well-off translate readily into policy changes and that those of the not well-off—when they differ—do not. And Bartels finds that Senate votes, and implicitly therefore policy, are cross-sectionally responsive to the views of the well-off and not to the poor.

Elizabeth Rigby and Gerald Wright (chapter 7), focusing on state politics and policy, a wholly different realm, find clear evidence that the views of the poor are generally less well represented than those of the middle class and the rich. The pattern is especially striking on economic welfare issues and especially in poor states, providing an interesting bit of context to the story.

Thus with three research designs and three conceptions of policy, one result emerges: American politics represent more the views of the rich than of the poor. I concur.

Methodological Issues

Limited response validity is one of the limitations of survey research. Some respondents some of the time have no real attitude to report on a question they have not confronted and yet nonetheless respond to the question. This is the problem of nonattitudes (Converse 1964). Whether respondents choose the middle category of a survey question or pick randomly among the others, the result will be an absence of systematic association with other variables. This acts generally to attenuate all relationships. Thus, to the extent that random response exists, all observed relationships between public opinion so measured and other variables—such as, in this case, policy outcomes—will appear smaller than they actually are. As long as all are reduced equally, this is a nuisance that we live with.

But what if all are not reduced equally? That is a real prospect. Income class is related to education, interest in politics, and other indicators that tend to predict real attitudes rather than nonattitudes. So when upper-income attitudes are evaluated in studies of representation most of the signal they carry is real. Lower-income observed attitudes, in contrast, will contain fairly weak signals embedded in a good deal of randomness. At least this is a prospect that cannot be discounted. Consequently, if representation were in fact exactly equal by income class, we would expect to see instead evidence that the upper-income group was better represented than the lower-income group. Inasmuch as this defect is inherent in the measurement of opinion, almost any research design would be biased by the condition. (Minimum effects would be seen where opinion was aggregated rather than individual, because aggregation tends to reduce the effects of random response.)

This hypothetical argument about differing response precision finds an empirical test of sorts in the work of Christopher Wlezien and Stuart Soroka (chapter 10, this volume). The authors observe changes in policy and expect a thermostatic response. Following leftward movements in policy, typical respondents will move a little to the right (and vice versa) signaling that the changes have gone too far, relative to typical preferences of respondents. Because the thermostatic response is in general quite pronounced, it becomes a standard of "correct" response in the aggregate. Wlezien and Soroka find that the response is graduated by income group, smallest among the poor and largest among the rich. This is exactly what we would expect to see if the responses of poorer respondents are more laden with error and randomness than those of the rich.

Where the income groups compete, in a statistical sense, to explain policy outcomes, measurement invalidity may be compounded by multicollinearity to enhance the effect of both. Imagine that representation were in fact equal and that the views of income groups were generally quite similar. Then the net views of each group would compete in trying to explain the same variance. The predictable effect of such competition, the classical multicollinearity issue, is that one will win the contest, explain nearly all the systematic variance that exists, leaving other coefficients near zero or even wrong signed (for a more complete exploration of this and other issues in the income representation context, see chapter 8, this volume). The winner among the three contestants will be the one with most valid and most precise variance, which we would expect always to be the better informed, more interested, upper income group. So measurement error plus multicollinearity can explain a result such as that reported by Bartels, even when true representation is exactly equal.

I do not believe that the Bartels result is totally a method artifact. But it seems likely that some proportion of it is.

Framing the Representation Process: Do Politicians See It Like Social Scientists?

Social scientists often frame their concerns in terms of group conflicts. And nothing comes more naturally than rich versus poor. So we wish to know how often rich and poor disagree and who wins when they do. But it is useful to remember that rich versus poor is an analytic convenience. Just because we find it useful to focus our attention does not mean that others use the frames we employ. And so we present to practicing politicians the choice: represent the rich or represent the poor. They get to choose. Represent the rich and they will alienate some poor constituents, some of whom do vote. Represent the poor and they will alienate some of their rich constituents, most of whom vote and do other things of value.

And then we encounter parallel publics in the longitudinal tradition that presents quite a different choice. If the public as a whole is moving left or right, should you follow it? If you do, the net utility is positive. You will please more people than you displease. When the public signals "time for a change," political expediency suggests that you want to be in favor of change.

Imagine being an ambitious politician. The group-conflict frame is not at all attractive. One choice may net out more positive than negative, but any decision that alienates some is to be avoided if possible. What you would like to do is please all of the people all of the time. You might often be forced to make decisions involving group conflicts, but given a choice you would often choose to avoid them.

Admittedly loose, this argument leads to the conclusion that real politicians will prefer responding to one-sided dynamic cues rather than wading in on one side of a group conflict. They should try to reframe their behavior as responding to what their constituents as a whole choose, rather than choosing to sacrifice one interest for the benefit of another. And the decisions we social scientists tend to frame as rich versus poor may often get reframed as responding to changes the public demands.

Who Gets Represented? Some Tentative Conclusions

Can it be simultaneously true that cross-sectional representation favors the rich and dynamic representation does not? Strangely, it can. Think of the dynamic case as a set of signals saying "move left" or "move right." Representatives may respond perfectly in a synchronous dance to these signals, each one from the most left to the most right taking the requisite number of steps at the right time. Then whether the center of all these policy actions is at the exact center of electoral opinion is a separable question. The whole distribution may be moving to the opinion music, but with a small but constant bias in favor of the views of the rich.

To illustrate this scenario I have borrowed a figure from Joseph Ura and Christopher Ellis (2008) showing a 10-item scale emulating public policy mood for four income quartiles from poorest to richest (see figure 12.2). To reduce visual clutter, I have deleted the second and third "inner" quartiles. Focusing on the (dashed) public opinion lines, we can see that the richest quartile is usually more conservative than the poorest (and others as well), but not dramatically.

Now imagine hypothetical policy responses. One I'll refer to as unbiased is just an equally weighted average of the views of the four quartiles. Another line, biased, is a rough approximation of the Gilens or Bartels scenarios. It is constructed by weighting the richest quartile at 4/7, the second richest at 2/7, the third at 1/7, and the fourth at zero. These weights would produce regression coefficients roughly in the ballpark of Bartels's result. The two solid lines in the graph are the hypothetical policy response of representatives: one for those who responded perfectly to the changes in public opinion, and one for those with a constant bias in favor of the views of the rich.

This is not a real result, so the numbers just reflect my assumptions. But, like reality, I think, the dynamics are an important share of the variance and the bias produced by differential response is modest. But a modest bias that is repeated at every policy opportunity can have quite immodest effects in the long run. Imagine that Congress changes the tax code just a little every year—not too far from reality—and each time has just a minor tendency to bias the result in favor of the influential rich.

Figure 12.2   A Hypothetical Vision on How Biased Response Cross-Sectionally Might Combine with Perfect Response Longitudinally to Produce Actual Representative Outcomes

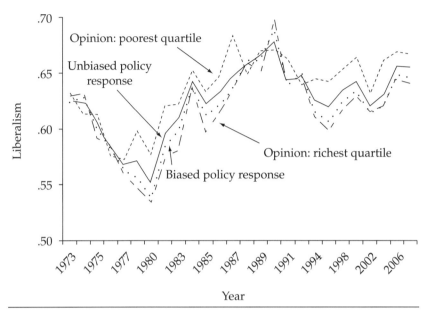

Source: Author's compilation based on General Social Surveys (Davis and Smith, various years) and on Ura and Ellis (2008).

That would produce a substantial and meaningful bias in the long term. And that would find its way into heightened income inequality.

So, opposite as the two conclusions seem, I conclude that they might both be true.

Notes

1. Some of this argument is developed in another work (see Stimson 2009).
2. The missing data category here, "refused," is somewhat problematic. Almost 9 percent of respondents, it appears to be the case that those who refuse to give their incomes are disproportionately high-income people. By self-identified ideology, for example, they are more conservative than the high-income category.
3. It is worth noting that these data were collected before the 2008 presidential campaign became focused on redistribution as a red-hot issue in the guise of Joe the plumber. A postelection survey might show even stronger results.

References

Bartels, Larry M. 2008. *Unequal Democracy: The Political Economy of the New Gilded Age*. Princeton, N.J.: Princeton University Press.

Converse, Philip E. 1964. "The Nature of Belief Systems in Mass Publics." In *Ideology and Discontent*, edited by David E. Apter. Ann Arbor: University of Michigan Press.

Davis, James A., and Tom W. Smith. Various years. *General Social Surveys, 1972–2008* [machine-readable data file]. Principal investigator, James A. Davis; director and co-principal investigator, Tom W. Smith; co-principal investigator, Peter V. Marsden, NORC ed. ICPSR25962-v2. Storrs, CT: Roper Center for Public Opinion Resarch, University of Connecticut/Ann Arbor, Mich.: Inter-University Consortium for Political and Social Research [distributors], 2010-02-08. doi:10.3886/ICPSR25962.

Enns, Peter K., and Paul M. Kellstedt. 2008. "Policy Mood and Political Sophistication: Why Everybody Moves Mood." *British Journal of Political Science* 38(3): 433–54.

Erikson, Robert S., Michael B. MacKuen, and James A. Stimson. 2002. *The Macro Polity*. New York: Cambridge University Press.

Fenno, Richard F. 1978. *Home Style: House Members in Their Districts*. Boston: Little, Brown.

Leighley, Jan, and Jonathan Nagler. 2008. "Preference Variation in Voters, Non-Voters, and across Demographic Groups." Paper presented at the Conference on Homogeneity and Heterogeneity in Public Opinion. Cornell University. Ithaca, N.Y. (October 3–5, 2008).

Mansbridge, Jane. 2003. "Rethinking Representation." *American Political Science Review* 97(4): 515–28.

Page, Benjamin I., and Robert Y. Shapiro. 1992. *The Rational Public: Fifty Years of Trends in Americans' Policy Preferences*. Chicago: University of Chicago Press.

Stimson, James A. 2004. *Tides of Consent: How Public Opinion Shapes American Politics*. New York: Cambridge University Press.

———. 2009. "Perspectives on Unequal Democracy: The Political Economy of the New Gilded Age." *Perspectives on Politics* 7(1): 151–54.

Stimson, James A., Michael B. MacKuen, and Robert S. Erikson. 1995. "Dynamic Representation." *American Political Science Review* 89(3): 543–65.

Ura, Joseph Daniel, and Christopher R. Ellis. 2008. "Income, Preferences, and the Dynamics of Policy Responsiveness." *PS: Political Science & Politics* 41(4): 785–94.

Zaller, John R. 1992. *The Nature and Origins of Mass Opinion*. New York: Cambridge University Press.

Epilogue

Final Thoughts on Who Gets Represented

PETER K. ENNS AND CHRISTOPHER WLEZIEN

IN POLITICS, WHEN preferences diverge, some win and some lose. Who are the winners in U.S. politics? An increasing body of literature answers "the rich" (Bartels 2008; Gilens 2005; Jacobs and Skocpol 2005). Indeed, after four decades of rising inequality and income imbalances not seen since the Gilded Age (Danziger and Gottschalk 1995; Ryscavage 1999; Pikkety and Saez 2006, 2007; Bartels 2008; Hungerford 2008; Kelly 2009), it seems the rich must be getting their way. As Larry Bartels concludes, "our political system seems to be functioning not as a 'democracy' but as an 'oligarchy.' If we insist on flattering ourselves by referring to it as a democracy, we should be clear that it is a starkly unequal democracy" (2008, 287).

The chapters in this volume present a more nuanced answer to the question of who gets represented. We have seen that if we try to understand representation (and inequality) in terms of rich versus poor, we miss the full picture. First, studies of the rich versus the poor miss—by definition—those in the middle, and we have seen they matter quite a lot. Second, income is not always the defining cleavage in terms of the public's policy preferences. For example, partisanship, race, region, and education matter in important, and not always predictable, ways. Third, representation looks different depending on what policies we analyze and whether we study a single time point or over-time change. Finally, representation (or the lack thereof) can be mediated through parties, organized interests, and state resources. We believe these findings need to be better incorporated into studies of representation and inequality.

Knowing where policy ends up does not always tell us how we got there. Put differently, knowing who gets what—to use Harold Lasswell's words (1936)—does not always tell us who gets represented. This distinction has guided the research in this volume. We hope that it guides future research, and that scholars and students of representative democracy will consider what stakeholders want in the first place. The distinction matters not only for academics, however; it also matters in a practical sense. If our understanding of representation falls short, after all, so will our attempts to create change.

References

Bartels, Larry M. 2008. *Unequal Democracy: The Political Economy of the New Gilded Age*. Princeton, N.J.: Princeton University Press.

Danziger, Sheldon, and Peter Gottschalk. 1995. *America Unequal*. New York: Russell Sage Foundation.

Gilens, Martin. 2005 "Inequality and Democratic Responsiveness." *Public Opinion Quarterly* 69(5): 778–96.

Hungerford, Thomas L. 2008. "Income Inequality, Income Mobility, and Economic Policy: U.S. Trends in the 1980s and 1990s." CRS Report RL34434. Washington: Congressional Research Service.

Jacobs, Lawrence R., and Theda Skocpol. 2005. "American Democracy in an Era of Rising Inequality." In *Inequality and American Democracy: What We Know and What We Need to Learn*, edited by Lawrence R. Jacobs and Theda Skocpol. New York: Russell Sage Foundation.

Kelly, Nathan J. 2009. *The Politics of Income Inequality in the United States*. New York: Cambridge University Press.

Lasswell, Harold D. 1936. *Politics: Who Gets What, When, How.* New York: Whittlesey House.

Piketty, Thomas, and Emmanuel Saez. 2006. "The Evolution of Top Incomes: A Historical Pespective." *American Economic Review* 96(2): 200–05.

———. 2007. "Income and Wage Inequality in the United States, 1913–2002." In *Top Incomes over the Twentieth Century: A Contrast Between European and English-Speaking Countries*, edited by A. B. Atkinson and Thomas Piketty. Oxford: Oxford University Press.

Ryscavage, Paul. 1999. *Income Inequality in America: An Analysis of Trends*. Armonk, N.Y.: M. E. Sharpe.

Index

Boldface numbers refer to figures and tables.